Philosophy and Medicine

Volume 135

The Philosophy and Medicine series is dedicated to publishing monographs and collections of essays that contribute importantly to scholarship in bioethics and the philosophy of medicine. The series addresses the full scope of issues in bioethics and philosophy of medicine, from euthanasia to justice and solidarity in health care, and from the concept of disease to the phenomenology of illness. The Philosophy and Medicine series places the scholarship of bioethics within studies of basic problems in the epistemology, ethics, and metaphysics of medicine. The series seeks to publish the best of philosophical work from around the world and from all philosophical traditions directed to health care and the biomedical sciences. Since its appearance in 1975, the series has created an intellectual and scholarly focal point that frames the field of the philosophy of medicine and bioethics. From its inception, the series has recognized the breadth of philosophical concerns made salient by the biomedical sciences and the health care professions. With over one hundred and twenty five volumes in print, no other series offers as substantial and significant a resource for philosophical scholarship regarding issues raised by medicine and the biomedical sciences.

More information about this series at http://www.springer.com/series/6414

Rudolf Ramm

Medical Jurisprudence and Rules of the Medical Profession

Translated, annotated and introduced by
Melvin Wayne Cooper

Springer

Rudolf Ramm
Instructor at the University of Berlin
Berlin, Germany

Translated by Melvin Wayne Cooper
University of Texas Medical Branch
Galveston, TX, USA

ISSN 0376-7418 ISSN 2215-0080 (electronic)
Philosophy and Medicine
ISBN 978-3-030-25244-1 ISBN 978-3-030-25245-8 (eBook)
https://doi.org/10.1007/978-3-030-25245-8

This Springer imprint is published by the registered company Springer Nature Switzerland AG.
The registered company address is: Gewerbestrasse 11, 6330 Cham, Switzerland

Foreword

In this foreword I wish to address three questions – why Wayne Cooper is an exemplary person to have written this work; why the work is important today; and why today is a favorable time for this work to be done.

I met Wayne in 1989 when he uprooted himself from a highly successful cardiology practice in Lubbock, Texas (where he had previously been Chief of Cardiology at the medical school at Texas Tech University). He came to Michigan State University as our institution offered what he considered to be a valuable Ph.D. program in the philosophy of medicine. For a variety of reasons, he did not complete the Ph.D. at Michigan State. However, on the way to his eventual doctorate in the history of ideas, he also managed to obtain master's degrees in bioethics, history, and philosophy.

The bottom line is that Wayne, besides his proficiency in medicine and bioethics, is quite willing to take things slowly to complete a task with proficiency and integrity. I will leave the Introduction of the book to speak for itself as to what he had to do to become competent to translate Ramm's work and how few scholars would have been willing to engage in this extended program of preparation, especially later in life.

Why would anyone today be interested in reading Ramm's work? Basically, it is very important, in our understanding of the history of medicine during the Nazi period, for us to know that a book such as Ramm's was written. The idea of a manual on Nazi medical ethics appears on its face to be an oxymoron. Being aware of what the work contained and how it was conceptualized and organized seems essential for any further scholarship of the period.

Flying up to a higher altitude, why scholarship into Nazi medicine and medical ethics at all? I would suggest that to do sensible work today in either bioethics or history of medicine, we somehow need to deal with the tension between two apparently contradictory ideas: that the Holocaust was a uniquely terrible event in human history and that its perpetrators were, for the most part, people just like us, who were in turn enabled by the acquiescence of other people even more like us.

I can best explain the importance of this tension by turning each idea on its head. There have been two ways in which the Nazi period has been commonly trivialized in bioethics discussions. One is to make the Holocaust the bogeyman under the bed to be hauled out whenever we wish to attack a proposal without having very much by way of good reasons, but only a deep visceral suspicion. We then declare that maybe whatever is being proposed looks innocent at first but that it starts us down a slippery slope with Nazism at the bottom.

The other trivialization of the Holocaust is to depict the Nazis as a uniquely depraved gang of thugs, who share no human qualities with good people like us. Instead of the slippery slope idea, which seems to suggest that a second coming of the Holocaust is continuously imminent, we have the apparently reassuring idea that the Holocaust can never happen again because no group of people so uniformly evil is ever likely to reappear. That spares us the task of investigating the Holocaust to see whether it can teach us anything about behavior and policies that we'd be well advised to avoid in the future.

The current translation of Ramm addresses this tension. We have an opportunity to understand better how a manual of Nazi ethics appealed to ideas and feelings with which physicians today can identify and what was unique about the Nazi period that allowed such a collection of ideas, which perhaps in another social setting might have gone nowhere beyond a fringe group of zealots, to result in the devastation that ensued.

In presenting his work to an audience, Wayne Cooper makes a point that I have never heard made so compellingly elsewhere. Suppose that you were a physician in Germany in the early 1930s. Suppose that you cared about medicine as a profession, and not merely as a business. Suppose that you were worried about forces in society that seemed unfriendly to the profession of medicine. Suppose that your motives were truly *not* self-interest, but rather a genuine concern for medicine's stature as a learned, helping profession. Suppose that in addition to all that, you believed devoutly in preventive medicine and public health. What political party would attract your allegiance? It seems important for us to realize today that *only* the National Socialist Party, among the entire range of political movements in Germany, would fit this description in the mind of such a physician.

Understanding Ramm's manual is important, and today is an ideal time to do it. Let me use as an example the fact that in 2012, the German Medical Association officially adopted a resolution at its annual meeting accepting responsibility for the role of German physicians in the Holocaust. One might ask both, what took them so long, and why, finally, then? Germany had to go through a number of stages before it was fully ready to confront the events of the National Socialist period. Firstly, the sheer immensity of postwar reconstruction had to be dealt with. Secondly, a period went by where forgetting the horrors of the war appeared to be the only sensible posture. Many former Nazis were then active members of their respective communities, making it awkward for other Germans to inquire too deeply or to become too critical of the Nazi record. As these Nazis began to die off, the next generation took refuge in the refrain that all this happened a long time ago and it was silly to keep bringing up the distant past. Most of the rest of German society, however, was well in advance of German medicine in acknowledging responsibility and in issuing suitable apologies and making reparations where possible. The fact that it took German medicine so long to admit its own central and enthusiastic role in the Nazi regime adds further reasons why we need now to understand Ramm's work.

My point here is that it seems that we have arrived somehow at an especially favorable juncture to look at the history of the Nazi regime. A multitude of documents remains to be sifted through. A few survivors of the Holocaust are alive today to provide oral testimony, and other oral histories were recorded in earlier decades. Yet enough time has passed to put these events in a perspective and a context that allows careful historical assessment. Another thing that has happened in the meantime, tragically, is other instances of genocide, in the Balkans and Rwanda, proving yet again that we dare not imagine that humankind has advanced beyond such behavior.

I suggest, therefore, that this volume represents a solid work of scholarship, produced by an appropriate person at the appropriate time. We should pay heed.

Knoxville, TN, USA
February, 2019

Howard Brody

Preface

"Medical Jurisprudence and Rules of the Medical Profession" is constructed as a required series of lectures of the upper semesters of the plan of medical studies.

The need for a definition and arrangement of the substance of this series of lectures arose from my activity as the teacher representing this specialty for the University of Berlin.

I was aware during the formation of this plan of studies that some of its content will also appear in other lecture series and will likewise be dealt with from other viewpoints.[1] With the writing of this book, the essential written and unwritten principles of the profession came to be gathered together, and the important areas of medical ethics and the responsibilities of the physician as health educator have notably been included.

Since the true ideal conception of medicine is founded on an inner calling and a high ethos, along with rich knowledge and manifest ability, and additionally, the demands which are placed on one becoming a doctor are not small – those having to do with character, morality, and mental capacity – in order to avoid disappointment later, each student should test himself intensively to determine if he possesses the inclination and aptitude for the medical profession.

Even though the physician's course is steep and difficult, if he is guided by a constantly urging conscience, and proceeds in faithful duty, he will be accompanied by a joy of responsibility and a sense of readiness to make sacrifices. Only the

---

[1] The material in Ramm's text is the standard material presented by the Nazi educators in multiple forms. There is little in Ramm the medical student would have not heard literally hundreds of times previously. Indeed, the intellectual state of the German medical students at the time has been characterized as "appalling," because "they are picked because of the low number of their [party] membership card," and "preference is given to those with fathers in the party and mothers in the National Socialist Womanhood. Five times weekly they have to attend marching and combat exercises and lectures on the theory of race" (W. Weyers, *Death of Medicine in Nazi Germany: Dermatology and Dermatopathology Under The Swastika* (Philadelphia: Ardor Scribendi, LTD, 1998), 124)). The period from 1924 to 1943 was very active in the production of laws pertaining to the medical profession. Swoch lists 273 laws pertaining to the medical profession passed during this period (Swoch, 294–351).

idealist has these qualities at his disposal. Despite all concerns and difficulties, a pathway full of beauty and wonder opens up to him because he ascends to the heights which reveal the vision and insight of the spirit and the soul of the world, an insight which remains closed to common people in their life's wanderings.

Whoever undertakes this journey with a conscious awareness of the duties and responsibilities which confront him, and holds them in selfless devotion, will find in the rich and deep experiences that are allotted to him and in the successes that he attains in the struggle for the preservation of the Volks' health gratifying fulfillment of his life.

So this book should be a companion and a guide to the student of medicine and to the young physician for his established goal and an adviser to the young person in his choice of profession. But also the physician who is already established in practice will find many stimulating thoughts that he can put into practice for the promotion of the health interests of the German Volk.

Berlin, Germany
January 1942

Rudolf Ramm

Preface to the Second Edition

The welcome reception of the first edition of this book, *Arztlizche Rechts – und Standeskunde: Der Artz als Gesundsheitserzieher*, proves that in all quarters of the health profession there is currently interest in the ideas contained herein.

The new edition is amplified and expanded where necessary.[1]

Berlin, Germany
January 1943[2]

Rudolf Ramm

[1] Additions to the 1942 text are noted in the footnotes.

[2] In January 1943, the battle of Stalingrad was underway. It was widely known that the outcome of this battle would decide the outcome of the war and, as a consequence, the National Socialist philosophical viewpoint. Ramm's production of a new edition of his text does not suggest optimism, fatalism, or self-deception. One was not permitted to display any anxiety or doubt about the ultimate outcome of the war. The National Socialists continued to operate according to their plan of National Socialist philosophical viewpoint until the total collapse of the regime in 1945. They merely shifted the operations progressively back towards the heart of the Reich.

It was also widely known in Berlin that the Jews of Germany were being exterminated "in the east" (E. A. Johnson, *Nazi Terror: The Gestapo, Jews, and Ordinary Germans* (New York: Basic Books, 1999), 441; Fischer, 516). Himmler informed German journalists as early as November 1941 that the "biological extermination of all Jews in Europe has begun" (Fischer, 517). At one point Ramm proudly notes that there are few Jews remaining in Germany. It was widely known where they had gone and what was happening to them. Ramm was an impassioned believer in the National Socialist ideology. He constructs what was for him a Coherent National Socialist Philosophical Viewpoint. Goetz Aly has shown how enthusiastic most Germans were to be involved in the construction of the idealist National Socialist state (G. Aly, *Hitlers Volksstaat: Raub, Rassenkrieg und nationalaer Sozialismus* (Frankfurt am Main: Fischer, 2005)). And in "Final Solution," Aly focuses on the Holocaust from the perpetrators' perspective and concludes that the Holocaust was the result of a new organizational expertise, an indifference to human life, and a habituation to brutality (G. Aly, *Endloesung: Voelkerverschiebung und der Mord an den europaeischen Juden* (Frankfurt am Main: Fischer, 2005). He referred to the system as "Total Biologism" and quotes Heinrich Himmler, who referred to the construction of the society as the "socialism of the good blood" (Aly, *Endloesung,* 376).

Introduction to the Translation

Introduction: History of the Medical Holocaust from the Perspective of the Perpetrators

One of the greatest achievements of historical scholarship in the last half century has been the extensive investigation of the crimes of the National Socialist doctors during the Holocaust. One area which has been largely unexplored, however, is the perspective of the National Socialists, in effect, the perpetrators of the crimes. In particular, the incentives and values of the medical practitioners have been largely left unexplained and unexplored. One is naturally, at first, reluctant and even resistant to attempt to consider the perspective of the perpetrators of some of the greatest crimes against humanity that the world has ever known. But, unless one is prepared to take the unhistorical stance that the National Socialists were nothing more than a gang of criminals, one must seriously attempt to see their world from the perspective from which they acted.

In consideration of why there has come to be little historical material published from the viewpoint of the perpetrators, there seem to be several possible contributing factors: Few of the perpetrators survived long after the war, either committing suicide or being executed after the Nuremberg Doctors' Trial.[1] Additionally, the records left from archives and diaries of the Nazis do not explicitly mention and detail the thinking and motives behind their actions. Only one record of the Wannsee Conference, the meeting in which the "Final Solution to the Jewish Problem" was planned, survived the Nazi's systematic destruction of incriminating records, and this only gives a general outline of the plans, without detailed elaboration of the motives and values of the participants. Also, the National Socialists explicitly developed code words and euphemisms ("Final Solution") to cover up their criminal activities. Perhaps another reason for the dearth of studies from the perpetrators perspective is that there has been concern that this might somehow validate their

[1] U. Schmidt, *Justice at Nuremberg: Leo Alexander and the Nazi Doctors' Trial.* (Basingstoke: Palgrave, 2004).

behavior. However, the enormity of the crimes has been so well documented that there seems to be little risk of this ever occurring except by the most rigid Holocaust deniers.

One needs to know, if possible, the values and motives for actions of the perpetrators. While their philosophy of racial hygiene and its attendant anti-Semitism have been extensively investigated, the actual connections of these philosophies to specific actions have gone largely unexplored and unexplained. One can, for example, have a philosophy of medicine such that one believes that the teleology of medicine is healing and curing, but this philosophy can become manifest with the same act in plastic surgery of burn victims and in cosmetic surgery. One needs to know more than a perpetrator's philosophy; one needs to know what values and motives and what action guides and rules are called upon to dictate the specific application of that philosophy. Rules and ethics of the profession are specifically designed to guide the behavior and self-governance of the profession, and examination of these rules and guidelines should give us some clues to why the traditional philosophy of medicine was so distorted and dishonored by the National Socialist physicians.

The Standard National Socialist Text of Medical Ethics

Rudolf Ramm's text, *Medical Jurisprudence and Rules of the Medical Profession*, has been reported to be an influential manual for medical ethics in Nazi Germany[2] and is commonly quoted as representing the Nazi viewpoint of the position and responsibilities of the physician in the National Socialist society.[3] It interprets the National Socialist Weltanschauung (National Socialist Philosophical Worldview) and makes explicit how this world view is to be actuated by the true National Socialist physician. It would seem to be a good text to attempt to see the National Socialist medical world view from the perspective of its practitioners. Ramm's text could be viewed as being analogous to an Army Field Manual for the practicing National Socialist physician. Consistent with this function, one can see that Ramm's book is not the sort of medical ethics text which is common in modern Bioethics. It does not discuss philosophical theories of ethics or cases of moral dilemmas. Instead, Ramm's text attempts to construct a Comprehensive National Socialist Philosophical Viewpoint (*Weltanschauung*). Features which are consistent with this

[2]Lifton, R. J. *The Nazi Doctors: Medical Killing and the Psychology of Genocide.* (New York: Basic Books, 1986), 30; R. N. Proctor, "Nazi Doctors, Racial Medicine, and Human Experimentation," in *The Nazi Doctors and the Nuremberg Code: Human Rights in Human Experimentation, eds.* G.J. Annas and M.A. Grodin (New York: Oxford University Press, 1992), 29; Bruns F, Chelouche T. Lectures on Inhumanity: Teaching Medical Ethics in German Medical Schools Under Nazism. *Ann Intern Med.* 2017;166:591–595.doi:10.7326/M16-2758.

[3]Kater, M. H. *Ärzte als Hitlers Helfer.* (Hamburg: Europa Verlag, 1989), p. 296; Schmiedebach, P. "Aerztlich Standeslehre und Standesethik 1919 – 1945, in Baader, G. and Schultz, U. *Medizin Und Nationalsozialismus: Tabuisierte Vergangenheit-Ungebrochene Tradition?* (Berlin: Verlagsgesellschaft Gesundheit mbH, 1980), pp. 64–72.

National Socialist philosophical viewpoint are ethical, those which are not are to be abjured, expunged, and, as he states at one point, "eliminated." Ramm's text dictates the specific applications of the legal values and rules which emanate from this Weltanschauung to the developing medical students and practicing National Socialist physicians.

According to Bruns, "Ramm's book is the most important known historical source pertaining to the instruction of Nazi medical ethics…The book, which was written not only for students but also for postgraduates, received positive reviews in German medical journals."[4] The 1942 edition sold out within a year, and a second edition published in 1943 included an extended appendix of medical laws.

Transmitting the National Socialist Weltanschauung to Medical Students, Midwives, and School Children

Ramm was born on November 23, 1887, in Dortmund-Loettringhausen. He attended Gymnasium in Witten and Mannheim and studied pharmacy and medicine in Strasbourg, Munich, and Cologne. He took his "Approbation" (license to practice) as pharmacist and physician in 1913. He served in the "*Infanterie-Leib-Regiment*" during the war. After the war, he became a member of the Stadtrat and was an early member of the party, even before the *Machtergreifung*.[5] He became a member of the Nazi party and an *SS-Standartenarzt* (physician of the SS) in 1930. Elected a member of the Reichstags (NSDAP faction), he reportedly wore his SS uniform to meetings. His file reports that "he was an idealist and a very proficient speaker."[6] He was leader of the Reich's Working Community for Cancer Research and became leader of the Physicians' Chamber and KVD-*Landesstelle* (Territorial Division) "Westmark." In 1937, Ramm was appointed by SS Leader Heinrich Himmler to be "Führer im Rasse- und Siedlungshauptamt" (leader in the Central Department of Race and Settlements).[7]

---

[4] Bruns, 593.

[5] January 30, 1933, the date Adolf Hitler became Chancellor of Germany.

[6] National Archives and Records Administration, General Records of the Department of State, Washington D.C., United States.(NARA), Box No. PI-157 E-Soo HM 1992 377, Roll Number A3343 SS0-0068.

[7] Ich nehme Sie mit Wirkung vom 12. September 1937 as SS-Mann in die Schutzstaffel auf

und befoerdere sie zum Dienstgrad eines SS-Untersturmfuehrers unter gleichzeitiger Ernennung zum SS-Fuehrer im Rass und Siedlungshauptamt.

gez.: H. Himmler
SS-Gruppenfuehrer. (NARA,ibid.)

Ramm traveled in influential circles. In 1940, with Kurt Blome, a member of the Reichstag and the leader responsible for continuing education of physicians,[8] he accompanied Reicharzte Leader Leonardo Conti on an inspection tour through Danzig-West Prussia. Blome was one of the physicians charged in the Nuremberg Doctors' Trial. Conti would presumably have been charged, but he committed suicide in Nuremburg prison. In 1940, Ramm overtook the editorship of the *Deutsches Ärzteblatt*, which reports:

> The "*Deutsches Ärzteblatt*" serves to represent the ideal and material interests of the German medical community; it is at the same time the official paper of the Reich Physicians' Chamber and the German Fund Physicians' Union.[9]

He held this position until the last edition in 1945.[10] He was appointed as Lehrbeauftrager (lecturer) and instructor of *Medical Laws and Rules of the Profession* at the University of Berlin in 1942.[11] In addition to writing for medical students, he wrote for school children[12] and midwives.[13] The latter work was endorsed by Martin Bormann, Party Chancellory leader and close confidant of Hitler. As a committed Nazi with experience as a teacher and writer, Ramm was a natural choice to produce the texts.

Ramm's position can perhaps be indirectly confirmed by the following comment from a representative of his former publisher:

> Unfortunately, Mr. Ramm was a little problematic character, who represented with other people the NS – public health system with the change from normal doctor to "Gesundheitsfuehrer"… As you can see, Ramm's book has a strong burden of NS-thinking; after [the] war all these books were smashed and for this reason we have no copies anymore. Because a bomb destroyed a part of our publishing house in 1944 no archival material is available for this period esp. for Ramm's book, the same seems for the Humboldt University in this time.[14]

[8] Stockhorst, E. *500 Koepfe: Wer War Was Im 3. Reich* (Kiel: Arndt: 2000), 62–63.

[9] Ramm, 225.

[10] Swoch, 79.

[11] Degener, Hermann A.L. (Hrsg.) Wer ist's 1935, Deutsches Aerzteblatt 69 (1939, S. 561; Deutsches Aerzteblatt 70 (1940), S. 143, 269. Deutsches Aerzteblatt 72 (1942), S. 360, Horkenbach, Cuno (Hrsg.) Das Deutsche Reich, 1932, Reichstags-Handbuch 1920–1933, 1932, S. 500, Stockhorst, Erich, Fuenftausend Koepfe – 1985.

[12] Reich, W. "The Care-Based Ethic of Nazi Medicine and the Moral Importance of What We Care About," in *Muse* 2001 1: 64–74.

[13] (Ramm, R. *Richtlinien fuer die weltanschauliche Schulung der Hebammenschuelerinne* (from the Washington Archives).

[14] Personal communication, Joachim Oest (Degruyter publishing), 2006.

As a high-ranking medical leader, at the end of the war, Ramm was sentenced to death by a Soviet military tribunal and executed in August 1945.[15, 16]

Value of the Translation

Considering that Ramm's manual is only *one* text and offers only a limited view into National Socialist medicine and given the now thousands of texts on National Socialism, one might wonder what is the value of having the text translated into English. The major reason is that the text is a fairly short and readable *primary source* of direct action guides and rules for the practicing National Socialist physician. Essentially, all primary material pertaining to the Nazi time has had to be translated from the original German to make it accessible to English-language readers. Of course, the translation does not provide direct access to such material, but it does provide the reader with a more direct source, helping to bridge the distance between the reader and the original propositions. Since an almost unlimited number of texts and articles have made Nazi medicine the ultimate endpoint of virtually all slippery slope arguments, there continues to be much to learn from the *primary* historical material of the period.

Corporatism and Professionalization: *Stand* and *Beruf*

Throughout Ramm's text, there were two terms which presented frequent challenges in translation – *Stand* and *Beruf. Stand* means "standing position, position, state, estate, etc." *Beruf* means "occupation, trade, or profession." However, merely translating these words or their cognates as "position" and "occupation," respectively, would not have resulted in a clear meaning. Another meaning of *Stand* is "status," "rank," or "class." But translating the word as one of these would also have not created clarity. *Der Berufstand* is clearly "profession." *Standestaat* is a "corporate state." *Standesgemass* means "befitting one's social standing or rank." *Standesgewusst* means "conscious of one's social standing or rank.[17] A further meaning of *der Stand* is a "social group."[18] More formally, the neomedieval *Stand* was a body of members of a particular class, e.g., a *Landstand* (member of a *Stände*

[15] R. Swoch, *Aerztliche Standespolitik im Nationalsozialismus* (Husim: Matthiesen Verlag, 2001), 370; E. Klee, *Das Personenlexikon zum Dritten Reich* (Framkfurt: Fischer Taschenbuch Verlag, 2005); W. Suess, *Der "Volkskoerper" im Krieg, Gesundheitpolitik verhaeltnis und Krankenmord im Nationalsozialistischen Deutschland* (Munich: R. Oldenbourg, 2003).

[16] Bruns, F. *Medizinethik im Nationalsozialismus. Entwicklungen und Protagonisten in Berlin (1939-1945).* Stuttgart, Germany: Steiner; 2009.

[17] *The Oxford-Duden German Dictionary* (Oxford: Clarendon Press, 1990).

[18] *Langenscheidt's New College German Dictionary* (New York: Langenscheidt, 1995), 575.

body) owed his position to the ownership of a particular piece of property or the holding of a particular clerical or urban office (abbot, mayor, etc.).[19] The spirit of hierarchy (*Geist der Stände*) was considered to be essential to a well-ordered society. One must live in accordance with a quasi-hereditary *Standesehre* (conception of honor dictating the performance of the duties of every status).[20] This will often be the sense in which Ramm uses the word *Stand.*

The other word, *der Beruf*, means "occupation," "profession," "trade," or "career."[21] It can also mean an activity in a certain area of responsibility in which one requires a certain education.[22] *Beruf* has a long history in the German language, being the word used by Martin Luther to designate a "calling." He gave it a clear religious connotation, meaning a calling from God.[23]

I have most often translated each word as "profession." This is of course not entirely satisfactory, however, because Ramm, in addition to using it for modern times, uses the word in reference to the premodern medical community long before there was any semblance of what we would today characterize as a profession. It seems that Ramm's use of the two words is an example of a particular National Socialist way of using words.[24] And, like their other uses of words, his use distorts the meaning of the term to the point that his constitution of a "profession" bears little resemblance to the use of the term in the modern philosophy of profession.

A constitutive feature of a mature *profession* is that it is "self-regulating," that is, that it has an internally generated and adjudicated code of behavior. It is this process of internal self-regulation that has been, and is even today, the issue of contention of German medicine. An *occupation* (*Beruf*), which is more closely associated with a trade, is clearly a commercial enterprise. The two concepts, *profession* and *occupation*, overlap to a certain degree but are clearly not coextensive. In America, professionalization as a process was accomplished most dramatically with the adoption of the AMA Code of Ethics at the time of the founding of the organization in 1847.[25] The process did not proceed as smoothly in Germany partly because it was not until 1871 that the country was unified and, even then, each state continued to have relatively independent medical systems.[26] This process was also more closely tied to state and national politics than was the case in America. It is this dialectic between the two conceptions (profession vs. occupation) which appears to be reflected in Ramm's almost interchangeable employment of *Stand* and *Beruf.* The connections

[19] K Epstein. *The Genesis of German Conservatism.* (Princeton: University Press, 1966), 260.

[20] Epstein, 194.

[21] Duden, 143.

[22] Langenscheidt, 99.

[23] *Das Herkunfswoerterbuch: Etymologie der deutschen Sprache* (Mannheim: Duden, 2001).

[24] V. Klemperer, *The Language of the Third Reich: LTI – Lingua Tertii Imperii. A Philologist's Notebook* (London: Athlone Press, 1975).

[25] Baker, R. *The Codification of Medical Morality: Historical and Philosophical Studies of the Formalization of Western Medical Morality in the Eighteenth and Nineteenth Centuries* (Dordrecht: Kluwer Academic Publishers, 1993.

[26] H. Holborn, *A History of Modern Germany: 1840–1945* (Princeton: University Press, 1969).

of the medical community, the profession, and the politics are more appropriately designated *Standespolitics.* Ramm's work, *Standeskunde*, which is in the title, has been translated as "Rules of the Profession."

It appears that Ramm's use of the term *Beruf* is consistent with the characterization of a profession by Emile Durkheim in the "Functionalist" tradition. Durkheim viewed social evolution as a movement from the mechanical solidarity of tribal societies to the organic solidarity characteristic of industrial societies. He argued that primitive societies were characterized by a strong *collective conscience*, which he defined as "the totality of beliefs and sentiments common to average citizens of the same society." This seems to be the sense of profession Ramm meant by *Beruf.* According to Durkheim, we learn of social rituals that create not only solidarity but also symbols that we use for thinking. Our minds are made up of ideas infused with moral power by the groups to which we belong. Our social memberships determine that what we believe is real, and they place a moral sanction on the necessity of believing this and, contrariwise, a moral condemnation on doubting these accepted beliefs.[27] The memberships develop what Durkheim called the *collective conscience*, which he characterized in *The Division of Labour in Society* as the following:

> The totality of beliefs and sentiments common to average citizens of the same society forms a determinate system which has its own life; one may call it the *collective* or *common conscience*...It is, thus, an entirely different thing from particular consciences, although it can be realized only through them.[28]

The role of the state is to persevere in calling the individual to a "moral way of life." This leads Durkheim to the assertion that the state is "the organ of moral discipline."[29] Individuals must be conceived as component parts of an organism. It is likewise from their whole community that they derive their regulation, their position, and finally their existence, which must be qualified as "being within the group." The humanity of man is only conceivable within the human aggregation and, in one sense at least, as existing through it.[30] The more solidarity there is among the members of a society, the more they maintain various relations, whether it be one with another or with the group collectively.[31] We read that in the sphere of morality as in the other spheres of nature,

> Individual reason has no particular prestige as such. The only reason for which one can legitimately claim historic moral reality – there as elsewhere – the right to intervene and to rise above historic moral reality with the aim of reforming it, is not my reason, nor yours, but impersonal reason, which is only truly realized in science...This intervention of science has as its end the replacing of the collective ideal of to-day not by an individual ideal, but

---

[27] R. Collins, *Four Sociological Traditions* (Oxford: University Press, 1994), 188.

[28] Durkheim, in G. Ritzer, *Sociological Theory* 5th Ed. (New York: McGraw Hill, 2000), 82.

[29] B. Turner, in E. Durkheim, *Professional Ethics and Civic Morals* (London: Routledge 1957), xxxiii.

[30] *Civic Morals,* xlvi.

[31] *Civic Morals*, l.

> by an ideal which is also collective and which expresses not a particular individuality but a better understood collectivity.[32]

As the division of labor increases, so too does individualism. As a result, there comes to be a corresponding decrease in collective conscience and a shift to organic solidarity, characterized by the interdependence of roles and a lack of self-sufficiency that held people together.[33] For Durkheim, the state has the responsibility to "work out certain representations which hold good for the collectivity…[because] the State is the very organ of social thought."[34]

Another characterization of a profession is that of Eliot Freidson's which is of assistance in articulating Ramm's apparent meaning of the term *Der Stand*. According to Freidson,[35] an interaction between the concepts of illness and social deviation leads to the development of professions. He argues that in the course of obtaining a monopoly over its work, medicine has also obtained virtually exclusive jurisdiction over determining what actually is illness and thus how people must act in order to be treated as ill.[36]

> Medicine has the authority to label one person's complaint an illness and another's complaint not; medicine thus may be said to be engaged in *the creation of illness as a social state which a human being may assume.*[37]

And,

> By virtue of making itself the authority on what illness "really" is, *medicine creates the social possibilities for acting sick.* In this sense, medicine's monopoly includes the right to create illness as an *official social role.*[38]

Consistent with Freidson's reasoning, the National Socialist theory of racial hygiene was indispensable in articulating the meaning of *der Stand*, which is consistent with Freidson's reasoning. The profession of medicine, like law and religion, uses normative criteria (in the National Socialist case the principle of racial hygiene) to pick out what it is interested in, and thereafter, its work constitutes a social reality that is distinct from (and on occasion virtually independent of) physical reality.[39] Since the concept of illness is inherently evaluational,[40] medicine is a moral enter-

---

[32] *Civic Morals*, li.

[33] R. A. Wallace and A. Wolf, *Contemporary Sociological Theory* (Upper Saddle River, NJ : Prentice Hall, 1999), 21.

[34] B. Turner, in Durkheim, 1957, xxxiii.

[35] E. Freidson, *Profession of Medicine: A Study of the Sociology of Applied Knowledge* (Chicago. U. of Chicago Press, 1988).

[36] Freidson, 205.

[37] Freidson, 205.

[38] Freidson, 206.

[39] Freidson, 206.

[40] T. Szasz, "The Myth of Mental Illness" *American Psychologist* 15 (1960) : 113–18; C. Boorse "On the Distinction Between Disease and Illness" *Philosophy and Public Affairs* 5 (1975) : 49–68; A. L. Caplan "The Concepts of Health, Illness, and Disease" *Companion Encyclopedia of the History of Medicine*, W. Bynum and R. Porter, eds. Vol. I, 233–48 (London: Routledge, 1993).

prise like law and religion, seeking to uncover and control things that it considers undesirable.[41]

> It is because it is believed to be independent of human culture (though human culture may influence its prevalence and treatment) that illness is felt to be different, more "objective" and stable than such clearly social forms of deviance as crime. In this view, illness is biological rather than social deviance, subject to the same biophysical law in man as in mouse, rabbit, or monkey.[42]

In medical practices in countries other than National Socialist Germany, the "illness" is condemned rather than the person, but it is condemned nonetheless. The person is treated with sympathy rather than punishment, but he is expected to rid himself of the condemned attribute or behavior. Thus, while (ideally) the person may not be judged, his "illness" certainly is judged, and his "illness" is part of him. As Freidson notes, "moral neutrality exists only when a person is *allowed* to be or do what he will, without remark or question."[43] Moral entrepreneurs develop in this setting whose charge and aim are to find and control these illnesses. The major moral entrepreneurs in medicine are those seeking to influence public opinion and political policy so as to have the greatest possible influence upon recognizing and treating the recognized illnesses. This is where the National Socialists' conceptions of *Volksgemeinschaft* (Volk community), *Vorsorge* (preventive care), and Racial Hygiene came into play most forcefully. Since the person, the Jew or the hereditarily ill individual, was the bearer of the illness, he had to be expelled from the society, the *Volksgemeinschaft*, for reasons of preventive health (*Vorsorge).* This is an extreme form of the theory of illness called "contagionism."[44] It is the counterpart of Social Darwinism and an anti-Semitism which sought to expel the Jew from society by *any* means.

"The public spokesmen for the organized profession is the major moral entrepreneur." [45] Freidson further writes:

> Most of the activities of the active moral entrepreneurs of health are permeated by the tendency to see more illness everywhere around and to see the environment as being more dangerous to health than does the layman…He is likely to see a serious problem where the layman sees a minor one. They are biased toward illness as such and towards creating secondary deviance – sick roles – where before there was but primary deviance.[46]

---

[41] Freidson, 208.

[42] Freidson, 208.

[43] Freidson, 253.

[44] A. R. Aisenberg, *Contagion: Disease, Government, and the "Social Question" in Nineteenth-Century France* (Stanford: University Press, 1999); P. Baldwin, *Contagion and the State in Europe 1830–1930* (Cambridge: University Press, 1999); S. Jarcho, *The Concept of Contagion: In Medicine, Literature and Religion* (Malabar, Florida: Krieger Publishing, 2000); HAMJ Ten Have, "Knowledge and Practice in European Medicine: The Case of Infectious Diseases," in *The Growth of Medical Knowledge.* (Dordrecht: Kluwer Academic Publishers, 1990), 15–40.

[45] Gusfield, in Freidson, 254.

[46] Freidson, 255.

In this sense then, Adolf Hitler and the *Gesundheitführer*, Dr. Gerhard Wagner, were the moral entrepreneurs. It should be understood that Freidson is not using the term "moral" here in the usual sense of morality but to indicate the normative criteria for the constitution of the subject field of the profession. Hitler repeatedly referred to the Jews in terms consistent with a biological contagion, making the Jew the subject for the construction of the Comprehensive National Socialist Philosophical Viewpoint (*Weltanschauung)* and the action of *der Stand*, the profession. These conceptions of Jewishness and the hereditarily diseased individual as forms of illness to be removed from the National Socialist society are articulated specifically in Ramm's text. The elimination of the carrier of biological illness, according to the National Socialist physician, legitimated his practice of racial hygiene as the application of *Vorsorge*.

A profession is an occupation which has assumed a dominant position in a division of labor, so it gains control over the determination of the substance of its own work. Unlike most occupations, it becomes autonomous or self-directing. This is where the conceptions associated with *der Stand* and *der Beruf* overlap. The occupation sustains this special status by its persuasive profession of the extraordinary trustworthiness of its members. A calling *(Beruf)* achieves a certain status (*Stand).* The trustworthiness it professes naturally includes ethicality and also knowledgeable skill.

The National Socialist conception of racial hygiene was developed by an interactive relationship between the state and the profession (*Der Stand).* The mutually self-supporting nature of the profession and the national government explains the antipathy Ramm develops toward the private practice of medicine. A truly autonomous fee-for-service solo arrangement is inherently unstable because it will eventually fall under the dominating control of either patients or colleagues. In such a system of free competition, the physician will be able to count on neither the loyalty of his patient (with whom he has no contract) nor on that of his colleagues (with whom he has no ties and who are competing with him). Since his colleagues are competitors, he is not likely to solicit their advice or trade information, and he certainly will not refer his patients to them. Under these circumstances, a private practitioner is quite isolated from his colleagues and relatively free of their control, but at the same time, he is very vulnerable to control by his clients.[47] Consistent with this line of reasoning, in Ramm, we see the strong condemnation of non-National Socialist medicine and the *Kurierfreiheit* (freedom to advertise). Accordingly, the National Socialists were seeking to theoretically construct a concept of the profession (*der Stand*), which was a contrast to this capitalist orientation.

One can think of the National Socialist conception of *der Stand* as a state corporation which has an authoritarian and centrally led medical community. The professional (*berufstaendische*) orientation placed the whole of the state as well as the duty of the community to the community in the center of the National Socialist construction. This *Stand* was to subjugate itself to the "*Fuehrer* Principle," which

[47] Freidson, 92.

was the central foundation of the National Socialist ideology. The concentration of all power in the hands of a *Fuehrer* and Reich Chancellor corresponded to the destruction of democratic structures, the destruction of all forms of political cooperation and public control. In its place, there arose the ideology of the "emotional-irrational" connection of "*Gefolgschaft*" (obedience) to the political leadership.

The German doctors were passionately against the Weimar government's consideration of medicine as being just another commercial enterprise. To counteract this, the National Socialists' use of the term *der Stand* embodies Freidson's conception of professionalization of the profession, with an ethical dimension. All rights were state (füher) derived.

A profession (*Stand*) could only be spoken of as a corporation which organized its own life on the basis of its special occupational (*beruflich*) foundation and relationships, whereby self-administration in the National Socialist universalist sense could be a means to an end, a tool used to fulfill professionally the sense of the whole. Professional (*Staendish*) self-administration meant, according to the universalist concept, not freedom *from* the state for the purpose of increasing one's own power but rather the raising of one's own capacities of achievement as an ideal in respects to the purpose of the whole. It was considered to be a "free profession," but this meant freedom to serve the state and Volk.[48] The relationship to the whole determines the unity of the leadership, the force of authority over the profession (*Stand*) through the objective protection of the whole.

According to Otmar Zilk in 1937, "National Socialism has restlessly done away with the poison of the individualism of liberalism and Marxism."[49] Max Frauendorfer, director of the Party's Office of Corporate Organizations (*Amt fuer staendischen Aufbau*), leaned heavily on negative examples. Corporate organization in the Third Reich, he emphasized, had nothing to do with hypothetical medieval models; it was not autonomous; it had no mandate to represent special interests or restrict competition. Corporate development in Germany was *sui generis*, without models.[50] Andreas Pfenning, a sociologist, stated that corporatist organization "has to do with the realization of a historically necessitated task by our Volk."[51] This places the conception in the ethereal National Socialist realm so favored by Hitler.

All of this idealization of *der Stand* certainly engaged German theorists, but the reality of application was more mundane. Behind the hard unanimity of the official ideological principles was a real struggle, not about ideological principles but about the control and direction of professional power and economy. Rather than an orderly flow of power from the leader to the members, what occurred was a chaotic struggle for power and control.[52] What arose in place of the corporate structure was a hetero-

---

[48] In Swoch, 95–6.

[49] In Swoch, 97.

[50] Max Frauendorfer, in D. Schoenbaum, *Hitler's Social Revolution: Class and Status in Nazi Germany, 1933–1939* (Garden City, NY: WW Norton, 1980), 122.

[51] Andreas Pfenning, in Schoenbaum, 122.

[52] D. Kater, "Doctor Leonardo Conti and His Nemesis: The Failure of Centralized Medicine in the Third Reich," Central European History Vol. 18 (1985), 299–325.

geneous collection of quasi-autonomous "self-government" organizations, vertically constructed in a way intended to preclude any effective organization of dominant interest (poly-acracy). The result was a differential development of the government's relations with the profession by an uneven double structure with one side being dominated by the party and the other by the state.[53]

Personal Union vs. the Iron Fist: The Necessity of Medical Laws

At several points in the manuscript, Ramm mentions that someone in some administrative position is in "personal union" with someone in some other administrative entity. While this could mean that the same person held both positions, it could also mean that the two officials were to cooperate fully with each other. One can see how this might be necessary by examining the organizational chart at the end of this manuscript. The hierarchy of the Nazi medical administration, after Hitler and the Reich physician leader, became chaotic – a competition of competing competences. This was as Hitler wanted it. He seldom wrote direct orders, but instead, his highest lieutenants would listen to him patiently then take from his ramblings what he wanted to happen. They then had reasonable freedom in action. Hitler rarely intervened afterward. A statement of this sort of administration comes from the leader of Nazi women, Gertrud Scholtz-Klink:

> You younger people always look for written records. You don't understand that Hitler did not make decision on paper. I did just what all the other leaders did. When I wanted something, I spoke to Hitler. Or rather, I listened patiently as he rambled on and on. Eventually, he would get tired, usually after about an hour. Then, when his energy was spent, he would listen quietly. Then I had a receptive audience. You Americans have a saying about striking iron while it is hot. But I always knew to stay away from 'hot iron' – topics that made him angry. I waited until the iron had cooled off, until I knew I could count on persuading him, before making a formal suggestion. Sometimes that made my younger co-workers impatient."
>
> "Then you were satisfied with Hitler's policies on women?"
>
> "Absolutely. When we disagreed, I told him so. My voice was not loud but we accomplished much in silence."[54]

If we look at the organization of Ramm's text, we can see that it is more than a medical ethics text. It is more accurately a history of medicine and an ethics of medicine book ended by medical law. Observe the organization:

I. History of medicine as a profession ///
II. **Ordinance of Licensure →**
III. Public Health ///

[53] Kater, Doctor Leonardo Conti, 322.

[54] Claudia Koonz. *Mothers in the Fatherland: Women, the Family, and Nazi Politics.* (New York: St. Martin's Press, 1968).

IV. Nazi Party and Medicine ///
V. Physician's Responsibilities
VI. ← **Criminal Law and medicine**
VII. Medical Press

When in 1935 the government introduced a Reich Physicians' Ordinance supplemented by a Professional Ordinance in November 1937, the doctors found themselves tightly bound by a set of rules imposed from above with penal sanctions threatened to anyone who infringed them. According to Evans, disciplinary courts quickly became active in issuing warnings, meting out fines, and even suspending doctors who transgressed.[55] There should have been no doubt in the medical student's mind that his position in the society was established by and controlled by the law. He practiced only at the approval of multiple state bodies. And, should he wonder as to the consequences if he were to deviate from the standard set by the National Socialist *Weltanschauung*, he needs only to read on and learn that the penalties were not just civil penalties but criminal as well. The consequences of a physician's breaking a law could be the loss of civil rights. After one had served his term in prison, the Gestapo often would be waiting to take the individual into "protective custody," and he would then be taken to one of the concentration camps. Two questions arise concerning this dominant influence of the law in Nazi medicine:

Was it really necessary? As a group, physicians were traditionally nationalistic and conservative and widely believed in the truth of the central tenet of National Socialism, racial hygiene. Racial hygiene was at least accepted in principle by most medical faculties in the 1930s.[56] By 1935, virtually all of the physicians who had not been politically inclined to support the Social Democrats had been purged. Furthermore, consistent with the Nazi practice of Social Darwinism, those who were allowed to attend medical school had been rigorously selected for untainted racial characteristics and ideological reliability. According to Evans, the famous surgeon Ferdinand Sauerbruch complained about the poor quality of the new intake of medical students, many of whom had, he claimed, been picked because they or their parents were party members.[57]

Among the professions, the clergy and teachers were equally rigorously harassed about their adherence to the National Socialist *Weltanschauung.* In these professions, there were numerous examples where priests or teachers resisted the indoctrination of National Socialization in their field and were summarily relieved of their duties (gleichgeschaltet – coordinated). In contrast, there is in the current history of medicine in Nazi Germany no records of similar actions against doctors. So, why the huge threat of the law?

The answer to this question comes from the importance of medicine to the successful implementation of the central tenet of National Socialism – the practice of eliminative racial hygiene. The commitment of medical doctors was absolutely

[55] Evans, 2006, 444.

[56] Evans, 2006, 317.

[57] Evans, 2006, 318.

essential to the Nazis' eugenic plans. It was their responsibility to be on the front lines in the battle to eliminate undesirable genetic traits. The importance of medicine to the society can be seen from the fact that teachers of medicine made up roughly a third of all university faculty members by 1935, and the dominant position of medicine in universities was reflected in the fact that from 1933 to 1945, 59% of university rectors were drawn from the medical professions.[58]

Certainly, among the most highly selected group of physicians – those SS physicians who had attended the elite doctor training camps, such as the one Ramm mentions at Alt Rehse – the regime found willing participants in their eliminative racial hygiene. The following extended quotation from Hans-Henning Scharsach gives a depressingly realistic accounting of the activity of these physicians:

Deadly Duty: A Routine Day in the Life of a Physician at Auschwitz

It can be seen from the statements given by the physicians after the war that there was no trace of remorse. They did the work as a doctor that was assigned to them in order to keep the Volks' organism healthy as strengthen the Volks' community. Fanatic anti-Semitism had made them blind to the murderous sides of National Socialism. They were completely ideologically blinded by Hitler's assertion that "the Jew is our misfortune." Before their transfer to the Extermination Camp they might have held that the statement the "extermination of Jewry" was merely a propaganda phrase. Afterwards, it was used in earnest. At first they were shocked – but only for a short time. They subsequently took refuge in a particular National Socialist version of good and evil. The agreeable term "Final Solution" eased their task for it did not sound like mass murder and it encompassed both the end and the solution of a problem. The process of habituation was short and the creation of insensibility was total. Murder came to be referred to in routine conversations as *Sonderbehandlung,* "special treatment." The physician went to work just like anyone else in an office. In the eyes of the executioner the fate of his victim was a decided thing and was therefore irreversible. Those delivered to him were already dead. One cannot kill those already dead.

That the physicians did not regard their service as completely normal can be seen from the amount of alcohol that each consumed. Alcohol was the universal ingredient for socialization in the extermination camp. The recently arrived camp doctors could hardly bear the work. Community drinking with experienced professional colleagues helped them to make the transition from outsider to insider, from horror and revulsion, to daily routine. The practice of the *Selection* was the test of the novice. Afterwards, he belonged. He acted just like all the others, rebelled not, questioned nothing, showed no doubt, accepting the job just as it was. After three weeks he was integrated, becoming one of the three types, which the Auschwitz-Survivor Hermann Langbein – distinguished: (1) the reluctant actor, (2) the one carrying out orders obediently, (3) the enthusiast carrying out tasks diligently. Hardly any quit. As an outsider he would have had to bear the burden of being in an exceptional situation and no one seemed to have the strength to do that. Social cohesion was more important. If they were desperate, the newcomers sought out those of common backgrounds or interests (like Baverians vs. Preussians), common university backgrounds or anyone having similar general interests). The socialization process was favored by the isolated location of

[58] Evans, 2006, 316.

the camp. Far from any professional outer climate, away from family and circles of friends, the camp world existed without any sort of corrective. The outer medical contact of the doctor – as long as they were not taking part in experiments on human test rabbits – descended to the level of the SS doctor Enno Loling. This doctor was in the Economic Administration Section of the Main Office for the Organization of the Extermination Camps. He was an incompetent alcoholic, who simply inspected the camps in order to demonstrate his powerful position. He too was isolated: None of his colleagues bothered to burden themselves with the routine details of the extermination programs.

Auschwitz was a separated civilization – an enclave, in which all legal, economic, human and moral reflections had been removed. The only thing that happened here was reality. Because nothing else normal remained, the only valid standard was efficiency. Whoever succumbed to that ultimate value came to the conclusion that Auschwitz was an elite place in which to work. One paid attention to correct manners, faultless behavior and a clean uniform. If one could not get out of the unpleasant duty then one could nevert[59]heless be counted as one of the best. At every opportunity the leading SS physicians sought to display their overzealousness. Thus, even Eduard Wirths himself, regularly participated in the service at the ramp, in which, because of his position, he did not have to do. He acted as if he was catching up on the work which he had missed because of his duties. Camp Commander Rudolf Hoss, Wirth's superior, behaved similarly. He was always an eager observer of the whole process all the way through the murders and disposals, "in order to show that I not only gave orders, but that I was also ready to follow them," as he expressed after the war before the Nuremberg court.

So, it would appear that these elite physicians came to be willing participants. On the other hand, we have very little direct evidence that the average practicing physician willingly accepted the National Socialist *Weltanschauung.* Certainly, many doctors became members of the party, but it is unclear if this was commitment or opportunism. Consequently, one can reason that Ramm was required to write for the medical student and doctor who might resist the dictates of the regime. It was really not necessary that they accept the Nazi view, only that they act according to the law, else civil and even criminal punishment was to be expected.

So, Ramm's "Medical Ethics" is actually the "carrot" of the "carrot and stick" metaphor. This is represented by his terms, "personal union" and "whole of the whole." If the physician failed to follow the Nazi *Weltanschauung* philosophy, then he would have become subject to the same threat and intimidation as any other member of the German community. This was the "iron fist."

Mark Mazower[60] reports that there was actually a struggle going on in the higher circles of Nazi leadership from late 1941 between what was called the *Herrschaft* (a leadership class) vs. a *Füherschaft* (which emphasized the leader principle). The softer approach was represented by Werner Best and Wilhelm Stuckart, the author of the Nuremberg laws. The iron fist was touted by Hitler; Heinrich Himmler, the head of the SS; Reinhard Heydrich, the chief of Security of the SS, and later, the dominant leader of the Wannsee Conference in 1943 which established the program for the "Final Solution to the Jewish Question." So, we see in Ramm's text, with the

[59] (Die Ärzte der Nazis, Hans-Henning Scharsach, my translation).

[60] M. Mazower. *Hitler's Empire: How the Nazis Ruled Europe.* (New York: Penguin Books, 2008), 245–6.

juxtaposition of medical ethics and medical laws, the employment of this dual approach to the medical profession.

One area of needed future research is a more detailed determination of how willingly the average general practitioner participated in the eugenic activities. We know, for example, how many sterilizations were performed, each of which required a certification of medical necessity, but we do not know if the physicians who made these referrals were the official state doctors or the regular general practitioner, a group the Nazis sought to control with the passage and administration of the draconian laws.

Translating National Socialist German into English

Perhaps another reason for there being little historical material from the viewpoint of the perpetrators of the medical Holocaust has to do with the nature of the National Socialist language. Scholars have well documented how the National Socialists developed their own syntax and semantics. A philologist living in the Third Reich cataloged the manifest changes the Nazis brought to the language. He called the Nazi language "LTI," meaning the *Lengua Tertii Imperii* (Language of the Third Reich).[61] Much of this effort was carried out to explicitly use code words and neologisms to cover up their crimes. Translating their writing into English carries the dual risk of making the text appear screaming and dogmatic, like Hitler's speeches, or shallow and breezy. I have sought to overcome these threats by comparing Ramm's text with other contemporary National Socialist texts as well as popular German novels of the 1920s.[62]

---

[61] V. Klemperer, The Language of the Third Reich: LTI – Lingua Tertii Imperii. A Philologist's Notebook (London: Athlone Press, 1975).

[62] R. Michael & K. Doerr, *Nazi-Deutsch/Nazi-German: An English Lexicon of the Language of the Third Reich* (Westport, Conn. : Greenwood Press, 2002); W. Schmidt, *Geschichte der deutschen Sprache: Ein Lehrbuch für das germanistische Studium* (Stuttgart: S. Hirzel Verlag Stuttgart, 2004); C. Schmitz-Berning, *Vokabular Des Nationalsozialismus* (Berlin: Walter de Gruyter, 2000), 84; W. Benz, H. Graml, and H. Weiss, eds., *Enzyklopädie des Nationalsozialismus* (Stuttgart: Deutscher Taschenbuch Verlag, 2001); C. Berning, *Vom "Abstammungsnachweis" zum "Zuchtwart": Vokabular des nationalsozialismus* (Berlin: de Gruyter, 1964); V. Klemperer, 1980: LTI. Notizbuch eines Philologen. 6. Aufl. Leipzig, p. 29; Gerhart Wolff *Deutsche Sprachgeschichte von den Anfängen bis zur Gegenwart* (Tuebingen: A. Francke Verlag, 2004); Max Domarus, *Hitler Reden 1932 bis 1945: Kommentiert Von Einem Deutschen Zeitgenossen* (Loenberg : Pamminger & Partner, 1973); W. Maser, *Hitlers Briefe und Notizen: Sein Weltbild in handschriftlichen Documenten* (Graz: Leopold Stocker Verlag, 1973); H. Picker, *Hitler's Tischgespräche im Führerhauptquartier*, (Ulm: Propylaeen Verlag, 2003); J. Goebbels, *Tagebuecher: 1945* (Hamburg: Hoffman und Campe, 1977); Christopher M. Hutton *Linguistics and the Third Reich: Mother-Tongue Fascism, Race and the Science of Language* (New York: Routledge., 1999); H. Kaemper, "Die Amerikanisierung der deutschen Sprache," in *Die USA und Deutschland im Zeitalter des Kalten Krieges 1968–1990* (Stuttgard: Deutsche Verlags-Anstalt, 2001), 496–507; B. Brecht, *Die Dreigroschenoper* (Frankfurt am Main: Insel Verlag, 2004); A. Doeblin, *Berlin Alexanderplatz*

Reading Ramm's Text as a Textbook

As one reads Ramm's book, one is probably struck by the normality of the prose. It reads just like any other countless textbook one reads for a college subject. It is a cool detached presentation of the history of medicine, medical ethics, medical science, and biology. But, one must not let the calm demeanor of the text mislead the reader. One must note and acknowledge that Ramm is systematically instructing medical student of their *moral duty* to:

- Participate in involuntary sterilization
- Reveal professional secrets to state authorities
- Participate in medical experimentation without informed consent
- Threaten patients with the loss of social benefits if they refuse to follow medical advice
- Lobby state authorities to permit physician-assisted euthanasia

And, although one does not read in Ramm of recommendation that medical doctors must participate in the genocide of Jews, one can clearly come to understand that the state medical regime, including its leading moral authorities, would not condemn, and even encourage, such willing participation.

What is more, it is all stated coolly and rationally without the standard Hitleresque shrillness. It is, in fact, bland, or more accurate *banal*, as the classic statement of Hannah Arendt of Adolf Eichmann, the architect of the annihilation of the Jews, of the "banality of evil."[63] But what is different about Ramm, as compared with Eichmann, is that Ramm was not just following orders or just doing his duty. He was in fact creating the words and phrases which were meant to direct and justify the actions and beliefs of medical doctors as they participated in the enormous crimes of the medical society of the Third Reich. At no point in the book does he quote the architects of the "Final Solution." He writes the justification himself, in his own words, using phrases and language of the Third Reich which would have been known and accepted by medical students as correct and carrying the authority of the medical profession and the laws.

(Dusseldorf and Zuerich: Patmos Verlag, 1996); K. Mann, *Mephisto* (Hamburg: Rowohlt Taschenbuch Verlag, 2005); S. Zweig, *Vierundzwanzig Stunden Aus Dem Leben Einer Frau* (Frankfurt am Main: S. Fischer, 1983); B. Brecht, *The Threepenny Opera* translated by Eric Bentley (New York: Grove Press, 1949); B. Brecht, *The Threepenny Opera* translated by Marc Blitzstein, (New York: Decca, 1954); B. Brecht, *The Threepenny Opera* translated by Michael Feingold (Frankfurt: Ensemble Modern, 1989); B. Brecht, *The Threepenny Opera* translated by Ralph Manheim and John Willett (New York: Arcade Publishing, 1994); B. Brecht, *The Threepenny Opera* translated by Robert David MacDonald (London: Digital Jay, 1994); A. Döblin, *Berlin Alexanderplatz* translated by Eugene Jolas (New York: Continuum, 2003); K. Mann, *Mephisto* translated by Robyn Smith (New York: Random House, 1977); S. Zweig, *Twenty-Four Hours in the Life of a Woman* translated by Anthea Bell (London: Pushkin Press, 2003).

[63] Arendt H. *Eichmann in Jerusalem: A Report on the Banality of Evil* (New York: Viking Press, 1963).

All medical students, if they wished to be admitted into the profession, would have known at the time of graduation of their "moral" duty. Additionally, they would have clearly understood the legal risk if they refused or even questioned acting out these demands.

In this sense, Ramm's text is a horrible text. It should make all scholars of medical history and medical ethics shudder with horror and appreciate how profoundly significant and relevant their scholarship and teaching are to the behavior of their charges who will later assume the awesome responsibilities which come with taking up the role of practicing medicine. It is well known how important the role model of the revered professor is to the acculturation of the medical student into the ancient medical society. Ramm's book, as a textbook, is testament to not just his banality but also his evilness.

Contents

Part I: The Ideal Conception of Medicine and the Medical Profession Through the Ages

The art and science of healing are expressions of human culture. We can assume with justification that from the oldest of times they have been associated with the progressive development of culture and that they have been intimately intertwined in the ebb and flow of the human story of varied peoples.[1]

As far as we can illuminate from the darkness by ancient historical research we can firmly establish that it was precisely the Aryan Volk,[2] who, on the basis of the creative power of their race, achieved in peaceful and prosperous times, in the context of their high culture, a high grade of medical art and science, and whose bearers and promoters demonstrated such a high moral conception of their profession – in

[1] From the beginning, Ramm states that medicine, society and culture are intertwined. This is a foundational proposition of the National Socialist philosophical viewpoint of medicine. The practice of the medical profession (*Beruf* and *Stand*) is a culturally determined activity within a particular society. While the Nazis did not deny the advances made to medical science by strictly objective scientific investigations (many by famous German medical scientists who were Nobel Prize winners), the actual *practice* of the profession was determined by the culture within the society. This somewhat soft view of objective science influenced the quality of supposedly scientific studies done by Nazi physicians on concentration camp inmates. The majority of such studies have been found to be sloppily performed and provide very little if any scientific quality.(R. L. Berger, "Nazi Science – the Dachau Hypothermia Experiments," in John J. Michalczyk, ed., *Medicine Ethics and the Thrid Reich: Historical and Contemporary Issues* (Kansas City: Sheed & Ward, 1994, 89).

[2] Ramm establishes from the beginning the proposition that the origin of all creativity in medicine came from the Aryan Volk. Not only were they the creators of medicine, but they "demonstrated such a high moral conception of their profession…that we still view them today with reverence…" These mythical Aryan Volk were the foundation Volk of the National Socialist ideal. The regime's constant appeal to the people, *das Volk*, represented its firm belief in harmonizing the one (*der Fuehrer)* with the many (*das Volk*), of "linking ruler and ruled in some mystical bond of leadership."(Fischer, 344) Michael Burleigh notes that "the *Volk* concept was doubly effective in a new nation state in which belonging was considered to be derived through blood as well as culture, rather than through subscription to shared civic values or venerable institutions."(M. Burleigh, *The Third Reich: A New History* (New York: Hill & Wang, 2000), 95).

R. Ramm, *Medical Jurisprudence and Rules of the Medical Profession*, Philosophy and Medicine 135, https://doi.org/10.1007/978-3-030-25245-8_1

spite of the prevailing changes in medical customs – that we still view them today with respect as being exemplary and worthy of imitation.

We know next to nothing about the health-related activities of the primitive foundation Volk. By comparable observations of animals and primitive people still existing today, we can assume that originally only the instinctive activity of the individual existed. One such individual who was more highly developed applied his experience to the healing of certain injuries and illnesses. Through collection and exchange of these experiences and the passing of them on to descendants, there gradually arose a treasury of knowledge which specially suited people employed to become healers of their tribal compatriots.

We are indebted to this empirical side of the development of healing science for the knowledge of many methods of healing which are still in use today.

To a certain degree, primitive reason recognized the causes of the diseases which had been brought about by external factors, however, in the case of internal diseases, this explanatory capacity completely failed, therefore refuge was taken in the doctrine of evil spirits, which were thought to intend the victim evil or believed to take total possession of the body. One sought to conciliate these demons with presents and sacrifices, and thereby propitiate or remove the spirits by the employment of magic to conjure up spells. In a few primitive volk groups the magician developed, by virtue of his experience and through his aura, the art of healing, which he knew secured him as a mediator between demons and the sick, and thereby became a *medicine man,* whose life calling was healing and who, by virtue of the instruction of his younger tribal comrades in his art, saw to it that there were the necessary descendants.

A later conception, which considered sickness to be punishment by God for committed wrongs, which required expiation, entrusted the art of healing to the priestly class, whose influence and reputation rose through these activities. As a result, the empirical health science contained a *theurgisch*[3] component, which strived to achieve healing through sacrifice, prayer, self-chastisement, fasting and the like. However, it has been historically proven that, alongside the priestly physician in the old volk cultures there were always worldly physicians who actively performed the lower medical activities, like surgical interventions, while, at the same time, internal medicine remained the field of the priestly-physicians. In ancient Babylon and Egypt these latter physicians even retained a certain right to supervise the common doctors.

We know that in these two volk cultures the practice of medicine enjoyed a high reputation,[4] that also much of the progress in healing science can be ascribed to

---

[3] *theure* = *teuer,* meaning higher value, precious. In this context, Ramm seems to relate it to a religious rite.

[4] One of the major themes of Ramm's text concerns the reputation or social regard for the physician. He goes to great lengths to point out when a particular sort of physician was in high regard in the society, and gives details for his explanation for such regard. Michael Kater reports that the precariousness of the physicians' professional status in the Weimar Republic was translated into a continuous quest for social standing. There was the general tendency within society to emulate the

these physicians and that the practice of their medical arts was collected for the first time in a legal form, which secured for the doctor, in addition to his economic existence, a great degree of freedom in the practice of his profession.

Nevertheless, we must recognize that it was the continuous creative achievements of the Aryan who was the only founder of healing science and that other traditional peoples overtook this from the Aryan Indians and Greeks. His creativity and thirst for new knowledge thereby drove this development up to that level of human culture which was transmitted to Rome, Alexandria, Byzantium and Arabia, then to Germany and Western Europe; the brilliance of this knowledge enlightened the early and late middle ages and established the foundation for the development of modern scientific medicine. The true history of the medical profession is built upon this foundation.

The health science of the Aryan cultural volk of India[5] in its oldest Vedic period (±1800-800 before the time change) – named after the holy script corresponding to this time, the *Vedas* – was of a *theurgisch* character, which distinguished it from the volk medicine of other volk. Holy prayers to the Gods, magic and conjuring spells were at this time the expressions of the striving for healing. Simple belief in the curative and corrupting forces of nature dominated the field of medical activities; meanwhile, the surgeon achieved a considerable level of ability. The Vedic doctor began to attain a special status resulting in the freer practice of his profession.

At the beginning of the second, Brahman, period, from 800 on, only the caste of priests appears to have been in possession of healing science. Since, however, the Brahman priests did not practice surgery, there developed two new castes – the noble caste of true physicians and the lesser regarded caste of healing servants.

---

aristocracy and conform to the ways of authority. (*Obrigkeitdenken)* (M. H. Kater, "Professionalization and Socialization of Physicians in Wilhelmine and Weimar Germany," *Journal of Contemporary History* 20 (1985): 679) This will become another justification for the Comprehensive National Socialist Philosophical Viewpoint of medicine, and is a representation of the idealization of medicine. Ramm is saying to his medical student readers, "If you want high regard in the society, you must follow this medThe term "Aryan" came from the translation of French racist Count Joseph Arthur de Gobineau's nineteenth century treatise. The term was originally used to denote the common ancestors of the speakers of Germanic languages. However, under the influence of a book by the Englishman, Houston Stewart Chamberlain, *The Foundations of the Nineteenth Century,* published in 1900, the term came to represent the Germanic race in its struggle against the Jewish race. These two races were the only two racial groups that retained their original purity in a world of miscegenation.(R. J. Evans, *The Coming of the Third Reich* (New York: Penguin, 2004), 33).

[5] It appears that Ramm is joining the racist theories of Chamberlain with the linguistic theories of the origin of the "Indoeuropean" languages, also often referred to a "Indogermanic." Sociolinguists have spoken of languages such as English, German, French, Russian, and Hindi as Indo-European dialects. In this case the assumption is that there was once a single language, Indo-European, that the speakers of that language (which may have had various dialects) spread to different parts of the world, and that the original language eventually diverged into the various languages we subsume today under the *Indo-European family* of languages. Ronald Wardhaugh, however, points out that this process of divergence was not as clean-cut as this classical *"neo-grammarian"* model of language differentiation suggests.(R. Wardhaugh, *An Introduction to Sociolinguistics: Fifth Edition* (Malden, MA: Blackwell, 2006), 33)ical National Socialist philosophical viewpoint."

In these times, the status of the physician was very high. One of the 14 *Retuas*, consisting of precious things which were produced by the Gods through the mixing of the earth and the sea, was the learned physician. His activity encompassed not only the practice of internal medicine but also surgery. "Only the unification of medicine and surgery" said Susruta, "makes the complete physician." "A physician who abandons the knowledge of one of these branches is like a bird with only one wing" (Haeser).[6]

Training to become a physician began as early as 12 years of age and ended at 18. Each teacher was allowed to instruct only four to six students. Instruction consisted of working through a textbook under the leadership and oversight of the teacher. The students were chosen on the basis of their noble descent, morality, health and good appearance, as well as good intellectual predisposition and great manual dexterity. With a solemn commitment, the apprentice was admonished to be chaste and abstinent, to speak the truth, to eat no flesh and to follow the orders of the teacher in all things. *"A physician who wishes for success in his practice and his calling, a good name and eventually heaven, must pray daily for the welfare of all of the living, strive with all his soul for the healing of the sick and, even if his own life stands in the balance, he must do no harm to the sick and never think of going near another's wife, or his possessions. In his dress and other formalities he must be simple and keep away from bad society. His speech is to be clear, agreeable, true, appropriate and measured; he should always seek to awaken, defend and promote knowledge. For those people who have been made outcasts by the king or the volk, he should prescribe no medicine, even less so for horribly misshapen, degenerate, troublesome persons and the dying. The events in the houses of the sick are not to be blabbed about" (Haeser).*

The education of the prospective doctor according to these prescriptions led to the establishment of a highly ethical position for the physician in his profession.

The practice of healing science required the approval of the prince, while state organs enforced compliance with enacted regulations, especially proofs regarding prior education. The physician's honorarium was commensurate with the reputation of the profession. Medical ethics demanded that the poor be treated free of charge. The despised castes of huntsmen, and falconers, as well as the incurably ill, were not allowed to receive any medical help. Punishment was given for false treatment; the reward for the good physician was Indian heaven.

Despite the extension of their healing science and in spite of the construction of a high ethos of the position of the physician, the Indians did not carry their *theurgisch* thinking to its full extent, and thus limited the ultimate conclusion of their intellectual stance. It remained for the Greeks to take the step from *theurgisch* – empiricism to arrive at free scientific thinking.

The conspicuous manifold instances of individual similarities between Indian and Greek healing science – like the Indian aphorisms and Germanic magic

---

[6] Haeser, H.: *Geschichte der Medizin.* Gustav Fischer, Jena 1882; In the body of Ramm's text he spells the name "Haeser" whereas in the reference he spells it "H a {umlaut} ser."

blessings – find their explanation in their common Aryan root. It may have been that for the Greeks, that Astrology and Numerology, which probably had had an Oriental origin, had a certain meaning, so that in the beginning medicine was connected to a religious cult. Related to this is the fact that no other people had carried out the separation of the practical art of healing from religious activity as early as had the Greeks. With this separation there began the period where the progress of health science was tied to the personalities of single great men, who, through the founding of traditionally connected schools, impressed their stamp on whole centuries and over much longer periods of history.

Even though the healing science of Ilias (± 1000 years before the time change) was still based entirely on the characteristics of an empirically based volk medicine, we find already at this time men who, as a consequence of their special experience and practice, are considered to be professional doctors and who enjoyed a high reputation. "Because the physician," so says Homer, "is a man who is worth a host of others."[7] Medical activity, as reported in the Odyssey, is of the old familiar type, with the difference that soon religious-superstitious practices forced themselves into use, and, in the case of especially severe illness, conjuring spells were employed in addition to empirical treatment.

In the following periods, the art of healing turned even more to magical ideas and practices. Individual shrines to deities were erected to whom one would turn in an emergency for advice and consolation. Among these deities, there emerged in the seventh century *Asklepios*, whose cult extended over the whole Greek lands. The temple consecrated to him, in which the priests gave medical advice to the sick, gradually became an important place of pilgrimages. In this stage in the development of Greek healing science, where this particular medical temple threatened to overwhelm the empirical one, there was a great danger that its course – like that of Egyptian and Babylonian medicine – would disintegrate into a religious-mystical cult of fraud and deception. Before that occurred, however, the worldy physicians preservered and developed the science of empirical healing, ultimately adopting an entirely self-sufficient way of healing. In many places of cult practice, there appears to have existed a close relationship between the worldly and the priestly doctors, in which one supported the other to a certain extent and mutually shared the means of healing and methods of treatment. The free medical profession appears to have been.

prevented from growing old through transmission of the profession within blood relationships. Later medical descendants came to be educated in the *Asklepiade Schulen,* which arose in the vicinity of the Asklepios temple, since here is where the greatest number of sick people congregated. The most famous of these were the schools of Kos and Knidos, Kroton, Kyrene and Rhodes; Hippocrates (born about 460 before the time change) came out of the Kosian school.

The medical profession was open for each free person. Instruction began in boyhood and involved theory and practice at the bedside. At the completion of instruction

[7] *Iliad xi.514.*

the student was accepted into the Ascelpian guild after which he had to swear to the so-called *Hippocratic Oath*:

I swear by Appollo, the physician, by Asklepios, Hygeia and Panacea and by all Gods and Goddesses, in whom I take as my witness, that I will fulfill this Oath and these my duties according to my ability and understanding, namely to honor those who have instructed me in this (medical) art, to consider them like my own parents, to share his life's fate, to grant those desires that he needs, to hold his descendant lineage equal to my male brothers, that if they want to learn this art, to grant to teach them without payment and without incurring debt, and to communicate the directed lectures and the usual material of teaching to my sons as well to those of my teachers and the students which enter and are indentured according to medical law, but otherwise no one.

I will use dietetic means for the benefit and devotion to the sick according to my ability and understanding; if they are threatened however with peril and injury I will seek to protect them. Also I will administer to no one, even if requested, a means to cause death; nor share such advice; likewise I will give no woman a means of producing abortion. Honorable and pious I will form my life and practice my art. Also I will swear by God not to cut for the bladder stone, rather will leave this to those in whose calling it falls. In all houses, however, in which I am allowed to go I will enter only to care and look after the patient, holding myself away for each intentional and shame-bringing wrong, especially from sexual traffic with men and women, freedman and slaves. What I see or perceive in my activities as a physician or what I experience otherwise of humanity which should never be revealed, that I will protect in my deepest heart and will hold it to be unutterable.

The similarity in the wording of the Hippocratic Oath to the Indian Oath is unmistakable and conspicuous. Both testify to a high ethical conception of the medical calling, which was the meaning communicated from another source to the Hippocratic Oath. The Indian oath begins with bitter complaints about the incompetence of many who call themselves doctors without really being so. It demands from the Asclepios youth: natural aptitude, instruction from boyhood on, love of work and stamina. The knowledge which is equally removed from timidity as well as from carelessness is to be securely anchored through these alone. The script shows further that, for the doctor, a good general education is indispensable. It rejects reflexion as the method of human knowledge and sets observation in its place.

The Hippocratic doctors appear to us to have been men who, with respect to general and medical education, stood at the height of their time. They deserve to be placed even today among physicians to be idealized because of their honorable behavior and their high regard for the responsibilities of the medical calling. "The Art of Healing," as it was called in the Hippocratic writings, "leads to piety towards the Gods and love towards mankind. Where there is love of this art there is also love for mankind."

Just as medical instruction was a thoroughly private matter, likewise was the practice of medicine. Proof of a sufficient preparatory education was not required. Because of this, the quack flourished alongside the high standing idealized conception of medicine. The doctor carried out his practice either at a fixed location or as an itinerant. Treatment was delivered in private hours or in the *Jatreia*, a kind of ambulance, which however occasionally was used for an extended stay of the sick. Specialists in today's sense did not exist as internal medicine and surgery were practiced by one and the same doctor. In times of war and epidemics the municipalities employed doctors. Indeed, we find around the year 600, before the time change, in individual Greek colonies, full-time and salaried municipal doctors. By a special tax the community financed these positions along with the arrangements necessary to carry out the practice. These doctors had no right to demand an honorarium from the patient, however, as a rule, affluent patients provided them with gifts and natural produce; in later Hippocratic times, an honorarium came to be reimbursed in the form of money. In addition to the healing science of the educated doctor, there were still at this time other of practitioners, including teachers in the Gymnasium, as well as root gatherers and herbalists.

After Philip of Macedonia conquered the Greek lands and after the erection of the powerful empire of Alexander the Great, the cultural emphasis shifted to the east and, after Alexander's death, to the states which followed. At this time, Alexandria – the city at the mouth of the Nile named after Alexander the Great – became the center of medical education. The medical profession did not undergo any essential change; however, the community doctor appeared, who received in the second century before the time change the honorable title "Archiater," indicating that some of the private physicians of that time no longer stood at the level of this Hippocratic doctor in knowledge and professional ethics and had come to be therefore considered in a certain sense to be subject to this official physician.

In old Rome, the development of the science of healing and the medical profession did not achieve the level of that of the Greek lands or of the Alexandrians. The rough rural and warrior people of Rome contented themselves in the erection of their world empire with their primitive folk medicine. If one could not heal oneself one turned to the healing art of slaves and freed slaves. Only after the subjugation of the Greek lands was it possible for Greek culture to penetrate and thus for the Greek physician to also immigrate, although the practice of his profession was at first, because of its foreignness, very difficult. Because of that, it was only late that Greek health science experienced in old Rome a new flowering, achieving its high point in the work of Galen.

With the granting of citizenship to the free Greek physician under Caesar's reign in 46 before the time change, the medical community developed into a highly regarded profession, to which prominent Roman citizens who were educated by the Greeks also devoted themselves. Caesar Hadrian bestowed on the physician in 117, after the time change, important rights, which consisted of freedom from community service, burdensome offices and service in the army, etc. Later a fixed number of students were authorized for each administrative district; the practice of medicine was made dependent on authoritative approval and the education of doctors was raised to a state responsibility. The Romans also overtook from the Greeks the practice of appointing the community doctors, who also were called "Archiater." This title later became reserved for the personal physician of the Caesar. In addition to Archiater, we find army and navy doctors as Roman state officials. Additionally, the larger corporate bodies, like theaters, libraries and gladiator schools employed personal physicians to provide treatment. Guilds and free unions soon followed this example, creating institutions which can be considered to be the forerunners of the insurance funds and medical unions of our time. The official and employed doctors were salaried full time. The publicly practicing general doctor was in general dependent on what his patient would voluntarily give him because he had no principle right to an honorarium, which was only established under Justinian (527–565, after the time change). After that time, a mutually agreed upon honorarium was permitted.

In old Rome, to a large extent, medicine split up into daughter disciplines. There were specialists for surgery, dentistry, eye and ear healing science; indeed specialization went so far that one finds doctors who only practiced water curing or only operated on fractures, cataracts or bladder stones. The quack was in full bloom. The social status of the doctor was great; he was highly regarded and respected by his fellow citizens, while the specialist, because of the narrowness of his knowledge, did not enjoy any special privileges. In the times of the later Caesars, with the decline in morals, there was also a decline in the healing sciences to a point where it came to be considered to be nothing more than a poorly regarded trade.

Galen (136-201, after the time change) was a new high point and the real final branch in the development of the healing sciences of antiquity. His scientific thought corresponded predominantly to a humoral-pathological conception. His abiding contribution consisted in the collection and categorization of earlier theories into a uniform system of all areas of science and practical medical activities, which, because of his clarity and thoroughness, influenced the course of the development of medicine for one and a half centuries. Since Galen neither founded a school nor trained individual students, his life's work did not generate a legacy to be continued and cultivated. Galen's significance however lies not entirely in the founding of a medical system, but rather above all in that with him there came to be a temporary conclusion to a struggle which had existed between the schools of Kos and Knidos and had affected the entire development of medicine: the struggle between the conception of medicine as a science or as an art. While the majority of doctors in Hippocratic times defended the view that medicine is an art, Galen introduced proof through promotion of medicine and its auxiliary sciences that the conception of medicine is to be recognized primarily as a science.

As a consequence of the racial decline of Rome, political and cultural downfall soon followed, pulling medical science along with it into the abyss. Demon cults, astrology, alchemy and magic were companions and followers of the racial decline seen in the intellectual areas. The political inheritance of the state passed over to the Germans pushing in from the north, while in the philosophical and religious areas it was the doctrine of *primitive Christianity* which gradually took over the spirit and soul of the south.[8]

---

[8]This one sentence contains propositions discussed and contested by many historians. The background question is, "When did the Roman Empire fall?" Ramm's answer generally is consistent with a standard German (not just National Socialist) viewpoint. The Roman Empire did not "fall" but was assimilated by the Germans.(H. Kelling, *Deutsche Kulturgeschichte* (New York: McGraw-Hill, 1999), 43) For the Nazis and their supporters, the very term 'Third Reich' constituted a powerful symbolic link to the imagined greatness of the past, embodied in the First Reich of Charlemagne and the Second of Bismarck.(R. J. Evans, *The Coming of the Third Reich* (New York: Penguin Press, 2004), 460)

From out of the heap of political and cultural rubble at the end of the Roman empire, rebuilding elements formed, going through hundreds of years. The Christian religion of the middle ages oppressed all of intellectual life with depressing religious dogmas and hindered thereby the free unfolding of self-sufficient thinking in scientific areas.

A stroke of fate[9] handed down high Greek science to the east Romans and Saraceans and then through monks to posterity, which, after the liberation of the

---

But, at the same time, "in the philosophical and religious areas it was the doctrine of *primitive Christianity* which gradually took over the spirit and soul of the south." This is a proposition by Gibbon, that is, that it was the mystical aspects of Christianity which was the cause for the "fall of the Roman Empire."(E. Gibbon, *The History of the Decline and Fall of the Roman Empire. Vol. VII.* (London: The Folio Society, 1990), 334) Ramm cannot buy entirely into Gibbon's argument, otherwise there would be no Third German Reich. But, at the same time, he does not reject Christianity entirely. At least during the early years of the Regime, the Nazis did not want to antagonize the Christian community, because they needed their support against the centrist parties. They declared that the 'nationalist' revolution intended to put an end to the materialist atheism of the Weimar left and to propagate a 'positive Chrisitianity" instead, above confession and attuned to the Germanic spirit.(Evans, *Coming of the Third Reich,* 363) So, in his interpretation, it is "primitive" Christianity which took over the spirit and soul of the south.

The relationships between the two Christian faiths, Catholic and Lutheran, to the Nazi regime were complex and at times chaotic.(G. Lewy, *The Catholic Church and Nazi Germany* (New York: De Capo Press, 1964); D. L. Bergen, *Twisted Cross: The German Christian Movement in the Third Reich* (Chapel Hill: University of North Carolina Press, 1996); K. Meier, *Kreuz und Hakenkreuz: Die evangelische Kirche im Dritten Reich* (Munich: Dtv, 1992); C. E. King, *The Nazi State and the New Religions: Five Case Studies in Non-Conformity.* (New York: Edwin Mellen Press, 1982); J. S. Conway, *The Nazi Persecution of the Churches 1933–1945.* (New York: Regen College Publishers, 1968); E. C. Helmreich, *The German Churches Under Hitler: Background, Struggle, and Epilogue* (Detroit: Wayne State U. Press, 1979) and the regime took account of the religions only in the context of their political power. The regime did make political concessions to the various faiths, and signed a "Concordat" with the Vatican in 1933, but Hitler refused to listen to the Church's exhortations against the racial laws and sterilization of those who suffered from genetic diseases.(Fischer, 363) Children in the Hitler Youth were explicitly indoctrinated against Christianity. Evans reports that the following text was recited by 12-year-olds at the Nuremberg Party Rally of 1934:

We are the jolly Hitler Youth,
We don't need any Christian truth
For Adolph Hitler, our Leader
Always is our interceder.

Whatever the Papist priests may try,
We're Hitler's children until we die;
We follow not Christ but Horst Wessel.
Away with incense and holy water vessel!

As sons of our forebears from times gone by
We march as we sing banners held high.
I'm not a Christian, nor a Catholic,
I go with the SA through thin and thick. (Evans, *Third Reich in Power,* 250–1)

[9] Ramm does not tell what "stroke of fate" he is referring to. It can be reasonably assumed that he is referring to the fact that most of the Greek manuscripts of antiquity were in Arabia, where they were eventually translated by Arabian scholars. During the ninth century, the Arabs came into

spirit from religious chains, then delivered the fundamentals of the proud edifice of all of the modern sciences.

In the eastern Roman Empire it was the capital city Byzantium where the culture achieved a height equivalent to that in old Rome. Medical science was cultivated from the position which had thrived in Rome in its heyday, in which, just like in Greece, Alexandria and Rome, there was the same type of full-time salaried Archiaters.

We find at the beginning, just like in Greece, Alexandria and Rome, again the model of the full salaried Archiater. Justinian annulled this doctor system, which had to make way for a vocation of free doctors, and gave to the medical profession special legal protection and great freedom. At this time the Army Medical Inspectorate was strongly cultivated and, with the founding of sick and epidemic houses, the model of the hospital and institutional doctor was created. It has not been determined if these institutions also served for the training of doctors. Theoretical instruction was given by full-time salaried doctors in public lectures; in order to learn practical knowledge, the student attached himself to an older doctor. In addition, as in Galen's time, there were student trips for continuing medical education to the old famous educational institutes of Athens and Alexandria.

With the spread of Islam, *Arabian doctor*s became the collectors and defenders of the medical science transmitted from antiquity. During the three to four century high period of Arabian medicine, the doctors held a position equal to the highly regarded and honorable social position of Greek times. The Arabian physicians are to be thanked for arranging together the scientific material into instructional books and collected works, which had been at the time scattered over the entire cultural world. These, however, suffered a regrettable restriction of distribution because of prohibitions of pictures of the body and organs of humans, decreed by the Islamic religion. The examination of doctors, which was introduced in 931 in Bagdad, testifies to the seriousness the Arabic public brought to medical matters. In spite of that, quacks continued to flourish. Doctors and specialists decided at that time to join together in a union which served scientific and ethical, as well as economic, purposes. State organs practiced a certain oversight over the activities of doctors.

The education to become a doctor became a private matter, carried out either under the supervision of a recognized physician or by visiting a special physician's school which was connected to a hospital.

The west Roman Empire of the Goths and Langobards, who probably had already had contact with the science of healing of antiquity from their wanderings in the south, derived benefit from the medical treasures of the Arabians and of old Byzantium. An extensive darkness descended over the medical activities of these times, since written traditions hardly existed and the few manuscripts on hand permit no real picture of the medical conditions of the period.

---

contact with Greek science and philosophy, and the result was a cultural flourishing. A team of translators, most of whom were Nestorian Christians, made Greek texts available in Arabic. (K. Armstrong, *A History of God: The 4000-Year Quest of Judaism, Christianity and Islam* (New York: Ballantine Books, 1993), 170).

There has been transmitted to us however from around 500, after the time change, an order which was decreed by Theodosias the Great, the king of the Langobards, under the designation "Formula comites archaetrorin," in which the high conception which one had of the mission of the doctor at that time is given expression, and which speaks of an already strict organization of the profession. An abstract of the statement goes:

> *Of all the universally useful arts which the Gods have granted to weak humans, the beneficial science of healing appears to have achieved the most. This is because it is that art which stands like the kindness of a mother during the dangers of illness, which defends our human frailty against pain and which comes to our aid where kingdom and high honor can no longer give us aid. Those qualified in the law will be esteemed with high honors since they are burdened with the defense of a client. It is however much more glorious to turn away the dangers of death and to bring reassurance to those endangered, who tend to despair almost immediately. That is the art which enables sick people to see more clearly than they are able to see by themselves, which invigorates those who are unstable, strengthens those shaken and, with the wise vision of the future, is able to resist illness. And while the sick person struggles with the weakness of his body, this art looks much deeper than one would otherwise be permitted, apprehends more out of books than what mere observation of the sick affords, so that what becomes known from following a reasonable inference proceeds from unreason to become an almost mysterious prediction.*
>
> *Must it not now however be considered to be a neglect of common human concerns if no judge is set over such knowledge? Therefore, the doctors to whom we grant the right to hospitality should also have a head master. They should know that they are responsible for the account of their methods of healing. That which is occasionally undertaken by the individual is not to be considered to be the art, but rather only that which is to be read of in the books. If we all demanded to be merely left to the arbitrary use of our own power, then we would set up great danger for ourselves. A delay of the matter will only cause indignant questions.*
>
> *For this reason, after the conclusion of his course of learning, the doctor should also still have a teacher over him and should have time for books and time to enjoy the writings of his elders. No one has more cause to delve deeply and diligently into books than one who works for the health of his fellowman. Refrain, you zealous healers, from the terrible minor squabbling over the sick! Regarding that, however, if the one does not want to give up to the other, because of distracting contradictory objections, you know now of the one authority who you could ask without jealousy. A wise doctor takes advice gladly from others, especially those recognized to be experienced, who proves himself to be especially careful by making numerous examinations. With admittance into this art, you have committed yourself to especially serious dedications. You have sworn solemnly to your teachers to hate wickedness and to love purity. You are not free to voluntarily let your attention lapse regarding that which was just a short time ago committed to your knowledge and conscience. And in regards to that, you must carefully seek all that heals the wounded and strengthens the weak. It may be that an oversight is pardonable, but to sin against the welfare of the people must be regarded as a crime, like a murder!*
>
> *Your appearance is for the sick like the visit of a loved guest, for the weak, a rejuvenation, for the exhausted, new hope. Inquire in full possession of yourself if the pain can be suppressed, the sleep can be restored. Then the sick person will also question himself and you will be able to thus clearly say what ails him: because to the experienced doctor the pulse of the veins points out how the inner nature is suffering. Also the urine can be examined. Finally one must pay attention to the voice of the complainant and allow no remarkable symptoms to be belittled.*
>
> *Show yourself to be compliant to my court! Trust in us because that will certainly lead to higher reward. While others have to perform according to the wording of the laws, you*

are entrusted with the reign of that of an oath of office. A high right is established for you: You have the authority to burden even us with fasting. You can make decisions which oppose our wishes and, considering our welfare, can make decisions which may appear to us burdensome and cruel. Regarding that, you should always completely and entirely appreciate this authority which we ourselves would hardly arrogate over to another and which is granted to you against us.

We believe we have admonished you about this. These thoughts have induced me to entrust you today with the dignity of a leader of doctors, so that you are to be outstanding among all doctors. Your decisions should reconcile all the squabbling since only your judgment leads to success. You should be an umpire and skillfully mediate each disagreement. Thus should you of all physicians heal the sick while you wisely bring to an end damaging squabbling. It is a high office to have understanding people given as subordinates and, among those who become honored by the community, to take on yourself also a place of honor.[10]

The science of healing throughout the old German period resembles in general the mythological times of the Greek and Indian periods. The Germans of the north had a special God of physicians named Eir. The sayings speak especially of miraculous women who lived in crags and forests and who brought recovery to those sick who sought them in these places.

Later, the practice of healing science was transferred over to the Priests (*Druids*) and the priestesses(Sagas and *Alrunen*), who sought to heal the sick through miraculous sayings, songs and drinks. It was the responsibility of these women to care for the sick and wounded. Lay doctors arose among the Germans, especially as treaters of wounds.

In the time of the wandering of the Volk, the German tribes came in to close contact with Hellinsitic culture and assimilated to a large extent its educational structure. In the Goths we find, for example, well educated doctors who were not inferior in ability and knowledge to Roman doctors. The practice of the profession was subordinate to the oversight of the state. Laws defended the sick from arbitrary use of power and bad treatment and likewise shielded doctors from the thanklessness of those which they had cared for.

After Christianity took over, the whole educational system, including medicine, appears to have become the possession of the cloister and monastery orders, whose members concerned themselves, as priest-physicians, with the practical side of the science of healing.

From the ninth and tenth centuries, there are references to doctors who came out of the *School of Salerno* in southern Italy. There is indication in the history of medicine of a Salernian doctor congregation which enjoyed a high reputation while constructing a systematic worldly and intellectual school of healing science. Salerno owes its world reputation predominantly to the fact that it was for a long time the single college in which a high medical education could be gained, and further for its loyal protection of the Greek methods of healing up to the time of Arabian dominance.

---

[10] This paragraph comes before the prior two paragraphs in the 1942 edition.

There are also legendary tales of this college in the fourteenth century. Its successors evolved into the schools of Montpellier, Bologna, Padua, Neapel, Paris and Salamanca. The teaching staff was educated in the old colleges by the residential doctor, who had to have obtained the status of medical doctor as a consequence of a scientific education. Later, only full-time employed professors were members of the faculty. After the churches came to dominate the universities, we see mainly teachers who belonged to ecclesiastical orders. As a rule, there was in each medical faculty a teacher for "Theory" (botany, physics and chemistry) and one for "Practice," which designated the real medical specialist.

We know about the content and duration of medical studies from an edict of Kaiser Frederick II from the year 1224 The first medical law had been enacted in 1140 by King Roger in Sicily in which a state license was required to set up a practice. According to that edict, 3 years of study of the philosophy of the preparatory sciences were demanded, and only afterwards were the five continuous years of study of real healing science begun. After a final examination the young doctor had to spend yet another year with an older practicing doctor before he was able to set down a practice.

During the time of education it was possible for the young student to gain various academic levels, each of which determined another entitlement. The "Baccalaureate" corresponded somewhat to our old Tentamen physicum[11] and today's pre-examination; the "Licentiate," was expected to acquire the Baccalaureate and could legitimately practice under certain restrictions, and finally, following the completion of a state test, was given the title "Majester," and, after further work, finally was granted the doctorate. The university only instructed in theory; students gathered experience by accompanying the teacher on visits to the sick or by working with him in the hospital.

The doctor who was educated at a recognized college was not prevented from freely establishing a practice across state and country borders. The status of the doctor was very high, however there already were arising among them at that time materialistic representatives of the profession, who advertised in the vociferous manner of a barker in order to capture the favor of the public, thereby doing damage to the dignity of the doctor.

The question of payment for delivered services was regulated in the later middle ages by decreed taxes and authorized minimum charges. A contractual agreement for a higher honorarium was permitted and customary. The house doctor was paid either by an honorarium for individual service or by a flat-rate payment. The revenue received from the dispensing of medicine played a not inconsequential role in the income gathered from the practice of medicine. After the establishment of apothecaries this self-dispensing of medicines by the doctor was no longer retained. Later the doctor called on the apothecary in order to enter his prescriptions in a book

[11] The *Tentamen physicum* was an examination in natural scienes. Ramm may actually be referring to the *Tentamen philosophicum* here.

laid out for this purpose. The use of prescription sheets appears to have become common only in the sixteenth century.

In the middle ages, the worldly and clerical princes retained for themselves a personal physician, who was ranked between knights and simple nobles. Physicians who had gained their doctorate were equated with knights. In addition to the personal physician, the city physician, appointed by the state, constituted the medical officialdom; they fulfilled to a certain extent the tasks of the later District and current Civil Service Physician. With such a limited number of scientifically trained doctors it is not surprising that their social position rose and that they were respected everywhere. The religious element withdrew ever more from the practice of the science of medicine as a consequence of the prohibition of its churchly authority, but many free doctors were allowed to grant lower consecration, being enfeoffed as a Canonkus with a profitable beneficence. From the beginning of the fourteenth century, the worldly doctor predominated everywhere and enjoyed a great reputation. Surgery at this time was not considered to be a science or an art, but rather was taken to be merely manual dexterity or even handicraft.

Further development of health science became paralyzed in unfruitful scholasticism, the "misalignment between science and belief." Also the epoch of the "Renaissance" of health science in the fifteenth century was not able to generate an impetus to medical research, but became lost in fruitless collecting and translating of old medical writings. Only Paracelsus continued to gain new knowledge by carrying on observations of nature.

In the thirteenth and fourteenth centuries, Germans preferentially visited the Universities of Padua, Ferrara and Bologna; Paris hardly came to mind,[12] as opposed to Montpellier.

It is unmistakable that the more one looks to the earlier part of this time than towards the later part of the middle ages that the entire intellectual establishment retarded and strictly limited the development of all the sciences, especially medical and natural sciences. "The entire intellectual life was so dominated by religious ideas that even in medical textbooks and also in university instruction holy prayer came to be ordered, bible passages came into direct competition with medical treatment and churches, and confessionals played the role of our modern professional organization" (Diegpin).[13]

The Christian philosophical viewpoint promoted, on the one hand, a medical ethos, however also, in a certain sense, decreased and limited it. Thus, in contrast to antiquity, the church established the precept of standing by the incurably ill and unburdening his life until death. The church gave to the doctor the charge to get the

[12] Since the days of Robert Koch and Louis Pasteur there had been rivalry between the German and French medical systems. Ramm takes this opportunity to point out that Paris has not always been a center of medical learning. (L. Pasteur, "On the Extension of the Germ Theory to the Etiology of Certain Common Diseases," in *Medicine and Western Civilization,* D. J. Rothman, S. Marcus, and S.A. Eiceluk, eds. (New Brunswick: Rutgers University Press, 1995), 253–257; R. Koch, "The Aetiology of Tuberculosis," in Rothman, 319–329).

[13] Diepgen, P.: *Geschicht der Medizin.* Walter de Gruyter & Co., Berlin.

sick to go to confession and to withhold treatment in case of refusal. Preservation of professional secrets was demanded neither by the state nor by church authorities. It was made a moral obligation of the doctor, before the establishment of a practice, to undertake a fundamental education and to work basically through his cases in practice with the help of the existing literature. The doctor was made responsible for all damages he inflicted on his patients through inattentiveness or forgetting his duty. New not yet tested methods of treatment were to be tried out only with great care. A reasonable honorarium could be demanded from the wealthy. It was made a duty of the population to turn to the doctor and to use his medicine. Also the sick were urged to accurately make available all information which would aid the doctor's knowledge and his healing of the sickness.

In the subsequent centuries, in contrast to the middle ages, there was progressive growth in the development of healing science. Natural knowledge came to be discovered through the promotion of observation. Though at the time the then arising natural philosophy at first represented only a lively fantastic absorption in nature and in no way made its task a systematic investigation of nature, and likewise demonology, astrology, magic, dream interpretation and alchemy still partly dominated the practice of the health science, yet these can now be taken to represent a prelude to an exact investigation of nature.

So as not to wander too far off the topic, we should speak in the following account only of the development of the physician's profession in Germany; the remaining European countries will only be considered in so far as their progressive conditions gave an example to the medical community in Germany.

With the breaking up of the German Volk and its distribution into a multiplicity of artificial states, which feuded continuously with each other and were the playthings of foreign peoples, it is not surprising that healing science and the medical professional conditions in Germany did not make the progress at the time which one would have expected from the Volk of "Thinker and Poet," while other European volk, who had become a political and cultural unity through the erection of a national state, achieved the heyday of their culture earlier than the Germans, with whom a progressive development of healing science is inevitably connected.

The sixteenth century is characterized by wide swings in the areas of politics and society. Feudalism was destroyed, and many privileges had to be dispensed with in favor of the middle class in the flourishing city communities. The despotism of the Kaiser and the continued influential power of the Pope were broken up by the growing power of the princes of the realm. All classes of Volk became prosperous and were able to get an education. The already existing, and at this time dramatically growing, universities became institutional protectors of free intellectual life, and, from this time on, made enormous advances. In addition to the other sciences, the science of healing took on a new life.

The predominantly scholastic dialectic dominating the scientific areas gave way to newly created intellectual activities which consisted of the investigation of recently discovered antiquities as well as the observation of the processes of nature. In the sixteenth century it was the German *Vesalius,* coming from Wesel, personal physician to Carl V, and *Theophrastus Paracelus* (*Bombast von Hohenheim*), who are to be thanked for the dramatic advance in medical science.

Vesalius' significance is in the firm foundation he created in anatomy by his investigations on the human body, while the *service of Paracelsus* concerns the fact that he gave to medical thinking a new foundation of pathology. *Paracelsus' greatness* lay in his incessant drive for empiricism, observation of nature, and of experimentation, which he declared to be the single basis for the science of nature and healing. While his teaching at first had limited effect on the progress of healing science, many great physicians later built on his ideas and promoted a wider development of the science.

It must be especially mentioned how high Paracelsus held the medical profession and with what an honorable heart he served it. Thus no one more than he is to be valued next to the great Koer Hippocrates, because he bound ethics with this greatness and showed "Virtue" to be one of the four fundamental pillars of medicine. Good heartedness, unselfishness and attention to the welfare of his fellowman were the characteristic features of his nature. His high opinion of the dignity and the duties of the medical profession is seen in the expression, "A doctor is to be permitted to be no masked man, no old woman, no executioner, no liar, no undertaker, but rather he should be a genuine man." "Know thou that a sick person should be in the mind of the doctor day and night and he should carry him daily before his eyes, placing all his sense and thought into the appropriate treatment of sick people." "The doctor grows in his heart, he comes from God, and represents the natural light. The highest foundation of medicine is love."

In addition to these and other revolutions in health science, we find at the end of the 16th and the beginning of the 17th centuries, many doctors who still held on to Galenism and scholasticism. However, very soon "the fundamental characteristics of inductive research were raised to a philosophical principle, setting aside all prejudice, all superstition and all bondage to authority, with the goal of developing the power of mankind over nature by the use of the weapons of knowledge, which were thought at the same time to lead to fruitful discoveries. The explanation of nature and its laws would supposedly thereby be achieved so that natural things would reveal themselves experimentally instead of by forced rational derivation of their norms." (Sudhoff)[14,15]

The foresight and surveys of *Francis Bacon* (1562-1626), which had been gathered partly out of studies of antiquity and partly out of his own correct discovery of their importance, demanded from health science the collection of clinical facts, a careful history of sickness, the promotion of physiology through experimentation

---

[14] Meyer-Steinegg u. Sudhoff: *Geschichte der Medizin im Ueberblick.* Gustav Fischer, Jena, 1938.

[15] Ramm quotes Sudhoff approvingly regarding the introduction of "inductive science." He does not give us details of what he means by inductive science, but presumably he is referring to what A. F. Chalmers has called the "naïve view of science."(A. F. Chalmers, *What is this thing called Science?* (St. Lucia: U. of Queensland Press, 1982), 2) This interpretation is supported by his next paragraph where he presents an overview of the standard historical contributions of Francis Bacon to inductive science.

on animals, the avoidance of premature conclusions regarding the incurability of a condition, and a well considered plan in each case of sickness. Striving for a causal therapy, he further demanded methodological testing of all modalities of treatment, and in addition to the pleasant responsibilities of the doctor, the relieving of pain, the just treatment of patients and the lightening of death itself.

Paracelsus, Vesalius, Bacon and other great doctors, scientists and philosophers were the forerunners of a century by century progressive development of the science of healing up to modern times, which began with the rejection of old crystallized conceptions and led through natural science investigation to a state of medical science which is unrivaled. While these developments occurred through the widening of the horizons of the European cultural world as a consequence of the discovery of the new world, and also the discovery of the printing process, they came to be conveyed by the enormous intellectual impulses of the widest Volk circles. The growing pressure for natural knowledge led to technical discoveries in which many doctors took part and through which a growing sense of scientific research was promoted.

While in the sixteenth century there was hardly any change in the conditions of the physician's status in comparison to the previous centuries, there came to be in the seventeenth century a decided improvement in the reputation of doctors. The studies of scientifically educated doctors at first followed the old course, yet soon accelerated, such as in the instruction of students by the teacher at the bed side. Not just the fundamental knowledge of medical things but also a good general education in philosophy and natural science, history and legal studies marked the doctor who gained a doctorate.

In addition to the physician who gained a doctorate there were practicing doctors who acquired their education irregularly and were held in low esteem, but were still preferred by the non-affluent people in the treatment of an illness, rather than the few university educated doctors with their high honorarium. Many complaints were brought against the unscrupulous behavior and greed of many of these second-tiered doctors, who were frequently more quack than conscientious health practitioner. Thus individual state administrations enacted medical edicts which were supposed to prohibit the worst violations against trust and belief between the sick and the doctor and official doctors had to see to it that there was a guaranteed supply of organized medical provisions for the city and country. In this time also the first physicians' union for the preservation of the interests of the profession, named *collegia medica,* was formed, which strove to promote a medical ethos among its members.[16]

[16]The medical ordinance of 1747 resolved some of the problems in the conduct of medical activities. Physicians had to submit to an examination by the *Collegium medicum* (a formation of the medical society). They had to swear to fulfill their duties faithfully and attend their local medical society regularly. The *Collegium medicum* would henceforth conduct the mandatory examinations of apothecaries, surgeons, barber-surgeons, military as well as civilian, and all midwives. (M. Lindemann, *Health & Healing in Eighteenth-Century Germany* (Baltimore: Johns Hopkins University Press, 1996), 52–3).

The internist was always still more highly regarded than the surgeon, who had to share the practice of his Specialty with bathers and barbers. Soon however, there were negotiations by the surgeons with the representatives of internal medicine for equitable credit if they could show that they had devoted themselves to a regulated academic study of the science of treating wounds. Also, from Maximillian I on, the academically trained surgeon gained an honorable position in the conscripted army as a major doctor of large groups of troops and as a supervisor of the medical orderly.

The education of the doctor in the seventeenth century had hardly changed in comparison to the sixteenth century in spite of the progress of science and practice. Even though the university was only a teaching and not a research institution, and doctors in practice only grudgingly took up medical research, the doctor enjoyed a growing respect in wide Volk circles in the course of this period. Even though there was no *state*-installed doctor as such, it was the *medical faculties* who gave permission to practice the profession, while the state granted extensive protection to medical activities.

"For the preservation of the reputation of the profession" the doctors at this time, painstakingly held themselves back from "lower" activities, which included surgical and obstetrical interventions.[17] They attended on these activities as an advisor but kept their own hands off. The establishment of a diagnosis followed by the prescribing of a completed prescription was their main task; with that act they exhausted the application of their medical knowledge.

The demands which the doctors placed on their professional comrades were extremely high. For example, the *Helmsted Professor Conring* (1606-1681) demanded a careful selection of medical students according to their physical, intellectual and moral aptitude, and further demanded a fundamental education in which practical instruction was not to exclude theory and was to give a high general education, in addition to a fundamental knowledge of a Specialty. He placed demands on the intellectual and ethical qualities of the developing doctors, who were not at this time certified by the doctor colleges. This came to be a time when the moral aspect was encompassed into the ideal conception of medicine.[18]

---

[17] The main thrust of Ramm's text is to point out the overarching importance of a doctor's reputation within a society. The society is a reflection of the will of the state, which is a reflection of the Will of the Leader, which must be recognized as the entity of the most importance. The reputation, or regard, or moral worth or idealization of the practice of medicine does not come from within the profession, but from a sort of dialectic between the profession and the state. This characterization of the situation of the medical profession within the National Socialist state means that the profession must be constituted differently from that which has been described in standard sociology analyses. The Comprehensive National Socialist Philosophical Worldview of medicine represents a conceptually different construction of medicine.

[18] Ramm uses three different normative terms in this paragraph: *moralischen, ethischen,* and *sittlichen,* without appearing to make any distinction between them. Nina Rosenstand reports that *ethics* comes from Greek (*ethos,* character) and *morality* from Latin (*mores,* character, custom, or habit). (N. Rosenstand, *The Moral of the Story: An Introduction to Ethics* (Boston: McGraw-Hill, 2005), 11) Ramm conflates the terms because he sees them as one and the same when manifest in

As a rule, in the rural area, the doctor's honorarium was reimbursed in kind, and in the cities, if there was not already an established court, personal or city physician involved, by payment in kind as well as in money from taxes decreed by the authorities.

The surgeon gained in the seventeenth century an even greater reputation and became after a while recognized as equal to regular doctors. They also began gradually to take on obstetrics, which had previously been the domain of midwives, leading the practice to become more highly regarded. The lower sorts of surgery, like the removal of warts and the application of leeches, as well as cupping and bleeding, were still performed by bathers and barbers. In addition to these practitioners, quack doctors thrived and frequently caused enough problems concerning deception and exploitation of the volk that the authorities were compelled to intervene.

Greater attention was devoted to the care of soldiers, especially in Prussia, which was achieved through the introduction of field orderlies and doctors. Military hospitals and hospitals for civil society were erected in large numbers in almost all European states, the size and arrangement being determined by the size of the volk population.

The eighteenth century brought enormous growth to the natural sciences, especially physics, chemistry and botany and also to medical science. Unfortunately however, there were other intellectual streams which flourished, like natural philosophy, mysticism, mesmerism and others, which proved to be a hindrance to the progress of the exact sciences. Philosophy was especially damaging to the development of the science of medicine.[19] There were numerous medical systems originating from different concepts of the cause of illness and these delayed progress, being expressed and exhausted in poly-pragmasie,[20] above all in the ordering of elaborately constructed prescriptions. Only thus can the great success of the Homeopathy of Hahnemann be understood, "although it was nothing other than a therapeutic system built on a theory."(Meyer-Steinegg).[21] In spite of all the minute details which Homeopathy had to follow in the treatment of the sick, which brought it into discredit, the kernel of this teaching has been preserved up to today and has found recognition through its scientific underpinning.[22]The new spirit, which was drawn

the person of the physician in the Comprehensive National Socialist state. In emphasizing that the enterprise of medicine is a moral enterprise, he joins the conceptions of the National Socialist physician together with all features of the medical and healing systems. The means and end of this conceptualization are the same – Racial Hygiene.

[19] Ramm appears to be referring here to the philosophy of Friedrich Wilhelm Joseph von Schelling (1775–1854), who was a German Idealist philosopher. Schelling attempted to derive the world of objects from the world of the ego by turning consciousness upon itself as the only object of which we have immediate firsthand knowledge.(A. Margoshed, "Schelling," in *The Encyclopedia of Philosophy,* P. Edwards, ed. (New York: MacMillan, 1967), 7&8: 305–309).

[20] "Poly-pragmasie" appears to be a neologism of Ramm's, which is explained in the following phrase.

[21] Meyer-Steinegg. U. Sudhoff.

[22] Ramm gives an equivocal assessment of Homeopathy, the system of alternative medicine founded by the German, Samuel Hahnemann (1755–1843). (W. E. Bynum, *Science and the*

into the science of healing by the great doctors of the eighteenth century like Haller, Boerhaave, van Swietin and others, had a beneficial influence on medical relationships. This period is characterized as "The golden age of the medical profession." The ideal conception of medicine, which had not been seen since the heyday of Hippocrates, developed as a consequence of the idealism generally prevailing at this time.

The hour of the birth of the "house doctor" fell in this century as well. The respectable and well-off families bound doctors to themselves to provide for continuous attention and advice to the family. This custom had continued to thrive up to the most recent times until it regrettably was replaced, at the establishmen of social insurance, with the system of the fund doctor. How worthwhile the arrangement of house doctor had worked for the family and for the ideal conception of medicine can be taken from the demand of recent times for the re-introduction of both the family doctor and the house doctor.

Also in the course of this century the background and training of doctors were firmly established. The *Abschlusspruefung*[23] of a kind of Gymnasium was demanded as a *precondition* for certification to study, following which there was a more or less 4 year long period of education at the university. Permission to establish a practice as a doctor was made dependent on sitting for the doctor's examination under the auspices of the professors of the medical faculty. Since however some universities, for materialist reasons, allowed all too freely, indeed carelessly, the conferring of this honor, many states, for example Prussia in 1798, went over to introducing a special state test. These measures had resulted in such inconsistency that many states demanded, before permission was granted to establish a practice, that candidates sit for an exam given by a commission erected for this purpose.

Through gradually developing the education of the prospective doctor at the bedside, medical studies were successfully improved to the point that unmistakable progress was noted. Surgery and physician obstetrics manifested such great

---

Practice of Medicine in the Nineteenth Century (Cambridge: University Press, 1994), 182) Just as in his remarks touching on Christianity, Ramm is treading a fine line when he discusses "scientific" medicine and "alternative" medicine. In addition to Racial Hygiene, German medicine was 'enriched" by another new discipline, "natural health science," also referred to as "new German healing (*Neue Deutsche Heilkunde*." This subject will arise again later in Ramm's text. The new discipline exhibited a decided aversion to conventional specialized medicine with its often impersonal modes of treatment. In reaction to this perception of allopathic medicine, the number of "healers" and quack physicians increased greatly. Nazi doctrine held that official medicine was "Jewified" medicine and that medications given by Jewish doctors suppressed natural healing and had but a single purpose – to profit Jewish stockholders in the pharmaceutical industry. As a feature of the physician being a "whole of the whole," the National Socialists did not think in terms of mechanisms of disease or disturbances of particular organs but advocated "holistic" medicine in which the entire human being would be restored by living in a natural way. The principles of natural health science, as in Racial Hygiene, were rooted firmly in National Socialist ideology. Just as individuals were significant only as parts of a racially defined community, so, too, organs of the human body were important only in the context of the whole being (Weyers, 162).

[23] School leaving exam.

development in scientific and technical respects that they achieved a reputation comparable to that of the internist.

The entire public health service was put underneath a strict state ordinance. The Prussian state was the first of the German states to pass a medical ordinance which became the model for the remaining German states (1725). Also the education and social position of the military physician was improved under the Prussian king, and a specialized way of education was developed in the newly founded *Pepiniere*[24] which corresponds to our military medical doctor's academy of today.

Since the number of university graduated doctors was not large in comparison to the number of citizens, their financial and social position was very favorable. Rural regions were in general medically under-served. This situation induced the Kaiser, Maria-Theresa of Austria, to secure the material existence of the doctor practicing in the country through financial support from the state and the community.

The eighteenth century was also meaningful for the promotion of women (1734 in Halle) to doctor of medicine, which however as a rule was still an exception at the time.[25]

Quacks were dominant to a large extent in all areas and classes. "A considerable contingent of this sort was supplied by monasteries, who knew how to exploit with great cleverness their aura of holiness for an earthly purpose." (Haeser).

So the eighteenth century represented a time of fruitful development in all of the areas of both scientific and practical healing science, state medicine and the medical profession and provided the foundation for the turbulent developments of the nineteenth century.

Certainly the political and intellectual conditions in the first decades of this century did nothing to promote development. The movement towards freedom which came to almost all European countries, and especially Germany, as a consequence of the French Revolution, set off an extraordinary enthusiasm for all things high, beautiful and honorable, but came up against a narrow, worldly and religious despotism in the community, which partly stifled it quickly in the bud. Philosophy,

---

[24] In Prussia, from 1725 to 1825, there existed the category of military physician. Such a physician was usually educated at the military teaching hospital, the Charite (founded in 1724), and at the state military-medical academy, the Pepiniere (founded in 1797), both in Berlin. Such physicians usually entered a staff physician's career in the Prussian and later the other German armies. Kater reports that the existence of such physicians usually signified the unbroken preeminence of traditionalist ways, which was squarely opposed to rational, modernistic practices subscribed to by the professional-minded civilian teachers and students of medicine (Kater, 1985, 683). Such a climate of medicine strengthened the military aura of medical establishments and contributed to the conservative nationalism of the medical profession.

[25] In no part of the text does Ramm give a negative view of women in medicine. But, in fact, their position in National Socialist German medicine was very difficult. Even though the proportion of women among German physicians grew remarkably during the Nazi years, they were greatly disadvantaged in their quest for professional and economic independence. They were largely relegated to sex-specific areas of endeavor – pediatrics and gynecology. This situation reflected the National Socialist *volkisch* philosophical viewpoint assumption that surgery called for and represented the essential qualities of German masculinity. (M. H. Kater, *Doctors Under Hitler* (Chapel Hill: University of North Carolina Press, 1989), 89–109).

predominantly Shelling's pragmatism, won wide influence in medical investigation in the form of romantic natural philosophy and led for a time to the trivializing of medical literature. Very soon there was a turn away in research from this kind of speculation and return to the ideas of the outgoing eighteenth century. The German universities were at this time poorly supported financially by the states. Despite that, German and Austrian research, as well as French, produced good results so that medicine was built into an effective science. Appropriately, the medical lecture was also established and developed for the communication of scientific thought and technical knowledge. However, several European countries did not make this adjustment at all and others only in variously different ways.

England held firmly to its old establishment and exercised no state influence on the course and promotion of medical instruction. Since the course of study in England was fundamentally different from that in Germany, it should be described here briefly. In order to be introduced to the fundamentals of treatment of the sick, the young doctor was entrusted over the 1st year to the care of a doctor already established in practice. A visit to a medical Specialty school then followed, the duration of which was not firmly established, but varied from institution to institution. The Specialty schools were situated as a rule in various important hospitals, which employed a variety of different curricula. The conclusion of studies was confirmed by a diploma. Only exceptionally was the university sought out for the purpose of the study of medicine and only if one wanted to gain a greater reputation among doctors and the sick. There was no medical faculty in most English universities and even fewer institutions for clinical and practical instruction. Up to 1858, medical study in the university covered only theoretical matters while the gaining of practical knowledge continued to be left to the individual, since the state, up to this time, did not generally attend to the education of the doctor. It was not until that year that the state finally determined which corporate body was supposed to be recognized to have the right to hold physician examinations, which body was to give certification for the doctor to establish a practice, which was to establish a bureaucracy and especially how to direct complaints and demands for honoraria with the court, a privilege that continued to be denied to illegitimate healers. This arrangement did not however prove to be a success. After only 20 years (1881) one sees the forced establishment of new ordinances of education and testing, which however, because of lax implementation, brought no essential change to the existing conditions, and have been in practice with few alterations up until the present time.

In the United States of North America, and many other countries which were under the cultural influence of England, we find similar medical relationships. *Scotland* is the single remarkable exception.

The developing course of the medical system in France was entirely different. At the time of the French Revolution, there were two recognized institutions of medical education: Paris and Montpellier, to which Strassburg was later added. Very soon (1803), the state overtook the oversight of physician education along with the whole health care system, introducing obligatory testing according to the several individual divisions of study, and requiring at least 4 years of study before permission to take the final test and certification for the doctorate examination. In order to remedy the lack of doctors in the countryside, there was developed in hospital schools a minimal educational requirement before a short period of studies for second ranked doctors, who were then required to send difficult cases to the educated doctors at the university as consultations. From the middle of the nineteenth century on, this kind of doctor was progressively on the decline, and at the beginning of the twentieth century, physician education in all of France, including at the university and urban specialized schools, was directed more towards education for the height of the time. The social place of the doctor was especially elevated at the end of the nineteenth century, and the condition of the profession could be seen to be exemplary, although the French medical profession was still not spared a fight, especially against the incompletely educated "Officiers de Santi," and the quacks.

In *Austria-Hungary* the development of the medical system has taken a progressively pleasant course since the time of Van Swietan.[26] In 1804 the student period for becoming a doctor was extended from 4 to 5 years, the first three of which were for theoretical instruction and the last 2 years were for practical clinical education. From 1810 on, specific lectures came to be presented for individual semesters and the curriculum was broadened. In addition to the Doctor of Medicine, the title of Master of Surgery could be gained, which however required only a short course of study. Also obstetricians and eye doctors received their diploma after a shorter preparation and an easier test. Since 1872, there has been in Austria-Hungary only one class of doctors.

In the individual German states[27] the developing course of medical activities corresponded to the general evolution of events in other states, ultimately becoming adjoined to the regulations validated in Prussia and Austria. *Baveria* trained, in addition to the academic doctor, rural doctors and rural surgeons in special schools which were connected to hospital complexes. Since 1808, regular studies have lasted 3 years, followed by 2 years of practical education in the hospital or with a

[26] Ramm describes the medical system in Austria-Hungary approvingly. It appears that the feature common to both the French and Austria-Hungary systems which contrasts with the English system, and which is the source of his approval, is the state oversight of the system.

Ramm's developing argument, relative to the development of the profession (*der Stand*): The traditional conception of a profession is one in which there is internal self-discipline. The National Socialists were explicitly acting to construct an entirely different entity – one which had a unique relationship with the National Socialist government – an idealistic "whole of a whole," the Comprehensive National Socialist Philosophical Worldview. There is supposed to be the requisite internal self-discipline in which each individual physician is merely a part of the whole of the profession, but this entity is itself merely a part of the whole of the entire National Socialist society, which itself is merely one feature of the will of *der Fuehrer.*

[27] Ramm presents some of the details of medical education in the German states. The tone is generally approving, although he does reveal a continuing conflict between the "natural scientific roots" and the "philosophical" [roots] of medicine. His remarks suggest that lectures on philosophy and psychology were voluntary, a surprising proposition in a system where all activities of students were to be controlled, but this probably reflects the continuing contention within the faculties over the place of these disciplines. Detlef Bothe has reported of a continuous struggle between "Neue Deutsche Heilkunde" (natural healing methods) and "Schulmedizine" (university medicine). (D. Bothe, *Neue Deutsche Heilkunde: 1933–1945* (Husum: Matthiesen Verlag, 1991).

practicing doctor, followed by the state test which validated the establishment of a practice. Since 1858, there has been a regulation that after the first study year one must pass a test in the natural science specialties. This was followed by 4 years of study and 1 year of practice, before the final exam was to take place.

In *Saxony,* in addition to the high-valued university education, there existed academies such as the Dresden Academy, where 2nd class doctors for internal medicine, obstetrics and surgery were trained.

In 1825, *Prussia* completely reorganized the medical system, whereby there came to be the doctorate physician (physician for internal medicine or surgery) and wound physician, classes one and two.

For a doctorate, the Abitur examination of a Gymnasium and a study lasting 4 years at the university were required, while the wound physician could spend a portion of his education time at hospitals or special teaching institutions. For service in the public health service, special tests were prescribed. From 1852 on, there developed various demands concerning background and training for a unified education, and, in 1861, the previously demanded Tentamen philosophicum was replaced by the Tentamen physicum,[28] making it such that the natural scientific foundations of medicine took precedence over the philosophical. Yet it is to be wished that today those studying medicine would still attend a course of lectures on philosophy and psychology.

The *foundation of the Reich* in 1871 also brought to the medical profession a unified rule of education and term of studies. Through a close relationship of the military academies to the Berlin medical faculty the education of the military doctor was also elevated and made equivalent to the general doctor.

At the change of the century, the studies were extended to 5 years = ten semesters, to which were allotted equal time for pre-clinical and clinical studies. Then after the world war, in 1924, yet another semester was added, which was meant to provide for a better clinical education. Before the granting of state license to practice, a year of practice as a medical practitioner had to be done at specially designated hospital institutions. The degree of doctor of medicine was allowed only after the granting of the license to practice, even if the necessary scientific work and oral tests before the faculty had been taken.

While the appointment as a doctor also allowed the establishment of the right to practice, this said nothing of the maturity of the young doctor for practice. For that reason the Reich Physicians' Leader had demanded before licensure as a fund doctor a further practical education of at least 2 years duration. If the currently established requirements of the licensure ordinance are satisfied, then licensure is possible, with the best prepared doctor receiving preferential registration.

The progress of medical science, above all in the area of human genetics, and the multiplication of the relevant scientific instructional materials for the physician needed for that, soon led to the demand for a reform of college studies and for

[28] *Tentamen philosophicum* referred to the philosophical (thought) examination and *Tentamen physicum* to physical/empirical examination. The *Tentamen physicum* replaced the *Tentamen philosophicum.*

professional physician leadership. The National Socialist Party rang out the call for the abbreviation of all academic studies for the Jungehe,[29] which represented an independent demand by National Socialism for preservation of the Volk population.[30] From the general advice of the Reich Physicians' Leader, of the Reich Interior Ministry and the Reich Education Ministry, a new study and Ordinance of Testing for doctors was created, which came into force in June, 1939.

A judgment regarding the suitability of the current course of education cannot naturally yet be made. The shortening of the education time reflects the general demands, although it does appear to be possible only with the greatest of efforts to cover all the necessary study material.

---

[29]Youngster. Ramm is presumably here referring to the "*Jungaerzt,*" who were those younger doctors in the compulsory waiting period before they could apply for fund practice. These students were overwhelmingly members of the National Socialist Party. They were very poorly paid and not entitled to more than 4 weeks of vacation per year and were forbidden to undertake extracurricular medical activities to increase their incomes (Kater, *Doctors Under Hitler,* 13.)

[30]*Bevolkerungspolitics* – a specifically National Socialist term and enterprise in which medicine is mixed with politics according to the Comprehensive National Socialist Philosophical Worldview (Racial Hygene and population genetics).

Part II: Ordinance of Licensure

The *new Ordinance of Studies* which is now constructed as a part of the Ordinance of Licensure is significant for a shift in the training from the theoretical to the professional practical side.[1] The course of studies is as follows:

If the young student has served out his work service and military service, then, after completion of a preparatory test, a study of ten semesters is expected of him, of which four are allotted to pre-clinical teaching material and six to clinical subjects. Females and those unsuitable for military service must serve a half year of nursing service in a state recognized hospital or a clinic before taking up medical studies, while those suitable for military service must fulfill this pre-condition. In the Sixth Ordinance for the Implementation and Completion of the Ordinance of Licensure for Physicians from 28 December, 1942, the duration of necessary service was reduced from 6 to 4 months; the service can now be served out during holidays while the pre-clinical studies are completed.[2] During the holidays[3] – best during the long holiday after the third semester – the young student must serve out at least 6 weeks of rural or factory service, which means that he must undertake the same work as the rural or factory worker, for a reasonable payment,

[1] The National Socialists created a whole new body of codes for the practice of medicine. The Reich Physicians' Ordinance of December, 1935 and its supplement, the Professional Statue (*Berufsordnung)* of November, 1937 established, on a nationwide basis, a fixed body of codes governing professional conduct. The German physician became an individual of the larger Nazi sociopolitical system (the whole) governed by the Nazi leadership principle (of the whole). He found himself bound by a set of rules imposed from above with the threat of penal sanctions for infringement. Evans reports that Disciplinary courts were active in issuing warnings, meting out fines and suspending doctors who transgressed the rules (Evans, *The Third Reich in Power,* 444). By "practical side," Ramm means biological studies, particularly genetics and Racial Hygiene.

[2] This sentence is added to the 1942 edition.

[3] Students' time was rigidly controlled, even during holidays. Students were required to serve a period of time as a rural or factory worker – in order to come to understand the living and working conditions of the "creating" people. These were the common foundation Volk and were thought by the National Socialists to be the source of all of the good creative properties of the Aryan.

R. Ramm, *Medical Jurisprudence and Rules of the Medical Profession*,
Philosophy and Medicine 135, https://doi.org/10.1007/978-3-030-25245-8_2

in order to later have the necessary understanding, as a doctor, of the living and working conditions of the creative people. Rural and factory service can also now be served out in a health setting (an apothecary, a laboratory, an investigational institute and the like). The Specialty Group Leader of the Public Health Service directs the student to the appropriate place which is given to him by the Regional Department Leader for Volks' Health.

Likewise in pre-clinical studies the natural science teaching material has been decreased in favor of biology. Further, studies over the preservation of the Volk population, racial hygiene and the history of medicine are taken up in this part of the study as new supplementary specialties. The substantive authoritative grounds for this change is the insistence that the history of medicine is of eminent meaning and the studies for the preservation of the Volk population and racial hygiene are foundations for all the studies, without whose knowledge the doctor could not follow his new responsibilities as a caretaker of genetics and counselor for marriage.

During the first two semesters,[4] the young student should test himself to see if he is capable of bringing enough inclination and love to engage these studies and if his capacities correspond to the demands placed on him. At the same time, a decision must be made by the Specialty Group for Volks' Health, in agreement with the Dean's Office of the medical faculty, on whether the young medical student is mature enough in character, intellect and ethics to meet those demands which the Volk community and medical profession are required to place on him. Thus, there is guaranteed to be a certain selection of trainees. After the fourth semester, the medical pre-test is taken, which covers the subjects of anatomy, physiology, physics, chemistry, botany and zoology.

There is, however, the intention to again break up the medical pre-test into a pre-Physicum,[5] which covers the natural science specialties and is taken at the end of the second semester, and that of the true Physicum, covering the main courses of anatomy and physiology, which is to be taken after the fourth semester.[6]

This introduction of the change is anticipated to be achieved at the end of the summer semester of 1943.[7]

Those clinical studies beginning after completion of the appropriate pre-test have been restructured so that practical demonstration at the bedside has been moved more into the foreground. During the clinical semesters, 6 months must be spent in an internship at an outpatient practice in a poly-clinic, hospital or with a practicing doctor, at best in two parts, during the long summer vacation after the 7th and 9th semesters. Of these, one must consist of at least 4 weeks of training in obstetrics. Internships of less than 4 weeks will not be credited. More precise information is in

[4] Students were constantly judged according to their adaptation to the Comprehensive National Socialist Philosophical Worldview. Being allowed to begin a course of studies in medicine did not guarantee that one would be able to complete it.

[5] Examination ending the pre-clinical phase.

[6] This paragraph was added to the 1942 edition.

[7] This paragraph was added to the 1942 edition.

the "Pamphlet for the Intern." Clinical studies of today[8] in comparison to that found in the earlier Ordinance of Testing require an intensification of study in many scientific areas and demand experience in the new specialties, such as genetics, racial hygiene, social and defense hygiene. Pediatrics has recently experienced new developments which give it the same value as the main specialties of internal medicine, surgery and gynecology. After six semesters of clinical training, the state examination can be taken. The medical license is granted immediately after passing the appropriate medical test. During the clinical studies, but also after passing the appropriate examination, the doctor examination can be taken.

There have been various amendments enacted for the Ordinance of Licensure during the war, containing partly interim regulations, and partly implementing orders, which are given in the supplement.[9]

In order to free the medical profession of inappropriate, dishonorable and racially foreign elements,[10] the Ordinance of Testing considers it a cause for rejection of the application if the applicant is not in possession of civil rights, if his national or moral reliability can not be determined, especially if serious criminal or moral charges have been leveled against him, especially if he lacks the aptitude or dependability which is demanded of the medical profession as demonstrated by the commitment of a crime or by weakness of his mental powers or because of an addiction. Further, he is to be rejected if his or his spouse's origin can not be officially confirmed. In hard cases, the Reich Minister of the Interior can give permission for exceptions, with the agreement of the Reich Physicians' Chamber.

The Licensing Ordinance similarly captures the precautionary measures aimed at cleaning up the medical profession, which widens these instructions to the point where an applicant who has been declared unworthy by judicial judgment to practice the medical profession can not be granted a license. In the case where a criminal court judgment or professional judicial proceeding has been brought against an applicant the decision about the license to practice is set aside until the completion of the proceeding (& 3 of Reich Physicians' Ordinance). Physicians who are licensed in a foreign country can be established professionally to practice in Germany by the Reich Minister of the Interior; they are subject to the same duties

[8] Changes in the curriculum emphasized obstetrics, genetics, Racial Hygiene, social hygiene and defense hygiene. During the war, it became necessary to facilitate medical studies with a view to sending a maximum number of graduates into combat zones, but the cuts in the curriculum excluded the basic sciences of topographical anatomy and pathological physiology, while retaining the subjects pertaining to racial-eugenics (Kater, *Doctors Under Hitler,* 156).

[9] Appendix to the original text.

[10] This is Ramm's first expression of "*Gleichshaltung.*" *Gleichschaltung* proceeded along two related paths: synchronization of all government institutions and mass mobilization of all citizens for the National Socialist cause. The expulsion of Jewish assistants, lecturers, and professors of medicine from the universities began with the promulgation of the Law for Reconstitution of the German Civil Service of April 7, 1933. Jewish civil servants, including all university teachers of medicine, were subject to immediate dismissal unless they had been in office before 1914, had fought in World War I, or had lost a father or son in that war. Medical teachers received the extra benefit of exemption if they had risked their lives in a quarantine camp for an epidemic.

and rights of the German physician (& 11 of the Reich Physicians' Ordinance). This regulation is applied in a general sense for Specialty physicians.[11]

The license is rescinded if the essential pre-conditions have been falsely submitted, further with the loss of civil rights, and if the applicant has been found to be guilty of a serious criminal or moral failing, and if he has been expelled from the medical profession through a professional judicial judgment. If there is an overwhelming suspicion of a serious infraction of a professional duty, a temporary restraining order to suspend practice can be imposed until the final decision.

In contrast to the earlier Ordinance of Studies, which has been suspended, in which the completion of medical practical training took place between the state examination and the granting of the medical license, now at least a year long course as a compulsory assistant is required before permission is given to establish a practice; the rural quarter-year service applies to this requirement.

It is doubtful that this period of time of practical education of the young doctor suffices to make him sufficiently trained for independent practice. The Reich Physicians' leadership has proposed a plan which is to be recommended for the time being for each young doctor. According to this plan, the young doctor is to be trained for all practical activities in all important disciplines. It is assumed that one will spend in a 2 year cycle, 6 months training in internal medicine, 4 months each in surgery and trauma care, obstetrics and gynecology and pediatrics. Three months training should be specifically spent in the specialties of ophthalmology, dermatology and ear, nose and throat disease. The remaining 3 months are to be spent in rural medical activity,[12] of which 2 months should be spent under the leadership of an experienced rural doctor and the last month as the representative of the rural

---

[11] Interestingly, physicians licensed in a foreign country were licensed to practice in Germany. Presumably, they would have had to pass the racial and "moral" tests which Ramm mentions.

[12] Ramm gives more details about the rural medical activity. The first 2 months are spent under the supervision of an experienced rural doctor. The final month is spent as the rural doctor's representative. This activity was designed to give the developing physician an appreciation of medical practice among the "creating" Volk.

In practice, the actual experience of the medical student was more often not so idyllic. Ernst Rodin gives the following account of his rural experience during medical school:

> I was…ordered to volunteer for work on a farm to help with the harvest. The regional board in charge of these affairs placed me in the tiny village of *Maigen* in Lower Austria. The farmer had no idea what he was to do with this city boy, and I was given a minuscule room. It was actually smaller than most prison cells, with dimensions of roughly five by eight feet. It contained a bed, and on the wall there was a nail to hang the clothes, and that was it. I didn't need a room anyway, because there was no time to use it. From sun up to sun down there was work in the fields, and in the evening there were more farm chores to do in the house and barn. Misery had struck again. What made it even worse was that I was profoundly allergic to hay and sneezed my head off because antihistamines were not yet available. After not quite three weeks the farmer had had enough of me and sent me home… (E. Rodin, *War and Mahem: Reflections of a Viennese Physician* (Victoria, B.C.: Trafford, 1999), 125)

physician. Since during this time care has been specially taken to acquire a wider theoretical education through lectures, films, demonstrations at public hygiene institutions, health facilities and factories, it is assumed that the young physician, when he begins practice, will have at his disposal all the necessary knowledge and ability to meet the essential demands. Common knowledge will mediate the experience and the progress.

While we view as the goals of this course of training the equipping of the young doctor with a firmly defined theoretical and practical foundation in specific medical areas, the *Reich Specialty Group for Volks' Health of Reich Students' Leadership* aims to transmit the knowledge which is to enable the doctor to meet the responsibilities which face him as health leader of the German Volk. Through close cooperation of the Reich Specialty Group with all departments of the Reich Health Leadership it is therefore guaranteed that the young student of medicine will be introduced during his studies to the fundamental questions of health politics of the Main Office for Volks' Health of the NSDAP, whereby the relevant knowledge which was introduced in college will be completed. Also the Reich Specialty Group for Volks' Health of Reich Students' Leadership contributes importantly through its selection and extension of the Comprehensive National Socialist Philosophical Worldview of its members. Among its responsibilities include determination of assignments for completion of rural and factory service and the filling of posts for internship. It is anticipated that a close cooperation between the medical faculty and the Reich Specialty Group for Volks' Health will lead to an improvement in performance of the young student and will lead to a valuable alignment of Specialty and National Socialist philosophical relationships.[13]

The Organization of the Medical Profession

In order to be able to understand the current medical profession, we must trace professional associations somewhat further into the past to see how they have developed in Germany in the course of the past centuries. As described previously, we already see in the seventeenth century the beginning of physician associations, which arose in the medical faculty of the university as "*collegia medicorum.*" These took upon themselves mainly responsibilities in scientific and professional-ethical

---

[13]German medical students no less than other university students were expected by the regime to be committed to National Socialism. The quasi-extracurricular medical study unit, the *Medizinische Fachschaft,* was supposed to organize and monitor these students. Incorporation in the *Fachschaft* was compulsory. The group would organize lectures by ideologically firm faculty members outside of the normal curriculum on subjects pertaining to the National Socialist philosophical viewpoint (Kater, *Doctors Under Hitler,* 157).

The Main Office for Volks' Health of the NSDAP had been constituted by NSDAP staff chief, Rudolf Hess, in 1934, with Hess' friend, Gerhard Wagner, as head. Wagner was granted a new mandate as the regime's putative "health leader," with wide powers (Kater, *Doctors Under Hitler,* 22–3) Wagner will appear prominently later in Ramm's text.

areas. Their foundation can in general be traced back to the instigations of state supervisory authorities. It was not until the middle of the seventeenth century that we find several German cities in which the physicians themselves freely united together in occupational associations. However, the joining together into an occupational-professional community was very unusual up to the eighteenth century. Only in the nineteenth century can one detect a truly physician's professional life in Germany. The efforts and stated goals of these unions were to imbue the entire professional movement with greater meaning.

The ideas of the French Revolution also took hold in Germany, and the German medical community sought through professional connections to improve their relationships in ethical, social and economic areas, while seeking at the same time to win influence in the health politics of the state.

These efforts undoubtedly were taken to be justification to win influence in the *entire* political sphere including the promotion of a Reich devoid of the absolutism of the regime.

Various shortcomings in the professional life and the public health service demanded resolution and thus the call for reforms arose, which took place in the course of time. The fragmentation of the medical profession into various classes, which has been reported above, carried in its train increasing dissatisfaction such that, for example in Prussia in 1825, the medical career types shrank to three classes. New regulations arose pertaining to these. The doctorate physician required 4 years of university. The trauma surgeon was designated either first or second class. For the trauma surgeon of the first class, a 3 year study in a university or medical surgical teaching institute was required, while the surgeon second class gained his factual knowledge in the hospital or by practicing with a teaching master, attended only a few theoretical lectures, and was allowed to take his medical test before his medical colleagues. In all three of these categories, one was allowed to practice as an obstetrician, but only if he had experienced special practical and theoretical training in this Specialty.[14]

But even these measures were not entirely satisfactory, and very soon there was a demand from the responsible medical community for the creation of a unified medical profession. Equivalent training under equivalent conditions of practice was promoted to provide both a reliable benefit for the population as well as genuine collaboration of doctors. However, other grounds of dissatisfaction also drove the demand for reform, including the overfilling of the healing vocations in the cities, which led to dishonorable advertising and competitive methods. In many states, the

[14] In this paragraph, Ramm gives an entire constellation of problems and complaints burdening the developing medical profession of the early nineteenth century. These problems were predominantly associated with the rise of irregular practitioners and the rise of what was taken to be unfair competitive practices. These problems are essentially the same as those which led to the formation of the American Medical Association in 1847 and the construction of American Medical Association's Code of Ethics (R. Baker, *The Codification of Medical Morality: Historical and Philosophical Studies of the Formation of Western Medical Morality in the Eighteenth and Nineteenth Century* (Dordrecht: Kluwer Academic Publishers, 1993).

practicing doctor was subject to the supervision of the state doctor, who ultimately was even allowed to intervene in the treatment of the patients of the practitioner. Competition led to pressure on the doctor to advertise, making it so that he could not decline treatment; this was part of the medical system in need of reform. The movement of reform achieved its revolutionary high point in 1848 and 1849. *Virchow* made himself the spokesman of the German medical profession and demanded a reformation of the German public health service of the state in order to achieve the explicit goal of controlling epidemics. *His demand culminated in the erection of a German Reich Ministry for Public Health Service.*

Though it appeared at the beginning as though the reaction would fade and the new ideas would produce no influence on the activities of most of the German governments, the demands of this time did indeed have a lasting effect in Prussia, so that in 1852 the unification of the medical profession was implemented, a measure which was also adopted in 1869 in the North German Federation and later the whole Reich. *Since then there has existed in Germany only one state approved doctor with unified preparation and training.*[15]

Even before the foundation of the Reich, doctors' unions were recognized in the states of Braunschweig and Baden.[16] After the founding of the Reich, political interactions between doctors and medical administration functioned more uniformly than before and progressed stepwise towards the goal of the creation of a Reich Centrum of the Public Health Service. In 1867 the North German Federation made the decision to establish the Medical Police,[17] so that after the founding of the Reich, conditions allowed more unified principles, leading to vaccination laws, quarantine laws, laws covering nutrition, etc. Even though the wish of 1848 for a single Reich Health Ministry was unfortunately not fulfilled, certain progress was made so that in 1876 the Reich Health Office of the Reich Government was formed as a single advisory authority. It provides proof of the good intentions of the government of that time.

---

[15] Ramm notes that, since there was no national German community at this time, these efforts failed to take hold generally, but that they did have a lasting effect in Prussia, so that the medical profession was unified in this eastern state. After the formation of a national government, the unification achieved in Prussia was effected nationwide (R. Swoch, *Aertzliche Standespolitik im Nationalsozialismus* (Husum: Mattiesen Verlag, 2001), 20) Many of the changes to the medical profession instigated by the National Socialists would come from Prussia. The German Empire of 1871–1918 was militaristic in the highest sense and much of regimentation of the system of medicine followed this Prussian model (Fischer, 20).

[16] From early in the development of the medical profession, Germany had had doctors' unions. The first national professional union, the Deutsche Aertzvereinbund, was established in 1873. These unions continue to be politically active in present day Germany (D. Nowak, "Doctors on Strike – The Crisis in German Health Care Delivery," *N.Engl.J.Med* 355; 15: 1520–1522).

[17] "Medical policing" arose in Germany after the 30 Years' War (1618–1648) because of threats of plague and dysentery (Lindemann, 81). Such activities contributed to the preeminence of public health in German medicine (P. Weindling, *Health, Race and German Politics Between National Unification and Nazism 1870–1945* (Cambridge: University Press, 1991), 5)

Despite this favorable development for the health system and the medical profession, the legislators, in 1869 and 1871, acted grossly inappropriately[18] when they incorporated the medical profession into the decree of the *Reich Business Ordinance,* and thereby made it such that the medical community became a service profession in the service of the welfare of the state. The German Business Ordinance however brought along with its liberal viewpoint an even more extremely unfortunate consequence, namely the *freedom of advertising.*[19] The profession threatened to split into a mere treater of the sick of the worst kind. The reputation of the medical community came to be shamefully degraded by its inclusion among the commercial ranks. A revolutionary unrest empowered the entire profession, threatening a fight over the fundamental rights of the doctors.

The answer of the German medical community to the classification of the physician in the business ordinance was the founding of its own Physicians' Union Federation, which was accomplished at the National Science Conference in 1872 in Leipzig.[20] The ideas of health politics of its founder, Dr. Herman Eberhard *Richter,*

[18] **"...mit rauher Hand..."** literally, "...with a raw hand..." Physicians were most critical of the Reich government for including the medical profession in the Business Ordinance. It was considered to be an affront to the physician's professional nature to be lumped in with mere commercial enterprises. They attempted to have a specifically physicians' ordinance passed, but had to content themselves with "Physicians' Chambers," which were corporations within each state which worked on the politics of the profession. These corporations were established in Prussia in 1887, Hamburg in 1894, Elsass-Lothringen in 1898, Anhalt in 1900, Luebeck in 1902 and Mecklenburg in 1911 (Swoch, 28) This financial environment especially encouraged the idea of unification of all physicians' efforts into a single organization. It was in this context that the *Hartmannbund* was founded. From 1901 to 1923, the *Hartmannbund* organized 1700 strikes, predominantly for financial reasons. In 1913, it came to be the first successful Reich-wide association of the medical community. At yearly doctors conventions, in October of each year, there came to be consistently calls for strikes against the government (Swoch, 28).

[19] *Kurierfreiheit.* Likewise, the freedom of advertising was a sore point with physicians. From their viewpoint, advertising was beneath the dignity of a professional. A similar viewpoint had been expressed by the framers of the AMA Code of Ethics. This is one of the reasons, according to Swoch, that Dr. med. Hermann Hartmann (1863–1923) formed the „Hartmundbund", *Verband der Aerzte Deutschlands zur Wahrung ihrer wirtschaftlichen Interessen.* (Association of Doctors of Germany for the Protection of Economic Interests). In an open letter, Hartmann wrote:

> I say to you, money, money, money is the main thing. We demand for our difficult debilitating self-renouncing work a decent compensation, relief from man-servant taxes, then the value and honor of the profession will be preserved. (Quoted in Swoch, 23)

Even though many members of the *Hartmannbund* (as the association was called after Hartmann's death in1923) were also members of physicians' unions and the Hartmannbund's activities were explicitly designed to address the financial issues of medical practice, the physicians still considered themselves to be professionally superior to common businesses.

[20] The political response was the founding of the *Deutschen Aerztevereinsbund* (Physicians' Union Federation). It was decided that the activities of the private doctor must come to be a matter of state. This is in clear contrast to the development of the medical profession in America where it was (and still is) demanded that the medical profession should be independent. This conception of medicine as being responsible to the whole of the society, which is a fundamental tenet of the National Socialist philosophical viewpoint of medicine, actually originated, according to Ramm, as early as 1872.

culminated in the demand, *that the activities of the private doctor must become a component of the science of healing as a matter of state. The medical profession must gain an influential position in public life through which it would become useful as a whole of the whole*[21] *and indispensable for the Volks welfare;* it must be well organized and should not be allowed to squander its power of all against all.

Thus we find in subsequent doctors' conventions,[22] which gradually evolved from meetings of general interests to become solemn occasions, the demand for change in the business ordinance, for reformation of the relationship of the doctors to the state, for recognized representatives of doctors, and also for the annulment of the freedom to advertise.

At the tenth German doctors' convention in Munich in 1882, a "Fundamental German Doctor Ordinance," was demanded along with the establishment of professional organizations, which were supposed to be recognized by the state as advi-

[21] Ramm places the concept of medicine as being "a whole of the whole" (*als Ganzes des Ganzen*) in the development of the *Deutschen Aerztevereinsbund.* One may think of the concept of the "whole of the whole" as something "double coherence" in common law theory. Melvin Eisenberg explains that this embodies two ideals (MA Eisenberg. *The Nature of the Common Law.* (Cambridge, Mass.: Harvard Univ. Press, 1988). Applying this to Ramm's "whole of the whole" would mean that the body of propositions within the profession are to be internally coherent at the same time they are coherent with the body of propositions which make up the rules of the society at large. The fundamental proposition of both coherences was that of the Nazi's ideal of racial hygiene.

The goal of the association was to improve the economic situation of the physician in the entire Reich and to defend him from the thoughtless exploitation of the sickness funds. The *Hartmannbund* came to be more and more inclined towards mediating places of practice, providing information on insurance and legal advice. It operated a specialty book store, a loan and death fund, a widow and orphans fund, a fund for burials of a doctor's wife, an old age fund, and a department for life, accident, fire, etc. insurance. For these activities and the lobbying efforts with sickness funds and the state, there was a "strike fund," into which each member was required to contribute yearly. In January, 1901 the association had only 668 members, but by 1903 the membership had climbed to 10,000 members and in 1910, 94% of German physicians belonged (Swoch, 24).

[22] The yearly physicians' conventions were critically important affairs which were initially started for educational purposes but soon evolved into opportunities for political activity. Since the country was only recently united in a single Reich, this was often the only opportunity for doctors to meet and interact with their counterparts from other areas. At first there was fear that the medical community would split because of a second major association. But, at the first Reich-wide gathering of the Hartmannbund in June, 1901, a consensus was reached to attempt to achieve unification. Two years later a unification of the two associations was sanctioned. The *Hartmannbund* came to be an economic department of the *Deutschen Aerztevereinsbundes,* but retained some independent standing.

sory corporate bodies.[23] Even though there were erected in individual Territories[24] – in Prussia in 1887 – *Physicians' Chambers,* these new establishments did not entirely correspond to the wishes of the medical community, which demanded the establishment of a central common Physicians' Chamber in order thereby to place at the side of the Reich government a corporate body which would give advice on the various areas of the health system. *Instead of a state decreed Reich Physicians' Ordinance, the medical community had to be content with a declaration which stated the "Fundamentals of a Medical Profession. Ordinance."* The desire for a decree of a Reich Physicians' Ordinance was only fulfilled in the National Socialist states in 1935.

Meanwhile new concerns arose in the medical community because of the creation of "Sickness Insurance for the Moderation of Social Damages to the Laboring Classes."[25] At this time the German doctor community could not foresee what

---

[23] The doctors were organized enough at the tenth convention in 1882 to make specific demands of the Reich government. They failed, however, in accomplishing what they wished for – the enactment of a physicians' ordinance, which would have separated them from the hated Business Ordinance. Instead, they had to be content with a compromise agreement which merely outlined some of the fundamental principles underlying their conception of the profession. Ramm notes that it was not until National Socialist times, and even then only after the National Socialists had been in power for 2 years, that a specific Physicians' Ordinance was enacted.

[24] *Land* – 1 of the 15 territorial divisions of Republican Germany, each with its own government. From 1933 the Central Government controlled the Laender through Reichsstathalter.

[25] Out of the workers' movement of the latter half of the century came the movement for the establishment of insurance for those unable to afford the cost of health care in the case of work-related injury. With the founding of the German Reich, there were calls for state-supported welfare programs to mollify the miserable living and working conditions of the average German. Even before this there was a law, passed in 1854, requiring workers to become a member of a sickness fund. This law established self-administration of the funds, a situation which would come to be anathema to the medical profession. The industrial code of 1869 permitted, in addition to the compulsory funds, free funds for labor and work associations. Accident insurance was passed in1884, old age and invalid insurance in1889. Compulsory insurance was extended to all post office, telegraph, railroad administration, professional carriage and inland navigation and shipping workers. Lawyers, notaries, sickness fund and insurance administrators were added to the insurance funds as long as they did not earn more than 2000 marks a year (Swoch, 18). The employee's contribution was graduated according to income, while the employer had to pay half.

The members received free medical care as well as free medication. While it became difficult for some funds to meet their legal obligations, there continued to be demands for the introduction of a wider circle of the population, like family members and servants. This led in1911 to the Reich Insurance Ordinance (RVO) which bundled together sickness, accident and disability insurance. Revisions to this law were made in 1914 and 1936, but it continued in effect until 1988 (Swoch, 19)

The development of social insurance brought not only confrontation between doctors and the sickness funds, it also placed the determination of the amount of the honorarium in the hands of the insurance carrier and ultimately led to the oversight of the medical community by the insurance carriers, an intolerable situation for the physicians. The medical profession saw this development as threatening to its authority and position with the patient. Additionally, because certain classes of patients were required to be a member of the sickness funds and each fund had its own group of approved physicians, fund physicians had an enormous advantage over their colleagues (Swoch, 19)

disadvantages and dangers this sickness insurance held for the scientific practice of the profession and to the economic position of the doctor. With the great enlargement of the circle of the insured, the economic position of that great number of doctors who chose not to take up medical fund activities soon came to be threatened. Unfortunately there were more physicians who applied for employment with the sickness funds than were needed. Thus there gradually began an undignified run for health insurance fund places, a situation which was exploited by the sickness funds in order to decrease the physician's honorarium to a degradingly low level, leading to working conditions for the doctor which bespoke of scorn for their social feelings.

The physicians who were active in the sickness funds were not even granted an appropriate basic salary for their participation, for which they had to take on a terrible workload. One of the most important professional activities of the doctor, that of the trusting relationship with the patient, was taken away by this system as the insured patient was not permitted to have the doctor of his choice, but instead was required to take advice from the doctor committed to the sickness fund. There thus broke out the decades long fight over the free choice of doctor, which only ended in 1933, after the overtaking of power by the National Socialist Party.[26]

The literature does not tell us exactly how many people were covered by compulsory insurance, but Claudia Huerkamp has reported that 4.29 million or 9.2% of the population were in compulsory insurance programs. By 1914, according to Huerkamp, 50% of the population was compulsorily insured and thus were able to demand free health care (C. Huerkamp, *Der Aufstieg der Aerzte im 19 Jahrhundert. Vom gelehrten Stand zum professionellen Experten: Das Beispiel Preussen* (Goettingen: Vandenhoeck & Ruprecht, 1985), 195–9). This, coupled with the power of the administration of the sickness funds, markedly limited physicians' professional freedom. Thus, the sickness funds were in the position to bring doctors to economic dependency.

Ramm presents the rise of social insurance as a disaster for the medical profession. This most certainly was the general view among the medical community, even before the National Socialists. He points out that it was not the funds per se which threatened the medical profession but the fact that the supply/demand ratio of fund practice positions was against the physician. This competitive rush for fund positions led to the "undignified run" of physicians for places. In many localities the economy of medical practice made it such that a practicing physician could not survive financially without the supplemental income from a fund practice. Ramm notes that the fund governing boards exploited the situation by lowering the honorarium for treatment of a patient in the fund to a "ridiculously degrading level."

[26] Ramm points out another major sore point for the medical professionals – the loss of the "free choice of doctor." As he notes, this resulted in a decades-long fight over this issue.

Almost all sickness funds were closed civil law contracts with one or more physicians. Physician payment took place in yearly flat rate payments. In the 1890s there were over 23,000 sickness funds in localities, businesses, farms and mining operations (Swoch, 26). Of the numerous sickness funds, 1.1% had no more than 5000 members, 44.6% had fewer then 100 and many had only 10–20 members (Swoch, 26). The larger sickness funds had taken over the district medical system from the beginning, following which there were particular physicians designated and contracted for each district. Other sickness funds worked according to the principle of "limited free choice of physician" or even "free choice of physician," by which was meant that the patient could consult freely those physicians working in their fund (Swoch, 26). This *de facto* exclusion of physicians was a cause of complaint by the non-approved physicians from the beginning. Gerald Feldman notes that the anomalous situation in which trade-union methods were used to protect the

Even though the German Physicians' Union Federation had also noted how the ideal conception of medicine had suffered so much damage, it could not however at that time bring about a change in the situation, because the government lacked the understanding of these matters.

In this highly charged situation, the German medical community turned to self-help through the initiative of *Hermann Hartmann,* who was the first to call for a fight against the oppressive and exploitative methods of the sickness funds and to place himself at the forefront of the enraged medical community, which was

---

special interests of a free profession was reflected in the demand that the insurance funds hire all doctors who wished to work for them (G.D. Feldman, *The Great Disorder: Politics, Economics, and Society in the German Inflation, 1914–1924* (Oxford: University Press, 1997), 532). In the 1990s there were already loud complaints about the physician's honorarium, which was largely determined by the sickness funds and their boards, on which there was no medical specialty representation (Swoch, 26). These boards became the social-experimental field of the workers movement. The organized workers movement operated with a heavy hand within the boards and became a long standing thorn in the eye of the organized medical community. The two issues of honorarium and free choice of physician came to be constant contentious problems for the medical associations.

The issue of the "free choice of physician," can be found in the literature as far back as 1848 (Swoch, 27). The concept of free choice of physician was popularized at the end of the nineteenth century since the demand gave an opportunity for the doctor to demand a position in a sickness fund. Swoch reports that the "free choice of physician" was not universally accepted by physicians' associations and citizens' parties, but the movement for free choice accelerated. In 1900 the *Deutsche Centrale fuer frei Arztwahl* (German Central for Free Choice of Physician) was founded in Freiburg (Swoch, 28).

While these confrontations between the sickness funds and the doctors increased, the number of doctors also grew, putting the physicians' associations in a poorer bargaining position. In 1921, there were 36,186 doctors in Germany (or one doctor for every 1700 inhabitants), whereas in 1909 there had been 30,558 doctors (or one doctor for every 2400 inhabitants. In large cities, the most desirable places to practice, the 1921 ratio was 1:950 (Feldman, 532).

At the same time, the number of insured rose rapidly (Swoch, 27). At the beginning, the practice with fund patients had been nothing more than a supplemental activity, but as a consequence of the growth of the number of fund patients and the increase in the number of physicians, physicians became dependent upon being a member of a sickness fund to make a living. With the freedom to advertise (*Kurierfreiheit*), the competition for patients became fierce.

Another point of the sickness fund problem was the presumed professionally unworthy position of the fund physician when the fund boards, as "employer" of the fund physician, had turned down a physician, making it then appear that he was "unworthy." Physicians had been employees of municipalities in the past in providing for the health care of the poor, but the fund relationship of employer/employee was not considered to be compatible with their notion of a "free" profession. "The medical profession is a free one and is no state institution" (H. Schadewaldt, in Swoch, 27). Swoch reports that, on the other hand, there was frequent taking and offering of bribes and underbiddings by doctors in order to secure a fund physician position. Fund physician approval became evermore important for the security of the existence of the physician (Swoch, 27). The physician was in a very difficult position and a sense of unworthiness permeated the profession. Their very method of fighting the insurance funds worked against their personal conception of their profession and the representations of the profession did not gain much sympathy by their strike threats, and the publication of statements to the effect that "for we doctors to put ourselves on a brotherly basis with the workers means to lose the last remainder of our self-respect" (In Feldman, 533).

prepared for a fight (1900). The methods employed by the *Hartmannbund* in this fight against the health insurance funds were wise, effective and purposeful. The so-called organized free choice of doctor was raised up as the goal of the fight as well as the demand that all licensed members of the Hartmannbund should receive an adequate honorarium on treating patients in a local fund. In many localities and Territories of the Reich, this demand was forced through only after hard and courageous struggles.

In 1913, the decree of the Reich Insurance Ordinance came as a great disappointment to the medical community because in this law the government again gave in to the sickness funds on the regulation of its relationship with doctors; as a consequence, there came to be the threat of open battle between the contracting parties. Before this occurred, however, the Reich government intervened.[27] An agreement was closed between doctors and the sickness funds which represented to a certain extent a stand-off in the battle. On the grounds of this agreement, the sickness funds were no longer free in the choice of their doctors; specifically they had to permit at least one doctor for every 1350 persons, and 1000 in the case of family treatment.

Even though a truce reigned between the fighting parties during the world war,[28] after the war, the fight again rose to its old intensity when the funds, on the grounds of their good relationship to the government system, strove to claim rights which were intolerable to the medical community. In 1923, the Reich Committee for

---

[27] A strike in the south German states in 1913 was settled by the government with the so-called "Berlin Agreement." The sickness funds had to make great concessions, including agreeing to collective contracting partners on the physicians' side, concessions on the free choice of physician and the allowance of a rise in the number of fund physicians. The real catalyst for the settlement was the threatened general strike which would have been devastating at the time. State intervention in the mediation process here coincided with its interest to narrow or withdraw the social democratic movement from self-administration of insurance (Swoch, 29).

[28] The First World War led to a break in the efforts to protect the Volk population. "Volk power" came to be emphasized in contrast to the welfare of the individual patient. The physician associations worked hand in hand with the government since it was clear that all power had to be put into the war effort. The physician was, like the entire population, one of the economic victims of the war, but there was no protest.

When, in November, 1918, the government extended the obligation of insurance to cover wider circles of clients and at the same time limited the rise of honorarium paid doctors, the medical community reacted with widespread protest. Many doctors believed that with the collapse of the German Reich they had lost their own personal highly regarded professional status. This led many to protest the changes without really being associated with the rightwing extremist groups. The majority of the medical community rejected the Weimar Republic. Various associations wrote letters of support to the Volk representative, Friedrich Ebert (1871–1925). Among them were the *Deutsche Aerztevereinsbund* and the *Hartmannbund,* which also sent similar letters to the Hitler regime to place themselves in the correct light at the appropriate time (Swoch, 30). Certainly the National Socialist ideology stood essentially closer to the ideology of the physicians than the Weimar government because giving equal rights to the underclass was a thorn in the eye of the medical community (Swoch, 30). The doctors therefore became the most strike-experienced and militaristic group of the citizenry. The Hartmannbund had a militaristic physician leadership and authoritarian constitution. Doctors' strikes came to be the "best weapons of defense" (Haedenkamp, in Swoch, 30) and were utilized as defensive weapons against worker-strikes as a means of economic confrontation (Swoch, 30).

Doctors and Sickness Funds was established, which set up guidelines for the relationship between doctors and sickness funds, and essentially constructed a peace between the parties. It was decided in 1931 for the first time to legislate, through a state emergency ordinance, the free choice of doctor and at the same time to license one doctor for every 600 insured. *The Fund Physicians' Unions*, which were newly founded by the ordinance, took over the important challenge of self-administration, which consisted of overseeing the activities of its members as well as the distribution of all of the reimbursements from the sickness funds. From this time on, the sickness funds paid to the medical community of its district a fixed amount for each insured, taking the fluctuation of the basic salary into account.

In retrospect, we must maintain that the German medical community has to thank solely the fearless and idealistic fighter, Hartmann, for the maintenance of its professional freedom, a freedom without which a high standing ideal conception of medicine would be unimaginable.

The victory of the National Socialist revolution[29] also meant for the medical community the breakthrough of a new attitude of mind. The dominant

---

[29] Ramm now turns to the "Comprehensive National Socialist Philosophical Worldview." The notion of a National Socialist philosophical viewpoint (*Weltanschauung)* was very important to the Nazis. Hitler told a meeting of Party members in March, 1934, that the victory of a Party was nothing more than a change of government and that he National Socialist revolution would achieve its final victory only when it was accepted by all Germans, something he estimated might take years or even generations (Schoenbaum, 50)

The medical community was very clear that it supported the new regime, even publishing in the "Deutsche Aerzteblatt on 30 Mar 1933 and in the Aerztlichen Mitteilung" of 1 April, 1933, a "Homage telegram," in which the top medical associations, the *Deutsche Aerztevereinbund* and the *Hartmannbund,* earnestly offered to the "Herr President," the joyful creed of the German medical community to be a sacrificing service for the fatherland and the health of the Volk, additionally sending greetings to "Herr Reichskanzler," and vowed to him to fulfill their duty as servants to the health of the Volk. Fourteen days later, there was a renewed greeting to the Kanzler, which expressly stated the medical community's viewpoint: Adolph Hitler was not only assured of the "joyful willingness" of "selfless cooperation in the new construction of the state and the Volk," the medical community showed itself to be prepared "in the sense of the new spirit of state and Volk to adapt the spirit and forms of their organizations to the new demands which are today placed on us" (In Swoch, 92).

The physicians believed that in the newly defined position of the medical community in the society, the long longed-for high valuation of their profession had been achieved by its being expressed at the state level. The health system, according to Julius Hadrich in 1933, belonged to the direct state organs which had to protect the state's interest in its first line and not just economically: "This new valuation is valid especially for the medical community because the National Socialist state, because of its Racial Hygiene goals, needs the physician urgently as one of its official co-workers" (Hadrich, in Swoch, 92–3). "In general," Karl Haedenkamp stated in December, 1933, "the place of the physician in the state has fundamentally changed since the completion of national renewal. The politics of the states has come to be constructed in an outstanding way on biological knowledge, the care of the Volk health and the health of the entire Volk body of each individual has stepped to the foreground as a state political responsibility. Physicians have been awakened to new and serious duties for a secure foundation. While with these widened duties there are greatly more laws, these developments are objectively and morally justified in the interests of the state" (Haedenkamp, in Swoch, 93). As a professional ideal the service of the whole profession to the state and its institutions was validated. In May, 1934, after over a year of National

liberalistic-materialistic attitude, which had predominated up to that time, was replaced by the Comprehensive National Socialist Philosophical Viewpoint. The leadership of the profession went over immediately in 1933 to the National Socialist German Physicians' Association (*NSD – Aerztesbund*), which had been founded at the party convention in Nuremburg in 1929 as a philosophically National Socialist fighting comrade unit within the German community and had won an increasingly higher reputation and acceptance within the German medical community and the general academic health profession. On 24 March, 1933 the leader of the NSD-Physicians' Association was Dr. Gerhard *Wagner*,[30] State Commissioner of the two top physicians' associations. On 2 April, 1933, the formal appointment of the spokesmen of the top medical associations for this new ordinance of medical professional relationships took place in Leipzig. This day is memorable in the history of the German medical community for when the parliamentary-liberal epoch had to make way for the leadership principle.[31] From this day forward, important regulations concerning the profession were no longer to be made by majority decision but rather by direct order from the leader of the profession. As early as 27 April, 1933 the Territorial and Provincial associations of the Hartmann Federation and the German Physicians' Unions Association were taken over by the authorized representatives of Dr. Wagner, who were delegated from the NSD – Physicians'

Socialist domination, Haedenkamp wrote, "With this increasing influence of the medical community on the future formation of the health care system, health education and health care administration, something has been won, though this influence is exercised completely free from professional-egoistic considerations and for the benefit of the entirety of all Volk comrades. Based on the ability of his knowledge of facts and educational preparation, it is fitting that the physician is the leader in the area of Volk health, but not as its ruler, but as its first servant" (Haedenkamp, in Swoch, 93). This was the Comprehensive National Socialist Philosophical Worldview.

This unselfish and submissive and honorable posture was the first assumption for the "new regulation" of physicians' professional politics (*Bevolkerungpolitiks)* and the health care system, for the introduction of the authoritative leadership, of the "Leadership train of thought" (Swoch, 93)'.

[30] Dr. med. Gerhard Wagner (1888–1939) became the first leader of the medical associations. He was born in Neu-Heiduk/Oberschlesian. He took his medical studies at Munich in 1912 and served as a field physician in the 18th Baverian Infantry Regiment from August, 1914 to December, 1918. He was a Freikorps fighter then general practitioner in Munich. He entered the NSDAP in 1929 and became a close personal friend of Deputy-Fuehrer Rudolph Hess. In time he carried these titles: *Fuehrer des NSDAB; Kommissar des Deutschen Aerzteverinsbundes and des Hartmannbundes, Praesident des Reichsgesundheitsamts, Fuehrer der Deutschen Aerzteschaft (Reichaerztefuehrer), Leiter der RaK, Haputdienstleiter in der Reichsleitung der NSDAP* (Swoch, 377)

Wagner was a rabid anti-Semite and a hardliner in regards to who was a Jew, but failed to make a strong case when the Nuremberg laws were being adopted by Hitler in 1935, reportedly because he spent his time in Nuremberg offsetting boredom by playing with a toy tank (M. Burleigh, *The Third Reich: A New History* (New York: Hill & Wang, 2000), 295)

He died of an undisclosed, but allegedly "vicious, "illness at the end of March 1939 (Kater, *Doctors Under Hitler, 24).*

[31] The German medical community was reorganized according to the "leadership principle," whereby all major decisions were to come from the leader.

Association.[32] By far the greatest part of the medical community gladly greeted the overtaking of leadership by the NSD – Physicians' Association, in the hope that the medical community would in the National Socialist Volk community again regain a high reputation and recognition. It was assumed that there would be elimination of unsuitable and politically unbearable elements, the restoration of professional discipline and the re-construction of a high professional ethos as a guiding principle of medical treatment.

One of the first measures of the National Socialist Physicians' leadership was the cleansing of the profession of politically un-reliable and racially-foreign elements, so long as the medical benefit for the Volk population was not endangered. If one considers that in 1933 in Germany out of 50,000 doctors 13% were Jews, that of this percentage over 60% were in Berlin and in Austria 67% were in Vienna, then one can appreciate the terrible influence that the Jews had in the medical community and the influence they had had on the legislation of health measures up to 1933. One can however today already grasp the blessings which are important to life and to our Volk in the offices of the states that have emerged after the forceful expulsion of the Jews from the professions.

It was the Jew who forced some German doctors into a crass materialistic employment of professionally unworthy methods of competition; the Jew who endangered the German Volk, and the one who, through extension of his soul-poisoning ideas, enabled the destruction of germinating life while generating the impression, through his methods of advertising in wide circles of the population, that he was indispensable as a medical researcher and medical practitioner.

The NSD – Physicians' Association had already for years taken on a psychological rearrangement of the German doctor, binding him to his Volk and hammering into him that he himself was not allowed to feel that he is a member of a preferred profession or a representative of an academic caste, but rather that the doctor is called to the service of the Volk and, as a leader in the area of health, would have to bear in his character a terribly great moral duty and responsibility to the whole Volk. Today no full-blooded German will allow himself to be treated by a Jewish doctor. Since 1938, each Jew has had his license taken away; he is allowed to be only a

[32] The NSD-Aerztebund had been founded by the Ingolstadt surgeon Dr. Ludwig Liebl during the party rally at Nuremberg in 1929 to promote the interests of Nazi doctors in the Weimar Republic. Among its activities was the cultivation of a relationship with the *Hartmannbund* (Kater, *Doctors Under Hitler,* 24). After the political takeover in 1933, Wagner, at the behest of Hitler and Hess, used the NSD-Aerztebund primarily as a political weapon against the still existing bourgeois physicians' associations (Kater, *Doctors Under Hitler,* 107).

sickness-treater for the increasingly small number of Jews still living in Germany.[33] It is expressly forbidden for him to treat a full-blooded German.[34]

In pursuit of simplification of organization, the branches of the Hartmann Federation and Physicians'-Union-Federation were joined together in 1933; the home of the German Physicians in Berlin became their headquarters. The Fund Physicians' Union, previously created in 1931, was joined to the German Fund Physicians' Union in August 1933 by ministerial ordinance, which on 2 November, 1933 received special articles of association.[35] The German Fund Physicians' Union

---

[33] In 1943, it was widely known that the Jews were being exterminated in the death camps. The terms "relocated," and "special treatment" (*Sonderbehandlung)* were part of the LTI, so Ramm's disingenuous remark, "**the increasingly small number of Jews still living in Germany**," seems particularly disingenuous.

Alexander Mistcherlich and Fred Milke, in 1947, published documents from the Nuremberg Doctors' Trial and concluded, "only the secret consent of the practice of science and politics can explain why the names of high-ranking scientists are constantly dropped during this trial, of men, who perhaps did not right off commit any crime but took advantage of the cruel fate of defenseless individuals" (A. Mitscherlich and F. Mielke, eds., *Das Diktat der Menschenverachtung* (Heidelberg: Verlag Lambert Schneider, 1947), ii). They could very well have been referring to Ramm.

[34] On April 1, 1933, there were from 8000 to 9000 Jewish physicians practicing in Germany. By the end of 1934, approximately 2200 had either emigrated or abandoned their profession (S. Friedlaender, *Nazi Germany and the Jew, Vol. 1:The Years of Persecution, 1933–1939* (New York: Harper-Collins, 1997), 225). The official listing of the country's physicians for 1937 identified about 4200 Jewish physicians, still too many in the eyes of the Nazis. The total elimination of Jewish physicians in the Third Reich began with an order by Rinehart Heydrich's SD on April 6, 1937 to compile systematic lists of all Jews active in the medical profession throughout Germany (Kater, *Doctors Under Hitler,* 200). Wagner convinced Hitler to exclude Jewish physicians from practice, so Hitler decreed on July 25, 1938 that by September 30 all Jewish doctors were to be decertified (Kater, *Doctors Under Hitler,* 200). Dr. Leonardo Conti, the erstwhile Health Leader argued that "every nondegenerate woman must and will internally shrink from being treated by a Jewish gynecologist; this has nothing to do with racial hatred, but belongs to the medical imperative according to which a relation of mutual understanding must grow between spiritually related physicians and patients" (Friedlaender, 1997, 30).

Note that Ramm even takes away the designation "doctor" and calls the Jew a mere "sickness-treater." On October 3, 1938, the Reich Physicians' Chamber had demanded of the Minister of Education that Jewish physicians, now forbidden to practice, should also have the title 'Doctor' taken away (Friedlaender, 1997, 259).

Some people insisted on seeing a Jewish doctor. If they did so, they were likely to come under the surveillance of the authorities and receive a letter from the Gestapo like the following:

> *I came to know that you are under medical treatment of a Jew. But Germans attend only German physicians. The Jew is not a German. It shall also serve for your information that you receive your public benefits from the German people and not from the Jewish people, who only enjoy hospitality in Germany. I hope that this instruction will suffice to enable you to act as a German in the future. I shall conscientiously oversee the success or failure of my admonition and warning. In the case of nonobservance, we will have to deal with this affair in a different manner. Heil Hitler!* (In Weyers, 96)

[35] The joining of the two traditional physicians' unions was merely a stepping-stone for the establishment of specifically National Socialist health and medical organizations. In the spring of 1936 the property and regional apparatus of the *Hartmannbund* was taken over by the *Kassenaerztlich Vereinigung Deutschlands – KVD.* Likewise headed by Wagner, the KVD was to oversee the certi-

(KVD) was the forerunner of the much sought-after reconstruction of the medical community which was achieved with the Reich Physicians' Ordinance, which culminated in 1936 in the Reich Physicians' Chamber and German Fund Physicians' Union. The Reich Physicians' Chamber and the German Fund Physicians' Union are both corporate bodies of public law, whereas the KVD is a department of the Reich Physicians' Chamber[36] with special independence.

The German Fund Physicians' Union (KVD)

The *German Fund Physicians' Union* is the successor to the Fund Physicians' Union; it encompasses the whole Reich and is the sole representative of the German medical community, empowered to regulate the medical benefit in social insurance, private insurance funds, the Reich Benefit, as well as voluntary service, etc. The Reich Physicians' Leader is leader of the KVD and appoints a permanent Vice-Representative for the KVD. The KVD also has the responsibility to negotiate contracts with the community and with welfare organizations concerning the medical benefit for the circle of Volk entitled to them. Further, it makes arrangements for honoraria for physicians who perform examinations for medical unions, and health and life insurance companies. It specifically regulates the relationships of fund physicians with each other, and is responsible for fund work licensure or termination of a doctor. It exercises oversight over the economic viability of all treatment modalities, reviews physician performance and orders the distribution of all the reimburse-

---

fication and regional deployment of all fund doctors (Kater, *Doctors Under Hitler,* 22) Swoch called the KVD the "First Professional Corporation for the Physician" (Swoch, 108).

The erection of the Fund Physicians' Union (KVD) on December 12, 1931 was the beginning of the transfer of the Hartmannbund to a public-legal corporation. Virtually all of the decisions relative to fund physicians' activities were put into the hands of the medical community. The Hartmannbund was no longer a free professional association but became a legal corporation standing under the oversight of the state. It regulated the licensing of physicians for fund practice as well for termination. Further it oversaw the fund physicians' activities regarding their economy. It determined the preparation for tests for a physician's performance as well as refereeing the result. It distributed the honorarium of the fund physician. The KVD also undertook the means to orient the physician towards genetic-biology. Among its wider responsibilities were the unification of compensation for the activity of experts and the introduction of investigations over means and measures of cure. It especially regulated the relationships between physicians. The KVD therefore had great importance for each fund physician and for each physician who was applying for a fund position. Reimbursement for a physician's activity with fund patients went directly to the KVD which distributed it directly to the physician (Swoch, 109). This decreased the direct influence of the sickness funds on the physician and replaced it with the KVD. Karl Haedenkamp believed that this arrangement meant that the power struggle between the physician and the sickness fund had been decided in the favor of the physician (Swoch, 109). What the physicians did not realize at first was that their individual power had been overtaken by the KVD and they were even more powerless than before the "*Machtuebergreifung*."

[36] *RAK*

ments which are paid from the sickness funds to the Reich Leadership of the KVD. It is entitled to implement and coordinate preservation of the Volk population (*bevolkerungspolitiks*) and genetic-biological viewpoints and such, and to reconcile differences in these areas. For these purposes, it manages an account to make adjustments for physicians with heavy family burdens as well as an account for physicians working in disaster areas.[37] The family burden account grants to each physician an expense allowance of up to 50 marks monthly for 3 children or more, and the disaster area account grants additional benefits to secure economic existence for the physician who works in the middle of a poor population or in a border area, and thereby stands at an especially important political-health post.

The KVD is structured according to Territorial divisions (*Landstelle)* and District divisions (*Bezirkstelle*). The *Landstelle* encompasses more-or-less the area of the former German Laender or Prussian Territories or the newly formed Regions.[38] The *District divisions* consist of the consolidation of several fund-physician unions of the old laws into a general administrative and accounting organ. The Department Leader of the KVD is assigned and dismissed by the Reich Leader. Disciplinary power is transferred over to the Department Leaders,[39] which gives them the authority to determine punishment, and in exceptional cases, fines up to RM 1000 with exclusion from the activities of the medical fund (s. & 8 of the KVD – Articles of Association). In the Articles of Association of the KVD, which are approved by the Reich Labor Ministry, it is expressly stated that the licensure of the physician for medical-fund activities is a task of the KVD and is regulated through the decree of the Licensing Ordinance. It is also the KVD that regulates the relationships between individual physicians to the sickness funds and represents a physician in his relationship with the sickness-funds. In that connection, the KVD's activities include licensure of the physician for fund practice, as well as the oversight of a fund physician's activities and honorarium.

The licensure of activities in the sickness funds occurs, as we have seen, by the doctors themselves[40] and in fact by special licensure committees, which exist in the individual Territorial Divisions of the KVD. The sickness funds and the insurance

---

[37] This is an interesting and very important feature of KVD activities. It appears that a physician who was especially aggressive in carrying out the Comprehensive National Socialist Philosophical Worldview might receive greater compensation. It can be seen that the KVD had enormous power to make certain that the physician practiced according to the Comprehensive National Socialist Philosophical Worldview. By controlling his relationship to the sickness fund the KVD was in the position to make certain the physician practice according to this worldview even if he was not a member of the Party.

[38] *Gau* – Region – the main territorial division of the Nazi Party, Germany was divided into 42 Gaue.

[39] *Amtsleiter* – official appointed for special duties in the central Reich directorate of the NSDAP

[40] One of the major complaints doctors had had against the previous administration of the sickness funds was that they were administered by non-physicians. The administration of the sickness funds by physicians was counted by Physicians as one of the assets of the overtaking of power by the National Socialists. In fact, however, the doctors actually lost power and privileges because all of their activities had to be filtered through the National Socialist associations.

carriers do not participate. Independent contractual relationships between individual fund doctors and sickness funds are not permitted; they are allowed only between the sickness fund associations and fund physicians of the German Fund Physicians' Union. The rights of a fund physician regarding the fulfillment of his obligatory duties are granted to him solely from the KVD and not directly from the carrier of the insurance. The KVD arranges for the sickness funds to provide an adequate supply of physicians for the insured. The disciplinary power of the KVD regarding the physician, mentioned before, empowers it to initiate training programs and to punish violations of a fund physician's obligations. Disciplinary authority includes a special disciplinary court proceeding by the professional court of the RAK in the case of unprofessional behavior. Disciplinary punishment is imposed by the leader of the Territorial Division of the KVD.[41] The Reich Leader of the KVD can alter or rescind the declared verdict. Permanent exclusion from fund practice may be decreed only by the licensure committee and for that reason this function was turned over to the Reich Licensure Committee.

In this connection it must be mentioned that supervision over the KVD, as well as over all social insurance, is exercised by the Reich Labor Ministry. *The Advisory Physician Service* has likewise now been placed under the supervision of the Reich Labor Ministry, since it no longer has any responsibility towards individual sickness funds or the like, but rather has been implemented as a community service of social insurance. It has been transferred over to the sickness fund department of the Territorial Insurance Institutes for Insurance of the Invalid. Since this again, like all standard arrangements of social insurance, is overseen by the Reich Insurance Office, and ultimately is under the authority of the Reich Labor Ministry, the right of oversight over the Advisory Physician Service is given over to the Reich Labor Ministry. Prior to this regulation, the Advisory physician was an employee of the sickness funds and had to work under their direction. The relationship of the Advisory doctor to the treating doctor (as also to the insured) has without a doubt improved through the formation of the Advisory Physician Service, even though the advisory doctor system has at no time enjoyed complete sympathy from either the insured or the fund doctors.

The Land Insurance Institutes as a rule employ the advisory doctor, who is typically a Civil Service Physician, but can also be some other official physician. The Advisory Physician Service's responsibilities consist of checking out one's incapacity to work and suitability for insurance. Further, the Advisory physicians are to advise the sickness funds concerning the application of their legal responsibilities, namely those relating to preventive measures.

Also the Industry Physician Service,[42] which oversees hygiene in industry and the prevention of industrial illnesses, is under the Factory Inspectorate of State Oversight of the Reich Labor Ministry.

---

[41] Ramm himself was a leader of the Territorial Division, "Westmark."

[42] Since the National Socialist society was essentially in an industrial growth economy from 1934 on, there were increasing demands for longer working hours in industry. The inescapable corollary of longer working hours was a deterioration of workers' health. Grunberger has reported that as the

So we could maintain that a certain worthy place has finally been achieved by the physician in regards to social insurance,[43] which sets him in the position, in regards to the fund activities which the Volk community transferred over to him, to bring a certain degree of harmony to his professional ideal. This harmony is never to be complete because sickness insurance – as material assistance, like all social insurance – is fundamentally disconnected from what has led to the sickness – that is, a weakening of the will to health brought about by a lack of education.[44] One of the most unfortunate accompaniments of sickness insurance is the destruction of the trusting relationship between doctor and patient, which is essentially caused by the growth of greed of the insured and the numerous unnecessary attempts by the doctor to satisfy the material wishes of the "sick." Also the complaints of the doctor over the unbearable burden of the accumulating accounting clerical work associated with this activity deserves serious consideration.

Even though the sickness insurance of today provides considerable measures within its legal framework in preventive health, the National Socialist movement does not acknowledge *today's* system of *sickness insurance* to be adequate to be able to satisfy the demands of the National Socialist philosophy. For the proper training and leadership of our Volk, the preservation and promotion of health towards the greatest possible encompassing provision of the genetically ill with pure measures will have to be made a priority before the limits of possibility are

---

peacetime industrial labor force expanded by approximately 50 per cent (from 13.5 million in 1933 to 20.8 million in 1939), the number of accidents and illnesses connected with work increased by one and a half (from 929,000 to 2,253,000). The incidence of occupational diseases more than trebled (from 7000 to nearly 23,000), and fatality increased two and a half times (from 217 to 525). Eventually industry retained over 4000 physicians – mainly working part-time – but this demand did decrease the availability of medical care to non-industrial sectors (Grunberger, 221). A part of this picture was the observation that during the Third Reich both industrial physicians and fund physicians were less ready to grant medical certificates and became more insistent on an early return to work than previously (Grunberger, 192). We will see later in Ramm a discussion and justification for this practice.

[43] Ramm is here asserting that the physician has achieved a "**worthy place in social insurance**..." The context of this remark is that physicians had previously considered the social insurance movement to be the greatest threat to their professional ideal. By placing physicians in the position of administering the funds the National Socialists believed they had been able to move the administration of the insurance funds towards the professional ideal.

[44] But, even with administration of the insurance funds, the National Socialists believed that the idea of social insurance had a certain corrupting effect on the insured person, by "weakening his will to health." But the acceptance of social insurance was so widespread that even the National Socialists did not believe that they could abolish the system, which they viewed as being one of the outgrowths of the "Marxist-liberalist" past. They did however manage to change the administration of the funds by placing loyal National Socialists in position of leadership.

Rather than provide "material assistance," the National Socialists would have ideally considered a sick individual as being one who had lost his "will to health." If he was unable to regain this lost will then he would be considered to be one of the nonproducing drags (the "sick") on the society, and therefore expendable. The entire society was constructed as a Social Darwinist experiment, as Kater writes, "The archetypal Nazi held a holistic view toward medicine, tempered with notions of Social Darwinism (Kater, *Doctors Under Hitler,* 25).

achieved. The social-political efforts which have up to the present time determined the character of the sickness insurance must be subordinated because of the change of objective health aims.

An ultimate statement from the party and state has not yet been given. After the end of the war the give and take of the new plans will have to be weighed in order to find a satisfactory and justified solution.

In the public interest and out of pure objective grounds, the planning as well as management and introduction of progress for the sick must still lay with the Reich Health Leader. Only by the arrangement whereby help for the sick is a service of the health leadership will the principle be maintained that all attention to the sick – including the provision of medical and nursing care as well as material provisions – must strive for that one goal, which is to promote recovery, and thus lead most rapidly and fundamentally to the restoration of performance capacity.

Reich Physicians' Chamber

With the Reich Ordinance Decree of 13.12.1935, which was put into effect on 1.4.1936, the struggle of over a century of the German profession for a central professional corporation of physicians was finally accomplished through the founding of the *Reich Physicians' Chamber* (RAK).[45] This occurred certainly not in the sense of a representation of the interests of the doctor or of a possible application of influence on the formation of laws – as the demand had previously been placed – on the contrary, the Reich Physicians' Chamber was created as an organ of the state, to be able to transfer to the state the responsibilities for the introduction and completion of contracts. It is the representative of the German medical community, with the characteristic of a corporation of public law, and is situated in the main city of the movement, Munich.

The responsibilities which the state placed on the Reich Physicians' Chamber were clearly outlined in & 19 of the Reich Physicians' Ordinance, where it says: "The German medical profession is called to work for the welfare of the Volk and Reich, for the maintenance and improvement of the health, the genetic wealth and the race of the German Volk."

The Reich Physicians' Chamber works on all measures which are given from the states in these areas, while it works with the government on modeling laws and

[45] Kater reports that Wagner wanted to establish a corporate body beyond the KVD for two reasons. The first was that the KVD covered only fund physicians, leaving non-physicians outside of his control. The second reason was that Wagner, as head of the KVD, was partially dependent on the Reich labor ministry because its jurisdiction covered matters of public insurance, including medicare (Kater, *Doctors Under Hitler,* 22). With the Reich Physicians' Ordinance of December 13, 1935, membership in the Reich Physicians' Chamber (RaK) became compulsory for every German physician (Kater, *Doctors Under Hitler,* 23). Thus another level of National Socialist control was established over the physician, giving an additional opportunity to be certain that the Worldview was inculcated into his practice.

arranging for the implementation of legal regulations or ministerial ordinances, establishing experts and subspecialties for special cases. All physicians, with the exception of doctors of the Wehrmacht, Waffen-SS, police and Reich Labor Service are placed under the professional oversight of the Reich Physicians' Chamber, and as a consequence, have to follow its advice and directions as long as such activities do not conflict with medical officials or medical employees of the Reich, the Territories, the community, the Reich insurance, or come under the Advisory Physicians Service.

The Leader of the Reich Physicians' Chamber, the "*Reichaerztefuhrer* "is called and dismissed by the Fuehrer and Reich Chancellor, on the advice of the Reich Minister of the Interior and the Party Chancellery. He has a permanent Deputy, whose appointment and dismissal is to come from the Reich Physicians' Leader with agreement of the Reich Minister of the Interior and Party Chancellery. An advisory committee stands at the side of the leader of the Reich Physicians' Chamber according to & 23 of the Reich Physicians' Ordinance. The Reich Physicians' Chamber has created under-departments of the Physicians' Chamber and Medical District Union, whose leaders and deputies are to be assigned and relieved by the Reich Physicians' Leader, and to whom an advisory board serves.

Each physician belongs to the Medical District Union, which has its place of residence in its local district (& 35). Each physician must report to his relevant Medical District Union on setting up his practice or on moving. Also he has to report on receiving recognition as a Specialty physician or on changing his Specialty, and, in case of marriage or re-marriage, he must present the certification of origin of his spouse. The Medical District Union, just like the Physicians' Chambers and the Reich Physicians' Chamber, produces a *Physicians Index,* which lists the member doctors in its district, those whose license has been rescinded, and those whose license has been denied, as well as those physicians whose practice of the profession has been temporarily prohibited or those whose authority to practice the profession is called into question.

The Reich Physicians' Chamber can create special departments for special matters. As previously stated, the German Fund Physicians' Union contains a special department whose leader is in personal union to the Reich Physicians' Leader and who names a permanent deputy for these responsibilities.

The Reich Physicians' Chamber raises contributions from the physicians on the grounds of the *contribution ordinance* of 25.6.1936. This establishes a gradation of contributions from physicians who in the process are setting up a practice, employed physicians, physician officials as well as for voluntary physicians. The contributions can be forced to be paid in the event a submission is not freely delivered (& 43).

The responsibility of joining together of physicians for general work and making them aware of their responsibilities are part of the wider assignments of the *Reich Physicians' Chamber*. It has the special responsibilities:

1. To bear the burden for the existence of a morally and scientifically high-standing profession of medicine.

2. To watch over the maintenance of physician professional honor and the fulfillment of professional duties.
3. To promote physician education.
4. To care for the training and continued education of the physician and to create the facilities required for this.
5. To generate thriving relationships of physicians with each other.
6. To plan for the regular distribution of physicians in the interest of providing sufficient attention to the population, and
7. To make arrangements for the welfare of physicians.

It is especially appropriate to make these arrangements to protect physicians and their offspring in the case of pressing emergencies.

Other tasks can be transferred over to the Reich Physicians' Chamber from the Reich Minister of the Interior. In the current war this has been put into use in the allotment of foodstuffs from the Physicians' Chamber to the sick and, in agreement with the appropriate government departments, the regular deployment of physicians for distribution to the civil population.

In the areas of training and continuing education, the Reich Physicians' Chamber has made the regulation that each physician up to 60 years of age has to undergo a 3 weeks continued education course every 5 years. Additionally, each physician is given the opportunity to complement his knowledge through participation in courses and instructions at the Academies for Physicians' Continuing Education, and at weekend courses and seminars. The sessions of the Physician Leadership School at Alt-Rehse[46] provide the training for the Comprehensive National Socialist Philosophical Viewpoint.

In order to regulate the relationships of physicians in regards to disputes with each other, in each District Union a standing *arbitration committee* is planned. Also disputes between physicians can be decided by a third party if the others agree. In case a search for arbitration is unsuccessful, the leader of the Physicians' District Union can make an arbitration decision if the participants have renounced further pursuit of their rights and submitted themselves to this demand (& 50).

Regarding arrangements by the Reich Physicians' Chamber for the welfare of elderly or impoverished physicians or their descendants, it is unfortunately due to the complexity of the times that since the Reich Physicians' Ordinance has come into effect the existing Elderly and Invalid insurance in the old fund districts or for private reasons has not yet succeeded in introducing uniform provisions for elderly physicians. Each physician has merely been given the duty to purchase insurance which provides him in old age or sick days. It accordance with & 46 Appendix 2 of the Reich Physicians' Ordinance, which was decreed on 30.12.1937, it was determined:

> In the Physicians' Chambers in which there is no arrangement for support, departments of *Physicians' Insurance* will be established. The Leader of the Physicians' Chamber is likewise Leader of this department; a committee stands advisory to him and makes decisions

[46] More will be said about the Physician Leadership School at Alt-Rehse later in the text.

regarding being released from the duty to serve. The support will be transferred to a contracting business; specific guidelines for minimal participation will be made. Physicians are freed from the duty to participate if they are more than 40 ½ years old; on application, physicians can be released with sufficient life insurance and married female physicians can be released under special conditions.

In Bavaria, in 1923, there was established, right after the stabilization of the Mark, a legal provision for elderly physicians and their descendents (Bavarian Medical Benefit), to which physicians, veterinarians and dentists were required to join. It is to be raised from a 7% duty tax on professional income. The basic pension amounts to 1200 RM, for which a bonus of 320 RM is to be paid. An additional pension applies here which amounts to 1/7 of the bonus over the basic pension. Child bearing, death, widowhood and orphan funds will be paid. Recently, the Regions of Donau and the Alpine lands, as well as the Regions of West Mark have been included.

In order to protect needy physicians and their families from pressing emergencies the Reich Physicians' Chamber has created special *welfare* arrangements which grant support on application. A legal entitlement does not exist. The Physicians' Chamber to which the physician belongs, or in which district the physician has last practiced, provides the support.

On the grounds of & 14 of the Reich Physicians' Ordinance, on 5.11.1937, the Reich Physicians' Leader, with approval of the Reich Minister of the Interior, decreed a "*Professional Ordinance for the German Physician,*" which highlights the special duties of the physician in his profession and his private behavior. Infringements against the professional Ordinance will be disciplined in light cases on grounds of & 53 and in severe offences on grounds of & 57 Abs. 1 RAO with punishment coming from a judgment of the professional court. *Disciplinary Punishments* are administered by the leader of the Physicians' Chamber and consist of a warning, reprimand, fines up to RM 1000, and exclusion from participation in public welfare treatments for a period of the duration of the punishment. The judgment about the severity of a professional crime above all takes into account the motive out of which the transgression was committed. Earlier transgressions by the physician are brought into consideration for the determination of punishment. The fine is to fit the economic circumstances of the physician. The physician can within 2 weeks file a complaint against the declared punishment by the Physicians' Chamber to the responsible Reich Physicians' Chamber, whose decision is final. Such an appeal leads to the postponement of the punishment. Physician officials, for whom a state ordered process of punishment exists, are not subject to the punishment authority of the Reich Physicians' Chamber, because their practice is in public welfare, from which they can be excluded for a particular time or for the duration of the punishment.

In order to avoid disciplining the physician twice for the same offense against the professional Ordinance, the authority for punishment has been transferred in recent times from the leader of the District Division of the KVD to the Territorial Division leader who is at the same time the Leader of the responsible Physicians' Chamber. The Disciplinary Ordinance of the Reich Physicians' Chamber of 20.6.1940 does not take away the right of the physician to appeal his case to the Professional Court, according to & 57 Abs. 2 of RAO.

The jurisdiction of the Medical Professional Court extends to the same personal circle that is included in the disciplinary Ordinance. Professional judicial proceedings should be initiated only for severe crimes. A professional judicial proceeding can be opened in a case in which for the same offense a criminal judicial proceeding before an ordinary court proceeding is to be carried out; it must however be set after the conclusion of the criminal judicial proceeding (& 57). A professional judicial proceeding is to be opened on the application of the oversight authorities or the Reich Physicians' Chamber. Also a physician can apply a professional judicial proceeding against himself, to clear himself from the suspicion of a professional offense (& 57).

For the individual Physicians' Chamber Districts, *District Medical Courts* are to be established and for the Reich Districts, a *Medical Court of Justice* is to be established. The seat of the District Court is that of the Physicians' Chamber, the seat of the Medical Court of Justice, like that of the Reich Physicians' Chamber, is Munich (& 58). To avoid overloading the District Courts, various panels of judges can be erected inside various chambers, as well as in the Medical Court of Justice. The District Medical Court is constituted of a judicially qualified chairman and two physicians as members, the Medical Court of Justice with two judicially qualified judges, one of which serves as chairman, along with three physicians as members (& 59), so that in each instance of oversight, there remains a feeling of justice.[47]

The accused can as well make use of a lawyer or a judicially qualified official in disciplinary proceedings, as well as in professional judicial proceedings (& 66).

After the opening of a professional judicial proceeding there can be imposed against the accused physician a temporary prohibition of medical practice by a decision of the District Court, if it is to be expected that he will be declared in the professional judicial proceeding to be unworthy to practice the profession (& 74, Abs 1). This prohibition is rescinded if in the proceedings it is determined or acknowledged that he has not been established to be unworthy to practice the medical profession or the proceeding is discontinued (& 75, Ab 1).

The Reich Physicians' Chamber, the overseeing authorities and the accused can appeal the judgment of the Medical District Court; the Medical Court of Justice makes the final decision (& 76 & 77).

Oversight over the Reich Physicians' Chamber and general state oversight over the course of business of the Medical Professional Courts were transferred over to the Reich Ministry of the Interior, which has transferred its oversight authority regarding the Physicians' Chambers and the Medical District Courts to the middle administrative authorities. The oversight authorities are to be invited in a timely

[47] On the Physicians' District Court sat two judges and two physicians, so that "**there remains a feeling of justice.**" Ingo Mueller reports of the courts of the Third Reich, "the purpose of a trial now became not so much to determine whether the accused had broken a law, but rather 'whether the wrongdoer still belongs to the community.'" (I. Mueller, *Hitler's Justice: The Courts of the Third Reich* (Cambridge: Harvard University Press, 1991), 79).

manner to the conferences of the Reich Physicians' Chamber, the Physicians' Chamber and the Physicians' District Union; their representatives are to attend the proceedings each time (& 80 & 81).

Repeal of the Freedom to Advertise[48] and the Decree of the Healing Practitioner Law

As I already presented in the history of the ideal conception of medicine, the Business Ordinance for the German medical community, upon which the practice of healing science was fundamentally established, and decreed immediately after the erection of Bismark's Reich, brought not just a degrading participation in commercial enterprises, arising from the liberal-democratic ideology, but also guaranteed to the entire German Volk the so-called freedom to advertise. Historians place the responsibility for this time on conflicting positions of government and political parties, which loudly clamored for increasing scientific and commercial education for the individual professions and demanded heightened performance from doctors for the maintenance of that highest good of the world, that is, health. At the same time, however, each Volk comrade was allowed to entrust his precious property to any idiotic, unscientific charlatan and folk-deceiver, without there being any legally decreed regulations which would have prohibited this nonsense. In the course of time the freedom to advertise was restricted to a few circumstances, thus making certain activities reserved to be exclusively medical activities, such as the advising of authorities and public corporations in the areas of healing science, the treatment of sexual illnesses and defects of sexual organs, vaccination against small pox, and later, after the *Machtuebernahme*, the interruption of pregnancy and sterilization for the prevention of hereditarily sick offspring. In addition the freedom to advertise was further limited by prohibiting the practice of obstetrics by non-physician females who were not midwives, and by prohibiting the practice of healing science in the community by non-approved practitioners. Further, apothecaries were not allowed to distribute certain strongly effective medications and such which required a receipt, on the prescription of a non-licensed practitioner. How many nameless misfortunes, which were perpetrated by the ungoverned freely given arts of medicine by those uneducated unscientific medical practitioners, which must have prematurely killed an enormous number of people who could have been rescued with appropriate use of medical help, only can be estimated by the physician to whom the cases were transferred for treatment, yet it was too late!

---

[48] *Kurierfreitheit* – Ramm opens this section with a polemic against the inclusion of the medical profession within the Business Ordinance, in which "**…any idiotic, unscientific, charlatan and folk-deceiver…**" can practice medicine. Being including among the commercial enterprises was an affront to the professional being of the German physician. It was against this conception of medicine as a commercial enterprise that the National Socialist physicians believed they were constructing their *Stand.*

After the establishment of the National Socialist philosophical view, the rights over one's individual body of the liberal times were replaced by one's duty of health, which each Volk comrade had to fulfill conscientiously in the interests of the preservation of the whole Volk.[49] To enable the Volk comrade to perform this duty, the National Socialist state could not tolerate the situation where a part of the Volk community would be delivered to some quack in the emergency of an illness, so there came to be a demand by the Reich Physicians' Leader, Dr. Wagner, for proof of competence for all who wanted to practice healing science professionally and commercially.[50]

It was not all too difficult to find a reasonable way to select out the really serious capable healing practitioners, since for years, out of the great number of those non-approved healing sciences, a special professional group had been identified, and that was the *healing practitioner* whose acceptance into their organization had been made dependent on the fulfillment of special pre-conditions. This group had worked to cleanse their medical system of dishonest and incompetent elements.

The fight for the abolition of the freedom to advertise and that over the form of the wider practice of healing science by non-medical people lasted years and led finally on 17 February, 1939 to the decree of the law concerning the professional practice of healing science without appointment (Healing Practitioner Law).[51]

---

[49] In the National Socialist state one lost all rights over his own body which became the property of the state.

[50] *gewerbs* – Ramm is making this contrast between *Beruf* and *Gewerb* in order to point out the contrast between the practice of medicine as a profession as opposed to practicing merely for money. Thus the Reich Physicians' Leader has jurisdiction over both professional and commercial health practitioners.

[51] The National Socialists had created for themselves a potentially contradictory situation in regards to natural healers. They constructed their medical Comprehensive National Socialist Philosophical Worldview on the basis of the Volk, which, being ideally rurally based, favored natural lay healer. But they also at the same time sought to keep the politically supportive professional community of the university medical doctors, who were naturally conservative. The problem was compounded by the fact that Rudolph Hess, the Deputy Fuehrer and Gerhard Wagner both were enamored with methods of alternative healing. Wagner wanted to create a synthesis between Nazi naturopathy – what was called "*Neue Deutsche Heilkunde*" (New German Healing), and what he called "academic medicine" (*Schulmedizin).* He envisaged the infiltration and gradual conversion of the traditional teaching body through the appointment of his own people into positions of trust. A new teaching hospital was constructed in Dresden in 1934, named *Rudolf-Hess-Krankenhaus*, which was supposed to disseminate the new methods of healing (Kater, *Doctors Under Hitler,* 120–1)

The "**special professional (*Beruf*) group"** Ramm refers to was the "German Healers' Union," a group of lay healers. This group purged its ranks of the most unsavory characters in order to improve its credibility (Kater, *Doctors Under Hitler, 37).*

The Healing Practitioner Law called for specific certification for lay healers, now labeled, "healing practitioners." There was compulsory membership in the regime-sanctioned German Natural Healers' Union. Kater reports that "any quack who could demonstrate requisite ability was allowed to graduate to the bona fide group of physicians after adopting the title, 'physician of natural healing.' Moreover, any with extraordinary talent could enter a medical faculty without the usual upper-school qualification and could advance to the licensure stage as a doctor medici" (Kater, *Doctors Under Hitler,* 38). Bothe reports that until Conti became Reich Health Leader, "Neue Deutsche Heilkunde," especially Homeopathy continued to compete successfully with "Schulmedizine" for the privilege of being the favored form of health care (Bothe, 270).

According to the wording of this law, those who desire to practice healing science without being a physician are required to get official permission. This permission is granted only to those who have practiced healing science professionally up to the present time. After approval of the application, those skilled in healing science are professionally designated "Healing Practitioner." The appropriate administrative authority[52] decides in agreement with the health department regarding the application. In case of denial, there is the possibility for the applicant to appeal to higher administrative authorities, the professional organization of the German Healing Practitioner community and the responsible Physicians' Chamber. Ultimately the Reich Minister of the Interior, in concert with the Party Chancellery, judges the appeal. The filing of an appeal does not postpone the implementation of the decision. Permission to practice as a health practitioner is not granted if the applicant does not possess German citizenship, if he or his wife is not of German or related blood, if he cannot demonstrate a completed grammar school education, if he is not in possession of civil rights, if it turns out that he lacks political and moral responsibility, especially, if serious criminal or moral failings are alleged, if he is disabled as a consequence of physical injury or because of weakness of intellectual or physical strength, or because of an addiction, or lacks the necessary inclinations for the pursuit of professional practice, and if it is shown with certainty that he plans to practice another profession in addition to healing science.

Whoever is granted permission to practice healing science on the grounds of this law is required to become a member of the German Healing Practitioner Community. Loss of such membership leads to the revocation of the licence to be a healing practitioner. Approval for healing practice can be rescinded by higher administrative authorities if subsequent facts come to light which would justify refusal of the application.

Since the law has also annulled the training schools of this professional class and prohibited their erection and maintenance for the future, the current group of healing practitioners encompasses all that will be licensed. One estimates the number to be from 3000 to 3500. Since healing practitioners are further prohibited from bringing in new recruits in other ways, then the time may not be too far in the future when healing activities of sick Volk comrades will be in the hands of only state installed physicians.

In order however to not exclude Volk comrades who possess a natural gift and capacity for the medical profession, it is possible under the special professional designation of "*Physician for Natural Science of Healing*" to practice healing activity, even without fulfilling the legally prescribed preparations to be a physician. In these cases, however, a proof of performance is required. To do that, the applicant must prove his healing capacities and special healing effects for at least 3 years, in which the proof is demonstrated in a medical facility during the course of up to 6 months, under the supervision of the responsible leading physicians. The

[52] Landrat – Lord Mayor.

"Physician for Natural Science of Healing" stands under the Reich Physicians' Ordinance just like every other state installed physician.[53]

Finally the law foresees that certain persons, through proof of special performance in the area of healing science may be given permission under facilitated conditions to study medicine. Among these are those who, without high school or having the school-leaving exams, on approval of their application, attend the university. They must however go through the same studies and acquire the same medical experience and are to be established as a physician under the same conditions, as those taking the usual course of medical studies.

Through creation of a legal foundation for organization of the ever important area of medical treatment of our Volk, an important step forward has been taken in regards to the maintenance and elevation of the health of the Volk. While not all wishes of the German medical community, which simply arise as a consequence of the feeling of responsibility for the nation, have been fulfilled, it has been the legal regulations of the practice of healing science which have provided definitive proof that the party and state take an interest in the fate of the sick, as well as in the maintenance of the health of common Volk comrades.

[53] Ramm is clearly ambivalent about these health practitioners. He reports of their credentialing rather dispassionately, then comments that the day will come when there will no longer be such practitioners. However, having said that, he allows that there are provisions for one who "possesses a natural gift" for the medical profession to be allowed to practice. It is clear that there has been political negotiation for the status of the healers withing the wider medical community. We can see the conflicts between those who believe that those practitioners with "natural healing gifts" and those who believe all practitioners must have only state-sanctioned privileges.

Part III: The Public Health Service and the Responsibilities of State Health Departments

At the time of the *Machtuebergreifung*, the public health service was completely splintered and its responsibilities were distributed among numerous disconnected authorities. As a consequence of this administrative weakness, despite their absolute importance, there was no centralization of Volk health activities. In addition to a state health system, there were municipal departments in cities, Districts, Territories, multiple insurance carriers and also numerous private organizations of Reich committees which pretended to serve Volk health, but in fact hindered the health system through the pursuit of their own selfish goals. Much of this occurred because of the struggle for power and not from striving to improve health; the weakening of the Volk and the disregard of its health-related problems were evident. Before fundamental changes could be carried out in this regard, all power of the Public Health Service, all existing organizations and all Reich committees had to be brought together and legalized according to a unified goal.

By the *Law For the Unification of the Public Health Service* of 3.7.1934, this intention was accomplished, although many obstacles arising from the inner administration and financial structures stood in the way.[1] First, all the branches of the Public Health Service were joined together with the Health Department, so that the existing responsibilities for the maintenance of health, for preventive medicine as well as for welfare were to be facilitated, together with the very important challenges for the renewal of genetic biology and the improvement of the German Volk. For financial reasons, the efforts went in general only into the establishment of the State Health Department, however the legislation let Municipal Health Departments continue while it established new departments in large cities. Both departments were put under the immediate legal jurisdiction of the Reich Minister of the Interior.

[1] Ramm describes the reasons for the unification of the Public Health Service and gives a broad outline of its hierarchical structure. Thus, the physician could carry out what Gerhard Wagner identified as the task of his Public Health Department: the "promotion and perfection of the health of the German people…and to ensure that the people realize the full potential of their racial and genetic endowment." (Wagner, quoted in Lifton, 30).

R. Ramm, *Medical Jurisprudence and Rules of the Medical Profession*,
Philosophy and Medicine 135, https://doi.org/10.1007/978-3-030-25245-8_3

The State Health Departments are under the jurisdiction of the city and Territorial District,[2] therefore to the Regierungspraesident,[3] which are municipally contracted to the Landrate[4] and, in district-free cities, to the Oberburgermeister.[5] Through the circular of the RMd of 1941 the leaders of the municipal health department are to be situated in the town council office of the cities. It is obvious that also the State Health Departments are to seek to carry out their responsibilities in close connection with the underlying administrative authorities, and on the other hand, it is the duty of the Landrat departments and cities to participate in all matters with the Civil Service Physician,[6] who is responsible for the introduction of the responsibilities of the Health Departments. Even though in some newly developed areas of the Reich there continue to be attempts to again place the State Health Department as a department of the Landrat, these measures represent without a doubt a serious disturbing backwards step and the placement of avoidable hindrances in the building up of the Public Health Service and demonstrate an insufficiently lofty estimation of this activity.

The Circle of Responsibilities of the Health Departments was constituted immediately as Health Police in the care of genetics and race, and gives advice regarding marriage, Volk health instruction, care of school health, advice to mothers and children and the care of those with tuberculosis, sexually transmitted diseases, physical disabilities, epidemics and addictions. Physician participation in the promotion of bodily health and physical education is expressly transferred over to the Health Department as also are court activities and Advisory Physician's activities, in so far as it can be permitted of the Civil Service Physician by the territorial law. Also in the area of social insurance the physician of the Public Health Department is to take over the activities of the Advisory Physician with the agreement of the supervising bureau. The area of jurisdiction of a Health Department extends to the city District or Territorial District. As a rule, only one Health Department is planned for each city-district or Landkreis, yet there are exceptions, e.g. in large cities. In urban districts with over 400,000 inhabitants, district branches of the Health Department can be established whereby the entity of the district branch represents the Health Department of the relevant city.

Of the wider responsibilities which are transferred over to the Health Department, one will be mentioned:

---

[2] *Landkreis* – Rural sub-division of a Regierungsbezirk (which was a sub-division of a territory) in Prussia.

[3] *Regierungspraesident* - Senior administrative officials in a Regierungsbezirk.

[4] *Landrat*-The chief authority in the administration of a Landkreis. Frequently the same man as the Party Kreisleiter.

[5] *Burgermeister* – mayor of a town or city.

[6] Kater reports that, initially, the time-honored *"Amtaerzte,"* were required to possess good academic records, a certain amount of field experience and the ability to pass additional examinations. But, as early as spring 1935, because more attractive options were available elsewhere, certain prerequisites for an *Amtzerzte* came to be lowered.

It is the responsibility of the Health Department to make a list of the medical practitioners as well as oversee the healing science practice of those individuals without state licensure. Further responsibilities include oversight of apothecaries and their personnel and attending to the regular medical benefit for the district. The Civil Service Physician has the special duty of overseeing trade in medicines and methods of healing, and trade in poisons within the apothecaries and drug companies, and planning tests for the authorization of trading in poisons. He is entitled to oversee midwives, which he tests at certain times and arranges for their continuing education. But also other medical assistants, like health care workers, supporting personnel, nursing personnel, disinfection and autopsy workers are all under the supervisory professional activities of the Health Department. Further, the Civil Service Physician has the responsibility to attend to the implementation of public hygiene in the city and the country, especially seeing to it that the grounds and the air are clean, seeing to the suitability of living places and youth hostels and especially overseeing the provisioning of water and the disposal of sewage. Trade in food stuffs and everyday objects of use are to be likewise controlled **as** regards to hygiene by the Health Department.

The Civil Service Physician's work extends to the protection and fight against communicable diseases and oversight of small pox and diphtheria vaccination and inspection of places of business and concessions.

For the purpose of implementation of the Law for the Prevention of Genetically Ill Offspring and Law for a Healthy Marriage,[7] the care of genetics and race becomes one of the most important responsibilities of the Public Health Department. Also it is foreseen that the Civil Service Physician participates in the granting of permission for marriage, as well as in the appropriate tests for immigrants and their families.

As a further important service to Volks' health, the Public Health Department works in the struggle against abortion and all matters pertaining to advising a mother as well as in the care of the health of infants and children. Further, the activities of the Health Department extend to the fight against tuberculosis and sexually transmitted diseases, care of cripples and the struggle against the dangers of alcohol and drug addiction.

[7]The Public Health Department was responsible for the implementation of the "Genetics Health Law," and "the Law for a Healthy Marriage." The so-called "sterilization law", promulgated in July 1933, served throughout the Nazi period as the model of all eugenic legislation. It introduced compulsory sterilization for persons suffering from a variety of mental and physical disorders and in the process defined the groups to be excluded from the national community. This legislation was followed in October 1935 by the Marriage Health Law, which mandated screening the entire population to prevent marriages of persons considered carriers of hereditary degeneracy, particularly those covered by the sterilization law.(H. Friedlaender, *The Origins of Nazi Genocide: From Euthanasia to the Final Solution* (Chapel Hill: U. of North Carolina Press, 1995), 23) Henry Friedlander reports that the exact number of persons actually sterilized are not available, but states that "it is generally agreed that at least 300,000 persons were sterilized during the years preceding World War II"(Friedlaender, 1995, 30).

Considering the large number of responsibilities transferred over to the Health Department, it is understood that not all of these are to be attacked at once, but only the most important are initially to be taken on. The reason for this is the deficit at this time of appropriate physicians and the relevant knowledgeable allied personnel, along with the appropriate financial support from the state, which currently has to deal with the most important basic human challenges.

The leader of the Health Department carries the name *Civil Service Physician*. He is, as a rule, a Reich official, but can also be a community official of the municipal Health Department. Each Civil Service Physician position has a permanent representative who is supposed to be, if possible, likewise an official physician. In Districts under 50,000 inhabitants, in general there should be no additional fully salaried physicians other than the Civil Service Physician in the Health Department. For those cases, but also for the larger Health Departments, the physicians are expected to be either a candidate for the career path as a Civil Service Physician or a practicing physician who carries out the responsibilities of the Health Department in an associated office. The Civil Service Physician has to provide special proof of credentials to lead a Public Health Department. Among these are included: (1) Licensure as a doctor, (2) Possession of the degree of Medical Doctor from a university of the Reich. (3) Passing a state physician's examination. (4) Long practice experience as a physician after attainment of the appointment as a physician. However, regarding this requirement, the Reich Minister of the Interior can declare a shorter independent period of practice to be sufficient.

The state physician's examination assumes participation in a series of lectures at the State Medical Academy in Berlin or Munich, which originally took 3 months, but since 1935 has been shortened to 2 months. Certification for a physician to take the test can occur with physicians who were licensed on the grounds of the Ordinance of Licensure of 1939, as early as 2 years (including the compulsory quarter year in the country) after licensing. This period of time had been set at 1 year for physician's licensed according to the Ordinance of Testing of 1901.

A further relaxation involves the decision to allow the test before participating in a state course of medical instruction, and the special courses of pathological anatomy, hygiene, bacteriology and legal medicine, as well as before serving as an assistant at a psychiatric clinic, whose period was set from 12 to 6 weeks. Whoever has served at a psychiatric clinic receives credit for this time spent. The practical oral part of the test can be taken before submission of the written work. Further relaxation is foreseen for physicians already predominately active in the Public Health Service when there has been a demonstration of favorable performance in public health areas.

The official physicians regularly active in the state Health Department do not have to take the state medical test; they are under the jurisdiction of the Civil Service Physician.

The Regierungspraesident as a general rule forms the oversight authority for the state as well as for the municipal health office. A physician who carries the designation *Government and Medical Adviser* is assigned to him as advisor and worker and is a member of the Government Collegium. His responsibilities extend to Specialty areas of the Public Health Department and to special areas which were recently placed under this administrative unit. In the new Reich Regions, these responsibilities are taken over by an official physician with the service designation "Government Director." In many of these Reich Regions there is a close relationship between the leadership of this office and the leadership of the Gau Office for Volk Health.

In the course of the unification of the state administration the necessity arose to transfer responsibilities of the state Public Health Service to the Oberpresident[8] of the Prussian Territories and to integrate the health service. The position of *Leading Medical Official (Landesrat or Regierungsdirektor)* as the presiding officer was created for this purpose. The Leading Medical Official, in the context of the empowerment authorized from the Oberpraesident[9] of the Reich Ministry of the Interior, is authorized to distribute objective instructions from these for the implementation of responsibilities to the Territorial associations.[10]

State Industrial Physicians (in the whole Reich, 48) are frequently also assigned to the Regierungspresidents. The working area of these Industrial Medical Advisors include advice and support for the officials who oversee industry and mining for questions pertaining to industrial hygiene; further their responsibilities include the dissemination of knowledge about occupational diseases and the improvement of general industrial hygiene in working areas. They have the right of regular inspections of all businesses in their administrative districts. The Industrial Medical Advisors are under the jurisdiction of the responsible Regierungspresidents for their official locality and ultimately are under the jurisdiction of the Reich Labor Ministry. Since the establishment of the German Workers Front and their office, "Health and Volk Defense," which supports and extends the efforts of industrial hygiene through medical care in the industry, especially through prevention from and fight against industrial diseases, there has developed a clear working relationship with the Industrial Medical Councils, which has consequences for the welfare of the working German public.

The "*Physician Service in Labor Compartment,*" which was established by the Territorial Working Offices and labor Exchanges, should likewise be mentioned.[11]

Since the question of the appropriateness of work practices plays a decisive role in the composition of a work environment, and further, since this depends to a high degree on the health situation, the judgment of the physician is of great significance regarding circumstances of each practice, keeping in mind the health and economic circumstances of the Volk. In a general sense, the physician also assists the Labor Department in giving occupational advice to adolescents.[12]

A new important responsibility has arisen during the war; this consists in the prevention of the introduction of epidemics from foreign work places.

---

[8] *Oberpraesident* – The senior administrative official in a Prussian Territory.

[9] *Oberpraesident* – the senior administrative official in the Prussian Territory.

[10] This paragraph was added to the 1942 edition.

[11] This paragraph was added to the 1942 edition.

[12] This paragraph was added to the 1942 edition.

In order to justify the great responsibility which is connected to the Labor Department, the *General Agent for the Labor Department* has conceded to the Reich Health Leader the exclusive right of oversight and advice in all health-related questions associated with labor activities.[13]

The law for the unification of the Public Health Services also led to a consolidation of all departments and organs which serve Volks' health into the Reich Ministry of the Interior. The Department of Volks' Health at that time was enlarged by the integration of the Prussian Medical and Veterinary Department of the Prussian Territorial Health Councils and the State Medical Academies in Berlin and Munich, which had as their responsibilities the education of the Civil Service Physicians.

Besides that, the Reich committee for Volks' Health Service was annexed to this department to achieve complete unification of all that had to do with preservation of the Volk population, genetics and racial care as well as with all the labor associations and scientific unions which serve health care and health promotion.

After the naming of the Reich Health Leader, *Dr. Conti*, to be the State Secretary,[14] the Department of Volks' Health was connected in terms of the care of social welfare to the Reich Ministry of the Interior in the Department IV "Public Health Service and Volks' Care," and placed, together with Department III "Veterinary Administration, in the state service district of *Dr. Conti* as state secretary for Public health, Volks'Care and Veterinary Science (For that see Fuerher Decrees of July 1942 (& 75).

The *Reich Health Departments* serving Volks' health matters for scientific research, and especially as an advisory and examining organ of the Reich Ministry, like the *Robert Koch Institute,* which has the responsibility for research and fight against infectious diseases, and the Institute for Water and Air Quality, belong to this bureau.

---

[13] This paragraph was added to the 1942 edition.

[14] On the death of Gerhard Wagner, Leonardo Conti (1900–1945) was named Reich Health Leader. Conti was born in Lugano, Switzerland. He attended the Friedrich Wilhelm Gymnasium in Berlin. He served in Field Artillery Regiment 54 in World War I. After the war, he was involved early in anti-communist and anti-semitic agitation and publicly debated Karl Liebknecht, one of the leaders of the communist Sparticist revolution, who was later murdered. He participated in the Kapp putsch in 1920. He undertook his medical studies in Berlin and Erlangen from 1919 to 1923. At first he practiced as a general practitioner in Munich, where he was not a member of the sickness fund. He first entered the Sturmabteilung (SA) in 1923 but transferred to the Schutzstafel (SS) in 1930. His major patron in the regime was Ministerpresident Herman Goering; thru Goering Conti became Prussia's commissar of health and the Berlin executive of the NSD-Aerztebund. Conti was reported to have a rather colorless personality. He was always at odds with others who vied for leadership of medicine, first Wagner, then after Wagner's death, with Karl Brandt. (Swoch, 358–9)

Kater reports that Conti was unable to satisfactorily reconcile the duplicate institutions of the KVD and the Reich Physicians' Chamber and this failure was exploited by his major rival after Wagner's death, Doctor Karl Brandt, Hitler's personal physician. (Kater, *Doctors Under Hitler,* 25) Conti committed suicide, by hanging himself with his shirt, in the Nurmberg prison in 1945.

The Robert Koch Institute and the Institute for Water, Ground and Air Hygiene were previously institutions of the Prussian state. On 1 April, 1942, both of the Institutes were declared Reich Institutes.

Since many responsibilities of the Public Health Department affect those of the Department of Volks'Health of the NSDAP, the Health Care Service of the HJ, the Office of Health of the NSV, the Office of "Health and Volk Defense" of the DAF and the Medical Services in the Labor Department, it is necessary to work closely together to avoid unnecessary duplication of effort.

Part IV: The National Socialist German Workers Party as Guardian of the Health of the Volk

While the responsibilities of the states in the internal political area consist of the organization, administration and protection of volkish life, the party has the responsibility to lead the German people in all areas of their common expression of life and to educate them to fulfill their political and biological responsibility.

For the recognition and survival of a Volk the most important determination is the sum of its pre-existing strengths and capacities. The greatest power and the best capacities will develop however only in the body and soul of a healthy Volk. Recognizing this, the party takes as one of its most essential responsibilities the maintenance and promotion of a healthy genetic makeup and racial purity of the German Volk, which represents, according to scientific and practical experience, the fundamental pre-conditions for the undisturbed health of each generation.

In the years of struggle the *National Socialist German Physicians' Association,*[1] which was founded at the party convention in Nuremberg in 1929, was the faithful

[1] The National Socialist German Physicians' Association (NSDAB), staffed exclusively with physician members of the NSDAP was the spearhead in the regime's drive to coordinate all medical doctors in the Reich and eventually use them for its purposes.

The NSDAB saw itself, from its founding in August 1929 at the party convention of the NSDAP, not as a professional organization but rather as a fighting organization of the party. It was not to be seen as a descendant of or subordinate to the two top physicians' associations. According to Ordinance it understood itself to be a collection of such physicians, "who are members of the NSDAP in order to act in the medical professional union and in the professional life according to the principles of the NSDAP in professional feeling with the party leadership and in order to inject thereby the German medical system with National Socialist spirit" (Swoch, 107).

With the Machtuebergreifung the leadership of the medical profession came to the NSDAB with the special assignment of "*Gleichschaltung*," meaning "coordination," or, essentially expunging all Jewish doctors from the profession. Its "*Gleichschaltung*" authority extended over the medical professional associations, the physicians' Chambers and the medical administration. Since Gerhard Wagner was the leader of the NSDAB he also took over the leadership of the "*Gleichschaltung*."(Swoch, 107) After the "*Gleichschaltung*" had ended the primary assignment of the NSDAB had also ended. Foreseeing its decline, three institutes were founded whose areas of responsibility made the NSDAB superfluous: The *Aufklarungsamt fuer Volksgesendheit*

R. Ramm, *Medical Jurisprudence and Rules of the Medical Profession*,
Philosophy and Medicine 135, https://doi.org/10.1007/978-3-030-25245-8_4

adviser to the party in all questions relating to Volk health. It is to it's historical merit to have placed the appropriate men in the party offices and state health apparatuses and to have delivered new ideas for its expansion. The Comprehensive National Socialist Philosophical Viewpoint of these men and their knowledge of the corresponding revolutionary thoughts and revolutionary deeds would come to guarantee the maintenance of the racial purity of the German people, as well as come to maintain and increase their physical and psychological health.

The establishment of the *Main Office for Volks' Health of the NSDAP* took place on 14 June, 1934. It was entrusted to Dr. Wagner, at that time leader of the National Socialist Physicians' Association who had been since 15 May, 1935 the trusted man for all questions pertaining to health for all party organizations, with the entitlement to deliver binding instructions to integratively secure and improve them. That is why it was further decided through the Ordinance of Implementation of the Reich leadership of the party, that the office leadership of the Regions and Districts was also to be integrated, especially all party departments, including the organizations of industry – with the exception of the military medical service of the SA,[2] SS,[3] NSKK,[4] NSFK,[5] and HJ[6] (including BdM[7]) – and that this leadership should apply to all responsible situations of importance in the health of the Volk. Without approval of this leadership office of the party, none of the bureaus, central or local, are authorized to distribute instructions regarding Volk health. At the same time, expert advice councils in the Regions were dissolved, being superfluous. Only the expert advice of the Reich leadership remained the advisory organ for Dr. Wagner, who was named at the same time to be Department Leader of the Main Office for Volks' Health. In the Regions and Districts the respective Region and District men of the National Socialist Physicians' Association overtook the Regional and District offices for Volks' health, subject to the agreement of the top personnel of the respective Regional and District Departments of Volks' Health.

Dr. Wagner,[8] at the Reich party convention of 1935, proposed that the highest goal of his office is "the promotion of health for the entirety of the German people,"

(Enlightenment Office for Volks' Health) was founded in April 1933 and from May 1934 it was called the *Rassenpolitisches Amt der NSDAP* (Racial Political Office of the NSDAP); the *Sachverstaendigenbeirat fuer Volksgesundheit* (Specialty Secretariat for Volks' Health) was founded in August 1933 and became in May 1934 the *Amt fuer Volksgesundheit des NSDAP* (Office for Volks' Health of the NSDAP) and finally the *Reichaerztekammer (RaK),* the Reich Physicians' Chamber. The founding of these institutes had for the NSDAB, a political disempowering and weakening effect (Swoch, 107).

[2] *SA – Sturmabteilung.*

[3] *SS – Schutzstaffel*

[4] *NSKK – Nationalsozialistische Kraftfahr-Korps*

[5] *NSFK –Nationalsozialistische Frei-Korps*

[6] *HJ – Hitler Youth*

[7] *BdM – Bund deutscher Maedel.- League of German Girls.*

[8] Wagner, being an "old fighter", and the founder of the *NSD-Aerztesbund* whose close friend and regular patient was the Deputy Fuehrer, Rudolf Hess, was in the position to dictate his own portfolio, since it was subject to review and approval only by Hitler. (Kater, *Doctors Under Hitler,* 23);

and "that this be extended in its entirety to the generally achievable genetic and racial biological capacities; that his health leadership is to serve the Department of Volks' Health in community work with all party organs and state bureaus, be they in the German working front in the setting of human leadership, be they in the National Socialist Volks' Welfare as a help organization of the National Socialist German Workers Party when it encounters emergencies involving otherwise genetically and racially worthwhile Volk comrades, or be it through supplementing corresponding state functions."

It has been already noted above that the Main Office for Volks' Health is a leadership office. That means, accordingly, that implementation of the measures arranged by it are the responsibility of the individual party sections and connected associations. The Hitler Youth, the German Working Front and the National Socialist Volks' Welfare are the largest of the relevant organizations which serve this purpose.

When, after the death of Dr. Wagner, *Dr. Conti* was named "Reich Health Leader" and Leader of the Main Office for Volks' Health, he was given, with this designation, a far greater range of responsibilities in the party than before, and by virtue of being named to be State Secretary in the Reich Ministry of the Interior and with the transference of all state health and Volk care to his responsibility, he increased substantially his area of responsibilities in comparison to his predecessor.[9]

As a further worthy step towards the unification of the Public Health Service the *Fuehrer Decree Concerning the Sanitary and Public Health Service* of 28 July, 1942 is to be noted.

"The personal and material domain of the Sanitary and Public Health Service requires a unified and systematic arrangement. I determine therefore the following[10]:

1. For the area of the Wehrmacht I entrust the Army Sanitation Inspector as Chief of Wehrmacht Sanitation Service, with the continuation of his prior responsibilities in connection with all general responsibilities in the area of the sanitation service of the Wehrmacht, the Waffen-SS and those organizations and associations subject to or connected to the Wehrmacht.[11]
   The chief of the Wehrmacht Medical Service represents the Wehrmacht in all general medical service matters of the Wehrmacht departments and the associations and organizations subject to or associated with the Waffen-SS, and represents the interest of the Wehrmacht to the civilian administrative authorities with regards to health matters.[12]

(M. Kater, "Doctor Leonardo Conti and His Nemesis: The Failure of Centralized Medicine in the Third Reich," *Central European History* 18 (1985): 299–325).

[9] Kater reports that Conti was rather colorless and had a more difficult time managing the conflicting political currents of the positions he took over from Wagner and was ultimately overshadowed by Hitler's personal doctor, Karl Brandt. (Kater, *Doctors Under Hitler,* 25).

[10] This paragraph was added to the 1942 edition.

[11] This paragraph was added to the 1942 edition.

[12] This paragraph was added to the 1942 edition.

To arrange the coordination of these responsibilities there has been primarily placed under him a sanitation officer of the Navy and the Air Force with the position of Chief of Staff. Fundamental questions regarding the sanitary service of the Waffen-SS are to be decided in agreement with the Sanitation Inspector of the Waffen-SS.[13]

2. Dr. *Conti*, State Secretary in the Reich Ministry of the Interior and the Reich Ministry Leader, is responsible for the unification of the civilian health service by appropriate means. Responsible departments of the Central Reich authority and their subordinate offices are also under his jurisdiction.[14]
3. For special responsibilities and negotiations for settlement of requests regarding physicians, hospitals, medications, etc. between the military and civil sections of the sanitary and health services, I authorize Professor Dr. of Medicine Karl *Brandt,*[15] who I place personally under me and who takes immediate instructions from me.[16]
4. My authorized representative for the Sanitary and Public Health Services is to lecture regularly about fundamental procedures in the Wehrmacht Sanitary

---

[13] This paragraph was added to the 1942 edition.

[14] This paragraph was added to the 1942 edition.

[15] Hitler named Professor Karl Brandt to the post of sanitation and health plenipotentiary. According to Kater, this action was taken to isolate Conti (Kater, *Doctors Under Hitler,* 25).

Brandt was born in 1904 in Muehlhause, Alsace. He came from a family of doctors who were all conservative mid-ranking civil servants and state-employed physicians, loyal to the monarchy and the authorities. He studied medicine at the University of Jena, Freiburg, graduating in 1928. He did his internship at the Bergmannsheil Hospital in Bochum and then in 1935 transferred to the Surgical University Clinic in Berlin. He became a member of the NSDAP in 1932 and joined the SA in 1933. After providing emergency treatment for Hitler's adjutant Wilhelm Brueckner in August 1933, he was appointed Hitler's escort physician in June 1934. He was constantly in Hitler's entourage and "enjoyed the ear of the Fuehrer."(U. Schmidt, *Justice at Nuremberg: Leo Alexander and the Nazi Doctors' Trial* (New York: Palgrave, 2004), 129–130.

Brandt was involved in the planning and organization of the Nazi 'euthanasia' program, consisting of the murder of tens of thousands of handicapped children and adults. He was convicted at the Nuremberg Doctors' Trial of complicity in concentration camp experiments (specifically experiments on epidemic jaundice on prisoners in Auschwitz, Mustard gas experiments at Sachsenhausen, high altitude experiments at Dachau, freezing experiments at Dachau, malaria experiments at Dachau, bone, muscle and nerve regeneration experiments at Regensbrueck, seawater experiments at Dachau, sterilization experiments at Auschwitz, and Spotted Fever experiments at Buchenwald and Natzweiler) (G. Annas and M. Grodin, *The Nazi Doctors and the Nuremberg Code: Human Rights in Human Experimentation* (Oxford: Oxford University Press, 1992), 97–99) and sentenced to death for "War Crimes, Crimes against Humanity, membership in an organization declared criminal."(Schmidt, 261) He offered to undergo the same experiments on himself, but this was denied. He was executed by hanging on June 2, 1948. (L. Heston and R. Heston, *The Medical Casebook of Adolf Hitler: His Illnesses, Doctors and Drugs* (New York: Scarborough, 1979), 97. A detailed biography of Brandt and his evolution as Hitler's doctor to where he comes to oversee the euthanasia program is in U. Schmidt, *Karl Brandt: The Nazi Doctor* (New York: Continuum, 2007).

[16] This paragraph was added to the 1942 edition.

Service and civil Public Health Service. He is entitled to insert himself into responsible negotiations."[17]

Professor Brandt leads as the authorized representative for the Ambulance and Health Service with the designation "*General Commissioner for Sanitation and Health Service of the Fuhrer.*"[18]

In regard to the civil health service, this decree empowers the Reich Health Leader to take all appropriate steps for the unification of the responsible Departments of the highest Reich authorities and subordinate departments.

The rights and duties of the offices for Volk Health were endorsed by a special instruction from the party of 1 May, 1940 and extended so that all departments, and connected associations of the party, were directed to educate and instruct the Main Office and those subordinate bureaus, unsolicited, about the important procedures in the areas of health leadership. To the bureaus of the Main Office the right to demand reports and to examine all relevant matters and situations was especially acknowledged. Further, it was determined that under the leadership of the Chairmanship of the Leader of the Department of Volks' Health, regular lectures to the leaders of all Health Departments and relevant associations were to be established, in which the most important questions concerning Volk health are to come under discussion. The sessions between labor communities, party bureaus, state bureaus, social service bureaus and other institutions having to do with health matters are transferred to the responsible leader of the Department for Volks' Health as the representative of the party, as long as the highest authority himself does not represent the party.

In many Regions in recent times the Regional office leader has been placed as *Regional Health Leader for Volks'Health* in order to bring into one place all power and facilities of the Region which serve Volk health and thereby link them so that they can dedicate themselves to a common goal. The *Regional Health Advisory Council* and *Regional Committee for Volks' Health* stand at the side of the Regional Health Leader as an advisory organ.[19]

Labor communities were established in individual Districts of these Redions under the Chairmanship of the District Office Leader for Volks' Health, who has to watch over health matters of his industrial regions.[20]

In the individual Districts of these Regions there were constructed by the Chairman of the District Department Leader for Volkshealth working communities (*Arbeitsgemeinschaften*) which go through the German Labor Front to attend to the health care provided by industrial physicians to working comrades in work places and to the research of new ways to increase production in the industries, while at the same time improving the health situation of their employees.

[17] This paragraph was added to the 1942 edition.

[18] This paragraph was added to the 1942 edition.

[19] This paragraph was added to the 1942 edition.

[20] This paragraph was added to the 1942 edition.

The office of "Health" of the National Socialist Volks' Welfare is required to work on all health questions of National Socialist Volks' welfare and especially with social insurance carriers and departments of state health services. Also, it addresses additional health concerns for those Volk areas for which other accounting carriers can not be made to accommodate. The questions which come up here are those of tuberculosis relief work, quarantine for health reasons of sick and exposed party comrades, as well as issues regarding sanitation in disaster areas. The relief work "Mother and Child," infants and small child welfare, orphanage placement, child placement, etc. stand under the Department of the NS Volks' Welfare, in regards to care and advice on health.

These two offices standing under the leadership of the Main Office are organized right up to the District level as well.

After the erection of the Main Office for Volks'Health,[21] the *National Socialist German Physicians'Association*[22] was re-organized as one of those offices standing in a secure association with the party, and placed under its care. To qualify to be a member one must be a Party member. Party candidates and worthy non-party candidates will be encouraged to be a candidate for the National Socialist Physicians' Association. The National Socialist German Physicians' League was immediately approved by the Supreme Party Court, with an independently standing Disciplinary Judicial Court; in the Regions there are Regional Disciplinary Courts. Its organization corresponds to and has close association with that of the Main Office for Volks' Health.

According to the party articles of association[23] which were established and approved in 1929 and unchanged since then, the National Socialist German Physicians' Association has the following responsibilities:

---

[21] In 1932, concordant with his assumption of the NS-Aerztebund leadership, Wagner was charged with broad responsibilities for health in the party realm. This was constituted as the *Abteilung Volksgesundheit,* the Department of Volks' Health. After the *Machtuebergreifung,* this was reconstituted on an official basis as the *Hauptamt fuer Volksgesundheit* (Main Office for Volks' Health). Wagner was granted a new mandate as the regime's "health leader" (Kater, *Doctors Under Hitler, 23).*

[22] The NS-Aerztebund existed officially as a branch of the Main Office for People's Health, and officially was an associated formation of the NSDAP (*angeschlossener Verband),* rather than, like the SA, SS, and HJ, an integrated one *(eingegleiderter Verband)* (Kater, *Doctors Under Hitler,* 292).

[23] The NSDAP was the predominant ideological organ for educating physicians in the "National Socialist philosophical viewpoint." It major educational effort was towards the National Socialist view of Racial Hygiene and genetics. It is important to note that the NSDAP trained the physician in ideological matters (National Socialist philosophical viewpoint), so that, given that the central function of the physician was to attend to the Racial Hygiene of the Volk, the physician was to be an ideological organ of the NSDAP. This orientation represents the first "whole" of the "whole of the whole." This notion of the "whole of the whole" is somewhat like the sense of "double coherence" in common law. There is to be coherence within the profession and this coherence is to be consistent with the coherence of the entire society, so that the medical profession reflects the social conditions of the wider Volk society.

1. To place at the disposal of the Party the necessary physicians and specialists for all official party organizations and purposes, according to the directives of the Department Leader for Volks' Health.
2. To permeate the German medical profession and the whole healing and public health sectors with the Comprehensive National Socialist Philosophical Viewpoint and also provide a public validation of these principles.

   The Political Leaders of the NSDAP representing the side of the party in the National Socialist Physicians' Association will, through the responsible training office of the NSDAP, attend to and indoctrinate in an obligatory National Socialist philosophical way.

   The entire National Socialist philosophical political orientation of the spokesman of the National Socialist German Physicians' Association comes from the advice of the responsible training office of the NSDAP. The Department Leader of Indoctrination in the National Socialist German Physicians' Association does not train himself in the Comprehensive National Socialist Philosophical Worldview, but rather organizes the National Socialist philosophical orientation in harmony with the Indoctrination Leader of the NSDAP.[24]

   The training of specialists (in National Socialist philosophical basics) of the spokesman, members and candidates for the National Socialist German Physicians' League will be independently trained by the National Socialist German Physicians' Association. Furthermore, arrangements are to be made for transmission of the necessary knowledge of all important matters in the areas of Volks' health.

   Specialist training is the sole responsibility of the responsible training department of the National Socialist German Physicians' Association.
3. To mutually support and encourage professional opportunities in order to bring descendants to National Socialism and to educate these colleagues early in a National Socialist professional Philosophical Worldview.

The *Leadership School of the German Medical Profession* in Alt-Rehse[25] is the training site of the National Socialist German Physicians' Association. It was given

[24]The *NS-Aerztebund* did not originate the viewpoints but merely reports what the "Indoctrination Leader" directs it to report.

[25]The indoctrination training of the physician was to take place at the so-called Leadership School of German Physicians at Alt-Rehse, a resort on Lake Tollense in Mecklenburg. Ramm designates the Leadership school as a "character school of the German physician." This designation illustrates that from the National Socialist viewpoint the responsibility of moral training is to teach "character." At this point, no specific comments are made about what is meant by "character," but one can gather that what is meant is that the physician acts and articulates the precepts of the Comprehensive National Socialist Philosophical Worldview, particularly regarding Bevolkerungpolitiks – the preservation of the Volk through Racial Hygiene and genetics. Kater reports that the training courses consisted of a calculated admixture of work and relaxation, sports, study, games, indoctrination and restful contemplation. The course lasted 2 weeks and consisted predominantly of speeches, marches and military drills (Kater, *Doctors Under Hitler,* 67).

According to available material relating to the school, it served not only as an indoctrination school for physicians, but also as a school to train physicians to become "*Fuehrer und Erzieher*"

its designation in the summer of 1935 as the National Socialist philosophical educational institution. It is situated far from the academic college and far from the clinic and lecture hall. One can perhaps designate it as a character school of the German physician. During the powerful upheaval of the intellectual and moral structure of the German Volk, against which the National Socialist revolution was called, there was also a fundamental rearrangement of the ideal conception of medicine. The overpowering individualism[26] of the liberal age had also influenced the thinking of the physician and produced a purely individualistic professional conception of the physician and the entirety of medical science. The physician had always only attended to the individual case and his recognition of the health of the whole Volk was obscured or generally not yet awakened. It is true that many good physicians recognized the plight of the Volk and its uncertain future, which marched daily with the inexorable circumspection of racial decline and stepped with continuously growing clarity towards the day of the death of the Volk. There was however no way for them to stop this catastrophe. Many of them sought to reassure themselves by living on an island of "purely detached non-political professional existence."

A complete change first occurred when Adolph Hitler succeeded in snatching the German Volk back from the brink of decay and leading it in a few years of intense constructive work to that height of power and validation which today is the guarantor of its life and freedom.

During this political development period the physician also recovered his essence inside the German Volk community, regaining his due respect corresponding to the enormously responsible assignment and meaning of his efforts. A new physician leadership had to arise in order to be able to show the way from the doctrine of the individual to that of becoming the physician to the nation. Things about which the doctor had previously had little or even no concern became for him burning problems. The application of the knowledge concerning the meaning of racial hygiene

---

(Leader and Educator) of the Volk. (Unknown Author, "Der Aerzt als Fuehrer und Erzieher" *Deutsch Aerzteblatt.* 1935, 92: 563–567) Thomas Gerst has characterized the graduates of the course as the "conspirator community in the service of Nazi health politics" (T. Gerst, "Verschworene Gemeinschaft im Dienste der NS-Gesundheitspolitik," *Dtsch Aerzteblatt* 92A (1995): 1588–91). Unfortunately, the historical community has few records of the activities at Alt-Rehse because the records were confiscated and taken to the USSR by the Red Army in 1945. "Not one sheet has been rediscovered since then" (Personal communication from Dr. Volker Dahm of Institut fuer Zeitgeschichte, Munich-Berlin). Schoenbaum reports that 3000 doctors were members of the SS. (Schoenbaum, 228) It is likely that all would have attended the courses at Alt-Rehse.

A number of other schools were established by the Nazis to train medical personnel. The SA (*Schutz Abteilung*, or Storm Troopers) founded its own school in Tuebingen. The SA became essentially defunct after the Roehm purge in 1934. An SS medical Academy was established in Berlin in 1938 and the Nazi Nurses' Association had a "mother house" in the Rudolf Hess Hospital in Dresden (Proctor, 1988, 86).

[26] The Comprehensive National Socialist Philosophical Worldview was predominantly that the physician must view himself a member of the "whole" and each patient as a member of the whole Volk and that the purely "individualistic" conception of the profession must be replaced by this National Socialist philosophical viewpoint.

and genetic-biology, the penetration of the Volk-health questions with National Socialist thought, and the synthesis of university medicine with the teaching of a national biological science of healing rooted deeply in the Volk, belong from now on to his most meaningful important volkish responsibilities. The German doctor should not today merely treat sickness conscientiously: from now on, as a matter of highest duty, the most important area of his work is in genetics and health leadership. Biological and genetic doctrines are the roots out of which the Comprehensive National Socialist Philosophical Worldview has grown and out of which the German Volk received ever renewed powers in its healing process.

Fulfilling these new duties presupposes that each individual physician must change his attitude, and that the entire medical community must undertake a moral-intellectual renewal. In order to carry this through quickly, as the time demands, and, above all, to be able to make it accessible to medical descendants, the Physicians' Leadership School of Alt-Rehse was created.

Many doctors, old and young of all branches of the profession, have gone through the Leadership School. All have managed extraordinarily well to achieve detachment[27] from the responsibilities of everyday life and concentrate consciously on the great political-health questions whose resolutions were transferred over to the medical community, and have had awakened in them again the idealism without which the National Socialist physician cannot function. The attention to true comradeship makes each teaching course an incomparable experience for all participants.

The return and re-incorporation of Volk-German peoples to the Reich[28] during the current war gave Alt-Rehse a new opportunity to demonstrate its worth through the introduction of the returning Volk-German physician to the fundamentals of our National Socialist philosophical viewpoint and to the laws of biology and racial hygiene.

The *Racial Political Office* of the NSDAP and the *Office of Ancestral Research* of the NSDAP are placed under the Reich Health Leader. The leader of the Office for Ancestral Research is at the same time the leader of the Reich Ancestors Office. The decision falls under his jurisdiction in the situations where the relevant documents are lacking concerning the question of whether or not someone is of German origin and free of Jewish-tainted blood in the sense of the conditions for being accepted by the NSDAP, as well as the delivery of indisputable certifications from political leaders with certification of their origin in terms of the relevant party departments, and finally the issuance of certificates regarding the German-blooded origin of the Party member.

The *Racial Political Office* has the responsibility to oversee indoctrination and propaganda work to achieve a unified viewpoint in the area of Population and Racial

---

[27] The Leadership school at Alt-Rehse operated as an indoctrination camp. The physicians lived in barracks army-style, performed physical exercises and took hikes together in the countryside. An intense atmosphere of mutual indoctrination was fostered.

[28] German-speaking physicians from the conquered lands were required to attend the Leadership school so that they could also become indoctrinated in the National Socialist philosophical viewpoint (Kater, *Doctors Under Hitler*, 67).

politics. The *office works on all questions* which concern the above named areas, in cooperation with the responsible authorities; it is authoritatively involved with the legislature of the state in this.

The Racial Political Office is divided into the Regional Office and the service area of the District Delegate of the Party. Oversight of the Reich Federation "German Family" (earlier the Reich Federation of Large Families) is transferred over to this office from the NSDAP. This office has been given the responsibility to bring together the genetically healthy well-ordered families[29] of pure German blood and to make them into a political fighting population, injecting the National Socialist philosophy of preserving the Volk population for the maintenance and promotion of the pure-blooded genetically healthy German family. The Federation is divided into Territories, District, and Orts[30] branches.

---

[29] The Racial Political Office was charged with finding "genetically well-ordered families" and encouraging them to procreate by "injecting National Socialist population-political thinking." What this amounted to was pointing out to those families who had been determined to be of the highest stock of the Volk that they had a moral duty to procreate and have as many children as possible so as to perpetuate the genetic stock. This was a form of forced human breeding program.

Fischer reports that the wife of Hitler's lieutenant, Martin Bormann, soberly accepted her husband's revelation that he had finally succeeded in seducing the actress Manja Behrens. She was reportedly neither jealous nor upset; in fact, she suggested a ménage a trios on the grounds that such an arrangement would set an example for other Germans since such an arrangement would be more likely to produce more children. Gerda Bormann suggested to her husband: "You can certainly be helpful to Manja, but you have to see to it that Manja has a child 1 year and I have one the next, (*so dass du immer eine Frau hast, die gebrauchsfaehig ist*) (so that you always have a woman around who is ready to be used). Fischer reports that the historian, H.R. Trevor-Roper has called this "the Nazi principle of crop rotation" (Fischer, 356).

[30] *Land - One of the territorial divisions of the Republican Germany each having their own governments. Controlled after 1933 by the central government through the Reich Governor; Kreis – District; Ort* – "place", in this context means a town.

Part V: On the Essence and Work of the Physician in the National Socialist State

We have up to now spoken of professional, state and party organizations in whose context the activity of the physician unfolds and plays out. We have also already brought clearly to expression how difficult and full of responsibility the profession of medicine is. So we want now to consider which presuppositions the young Volk comrade who wants to devote himself to the medical profession must fulfill, which demands must be met, and what responsibilities must he be up to, in order to be able to meet the expectations of the honorable and richly responsible calling as a physician of the National Socialist Volk community.

The picture of the essence and impact of the physician has been represented variously in different epochs of history – often varying even in the generations immediately following each other. Culture, race and spirit of the times affect a physician's values and manner of engaging the prevailing problems, like all professional groups, according to the standards of the times. Times of racial and cultural decay give to each Volk as well as to the medical profession its special character, just as epochs of high culture have likewise practiced their definitive influence on the knowledge and capabilities of the physician, on his ethos and on his place within his Volk. It testifies however also to the high worthiness of those people who at that time devoted themselves to the medical profession, that it took long periods of decay to detract from their ethical principles, and that the medical profession, as one of the few stabilizing and supporting pillars of culture, stood out from the general heap of rubble under which the ethics and morals of the great mass lay during the brief periods of decadence.

The famous clinician Nothnagle, a contemporary comrade of Bilroth,[1] in his inaugural Vienna lecture established the criterion of suitability to be a physician: "Only a good person can be a good doctor." Bilroth wanted to append to "the good person," the distinctive property of "well brought up," of which he understood to be

[1] Christian Albert Theodor Bilroth (1829–1894) was the first person to successfully perform a gastrectomy for stomach cancer. He worked as Professor of Surgery at the *Allegemeine Krankenhaus* of the University of Vienna (http://www.webhealthcentre.com/surgcor/sc_doctor.asp).

R. Ramm, *Medical Jurisprudence and Rules of the Medical Profession*,
Philosophy and Medicine 135, https://doi.org/10.1007/978-3-030-25245-8_5

the awakening of all talents which leads to the knowledge which makes others happy and cheerful and which must lead to good fortune and joy in the life of the doctor. Those of us who have experienced the coming and breakthrough of the National Socialist philosophical viewpoint in our Volk, and have become convinced ourselves of its incredible penetrative power to direct the course of the formation of the will and the heart of the German people, and know that all the great deeds and successes in war as well as in peace, which only lead back to its victorious effects, must place on the physician just the one *indispensable* demand that with all of the other good characteristics which have been constantly demanded from the physician, this National Socialist philosophical viewpoint must penetrate the deepest, so that he becomes a leader and model to his Volk in all areas of expression of human life. Only *the* physician of our time who is a true National Socialist will be a pillar of the Volk community and a cooperative creator of the German future, which means a Volk comrade who not only outwardly but also in his inner heart, makes the *biological laws* the unique guiding principles of his life and behavior and, as a tireless pioneer and preacher, convinces his Volk of the correctness and real truth of these laws. Only with this attitude is he to be an intellectual and moral leader of his Volk.

From within this unshakable Comprehensive Philosophical Viewpoint must the National Socialist physician fulfill his mission, which consists, not only as before, in the healing of physical and emotional wounds, consoling his fellow man during misfortune and in the administering of relief at the end of life, but additionally gives this mission priority over his duty to the individual. He becomes thereafter the protector of the genetics of his Volk and sets his heart on the education of all Volk comrades for health, so as to achieve the best possible development of all the pre-existing genetic traits; he will mature thereby from an individualist physician of the past to a true Volk physician.

Who should now be a physician?

Only a physically and psychologically healthy and strong young Volk comrade – man or woman – should choose this profession, which requires so much personal sacrifice and so much moral and physical strength. Only that one who is master of his passion and ambition, only those fully-matured in spirit, disposition and character, are suited for this beautiful, and frequently so difficult, profession, which burdens the soul so extraordinarily. A feeling of duty, consciousness of responsibility, readiness to help, a sense of sacrifice and infinite generosity must stand in the foreground of the structure of the character of the physician, while fundamental scientific knowledge and technical ability must be the weapons which he learns to forge during his study and education time under the leadership of a master and which during his entire life he will let become neither rusty nor blunt.[2]

---

[2]This paragraph gives both the prerequisite conditions for becoming a physician and the resulting moral responsibilities.

Kater reports that the demands relating to the need of doctors for the Wehrmacht caused the regime to take a year off of the traditional 13-year curriculum in early 1937. It should be noted that this was over 2 years before the outbreak of the war. In 1939, in expectation of an armed conflict, significant cuts were again made in the medical curriculum. The curriculum was again shortened

The inclination to become a physician as a choice of occupation must be already well established and tested in the first semester of study. It is of great importance to determine that the physician candidate arises from a well-ordered genetic-biologically flawless family, has grown up in a well-ordered family and was raised to be an honorable conscientious human being. An old home, schools, Hitler Youth and BdM and later college, as well as the faculty and the Specialty association of Volk health of the National Socialist Students' Federation, to which every medical student must belong, are to us the guarantor for high intellectual capacities, moral quality and character traits of the probationer.

The meaning that party, state and profession attach to the *racial purity* of the physician is demonstrated by the determination that before the student can begin medical studies the same demands as that for officials must be fulfilled, which means, that the ancestral line back to the grandparents is to have no element of foreign blood, especially no Jewish blood.[3]

The young medical student should not use *his study time* just for the appropriation of medical knowledge and capabilities, because that can never be fundamentally enough; he should also acquire knowledge in areas bordering on medicine like philosophy, psychology, volk-economics, and beautiful arts, and, through interactions in the university, learn to treasure the overwhelming value of the wonderful German Volk culture which manifests itself in many ways in the various branches of our Volk. Out of the understanding of the racial structure of our Volks-soul will he gather knowledge regarding the process of how the individual soul comes to expression in mankind in healthy and sick days. This soul contains great significance for the biologically thinking physician for comprehending how leadership and healing can achieve a conceptual unification of body and soul.

An especially fortunate influence on the psychological capacities of the physician occurs if fate has at some time thrown him into the position of sickness, whereby he can study the correlates and psychological manifestations of his own body.[4] How much greater would be the understanding of many physicians for the

---

in 1943 and 1944. In place of the traditional subject matter many courses turned to emphasizing Racial Hygiene and military medicine (Kater, *Doctors Under Hitler,* 152).

[3] Bela Bodo has reported that, just like the entire German population, medical students were required to undergo rigid anthropological and racial examinations as an integral part of the admission process to university. These exams were repeated at various times during the course of studies (B. Bodo, "The Medical Examination of Biological Selection of University Students in Nazi Germany," *Bull. Hist. Med.,* 76 (2002): 719–748).

[4] Ramm wishes for each medical student to himself become ill. But note that he does not wish this so that the physician can come to understand empathy for the sick patient, but rather that he can learn how to raise his psychological defensive capacities for resistance, that is, his "*will*". Presumably, then, this experience is to be of use to apply in his practice to urge his patients to activate the same psychological will. This approach to the sick gives the physician an infallible excuse for the failure of any form of therapy – the patient failed to have enough "*will*" to make himself well. Psychologically blaming the patient for failure to make himself well is an extension of the theory of disease which follows from Social Darwinism, that of "contagionism" (A. Aisenberg, *Contagion: Disease, Government, and the "Social Question" in Nineteenth-Century France* (Stanford: University Press, 1999)). In this theory of disease, the ill person is

psychological state of their patients and how much more intensive would they be in regards to the re-strengthening of their psychological capacity for resistance relative to fighting the influences of sickness, if they themselves at one time have had to overcome a serious illness!

If now the young medical student, after assiduous studies, has taken his state exam before the state testing commission, the *Licensure as Doctor* will be granted to him by the Territorial authorities.[5] When he has completed the studies which lead to his promotion to doctor, he is then also entitled to officially receive this academic degree. According to the most recent regulations, the young physician has to seek to accumulate and deepen his practical knowledge at clinics or in hospitals for the period of a year. Then he must serve out the rural quarter-year.[6] Only after fulfillment of these regulations is he entitled to establish his practice as a self-standing physician. The licensing for fund practice and the determination of the place of practice are part of a special proceeding of the licensing committee established by the Territorial Division of the Fund Physicians' Union of Germany.

It becomes an important responsibility of the Reich Physicians' Chamber to make available a regularly cycled course of education, as was previously mentioned, through regularly planned appointments of young physicians as assistants in sickness institutions and with practicing physicians.[7] Even though today the Reich

---

himself found to be responsible for his own illness. If, then, one is responsible for his own illness, he must be responsible for his own cure. Such reasoning regarding the etiology and treatment of diseases buttresses many public health preventive medicine and alternative medicine theories of disease (P. Baldwin, *Contagion and the State in Europe 1830–1930* (Cambridge: University Press, 1999); S. Jarcho, *The Concept of Contagion: In Medicine, Literature and Religion* (Malabar, Florida: Krieger Publishing, 2000); HAMJ Ten Have, "Knowledge and Practice in European Medicine: The Case of Infectious Diseases," *The Growth of Medical Knowledge* (Dordrecht: Kluwer Academic Publishers, 1990), 15–40).

[5] The various stages from medical student to ultimate establishment as self-standing physician are presented. By the time the physician was allowed to establish his independent practice he would have been exposed to the National Socialist philosophical viewpoint in medical school, during countless lectures and conferences, during the practical year and during the rural quarter-year. Finally, he would have to apply for fund practice. Approval for fund practice would likewise depend on acceptance and mastering of the Nazi National Socialist philosophical viewpoint.

[6] The young physician was required to spend a year in a rural setting in association with a local physician. Evans reports:

> At times, Nazi rhetoric might seem to envision a Europe of peasant farmers, of Germans united by ties of 'blood and soil,' enslaving and exploiting members of inferior races in a pseudofeudal world shorn of the complexities and ambiguities of industrial society; de-industrialization and de-urbanization would be the essentials of the final incarnation of the Third Reich on a European scale. (Evans 2005, 502)

[7] After establishment in practice the physician was required to participate in continuing education courses on a 2-year cycle. The courses emphasized Racial Hygiene and preventive medicine.

Ramm makes it clear that the "voluntary fulfillment of this authorized demand" will be taken into account when it comes time to be chosen for privileged positions, such as approval for fund practice.

It can be seen that the physician who had agitated against the self-administered sickness funds before the coming of the National Socialists had managed to become a member of a profession

Physicians' Leader recommends a regularly cycled 2 year period of practical education after the granting of the license, this is required only to learn those technical and artificial treatments to be employed to treat illness and to maintain health when they are well. The voluntary fulfillment of this authorized demand of the profession can be supported by emphasizing that the licensure authorities give priority for licensure for the establishment of a practice to the prepared physician. But also the young physician who seeks to bypass this demand through renunciation of licensure for fund practice by going into independent private practice will in the future have to acquire this broader practical education, since it is intended to make participating in sickness insurance and planning for the establishment of the Reich Physicians' Chamber a duty of each physician in peacetime, as it now already is in the war, because otherwise the supplying of physicians for the recovered or newly won areas of the Reich would be called into question or made even impossible. It must hereby be expressly maintained that only *the* physician who is prepared to place into evidence his preparations to take over a post given to him by the Physicians' Chamber in a medically poorly supplied area for the 1st years of independent practice will acquire a right to have his wishes fulfilled regarding putting down his practice and the nature of his medical activities.

The Education as Specialty Physician requires courses of education which are additional to those of the general practitioner. It is desirable for each Specialty physician to acquire the fundamental education of the practical physician so as to deepen his general knowledge and abilities in the areas bordering his own Specialty; the young physician will likely be pressured very frequently into Specialty physician education through many extensive circumstances, such as perhaps accidentally taking an assistanceship in a clinic or somehow an opportunity is offered to him during the course of his general education.

The Specialty Physician Ordinance, which is part of the Professional Ordinance for the German physician decreed on 5 Nov 1937, provides binding regulations for a comprehensive education of specialist physicians, and regulates the large specialties of internal medicine, stomach, intestine and metabolic diseases, lung diseases, childhood diseases, surgery, female diseases and obstetrics, diseases of the urinary tract and pathology, such that there is to be a purely Specialty education[8] of 4 years

---

which was indeed administered by professional colleagues. But the cost was that the physician who wanted to practice had to practice according to the National Socialist philosophical viewpoint if he wanted to survive. Even if he harbored secret doubts or objections to the genetic-biological conceptions of the Nazis he would have not been able to act on them without jeopardizing his own professional life, if not his actual life.

[8] Ramm discusses the development of specialty education. Germany was traditionally more advanced in certification of specialty medical training than were other countries at the time, since many of the specialties, especially surgical specialties, originated in Germany. But the specialists' approach to medicine, which emphasized the technological aspect of medicine, conflicted with the National Socialists' holistic approach to medicine. "The archetypal Nazi held a holistic view towards medicine, tempered with notions of Social Darwinism" (Kater, *Doctors Under Hitler,* 25). The individual physician was part of a "whole" and the community itself was just a part of the larger "whole" of the *Volksgemeinschaft.* For the first few years of the regime medical specialism

besides a 1 year general physician or internist activity. The Specialty physician for internal medicine, instead of this, may have a year of general medical, surgical or gynecological education. The specialist for teeth, mouth and throat disease must take the present test as a dentist besides presenting the previously mentioned documents. For the individual specialties there are accepted regulations in the Specialty Ordinance concerning the decreed course of education. The time in which one pursues his own practice can not be counted for the prescribed education time to become a specialist physician; on the other hand, up to a quarter year substitute activity with a specialist physician can be counted. Besides that, up to a year of formal education in a related field can be counted.

The Specialty physician should be master of his Specialty area and be in full command of this both scientifically and practically.[9] Therefore his formal education should as a rule be taken at a Reich university or medical institution and be led by a specialist physician. Only the larger medical institutions, in which it is most likely that there are many specialties represented, will be appropriate for Specialty physician education. It is expressly demanded that the formal education of the Specialty physician extend to all areas of the Specialty. The formal education time in a hospital where diseases belonging to other specialties are treated will be counted proportionately and only up to at most half of the prescribed formal educational time. An outpatient clinic and such can be counted up to a half and at most up to 1 year of the formal education time. An exception is the formal education at a university outpatient clinic, which is counted in its entirety when it is established as a permanent department.

During the formal education time the prospective Specialty physician must hold an assistanceship in a Specialty department or an equally responsible voluntary or supporting physicianship, otherwise this time cannot be counted. Also, formal education in foreign countries can be recognized if their demands are equivalent to those required in the Reich. By the addition of the Specialty of pathological anatomy

---

was distinctly unwanted because it was inconsistent with the Nazi idealist idea of the family physician of "*Blut und Boden*," (blood and soil), that view of the everpresent rural family practitioner at the bedside of the ill person in the rural cottage. There continued to be demands for specialists, especially in the large cities, so the Nazis ultimately spelled out the specialists' training in more detail in a followup physicians' ordinance of 1937. Consistent with their philosophy, they constructed a hierarchical specialty system. The surgeon was at the top of the hierarchy because they more traditionally fitted into a military style male-oriented regime. "It is no accident that the few natural representatives of the master race usually turn to surgery. Here, if anywhere, strong will and action are evidently still decisive" (In Kater, *Doctors Under Hitler,* 28). The surgeons' percentage of the total number of specialists in Germany increased from 10.0% in 1935 to 15.3% in 1937, and in 1939, 25.1% of new specialty certifications were in surgery (Kater, *Doctors Under Hitler,* 29). Surgery was followed in order by Internism, Gynecology and Pediatrics (Kater, *Doctors Under Hitler,* 29).

[9] Ramm presents a discussion of rights and responsibilities of the specialty physician. As in others areas previously noted, the National Socialist government was intimately more involved than other countries of the time in regulating the practice relationships of generalists and specialists. In the United States, even today, these relationships are regulated, if at all, by professional bodies rather than government agencies.

there are now 15 specialties in the Specialty Physician Ordinance in which a special formal education can be acquired for the Specialty physician title.

The recognition as a Specialty physician is granted by the responsible Physicians' Chamber for the applicant when the required documents for the request are submitted. In each Physicians' Chamber there exists a *Specialty Physicians' Committee*, which examines in every detail the submitted documents and then reports to the Leader of the Physicians' Chamber regarding the nature and duration of the activities of the applicant, and whether the application is to be certified or rejected. The decision of the Physicians' Chamber can, in the case of a negative determination, be challenged within 2 weeks to the Reich Physicians' Chamber, whose decision is final.

The recognition as a Specialty physician is valid for the entire area of the Reich. The practice of several Specialty physician designations and the connecting of a Specialty physician practice with a general physician designation are prohibited. In the situation where, in the course of his occupational practice, it should occur that the physician no longer possesses the inclination to practice as a Specialty physician, the recognition as a Specialty physician can at that time be rescinded by the responsible Physicians' Chamber.

As a consequence of his special education, there are certain limitations in the practice of the specialist physician to which he has to attend. Thus he is not allowed to practice as an Advisory Health Insurance Examining Physician. He should limit himself essentially to his Specialty, and cases which belong to another Specialty should be turned over to the responsible physician. To practice his Specialty activity he must procure the necessary furnishings, instruments and tools which are presently the requisite tools of his Specialty. The Specialty physician should be certain that his visiting practice does not become a general house physician's activity, so as not to alienate the family from their house physician. Specialty physicians who are leaders of the larger hospitals or departments should practice in general only clinic hours and consultative activities. A substitute for a Specialty physician should only be a physician of the same Specialty.

Physicians who were licensed to practice before 1.1.1935 will be entitled in the interim regulations to a shortened formal education time of around 1 year. Specialty physicians who previously had a double designation are permitted to carry only *one* Specialty physician designation, as already stated, from the starting point of the decree of the Specialty Ordinance; they can however continue in the previous combined areas, with the certification of the responsible Leader of the Physicians' Chamber and the KVD, if they can prove a formal education as a broader Specialty physician.

If the young physician has completed his formal education, nothing stands in the way of his either founding a new or taking over an old practice. It is however to be noted that licensing for a practice is dependent on the decision of the licensure committee. Therefore it is important that, in the choice of the place where one prefers to establish a practice, one determines either that he prefers a place where licensure by the fund is guaranteed at the beginning or where licensure is possible for the future. Without ongoing consultation with the responsible Department Leader of the

District or Territorial Division of the Fund Physicians' Union of Germany, no young physician should be allowed to prepare to lay down a practice, because this alone is the opportunity for professional comrades to give objective advice to the young physician and protect him from injury. How often it has occurred that a young physician, in the enticing proposal to be soon self-sufficient, has undertaken a house somewhere or an established practice with living space at an exorbitant price, leaving him or his heirs in debt for years! Only after consultation with his responsible Department Leader does he gain insight of how much apprentice premium he is required to pay for this over-hasty action which is taken without the fore-knowledge and cooperation of his professional organization.

Since the Leader of the Physicians' Chamber has to give his certification for each assumption of a practice and can also have influence over the real value of the undertaking and, in case the real value of the practice comes into question, the determination of this also can be attached to his certification; thus each young physician must expressly receive certification for the founding of his practice, and only act in agreement with the responsible Department Leader.

Out of this necessarily close cooperation with the professional organization arises the demand that it is seen as an obvious duty that each young physician who newly comes into a Region or in the Bezirk[10] Physicians' Chamber, whether as an assistant physician or a self-standing physician, should introduce himself to the responsible Department Leader. To these I would like to add the District and Regional Department Leader of the Office of Volks' Health, the Leader of the District Office of the Fund Physicians' Union of Germany, the District Union of the Physicians' Chamber, and finally the Leader of the Physicians' Chamber and the Territorial Division of the KVD, especially the Civil Service Physician of the District. It is in any case better that the neophyte stands out to the leaders of his professional organizations through conduct corresponding to the demands of courteousness and good breeding than that he shows his presence in the Gau through his first violation of the Professional Ordinance. I hold further to the demand of comradeship that one should make oneself known to physicians living in his vicinity through a short visit and in this way construct good relationships that are self-evident among National Socialist physicians.

No one would believe that he can avoid the obstacles of life and profession undisturbed without the comradeship of others and without the defense of a professional organization. And how it is fortifying if one has a helper in the fight and how soothing it is if one can gain for oneself good advice or find protection from help from his Department Leader or some other professional comrade during danger or misfortune!

How often will false conclusions and results be drawn from the testimony of patients about statements and treatments by a neighboring professional comrade

[10] *Bezirk* – Administrative sub-division of a Prussian Territory (roughly the size of an average English County).

because one does not know the other and therefore associates with him things which one could at the beginning from closer familiarity expose and determine to be untrue.

Polite and tactful – one word – *comradeship should be the relationship of physicians with each other.*

Because of the nature of the occupation of medicine it is unavoidable that occasionally one physician will come into conflict with another. Often the occasion occurs that in a sudden serious illness of a volk comrade, that three or four physicians, who were called, each arrive at the bedside at the same time because one or the other was not immediately available. In this case one must leave the field of activity to the first arriving physician, unless one of those present is the house physician, who has a natural priority.

It will further regularly happen that a patient for whom one physician has not fulfilled his wishes turns to another and seeks to represent the first physician as incompetent, malevolent and unsocial. It belongs to the duty of decency that one doesn't' transmit to any authority this reproach, but rather seeks out the professional comrade to apologize and set things right. One should take special care to set straight a complainant or slanderer who passes sentence on the manner of treatment of a professional comrade after it has been misrepresented. One should always consider that what happens today to a professional comrade can happen tomorrow to oneself and that the reputation of one physician is one's own reputation and that the prestige of the whole medical community plays out on oneself. The thought is to be rejected that with a profession like that of the physician that if one puts oneself individually over to the side that there will be a special value forthcoming for him in the Volk community. If one stumbles or certainly if one falls then that produces a fleck on the blank shield of honor of the whole profession, and if the respect for the whole medical community sinks, then no one can believe that he is an exception. Therefore, it is a duty of honor of each representative of the profession that he not only justify the trust of his Volk comrades in himself, but that, additionally, he places himself in the position to defend the reputation and the prestige of his professional comrades and, if he sees that the other intentionally or unintentionally injures the honor of the profession, then he should in a comradely way make it known of this injurious behavior and only take steps to notify the professional representative if this one is incorrigible or malevolently rejects the comradely advice.

In office hours the physician is allowed to advise and treat every patient who seeks him out. He is permitted to make sickness visits only to patients who can not get medical treatment in any other way. If he learns before carrying out the visit that the sick person has already sought advice from another physician then he must confront this behavior and, depending on the outcome of the visit, encourage him not to do this or he must combine generally his treatment with the prior physician's. If a physician subsequently becomes aware that a patient, behind the back of an other physician, causes a visit to occur, then the physician has to communicate this immediately and leave to the other physician the wider treatment and, only in the case where this one renounces the service, undertake further treatment oneself.

If a physician is called in an emergency to a sick person who is already under the treatment of another physician who is not available at the moment, then it is an obvious duty of decency to promptly inform the professional comrade of the means of treatment employed and leave over to him the wider course of treatment.

Rural places that are the residences of physicians should be visited by a non-local physician only with the agreement of the local physician.

When a physician requests another physician to accompany him in some unclear or difficult case one cannot refuse this request without extreme reasons. Likewise a request to a physician from a sick person or his family member to call in another physician should be complied with. With the supervision of a sick person by another physician this one should, after the conclusion of treatment, refer the patient back to the first treating physician if follow-up treatment is still required. Likewise it should be considered to be a professional duty that patients who have been treated by a substitute physician are to be given back to the first after he has again taken up his practice.

Substituting by physicians whose license is suspended or is affected by a provisional ban on medical activity is allowed to take place only with certification of the Leader of the Physicians' Chamber. Substitution by physicians who have renounced their medical practice is not permitted. With the death of a physician the widow or children are permitted with certification of the Physicians' District Union to establish a substitute for the practice for the duration of a quarter-year. In specifically designated cases the Physicians' District Union can extend this period.

The employment of assistants in a freely standing practice is permitted only with the certification of the Physicians' Chamber. A substitute or an assistant of a free-standing physician's practice is not allowed to establish his own practice in the same district for the period of a year, without the express consent of the Physicians' District Chamber.

Physicians who practice a welfare activity in an official capacity, especially in emergencies, must, in the context of this activity, limit this treatment and not allow it to alienate patients from their house physician.

Physicians in health spas and bath resorts should discontinue the treatment of their non-local patients at the end of the rest. Physicians who visit health spas and bath resorts during their own holiday are not to carry out their own practice while at the resort, so as not to insult the physician of the institution. It is a medical tradition that the patient who is admitted to a health spa or bath resort is not to bring with him a course of regimen and certainly not a course of treatment from his previous doctor during the duration of his stay at the institution. The healing plan to be proposed during the cure is the responsibility of the institutional physician.

In consideration of other physicians, it is forbidden to erect private clinics or hold other *free-of-charge office hours* or to distribute treatment by letter or to distribute discussion of methods of healing or healing processes in the daily press or in lectures, radio or film, or in advertisements in connection with one's own practice. In the times of the corruption of medical ethics, a bad habit was established in large cities and in many country districts whereby the physician who transferred his patient to one or the other hospital was to receive remuneration. Professional custom declares this "symbiosis" as being immoral and demands its punishment even if it occurs in surreptitious form.

The erection of a general practice in which there is an agreement with an apothecary is improper in any way in which there is for the physician an economic advantage.

The relationship with the apothecary profession is to be correct and polite. One should always consider that the German apothecary also has an important responsibility to fulfill in the care of the Volk, therefore he is to be recognized by the physician as a welcome and equally valuable fighting comrade.[11]

It is forbidden, from the standpoint of the profession, and liable for damages, in the course of practice as a doctor, to recommend patients to a particular apothecary or to designate an appropriate apothecary for this purpose.

To be expressly pointed out is that it is forbidden to promote or receive from the supplier any goods or services for the ordering and recommendation of any modalities of treatment. The *Testing and Critical Evaluation of Modalities of Treatment* and the publication of their results is dependent in all cases on the certification of the Reich Physicians' Chamber. The physician is permitted to neither promote nor accept any remuneration over and above his usual honorarium.

According to & 28 of the Professional Ordinance, the physician is required to present to the Reich Physicians' Chamber for certification all contracts which he has taken up regarding his occupational activities. Even though the qualifying conditions, which are foreseen in & 49, Abs 2 of the Reich Physicians' Ordinance, have not yet been implemented, *all* contracts are nevertheless to be obligatorily submitted to the responsible Physicians' Chamber for certification. It is even advisable to call in the advice of the Physicians' Chamber during the contract negotiations and before the conclusion of a contract so as to guarantee the uniformity of the contracts for the whole profession and to protect the individual from injury. How often has a physician or a Specialty physician, in the first joy of the possibility of starting his own practice or to be active clinically, not investigated a contract, which turns out in the future to be personally or economically unbearable.

In the process of implementation of the Law For the Professional Practice of the Healing Sciences (Healing Practitioner Law), the physician is required, through arrangement of the Reich Physicians' Leader, to grant to recognized healing practitioners, at their request, advice and aid in the treatment of their patients. It is however forbidden to support the unlawful activity of a quack.

---

[11] At the beginning of the Third Reich, many pharmacists believed that the coming of the regime would give them the chance to realize their long-term ambition of having their profession formally put on a par with medicine. These dreams were not realized, however, and their profession was absorbed into the Labor Front in 1934. They were totally *gleichgeschaltet* like the other professions and their specific contribution to the National Socialist philosophical viewpoint was the search for home-grown drugs to render Germany independent of pharmaceutical imports (Evans 2005, 439). As a consequence of the regime's holistic view of medicine, the health-insurance outlay on medicine prescribed per average case of illness dropped by a seventh, from 3.45 to 3.00 marks (Grunberger, 221).

Before taking over his own practice the physician must comply with all laws and regulations which have been decreed by the state and the profession. Through these, come the rights and privileges, the duties and responsibilities, the instructions and binding orders of the physician, which serve as guiding principles in regards to sick and helpless people as well as to the Volk community. It is self-evident that in an occupation which has been entrusted to care for and promote the highest good of the individual person as well as the health of the Volk community, that not all responsibilities and duties can be put down in the paragraphs of laws and regulations, and that in addition to these there are even higher moral viewpoints completing the obligations of the physician, which arise in the concept, "*Medical Ethics.*"

Out of tradition, each profession and each occupation cultivates a special professional honor and demands from its members a definite moral attitude in its individual Volk-comrades in regards to the Volk community. None of the occupations are given or enabled to have any deeper insight into human wishes and desires, of human suffering, in short in the purest feelings of psychological life, than the physician. The basis for the revelation of these psychological secrets and needs is the unbridled trust of those who seek out the physician for understanding, advice and help. Thus it is self-evident that with this close psychological relationship of the physician to the sick or advice-seeking Volk comrade, a feeling of pure harmony and high responsibility, and also a deep understanding of human nature is expected, which is over and above the common degree of understanding and above common ethical standards.

What the Volk community and each individual Volk comrade may expect from the physician is brought to expression in the first paragraph of the Reich Physicians' Ordinance: "The physician is called to the service of the health of the individual person and the entire Volk. He fulfills a publicly regulated responsibility through this law. The medical occupation is no business enterprise."

The legislature has given the Reich Physicians' Chamber, on the grounds of &14 of the Reich Physicians' Ordinance, the task of regulating medical responsibilities of the profession through the decree of a *Professional Ordinance* and has accomplished thereby the protection of professional honor. The Reich Physicians' Leader decreed this Professional Ordinance on 5.11.1937, wherein, by widening the physician's duty, the demand was placed on the medical community "to work for the welfare of the Volk and the Reich for the maintenance and improvement of the health, the genetic makeup and race of the German Volk and to fulfill these responsibilities in the sense of the Comprehensive National Socialist Philosophical Worldview." Especially each physician is charged "to incorporate himself into the organization of the professional corporate body of his profession, the Reich Physicians' Chamber and the Fund Physicians' Union of Germany, and as a consequence to carry out their administrative directions."

It is clear to each person entrusted with the essence of the physician's profession that a professional Ordinance can not deal exhaustively with all medical professional duties and that there are certainly pure moral demands which can be taken to be striving for the medical ideal which are perpetual, like those already laid down in the Hippocratic Oath and which thereby have created estimable medical ethics up to the present time. The deeper this unwritten law becomes incorporated into the soul of the physician, the more encompassing it comes to be expressed in his actions, the more pronounced becomes the bearer of such a professional conception, the more will he come to be an effectively good physician, as a representative of the ideal that we recognize in the concept of the "The Ideal Conception of Medicine." Early in the course of his development, the individual reveals if he is going to strive for this ideal and how close he will be able to achieve it in his professional practice.

The *personality of the physician* must be of a firmly National Socialist philosophical nature and reach a high grade of completeness which arises out of three roots: *His nature as a human, his education and his calling.*

As a human, the physician must be fully adequate, well formed and harmoniously proportioned in body, clear and sharp intellectually, and deep, strong and kind in his soul. He must carry in himself the striving to possess the highest measure of knowledge and ability in the area of medical science, in the accompanying areas and in those of general education. With a sharp gift of observation he must combine a healthy judgment; he must be composed and stable in his behavior and must be free and resolute in his dealings with Volk comrades. With the seriousness of his nature he must pair in himself a joy of life and a joyful mood, characteristics which help him bear and frequently lighten the difficulties of his profession.

If we speak of the *calling* to be a physician then we understand this as encompassing the inclination for strong scientific thinking and a sense of artistic creativity. The struggle over the idea of the question of *whether medicine is an art or a science* has moved the hearts and souls of mankind from antiquity to the present. The history of medicine brings proof that the varieties of the conceptions of the nature of medicine were already cause for extensive discussion in the academies of Kos and Knidos. The representative from Kos was *Hippocrates,* under whose name the collection of Koisan efforts of this type were collected together. His contemporary was *Euryphon of Knidos*, as famous in his lifetime as the Koer (Hippocrates); many fruitful thoughts of his school were translated later than those hippocratically derived. Hippocrates and the Koisan school classified medicine as an art, while Knidos wanted the character of medicine to be known as a science. Today we know that medicine encompasses art *and* science, the art of healing (*Heilkunst*) and the science of healing (*Heilkunde*), and that the true physician must have at his disposal artistic aptitudes and scientific capacities if he wants to be up to the demands of the boundless trust of ill people.

Even without dividing up each Specialty area into the named characteristics in which in the course of time they have devoted themselves for better investigation and application, the profession offers sufficient possibilities for the application of various practices.

George G. Gruber[12] proposes an ideal picture of a physician's nature when he said: "The fulfillment of medicine's desires as it exists before us in its highest and

[12] Gruber, GB.: Einfuehrung in Geist und Studium der Medizin. Georg Thieme, Leipzig, 1934. – Von aerztlicher Ethik. Hippokrates-Vlg, St.

purest form is probably only possible if an artistically feeling and formed man skillfully brings his intellectual gifts to the science of the general welfare. These gifts are the achievements of an *art*. Each case demands a renewed sensitivity. And they are achievements of applied *science* because each time there are fundamentally new considerations required. They are neither automatic nor just business-like because at no time do they represent identical objects, because lacking in them is the peculiarity of the continuously far from life repetition which is generated by the central purpose of systematically making money, making it such that this extraordinary responsibility both complicates and heals professional activity. In the physician there should come to be a feeling of responsibility of the highest sort of scientific conviction, artistic desires and technical ability. One wants to see as physicians personalities who bring a beautiful harmony of head, heart and hand."

The Professional Ordinance demands that the physician practice his profession scientifically and show in his behavior, inside and outside of the profession, that he is worthy of the attention and trust which the Volk community has given him. Since there exists naturally conditioned sympathy and antipathy between people – even within the same race – and the consequence of medical works is dependent on the pure psychological fiber which develops between physician and patient, this natural law should at no time be prevented from acting between the sick and the physician. The right of the sick person to choose his own trusted physician is to be recognized at all times – except for emergencies. This trusting relationship is always the principle upon which the necessary moral leadership of the physician for healing must be constructed.

But it is not just the trust of the *individual* volk comrade which the physician must cultivate, he must enjoy the entire trust of the *community* of his Volk if he wants to demonstrate the solemn meaning of the word in its highest sense. For that, it is necessary that he recognize his conceptual duty as an ideal in regards to the whole. The living of his own life must be exemplary in its impeccability and in the organization of his relationships. His own nature and that of his family must be expressed through the Comprehensive National Socialist Philosophical Worldview; each desire and action must correspond to its fundamental principles. The service to the Volk community, and especially that of his profession, should mean for him the highest law and should be the living embodiment and fulfillment of his life. He must be the bearer and conscious promoter of the culture. As representative and reporter of the National Socialist idea he should as a moral duty represent the elements of the party and state to Volk comrades and should work for their fulfillment.

An idealistic composure in each relationship and restless commitment to the intellectual-psychological renewal of our Volk, which was threatening to disintegrate under the influence of false and foreign racial ideologies, are the fundamental pillars on which the German physician must build his place of leadership, and which he needs for the resolution of the overbearing responsibilities transferred to him by the Volk community.

The instructions of the National Socialist Leader to the physician are threefold. They extend to:

1. Taking care of and treatment of the sick.
2. Care of the race and protection of the genetic wealth of our Volk and
3. Health education of the German people.

As old as the science of healing itself is the responsibility of the physician to stand by the sick and weak person during his physical and psychological suffering and to help strengthen him. Equally as important from the standpoint of the care of the Volk is the pure preservation of the blood through prevention of bastardization by bad qualities or foreign racial elements, as well the responsibility for the protection of the genetic wealth, the preservation and improvement of genetic predispositions and the complete eradication of the mass of bad genes.[13] Of the same value as these two in the leadership of the people is the education for health with the intention to raise the capacity for achievement by development of the good pre-existing properties in individuals, with the goal of achieving the highest possible strengthening of the psychological and physical strength of the whole Volk.[14]

The Physician as Manager of the Sick

The Responsibilities and Duties of the Physician in Practice

In the *help of the sick* the physician is not allowed to make any distinction between high and low, poor and rich. Each genetically healthy person must possess the same value for him whether he takes advantage of his help for money or demands it as God's wages. So that the physician is not brought to distribute his favors to the needy Volk comrade for filthy lucre, it must be seen as the highest duty of the professional state leadership to secure the physician's material support to a sufficient degree. The medical profession makes a claim on its members for all their psychological, intellectual and physical strength, so that in addition to their fight against sickness it can also lead to a fight for their own naked Being. How is one supposed to be a good physician if the care of women does not emanate from the threshold and one's own material existence and that of one's family is not secure? Lofty conceptions of medicine and the striving for money and possessions are mutually irreconcilable. Thus one must conclude that a noble ideal conception of medicine can thrive only on a secure material basis. Only an ordered economic relationship places the physician in the position to live up to an ethos which forges his conscience daily without his reflecting about the expected pay. This allows him to

[13] *Endloesung*. With the belief that the Jew represented the largest repository of this "mass of bad genes," this statement seems to justify the participation of the Nazi physician in the "Final Solution of the Jewish Problem."

[14] This paragraph presents the central paradox of National Socialist medicine – *Heilen und Vernichten* (to cure and to exterminate). (A. Ebbinghaus and K. Doerner, *Vernichten und Heilen: Der Nuernberger Aerzteprozess und seine Folgen* (Berlin: Aufbau-Verlag, 2001).

respond only to the difficulties of the pressing circumstances of the sickness and the degree of assistance required. Therefore one must strongly disapprove of making a distinction in treatments which begins with the establishment of two waiting rooms, one for private patients, the other for members of the fund, and ends with paying greater scrupulous attention to treatments of the wealthy sick. This is neither a professional – ethical employment of the physician for his needy Volk comrades nor a National Socialist conception of the medical profession. Likewise, the physician should guard himself against providing superfluous services, be it through too numerous appointments of the sick or too numerous visits to the house of the sick or even through treatment modalities themselves to the sick. The fund patient may, out of ignorance of the physician fund accounting system, take this attention to be fundamental or special, whereas the self-payer sees it as too much business and is inclined to reduce the calls to the physician by himself. The physician must lay great value on his behavior with his sick patients because their trust is grounded in this as much as in his ability. Friendliness and restraint in equal measures are encouraged without being overbearing, selfish and dogmatic, while the art of being a physician calls for sympathizing, consoling, with upright and always encouraging behavior. He must always remember that the sickness of the body leads to psychological weakness and that psychological sickness also creates physical damage. Neither crudely nor impulsively, but rather always calm, serious and self-possessed, he must expose infringements and unworthy unreasonable demands. He avoids making prognostications more favorable than probability allows, but he is also not permitted to lay unnecessary cares in the hearts of his patients and the family members if he does not share them himself.

What above all should be displayed by the physician towards girls and women who make demands for his advice is an irreproachable relationship. All medical actions and deeds must be born from an honorable intellectual attitude and a pure heart. The female sex is the bearer of the coming generation of our Volk and has therefore a justified right to be acknowledged by everyone in respect to its high responsibilities and achievements, especially by the physician.[15]

---

[15]This paragraph displays the National Socialist attitude towards women. Women had gained considerable freedom in the Weimar Republic, partly from the more progressive and egalitarian climate of the Republic and partly from the specific guarantees within its Constitution. There were 111 women in the Reichstag in 1920 and there was a higher representation in the professions. Sexual politics arose in the form of the League for the Protection of Mothers (BFM), which demanded free abortion and government financial assistance to unmarried mothers (S. J. Lee, *The Weimar Republic* (London: Routledge, 1998), 114).

The Nazis reacted aggressively to these liberalizing tendencies in regards to women. Women were placed on a high plane, while at the same time much was expected of them as child-bearers. Michael Burleigh refers to the Nazi attitude towards women to be a "mother cult." May 10 was the Day of the German Mother on the Nazi calendar, when the 'brave sons and brave daughters wove a coronet of flowers for their beloved, good mothers'. The Nazis made the date a high occasion. Youths from the HJ, SA and SS spread out through the country demanding contributions. In 1938, they established the award of Mothers' Cross for women 'rich in children.' If a woman was nominated for the award she and her family were scrutinized compulsively by the authorities. The criteria were designed to distinguish laudable, independent and orderly families 'rich in children'

The physician should not neglect to record his bedside observations in each case in order to be able to use them with later sicknesses and in case of transfer of treatment to another physician. Obviously, cases of illness which are unclear must be thoroughly worked through until a clear diagnosis is made. In cases where a clear diagnosis has not been established and cannot be worked out working alone, he should exhaust all possibilities to help the sick through consultation with other experienced professional comrades who are especially well trained in the area. The seeking of advice from other physicians in doubtful cases should be initiated by the treating physician himself; he should not wait until the sick person or the members of the family express this wish, for this always makes an unpleasant impression.

It is the highest duty of the physician to let great *scientific ability* prevail in the management of his sick people, which must extend not just to the choice of the correct means and methods of treatment but rather also to the frequency and number of times of its use. Above all, the physician is to be careful in the use of highly potent medical modalities and poisons and he should never forget to be certain that he has not ordered too strong a preparation.

The Professional Ordinance puts a very heavy emphasis on *protecting the physician's duty of silence* which is understood to be the protection of each secret that has been entrusted or accessible to him as a physician. As early as Hippocratic times, the physician had to swear, "What I see or perceive in my activities as a physician or what I experience otherwise of humanity which should never be revealed, that I will protect in my deepest heart and will to hold to be unutterable." The ideal conception of medicine has at all times taken this demand of the professional ethos seriously, with few exceptions, and attended to it as an ornament of each physician, which he fulfills his entire life. This duty of silence concerning secrets and observa-

---

from unworthy, dependent and dysfunctional 'large families.' Burleigh notes, "Women who received these Crosses could derive comfort from the claim that their bodies were the medium for the transmission of Nordic 'blood', even as they were being demeaned to the level of cows ruminating in the fields." (Burleigh 2000, 230–1) On Mother's Day in May, 1939, three million women who had given birth to four or more children each were invested with the title of 'Mother of the Reich' in special ceremonies held all over Germany (Evans 2005, 517). One leading eugenicists, Fritz Lenz calculated that a woman should be able to bear 15 children during her active childbearing years (Evans 2005, 516). If a woman had ten children, the tenth had Adolph Hitler as a godfather and the child would be named 'Adolph' (Evans 2005, 517). As a corollary to the Nazis' conception of the "triumph of the will," women were discouraged from taking anesthesia during labor and delivery because it went against the notion of the will overcoming adversity and it would be unfitting for women to undergo the supreme experience of their existence with their consciousness dimmed (Grunberger, 227).

However, many of the measures developed to encourage and support women in pregnancy were ahead of their time. Burleigh reports that the Reich Mothers' Service organized classes for pregnant women, to educate in child care and domestic science. By 1939, these courses had been attended by over 1.7 million women and provided instruction concerning the dangers of smoking or excessive drinking during pregnancy and infant care (Burleigh and Wippermann, 250). More commentary about women in Nazi Germany is in Ramm's "Guidelines for…Indoctrination of Midwifes."

tions entrusted to him is to be adhered to not only during the life of the patient, but even after his death.[16]

How often the case occurs that sympathy or curiosity urges the physician to make statements pertaining to patients entrusted to him, which can lead to harm to the patient.

If however a sickness, behavior or genetic trait conceals in the individual danger to the Volk community, then there is a higher viewpoint which transcends the duty of silence, leading to the duty to report and thereby serve to protect the community. We are thinking here of giving notice to the health authorities of overwhelming sicknesses and the reporting of genetic illness for the purpose of sterilization. The publication of an unreported sickness is authorized if the physician is released from the duty of silence by the individual or if a secret entrusted to him relates to a crime or an assault against the well-being of the Volk.

The duty of the physician in this regard extends to his own family members. Especially he must hold those he employs, like clinic help, nurses, assistants and interns to secrecy, since they likewise are obligated, just like the physician, according to the regulations of the Reich Physicians' Ordinance (&13).

Further, the Professional Ordinance makes it an obligation of the physician to resist all efforts which have as their goal the weakening of the Volk community and thereby lead to a decline in the number of the Volk. There is an iron law of his code of honor that the German physician agrees to perform an *abortion* only if there is a danger to the life of the pregnant woman. It has been precisely decreed in which circumstances this measure is justified. Therefore let this be a warning to each physician that anyone who does not keep to this prescribed way will have his license revoked by the Reich Physicians' Leader, even if there are mitigating circumstances for the perpetrator. *Whoever weakens the Volk community through abortion of a fetus is to be placed on the same plane as a traitor to the country and Volk.*[17]

---

[16] In this paragraph, Ramm appears to demand that the physician keep the secrets revealed to him in the course of his professional activities. However, in the very next paragraph he demonstrates the bold exception the National Socialists made to this traditional professional obligation. **"If however the sickness, the behavior or the genetic trait conceals danger to the Volk community in the individual, then there is a higher viewpoint which transcends the duty of silence…"** This reveals the principle substance of the National Socialist philosophical viewpoint – the protection and encouragement of development of the genetic wealth of the Aryan Volk, and the corresponding responsibility to betray a secret if it threatens the health of the Volk. This rule can clearly be interpreted to mean that a physician was obligated to reveal to the authorities any sickness, behavior or genetic trait which was considered to be a genetic threat. He states that the purpose of the reporting was sterilization.

Kater reports that Hitler personally decided to suspend medical secrecy in January 1943, (Kater, *Doctors Under Hitler*, 39) although the principle had already been breached in March 1942 when Conti started the process to establish a "health file" on every German citizen.

[17] Ramm makes the National Socialists' viewpoint on abortion very clear. Performing an abortion was equivalent to being a traitor to the country and Volk. The basis for banning abortion and contraception was not moral but genetic-biological. Sterilization courts could rule that pregnancy could be interrupted for eugenic reasons in a "racial emergency," if the future child was likely to inherit certain defects or had mixed (Jewish and non-Jewish) parentage (R. J. Lifton, *The Nazi*

The physician, especially the young professional comrade, should not let himself through false empathy and consideration of the social position of the mother, family relationships or other grounds, be influenced when unreasonable requests of this kind are made.[18] Good advice, reasoning conviction, clarification of the preparedness to undertake some other measure between the affected and her family or her

---

Doctors: Medical Killing and the Psychology of Genocide (New York: Basic Books, 1986), 42). Abortions were prohibited for only Aryans, while the eugenically unfit, Arab or African Germans, Gypsies or Jews, could have abortions. Robert Proctor reports that if the woman made "a good racial impression," permission to have an abortion could be granted only by SS or police authority, but was generally denied (R. N. Proctor, *Racial Hygiene: Medicine Under the Nazis* (Cambridge: Harvard University Press, 1988), 123). Burleigh notes that this is why the Gestapo (state secret police) agency responsible for the repression of abortion and contraception coupled homosexuality and abortion, since both had deleterious effects on the birthrate (Burleigh 1991, 233). Courts imposed jail terms of 6–15 years on doctors found guilty of abortionist practices. In the year prior to the Nazi seizure of power (1932), 43,912 German women applied for abortion on medical grounds; 34,698 of these applications were approved. In the 5 years between 1935 and 1940, however, there were only 14,222 applications for abortion in all of Greater Germany, and only 9701 of these were approved (Proctor, 122). Not all historians believe that the Nazi politics resulted in fewer abortions, however. Richard Grunberger reports that before 1933 the annual average of abortions was estimated to be between 600,000 and 800,000, as against between a million and 1 ¼ million births per year: a ratio of almost two to three. For the Third Reich, in 1938, every eighth in 1 ½ million pregnancies was officially listed as a miscarriage. Considering that during the preceding 4 years there had been a 50% increase in prosecutions against abortionists (1934: 4539 and 1938: 6983), and positing a 1:100 ratio of detected and indicted abortions as against ones which had actually been committed, he inferred that the decline in abortions after 1933 was not so much absolute as relative to an increased total of pregnancies (Grunberger, 239).

In Auschwitz, SS doctors were supposed to perform an abortion on *fremdvoelkish* (alien) women found to be pregnant. Pregnancy in a Jewish woman meant the gas chamber, if an abortion was not carried out by a Jewish prisoner doctor (Lifton, 149). Indeed, it was considered to be heroic activity for a Jewish doctor to perform an abortion on a pregnant Jewish woman to save her from the gas chamber (Lifton, 225).

[18] Illegitimacy was wholly irrelevant to the Nazi view of childbirth (Grunberger, 246). If the infant was racially pure and healthy, it did not matter at all whether its parents were legally married. The prioritizing of breeding in this morally neutral way led Heinrich Himmler to develop a program whereby his elite SS soldiers were encouraged to breed a master race – the *Lebensborn* (Well of Life) program. He founded a series of maternity homes, which sported a white flag with a red dot in the middle, for racially approved unmarried mothers (Evans 2005, 521). One single woman wrote of the experience:

> At the Tegernsee hostel, I waited until the tenth day after the beginning of my period and was medically examined; then I slept with an SS man who had also to perform his duty with another girl. When pregnancy was diagnosed, I had the choice of returning home or going straight into a maternity home…The birth was not easy, but no good German woman would think of having artificial injections to deaden the pain. (In Grunberger, 247)

Himmler issued the following procreation order to his elite troops:

> Only he who leaves a child behind can die with equanimity…Beyond the bounds of perhaps otherwise necessary bourgeois law and usage, and outside the sphere of marriage, it will be the sublime task of German women and girls of good blood acting not frivolously but from a profound moral seriousness to become mothers to children of soldiers setting off to battle, of whom destiny alone knows if they will return or die for Germany. (In Grunberger, 247)

partner, are as a rule the means to change a presumed misfortune and what is at first an unresolvable appearing situation into a fortunate outcome. How many young girls and women have threatened to end their own life if the doctor does not help her in her situation! *Almost all of these presumed strokes of fate are resolved in marriage and birthday festivals if the physician understands how to point out to the involved mother and father about the naturalness of these occurrences, and to the father his duty to the child.*

In addition there are however also cases where the physician as comforter in the misfortune must step up and seek to strengthen in the young mother the courage to go on living, by explaining that an unmarried mother and an illegitimate child have a right to attention and validation by the Volk community.

There is a moral duty for every physician to strengthen the desire to have children and thereby guarantee the future of his Volk. As a logical consequence of this, it must be taken to be self-evident that he can not carry out or recommend, without an extreme degree of justification, any means which leads to contraception, and further that he is permitted to perform an abortion and sterilization only in a legally determined capacity.

Thus it is one of the most noble responsibilities of the physician to protect a germinating life and to carefully guard over it to see that it is not destroyed by unscrupulous people by criminal means; likewise, he must seek to make easier the life of the older and weaker people, even if they appear to have lost their mental capacities through the severity of illness, and take them carefully into his protection so as to alleviate their pain and suffering according to his best ability up until the entry of releasing death. One should never forget – every experienced physician can attest to the fact – that many sick people who have been given up for dead become healthy again and thereby contradict all the physicians' predictions.

The question frequently arises if it belongs to the ethical duty of the physician to give, through some intervention or means, release from incurable suffering.[19] It can

---

In contrast to Himmler's SS, there was a taboo placed on teaching sex education in regular school. The subject was declared to be outside the provenance of both school and the Hitler Youth. Fourteen-year old boys and girls leaving school were given a brochure offering this advice: 'Health is a precondition of external beauty – choose not a playmate but a comrade for marriage – wish for as many children as possible' (Grunberger, 289).

[19] There is a common misconception that the Nazis were in favor of euthanasia for the incurably ill. (G. Pence, *Classic Cases in Medical Ethics: Accounts of Cases That Have Shaped Medical Ethics, with Philosophical, Legal and Historical Backgrounds* (Boston: McGraw-Hill, 2000), 87). In modern debates on euthanasia, one frequently hears that one must not take the first step of euthanasia because one is then on the slippery slope leading to Nazi euthanasia practices (M. Burleigh, *Ethics and Extermination: Reflections on Nazi Genocide* (Cambridge: University Press, 1997), 142). But the distinction made by the National Socialists must be remembered. The euthanasia program which was supported and encouraged was for those "useless eaters" who were mostly in mental institutions. This program began in 1938 and was carried out against both children and adults incarcerated in asylums. The program came to be known as the "Aktion T-4" program, named after the address of the program in Berlin – Tiergartenstrasse 4. Burleigh reports that, according to an internal T-4 reckoning, up to 1 September 1941 70,273 persons had been 'disinfected' (gassed). Further statistics, which took into accounts persons killed by means other than gassing, indicated

be asserted in regards to this, that it is probably one of the most difficult responsibilities in the life of the physician to look after a person who is incurably ill, to contribute to him courage and hope out of the greater strength of his own soul, and in doing so, to know that he speaks against his own conviction and that the untruth which is spoken in almost all answers to the question of the sick person, "Will I ever be well again?" is only born out of a good will to help and a deep love of humanity.

On the basis of existing laws, the physician is not authorized to shorten a life, even if this would mean release from unending and unbearable torment in the end stages of a sickness.

The Problem of Euthanasia extends however to people afflicted with intellectual and physical genetic illnesses who can never develop normally and are always arrested at some low developmental level, especially in people in whom sick genetic traits produce later disintegration of their intellectual personality. This merely vegetative creature places a terrible burden on the Volk community to the extent that it drives down the living standards of the remaining family members, and requires a person to care for it during the remainder of its life.

If a person is burdened by a terrible agony from an incurable suffering or if the intellect disintegrates from continuing derangement, then doubtless on the grounds of humanity, euthanasia would be appropriate to consider. It is the responsibility of the medical profession to be the forerunner in this consideration, and the responsibility of the state to confer this on him as a force of law.[20]

Among the special, legally anchored professional duties required of the physician includes the obligation to report various events and sicknesses. Thus it is required to report verbally within a week to the Professional Office of a birth, if the legitimate father or the midwife who is present for the birth is unable to make a report. In the case of a still-born or a child dying at the time of birth, the physician is subject to the same duty, however with the instructions that the notification is to be made in a written form on the following workday. Furthermore, every miscarriage that occurs prior to the 32nd week of pregnancy, as well as premature births,

---

that 93,251 beds had been 'released' by the program (Burleigh 1991, 153). The program has been extensively covered in literature on the Holocaust. (R. Rubenstein and J. Roth, *Approaches to Auschwitz: The Holocaust and Its Legacy* (Atlanta: John Knox Press, 1987), 142–143); A. Frewer and C. Eickhoff *Euthanasie Und die Aktuelle Sterbehilfe-Debatte* (Frankfurt am Main: Campus Verlag, 2000); M. Burleigh, *Death and Deliverance: Euthanasia in Germany 1900–1945* (Cambridge: Cambridge University Press, 1994)

In the present context, Ramm is speaking of the genetically healthy person who has an incurable illness. The National Socialist policy, being built on the genetic principle, did not require euthanasia of these patients. This distinction is made clearer in the following paragraphs.

[20] Despite what was stated on the previous page, Ramm actually makes a statement in support of euthanasia for incurable illness and calls for the medical profession to urge that this be accepted by the Reich government. This statement illustrates that there continued to be contentions between the medical community and the government over certain aspects of medical practice.

On the 1st day of the beginning of the war, September 1, 1939, Hitler authorized Reichs Leader Bouhler and Dr. Brandt to "extend the responsibilities of physicians still to be named in such a manner that patients whose illness, according to the most critical application of human judgment, is incurable, can be granted release by euthanasia." There is no documentary evidence that this was ever undertaken by any German physicians other than those involved in the T-4 program.

must be reported in writing to the responsible Civil Service Physician. There will be a punishment if the notice is not made. Also the interruption of a pregnancy is to be reported to the Civil Service Physician within 3 days.

Furthermore there are required reports for certain contagious diseases which are to be completed on special forms. These will be made available gratis from the police or the Health Department. The reports can however also even be completed in free form. The statutory obligation to report is not just for the illness but also if there is just the suspicion of an illness. The period for reporting is within 24 h of acquiring the knowledge of an illness, for tuberculosis it is 8 days and another 24 h in case of a death from tuberculosis.

There is also an obligation to report occupational diseases and, to be precise, the report must be made either to the insurance carrier (trade association) or to the responsible occupational physician.

Additionally, established genetic illnesses of the sort covered by the sterilization law or extreme alcoholism carry an obligation for the physician to report in writing to the Leader of the responsible Health Department. An exception to the requirement to report is in women who have reached 45 years of age, since it has been observed that, as a rule, women of this age are no longer fertile. There is also a duty to report a suspicion of these diseases The State Health Department will take further appropriate steps depending on the completed form.

The fight against venereal disease falls not just to the Civil Service Physician, but rather a deciding role falls much more on each physician who either diagnoses or treats this disease. There is a duty for the physician to bring to notice each venereal illness that he himself has not treated or not treated completely, and especially to search for the infection source, which is a measure which proved itself on the occasion of the Olympiad in Berlin.[21, 22]

---

[21] This paragraph was added to the 1942 edition.

[22] Ramm reports that the public health officials searched out the infection source (sexual contacts) of each case of venereal disease during the Olympiad in Berlin. Burleigh reports that, during the Olympics, the Nazis corralled 600 Sinti and Roma (Gypies) in a closed camp at Marzahn (Burleigh 2000, 373). No doubt this action was for security as well as sanitary reasons. The 1936 Olympic Games in Berlin were a great propaganda victory for the Nazis. Visitors to Germany for the Olympics discovered a Reich that looked powerful, orderly, and content. As the American liberal periodical, *The Nation,* expressed it on August 1, 1936: "[One] sees no Jewish heads being chopped off, or even roundly cudgeled…The people smile, are polite and sing with gusto in beer gardens. Board and lodging are good, cheap, and abundant, and no one is swindled by grasping hotel and shop proprietors. Everything is terrifyingly clean and the visitor likes it all" (In Friedlaender 1997, 180).

Hitler had, in *Mein Kampf,* addressed problems unique to medicine, particularly the fight against venereal disease. He simplistically proposed to fight syphilis by putting an end to the "prostitution of love." The fight against venereal disease became for dermatologists a means to secure a special place in the pantheon of the German medical community. The dermatologists formed "German Society for the Fight Against Venereal Diseases" and considered the fight to be predominantly a fight for the ethos of the society. Bodo Spiethoff, the leader of the society wrote: "In the fight against venereal diseases, everybody should be guided by the idea that, in the words of our Fuehrer, Adolf Hitler, the fight against this plague is not only one task, but the main task of the nations" (Weyer, 139).

Finally, the physician should, on the grounds of the dictates of the Law for Care of Cripples, inform the state Health Department within a month, if he diagnoses a deformity or finds signs of a threatened deformity in a person under 18 years of age. After the report is completed, the Health Ministry undertakes the necessary measures to address the issues of healing, recovery and qualifications for employment of the juveniles threatened by the ailment.

It should also be mentioned that the physician is to take all possible precautionary measures against the establishment of an epidemic by collaborating with other physicians in the struggle against all diseases which are dangerous and overwhelming to the community, and by using all the means available to him to limit their spread. He must especially encourage the enlightenment of the population and, wherever he encounters resistance or rejection, he must convincingly justify the legal measures. Thus the introduction of Smallpox immunization is not just the responsibility of the Department or Vaccination physician, but even more so the responsibility of the freely practicing physician; recently, cooperation in the introduction of Diphtheria prophylaxis through active immunization has been declared to be an area of responsibility of each and every physician.

The continuing education of the physician is of the greatest importance in order for the progress of medical science to be unstoppable. He must use his wide education diligently and energetically if he wants to stand before his own conscience and the criticism of his fellowman. Ludolf Krehl, the great Heidelberger clinician, once said: "The best of all things is to teach oneself to feel the drive for progressively more training." A continuing education in one's own practice is entirely possible if one works through his cases scientifically under the diligent employment of the scientific literature. Each practitioner should receive one or more scientific periodicals for the purpose of deepening and enriching his knowledge; especially, he must take part in scientific lectures which are organized by the medical community. From time to time there is the opportunity to attend weekend courses organized by the Physicians' Chamber or the Physicians' District Union, and thereby complement his knowledge and ability. There are often opportunities to search out a clinic or a hospital where one can for several days or weeks fill in gaps in one's knowledge, under the leadership of the Civil Service Physician or Chief Physician. It must be emphasized in praise that the German physician has at all times avidly sought out continuing education, and only a few have refused this in all respects. This notwithstanding, the Reich Physicians' Leader made continuing education the duty of the physician, in order on the one hand, to raise *all* physicians to the height of medical science and art, and on the other, to make the opportunity for continuing education easier and, through the erection of the appropriate organizations, to create the financial circumstances so that it is possible for each physician to acquire this education. On the grounds of the regulations decreed by the Reich Physicians' Chamber, each physician (and Specialty physician!), as long as he is not over 60 years of age, must

Despite their efforts, venereal disease became epidemic. It is estimated that by the end of the war 23% of all young Germans were infected with venereal disease (Grunberger, 249).

undertake 3 weeks of continuing education every 5 years in a hospital designated for that purpose, where he is to be informed about progress in all areas of medical science and technology and where he can extend his knowledge through practice in the laboratory and observations at the bedside.

One would have assumed that it would have been necessary to include obligatory continuing education to meet the needs of the physician. The opposite has been the case. The desire by physicians for continuing education has increased in the last few years such that we have had to limit the number of participants in the courses at the academies which were constructed for continuing education and at those where participation is voluntary.[23] This has been, all in all, a very pleasant situation which is rounded off with the lively interest in the new German science of medicine, which comes out of the synthesis of the scientific and traditional conceptions of the science of medicine and tropical medicine, which itself is important for the colonial activities of our Volk.

The hospitals and clinics to which the obligatory continuing education is transferred are scattered throughout the Reich; each Region has one or more of these establishments. The Reich Physicians' Chamber has at its disposal special academies for continuing physician education in Berlin, Dresden, Hamburg and Vienna, of which Berlin and Vienna serve for general continuing education, Hamburg for colonial continuing education and Dresden for continuing education in the new German science of healing. To these should be added in the future an academy for occupational medicine and another one for continuing education in trauma medicine in the Ruhr district.

How much value the Reich Physicians' Leader lays on voluntary continuing education of physicians as the completion of the duty for continuing education can be gathered from the arrangement which the deputy of the Reich Physicians' Leader for the Fund Physicians' Union of Germany, Dr. Grote,[24] decreed in agreement with

---

[23] Ramm notes that the desire for continuing education was so great that the number of participants had to be limited. Kater provides evidence that this was far from the case. He quotes from a Professor Karl Eimer in *Deutsches Aerzteblatt* in 1937, who said that doctors should volunteer more cheerfully for the courses "to avoid the hardships of quota conscription" (In Kater, *Doctors Under Hitler,* 36). Ramm ascribes what he reports to be the interest in the courses to enthusiasm in "the new German science of medicine," which is the genetic-biological conception of medicine he has presented in depth. Ramm implies that the interest in the continuing education courses is due to a scientific interest of the physicians, but it is likely that much of the interest was due to the pressure put on physicians by the National Socialists as well as the rewards for participating in, and the punishments for not participating in, the National Socialist philosophical indoctrination.

[24] Heinrich Grote had been a functionary of the *Hartmannbund* who crossed over effortlessly to the Nazis after the *Machtuebergrabung.* (Kater, *Doctors Under Hitler,* 61). As director of the KVD he carried out the expulsion (*Gleichschaltung*) of Jewish physicians from fund practice in 1934 (Kater, *Doctors Under Hitler,* 187).

Grote was born in Hannover in 1888. He took his medical training in Marburg and Berlin at the *Kaiserliche Wilhelm-Akademie fuer das militaeraerztliche Bildungswesen* (Kaiser Wilhelm Academy for Military Medical Education). He was wounded and received the Iron Cross in World War I. He entered the NSDAP in 1933 and was a *Sturmfuehrer* of the SS, ultimately becoming deputy of the Reichsfuehrer for the KVD as *SS-Oberfuehrer.* He was the one predominantly responsible for the incorporation of the *Hartmannbund* into the KVD. In May 1945 he was shot by Soviet soldiers (Swoch, 220).

the earlier representative of the Reich Physicians' Leader for Physician Continued Education Program, and, presently deputy Reich Physicians' Leader, Dr. Blome, which thereafter, on taking effect on 1.1.1939, granted compensation for voluntary participation in continued education (additional continued studies).

It is assumed that the courses take place outside the place of residence of the physician, last at least 6 days, and that participation is confirmed in writing by the course Leader, in accordance with the regulations. Compensation is not granted for courses of shorter duration. An exception to this consists of the short courses of at least 2 days duration which are organized in the context of international continuing education for specialists.

Compensation for participation in additional continuing education in addition to compensation for participation in required continuing education is permitted for at most 21 days in the course of 5 calendar years. Compensation for participation in required continuing education, additional continuing education, and that for the teacher courses amounts to RM 12 per day from 1.1.1939 on for the unmarried, and RM 15 per day for the married physician. It is raised one RM for each child under 21 for whom the physician is responsible. A per diem rate will be paid also for each day of travel to and from the meeting.[25]

Thus the possibilities for exemplary continuing education are offered to the German physician, of which he is enabled to make valuable use for the welfare of his patients and in the interest of the promotion of the health of the Volk.

Just as the physician in the practice of his profession must give his greatest effort and must strive in each case of illness to achieve the best outcome in the simplest way, he should also do his duty in the *presentation of expert testimony*[26] *and witness*

---

[25] Physicians were granted financial compensation for participating in the continuing education courses. Twelve Reichmarks is a substantial sum, given that the average gross earning of a doctor in 1933 was 9000 marks (Evans 2005, 445–6).

[26] Physicians were required to give expert testimony in legal cases, especially regarding the genetic health of his patients.

It cannot be underestimated how damaging to the patient-physician relationship was the threat of a physician's giving expert testimony against a patient regarding his genetic fitness. Patients who were unable to prove their pure ancestral history were judged for their genetic health on the basis of their physiognomy, a method which is notoriously unreliable. Even the "experts" acknowledged the subjectivity of the science. As the bureaucrats for ethnicity struggled with mountains of red tape and conceptual confusions produced by the racial laws, they turned to "racial scientists" for help. Support for Racial Hygiene courses in universities increased dramatically. Proctor reports that by 1936 professorships in Racial Hygiene had been established at Berlin, Bonn, Frankfurt am Main, Giessen, Hamburg, Heidelberg, Jena, Koenigsberg, Munich, and Wuerzburg, and racial science was taught in the medical faculties of all other German universities (Proctor, 79).

The problem of finding more refined criteria for classification of the races was one of the instigating factors which drove Nazi physicians, like Joseph Mengele, to continuously try to refine the criteria, by providing what was considered to be pristine "material" for study at the Kaiser Wilhelm Institute of Anthropology and Human Heredity and Eugenics in Berlin-Dahlem. He took detailed measurements of skull and body and various characteristics of nose, lips, ears, hair, and eyes (Lifton, 357). Lifton reports that women were selected at Auschwitz who were considered to be ideal specimen material for the anatomy museum of the Strasbourg University. They were transported to the concentration camp at Natzweiler, near Strasbourg, which possessed its own gas

and at no time let himself be induced to display a so-called "attestation for a favor." The testimony of the physician must, when viewed from the standpoint outside of the physician, be subjectively true, which means that it is dictated from his best knowledge and conscience. Any other behavior of the physician reduces confidence in his credibility as an expert witness and in his testimony and brings him into conflict with the professional law and, in certain circumstances, also with the criminal law.

Through a decree of the Reich Physicians' Leader one is prohibited from handing out declarations about genetic health or statements concerning unfitness for military service to the person involved. Only the authorities (Civil Service Physician or Genetics Health Court) are authorized to demand from a physician this sort of testimony. Each requested testimony and expert report must be produced in an appropriate period of time in order to be able to serve the intended purpose. It should be made a firm principle of each physician to make a punctual submission so as not to come under suspicion of carelessness or non-punctuality.

In the *activity* of the physician as *expert witness or expert before the court*, unconditional clarity of thought and expression are required in order not to become entangled in an embarrassing play of question and answer from the judge, state's attorney and defense attorney. The standpoint recognized at once as correct on the grounds of objective perception and judgment must be maintained during the proceedings with firmness and decisiveness against all efforts to alter it to the favor or disfavor of the accused, whereby, in the course of the proceedings, when a new viewpoint is submitted, a change becomes warranted.

To the duties of the physician established by the Professional Ordinance belongs in addition to the *keeping and storing of x-rays,* also *the regulated management of his index card file of sick patients,*[27] into which must be carried all that is essential

---

chamber. The women were given a sham physical examination for reassurance, then gassed, and the corpses were immediately transported to the museum (Lifton, 285).

[27] Physicians were required to maintain an index card file covering the important relevant details of each particular patient. It was to serve for later "examination and discovery." Ramm does not state so, but one can assume that the index card file would be made available to the authorities, particularly the Hereditary Health Court. Ramm states that the files are not to be published, but this would not prevent them from being made available to the authorities. This would be consistent with the totalitarian nature of the society. Richard Evans includes the medical profession among those institutions which were a part of a wide net of surveillance, including the Gestapo, the SA and SS, Criminal Police, the prison service, the social services and employment offices, the Hitler Youth, the Block Wardens, tax offices, railway offices and post offices (Evans 2005, 118).

The Nazis were obsessive with their index card projects. Department II, Subsection 112 of the Gestapo's pet project was the compilation of a card index of Jews (*Judenkartei*), which was intended to identify every Jew living in the Reich. The project was even expanded to compile another card index of the most important Jews in foreign countries and their mutual connections (Friedlaender 1997, 199).

Burleigh reports that "rabid professional enthusiasts" compiled an enormous number of files from the population to be used to promote the new role of doctors as "political soldiers" of the Fuehrer. Children were encouraged to devise family trees, which were to be co-opted by the authorities to determine who in the families should be considered for sterilization (Burleigh 2000, 355).

about each individual's care and illness, in order to be able to serve as a basis for later examination and investigation. The records as well as the x-ray pictures are to be preserved carefully at least 5 years after the completion of the treatment. Regarding their publication, there is, according to regulations, a duty of silence to be respected by the physician.

That there are aberrations in many physicians who make their guiding principle not the professional ethos but rather the desire for recognition and the striving for money, is proven by the law for *Prohibition of Distant Treatment.*[28] We understand this practice to be the expression of advice and treatment on the grounds of information given in writing or over the telephone to the sick person or his family member without an examination of the sick person having occurred. With justification, the Professional Ordinance rejects this bad practice, which comes from an unrestrained decadent time in which neither personal nor professional honor, neither breeding nor custom were held high, and all traditional values – honor, reputation, steadfast attitude, tradition – were disregarded or completely given up in favor of a purely materialistic existence.

A *Compulsion to Treat* does not exist for the physician.[29] It would however contradict the physician's ethics in the sense of a healthy Volk, as well as the Professional

---

[28] By this comment, Ramm reveals that not all physicians abided by the idealistic National Socialist philosophical viewpoint of medicine. He blames the problematic behavior on habits developed before the National Socialists took power. Kater has reported that antiregime activity among physicians was "inversely related to National Socialist association" (Kater, *Doctors Under Hitler,* 74). By this, he means that the relatively high participation of physicians in National Socialist organizations (NSDAP, SS, SA) conforms with the relatively low resistance to the Nazis. He reports that the most committed group of politically motivated resistors was among the Marxists and that "Aryan" physicians who had a proved record of Marxist activity in republican times were dismissed from hospital, *Amtsarzt,* or other employment situations and were ostracized from fund practice (Kater, *Doctors Under Hitler,* 76). One celebrated resistance group, designated the "White Rose," began in 1942, when the outcome of the war was still in doubt. It included several medical students, including Hans and Sophie Scholl, Alexander Schmorell, Christoph Probst, and Willi Graf. They spread anti-Nazi leaflets and tarred university buildings with phrases and slogans calling for passive resistance against the regime (Johnson, 305). One of their publicly circulated leaflets stated:

> Every word that comes from Hitler's mouth is a lie. When he says peace, he means war, and when he blasphemously uses the name of the Almighty, he means the power of evil, the fallen angel, Satan. His mouth is the foul-smelling maw of Hell, and his might is at bottom accursed. True, we must conduct the struggle against the National Socialist terrorist state with rational means; but whoever today still doubts the reality, the existence of demonic powers, has failed by a wide margin to understand the metaphysical background of this war. Behind the concrete, the visible events, behind all objective, logical considerations, we find the irrational element; the struggle against the demon, against the servants of the anti-Christ...Has God not given you the strength, the will to fight? We *must* attack evil where it is strongest, and it is strongest in the power of Hitler. (In Sax, 473–4)

These students were arrested, tortured and decapitated (Rubenstein, 223–4).

[29] In the following paragraph Ramm reveals a problem in which there was apparent conflict between the medical community and the legal community. He reports that in some legal quarters the law which provides for the obligation of a physician to assist in emergencies had been inappropriately extended to non-emergency situations. Ramm maintains that the physician must be allowed to decide for himself to whom and when he allots his help. We see here a trace of the

Ordinance, if the physician refused to treat a sick person without valid grounds. It is well known that there exists for *every* Volk comrade a duty to assist in an emergency occurring in the Volk community; the penalty for refusal or neglect of this duty is located in the penal code at & 330c. The paragraph states:

> *Whoever in cases of misfortune or general danger or emergency does not give help, although this is considered to be his duty by popular opinion, especially whoever does not carry out demands by the police to render help, although he can satisfy the demand without raising a danger or without violation of another more important duty, will be punished by imprisonment up to two years or with a fine.*

With that, the moral duty to give help in the named instance has become *in general* a legal obligation whose violation will be punished. However, it surprised and

---

professional umbrage taken by the medical doctor in the case where the courts decided that the physician has an obligation to treat a patient on a family's demand when the case is not an emergency. Ramm presents quite a rigid defense and doesn't appear to allow for any negotiating room in the confrontation. He defends professional honor against what is taken to be action by the courts beyond their jurisdiction. He takes as his ultimate defense the position that, if the physician is forced to work beyond his physical and mental capacity, he might himself suffer a physical breakdown.

The resistance Ramm displays here is evidence against the defense given by defendants at Nuremberg, which was that they were "just following orders" (Annas, 174). Daniel Goldhagen has presented the greatest amount of evidence against the view that the perpetrators of the Holocaust were merely following orders (D. J. Goldhagen, *Hitler's Willing Executioners: Ordinary Germans and the Holocaust* (New York: Vintage Books, 1997), 381–384). Goldhagen's book has been criticized its own extremism, but he does provide an insight countering the claim of just following orders.

The conflict illustrated here by Ramm is further consistent with the notion that the character of Nazi rule was polycratic, a term suggested by Martin Broszart (M. Broszat, *The Hitler State* (New York: Longman, 1981)). By "polycracy" is meant a pluralism of forces and the existence of different and often competing power centers held loosely together by their subservience to the Fuehrer (Fischer, 311). This thesis has been most extensively developed by the functionalist school of historians, led by Hans Mommsen (H. Mommsen, *Von Weimar nach Auschwitz. Zur Geschichte Deutschlands in der Weltkriegsepoche* (Berlin: Ullstein Tb, 2001)) and Goetz Aly (G. Aly, P. Chroust and Pross, *Cleasning the Fatherland: Nazi Medicine and Racial Hygiene* (Baltimore: Johns Hopkins, 1994); G. Aly, *Endloesung: Voelkervershiebung und der Mord an den europaeischen Juden* (Frankfurt am Main: Fischer, 2005) and most recently underscored by Winfried Suess (W. Suess, *Der "Volkskoerper" im Krieg: Gesundheitspolitik, Gesundheitsverhaeltnisse und Krankenmord im nationalsozialistischen Deutschland, 1939–1945* Studien zur Zeitgeschichte, no. 65. (Munich: R. Oldenbourg, 2003)

Another interesting feature of this debate is that the Comprehensive National Socialist Philosophical Worldview did have a "Good Samaritan "law. Ramm is here arguing that this law did not *require* that a physician come to aid in anything other than an emergency. But, *importantly,* no one disagreed that the requirement did not apply when it came to rendering aid to one considered to be outside of the Volk, i.e. Jews and other *Minderwertigen* (those of lower valued to the Volk). This shows one of the strongest arguments against those historias who have argued that medicine went "mad" in National Socialism.

The importance of this topic cannot be overemphasized. The single greatest debate among the Nazi officials at the Wannsee Conference, which planned the "Special Treatment" of the Jews, was the interpretation and application of the Nuremberg laws which determined who was or who was not a Jew.

troubled the medical profession to a large degree that after the decrees of these legal paragraphs in 1935, several courts went over to using these regulations as designating special professional duties of the physician. According to our interpretation & 330c of the StGb is no prescription for the Professional obligation of the physician, because it does not permit a sick person or a family member to demand treatment or a visit to a sick person by a physician, so to say, under threat of punishment if the situation of the sick person is reported to be threatening. The physician, being the one responsible for his reputation and his place in the Volk community, is to be allowed to decide for himself to whom and when he allots his help. The fulfillment of the professional obligation of the physician is strenuously supervised by the medical professional courts. The regulation of & 330c StGb speaks about a duty for everyone to provide help. The professional duty of the physician is based on an entirely different level than that which is encompassed in this paragraph of the penal code.

It is just natural that each physician should determine for himself his own professional obligations in certain respects out of his own drive. One is not however to demand impossibly from the physician, like has been increasingly done in many cases where there is an exaggerated interpretation of this law. A physician is just a human with a limited stock of physical and psychic strength that is to be demanded especially in times of epidemic and war but only up to the limits of his capacity to achieve. There comes a time when the physician under excessive prolonged demands has exhausted his last reserve of strength and requires a period of rest for himself.

In our experience the physician does a disservice to himself if he, in a general emergency situation, works more than his reasonable duty; in our experience he brings sickness and fever to himself, rather than help to others. Each physician sees his noblest responsibility to be to stand by each individual Volk comrade and also the general community in times of sickness, danger and emergency. It can not however be determined from & 330c StGB that sickness of the individual represents a *general danger* or *general emergency.* One should also not take from this law that the concept of sickness applies when there has been some misfortune. The physician will in general only very rarely refuse a demanded treatment. A special instance of this is seen in a physician's own illness or when a conflict with another duty of higher value occurs simultaneously, for example, with the delivery of a baby, or performance of an operation, etc.

The specialist physician is justified to reject all cases not conclusively in his Specialty. In cases of emergency, however, when another physician is not available, he must deliver the first help. A further valid ground for rejection exists in the case of a serious transmissible disease, if the physician, by undertaking treatment, would endanger his own patients. The inability to pay can at no time be submitted as grounds to decline to give treatment.

All *advertisements and inducements* are forbidden for the physician. The *announcement of the starting up of a practice* is permitted to appear at most three times in the local daily newspaper, as similarly in the *resettlement of a practice*, the return from vacation or the resumption of a practice after a long sickness. The *physician's sign* is not allowed to exceed a certain size and is allowed to show only the information certified by the Professional Ordinance and as a rule – with the exception of corner houses and living quarters lying hidden, where a second sign is allowed – is only to be put up in one place. With the resettlement of practice, a sign pointing out the direction to the new residence is allowed to be put up on the earlier residence for a half year.

An important question which is frequently in the position to disturb the relationship of the physician to his patients regards *the honorarium* that is demanded for the physician's treatment.[30] The two scales of fees to be found in force – the Prussian and the general German scale of fees – designate relevant valuations for the individual physician services, which vary from one to tenfold. In general, the physician will charge by the relative valuations that have in the course of time been put out as being locally reasonable. The lowest valuation is appropriate for the sickness fund account, welfare office and the like. The higher and the highest valuations of the scale of fees will be calculated as a rule in the case where there has been special difficulty in rendering treatment and in very well-off patients. Exceeding the highest valuations is permitted only with the certification of the Reich Physicians' Chamber, or on grounds of a specially written arrangement between the two participating parties. The physician has always grasped the great social meaning regarding those entrusted to him each day, and thus today the pleasant custom of treating directly relatives and friends as well as professional comrades and family members who have meager resources or the inability to pay has been certified by the Professional Leader. In order to do no harm to his remaining professional comrades who have perhaps not done as well economically, he should adhere to the local valuations of all local physicians.

The physician should also get accustomed to present his *fee bill* either immediately at the completion of his treatment or at least every quarter year. In the circumstance where there is a desire to establish an individualized fee bill, then this request must be certified. Since today there are often times when the Volk comrades who don't belong to a Reich certified health insurance fund are insured by private health insurance schemes, there have come to be demands for control of the accounting of these private health insurance funds.[31] The physician can reveal the sickness, without infringing upon the physician's duty of silence, if he has the agreement of the

[30] Another major sore point of the physicians with the sickness funds during the Weimar period was the honorarium paid. Ramm goes into specific detail regarding the scales of honoraria and gives some indication of how the valuations are to be determined. As can be seen, the physicians did not receive a fixed rate honorarium, but the fee was influenced by both the locally standard valuation and the degree of difficulty encountered in rendering treatment.

[31] Ramm reveals another apparent problem in the medical community – the case in which people insured by private health insurance might present fraudulent claims. Ramm reports that this is another condition where the physician may legally reveal details of a patient's sickness.

Jewish doctors were prohibited from having contracts with private health insurance funds (Kater, *Doctors Under Hitler*, 186). When some brave Jewish doctors argued that these private funds were exempt from their prohibition to practice, they were lectured by judges who said that the KVD, which had made the determinations, was an instrument of the Nazi regime and therefore was beyond the law (Kater, *Doctors Under Hitler*, 194).

one being treated or there are no demands of absolute medical principles standing in the way of this.

In this connection, in order to protect the physician from harm, a warning which demands urgent attention should be given. As a rule the private health insurance reimburses only a certain percentage of the amount of the charge to the insurance (in most cases 80%). In order to get reimbursement from the insurance for that part of the amount of the charge that is considered to be the responsibility of the insured, the patient frequently puts a demand to the physician to give him a bill of a higher amount or to give to him a receipt indicating a higher amount of honorarium, so that he may be paid the full amount. The physician performs a punishable offence in both cases, and certainly in deceiving or aiding and abetting deception; likewise if he gives out a receipt to the patient for an insurance company although he has not yet received his honorarium.

Another occasion where the professional law is violated occurs in the case where the person who is compulsorily insured by the legal health insurance fund requests the physician to treat him not at the expense of the health insurance fund but rather at his own expense. In these cases it is advisable to demand a written confirmation from the applicant, since it frequently occurs that the person treated transfers to the physician later on as honorarium this private calculation from his sickness fund. The physician is absolutely entitled to expressly demand payment if no sickness fund receipt is handed over to him. As soon as the sickness receipt is given over to him the owner is regarded to be a sickness fund patient on whom the contracts between the Physicians' Fund Union of Germany and the sickness fund are fully applied. In the cases where the patient was allowed to use the physician as a non-sickness fund patient, or if after frequent demands no receipt is delivered, then the physician is authorized to demand payment for this elapsed period of time.

Finally, I would like to say something more to the circumstance in which the physician is obliged to take into account the economics and social circumstances (family with many children!) regarding the amount and also the punctuality of the payment of his honorarium.

The employment of hygiene lessons which have been conveyed to him at the university and during his hospital education belongs to the ideal which the physician must transmit to each Volk comrade in all areas of his life style and in the practice of his profession. I mean here that there is a duty that the *waiting* and the *examining* rooms of the physician are to be found in an ideally clean condition and likewise furnishings must always be clean and orderly. Defective parts of the furnishings and the instruments are to be converted back to flawless condition without delay. One should not miss the opportunity to renew the painting and wallpaper in these rooms after definite periods of time. The physician should never forget to regard and to practice as a holy duty *the law of asepsis and antisepsis* and be true to the fundamental principle of medical treatment: primun nil nocere!

The physician must – with few exceptions – see each Volk comrade who makes a demand for a physician's help as a valuable member of the Volk community, who has been entrusted to him because of his knowledge and ability.

Who turns to the physician for help?

There are Volk comrades who bring to him either physical sickness or psychological suffering, people who are powerless to help themselves in the struggle for life, in whom the worry arises that he will not be a match for the illness and that he will in the future have to abandon his family to need and misery. Thus the sick person puts his faith in the physician and ties up this hope with trust in the ability of the physician, that he will return his full health to him again.

The physician must justify this trust through his participation in the suffering of the other, through his love of Volk comrades and his willingness to help. We know, however, that once in a while the best intentions of the physician come to be shattered through the obstacles presented by the process of recovery, many times however also through disobedience and mistrust by the patient or from false advice by those around him. Just as much of his psychological power and employment of his ability must be used in the healing of patients in whom favorable circumstances have already occurred, so much more are stringent efforts needed when complications set in, which have their origin either from the sickness itself or in the environment of the patient! What willpower it demands to conceal from the patient the danger in which he hovers, and how much kindness and philanthropy belongs to that duty daily from morning to evening, to strengthen through cheering up and pacifying the psychological turmoil of the patient and inspiring his will to become well. And if the victory in the fight against death is denied, then he must possess enough psychological strength to not despair from the single case and be philosophical enough to be able to say to himself that often fate is stronger than human will.

After such saddening experiences, in order to win back the necessary attitude towards the profession, he must steer his thoughts to the cases where he has succeeded in showing the way of nature to healing, where he, through his art, was able to return to the family its breadwinner or its mother, or where, through his skillful care, he has rescued and defended the mother and child in a birth and thereby achieved a successful family outcome.

The *good trusting physician patient relationship* is an essential factor in the favorable influence of the healing process. It rests, as was already made clear, on the pure close and harmonious psychological relationship of the two together. The trust of the community in the German physician in the last decades before the National Socialist revolution was represented by many, rarely objective, critics as being disturbed or diminished, and the guilt for that was falsely shoved on to the physician; moreover it can be maintained that a certain circle of critics in their egotistical interests carried the catch phrase "Crisis of Medicine" to our Volk so as to enlarge the number of the gullible who then turned uncritically to quackery, charlatans, astrology and magic.

This occasionally occurring problem in the relationship has to do not with a "Crisis in Medicine," but rather with a *psychological crisis of the German people,* which was introduced as a consequence of the hard conditions of the Versailles Dictat and resulted in the unpleasant political and economic conditions in the time after the World War. There should be added to that the overvaluation of technology, which had its cause in the overspecialization of health science, and which led to a limitation of the psychological side of physician treatment.[32] But the manner of implementation of sickness insurance also contributed a good degree of culpability to the production of this unwanted circumstance.[33]

In addition to really bad and unworthy physician behavior in conducting fund activities, there was likewise the overburdening of the physician by paperwork from petty cases of simulated illness which led to the demand for treatment more from greed of the insured person than through real sickness. In the past there were frequent disturbing applications of influence by the social security authorities on the relationship of the patient to the physician which drove both sides to anger and annoyance and estranged them from one another.

The upheaval which was carried through by the National Socialist revolution has also created change in this area so that today it is only when there is asocial behavior of an individual who exploits the basis for social insurance and unnecessarily burdens pure medical activities that there is a destruction of the generally good relationship of the sick person to his physician.

---

[32] Ramm will have more to say against the "overvaluation" of technology in medicine. The sociologist, Jeffrey Herf, has argued that before and after the Nazi seizure of power, an important element within conservative and subsequent Nazi ideology reconciled with modern technology the anti-modernist, romantic, and irrationalist ideas present in German nationalism and the manifestations of "means-ends rationality." He refers to the result as "Reactionary modernism" (J. Herf, *Reactionary Modernism: Technology, culture and politics in Weimar and the Third Reich* (Cambridge: Cambridge University Press, 1984), 1). According to Herf, technology came to express the soul and culture of Germany. It was this efficient use of technology which produced the efficient killing machine which ran the trains to the gas chambers at Auschwitz (R. Hilberg, *The Destruction of the European Jews* (New York: Bantam Books, 1986)). Herf argues that the reactionary modernist tradition contributed to the technological strength that made the war conceivable, although not winnable (Herf, 216). In the end, they only had the adequate technology to eradicate the European Jews (L. Davidowicz, *The War Against the Jews: 1933–1945* (New York: Bantam Books, 1986)). A similar point is made by Christian Pross, who wrote: "What for us today appears to be the contradictory nature of Nazism in fact explains its success: the connection between destruction and modernization…The functionaries of the Nazi state were extraordinarily young, and they consciously relied on the results of scientific research. To cleanse the body of the Volk of everything sick, alien, and disturbing was one of the dreams of the German intelligentsia" (C. Pross, in Aly et. al. 1994, 14–15). Hans Mommsen has argued that the use of bureaucratic and technocratic methods repressed any moral inhibitions among the perpetrators, turning the death of Jews into a technical problem of killing capacity (Mommsen, 224–53).

[33] In this paragraph we come to see the source of Ramm's passion – "the Versailles Dictat." Virtually all sectors of the German society angrily denounced the Allied peace terms at the end of World War I and believed that the victors wanted to shackle Germany as a nation with chains for perpetuity. There came to be a sense of historic grievance of the world against the Volk, since, with the loss of many peripheral German speaking lands, 13% of the German population was now marooned beyond its borders. They saw ethnic Germans under the thumb of the French in Alsace-Lorraine and the Rhineland and the Polish in West Prussia and Silesia. This situation contributed to an emotional intensification of *voelkish* thinking. From the same mix came the belief that those who established the Republic and overthrew the Kaiser were part of the 'November criminals,' as they were designated (Burleigh 2000, 247–8). Jews came to be particularly associated with the conspiracy which led to the "stab-in-the-back" (*Dolchstoss*) theory of the Versailles treaty (Fischer, 42–3).

The lawyer considers the relationship between the physician to his patients to be a silent contract of service in which the physician is duty bound to deliver the demanded help and the other party is duty bound to pay the usual or agreed-upon reimbursement. Out of this contract there is derived the obligation of the physician to ascertain the characteristics of the illness and to put into effect that treatment which appears to him on the grounds of his medical science and experience to be the most promising, the least painful, and the quickest in healing. For emergency operations he must make sure of the agreement of the patient or his legal representative, except in those emergency cases in which there is life-threatening danger. There is a duty to inform if mutilation or other bad consequences are anticipated with an operation. In regards to this, the physician must take into consideration the psychological constitution of the patient in order to not aggravate his sufferings. Among the most difficult situations that a physician faces, which the experienced physician can resolve, is when he must arrange for a person with a serious illness to write down his will and testament because of the interests of the family.

While the physician is also obligated to explain to the patient about the necessity and possible consequences of an operation and make its performance in general dependent on his agreement, there are often many cases in which the patient is obligated to endure the intervention if he wants to run no danger of losing his social security to which he is otherwise entitled.[34]

In the relationship of the physician to his patients the *liability of the physician* and his assistant plays no small role. Most legal proceedings against physicians are not because of a violation of the duty to explain or because of professional secrets, but rather are carried out because of unsatisfactory therapy brought about by presumably incorrect diagnosis which led to damages to the patient.[35]

How often is it with the death of someone or with the lack of success of an operation that the guilt is attached to the doctor in order to prove a professional error on the part of the doctor out of which there comes a claim for damages! Damages can however only be claimed if it is proven that the physician is at fault on the grounds of faulty treatment or negligence in establishing the diagnosis or in the application of therapy. Culpability is established in cases where the physician causes an injury

---

[34] In this paragraph Ramm reveals the true nature of the "informed consent" of the National Socialist physician. The physician is obligated to explain the operation and make its performance "**in general dependent on his agreement**," but he can make it clear to the patient that he might lose social benefits if he does not agree to the operation. This is an unheard of form of professional coercion which reveals how the National Socialist philosophical view of the obligations of the individual to the whole became manifest. The physician is free, indeed forced, to use his professional skills to make it such that the patient is able to return to the work force.

[35] With the previous paragraph in mind, this paragraph rings even more ominously. It states simply that the physician may be liable to the patient for damages brought about by incorrect diagnosis and/or therapy. One can see, however, along with the fact that every act of the physician is being overseen by the professional authorities, the damages to the patient might be those considered important to these authorities, rather than just to the patient or his family. For example, if a worker is unable to return to the work force because of wrong treatment, the physician might face civil or even criminal penalties adjudicated by the state authorities.

through *intention* or *negligence*.[36] It is regarded to be intentional treatment if, for example, the physician makes a different or more operations than is agreed to by the patient. The physician acts negligently if he does not take notice of the results of medical research and practice in his diagnosis and therapy. In order to avoid this accusation the physician is obligated to progress professionally and to maintain his knowledge and technical capabilities at the height of medical science and to test himself in individual cases to see if his knowledge and abilities are sufficient for the successful establishment of diagnosis and treatment of sicknesses and, in case the answer is negative, to transfer this patient to a suitable physician.

Also the application of natural healing and Homeopathy – both recognized courses of treatment – makes it necessary in each individual case to determine if the natural healing or Homeopathy corresponds to the rules of medical science, so that it does not run the danger of becoming complicated by a case of liability with all of its troubles – the engagement of expert witnesses, the calling of knowledgeable opinions and worst of all, a court proceeding.[37]

Negligence can be assumed in the establishment of a diagnosis if the patient was not investigated with all due care and technical means, like the Roentgen apparatus and the microscope, or if the results of medical science and practice are not sufficiently taken into account.

In regards to therapy, the physician acts negligently if he does not employ recognized healing methods or use recognized means of healing, for example, Diptheria or Tetanus serum. He is not allowed to employ any therapeutic means that he himself has not mastered, for example, an operation if he has not had the necessary training. Also belonging to this situation is where the physician does not have at his disposal the means of healing (e.g. Radium) which is required for successful therapy and instead employs a less promising therapy.

It can only be left to each physician to be trusted to make the relevant Reich-legalized decisions that do not commit an offence against the accepted concept of law.

A further case of physician's liability can occur if the physician writes or draws up a prescription which is illegible or uninterpretable and the patient is thereby injured. The physician should take special care in prescribing powerfully effective medication or narcotics, because any infringement of the enacted legal instructions will lead him to commit a criminal offence and be liable for a extra duty of compensation.

---

[36] Ramm explains that physician culpability is derived from the proof of either a bad *intention* or *negligence*. With the state requirement of continuing education, a physician could be charged with negligence if he failed to use what was considered to be the latest medical approach.

[37] The practitioner is obligated to determine if "natural healing and homeopathy" corresponds to the rules of medical science. Since these two forms of medicine are, by definition, outside of the rules of medical science, it is obscure how one is to make this determination. The regular doctors were decreed to assist registered nature healers at the latter's request. Any quack who could demonstrate requisite ability was allowed to be considered to be a bona fide physician by adopting the title "physician of natural healing" (Kater, *Doctors Under Hitler,* 38). It would appear that this paragraph is put into the text more as a political statement, than as a substantive statement.

The use of injections and radiotherapy (x-ray, diathermy, ultraviolet ray) as therapeutic means often have injuries as a consequence which are unavoidable, however, inflammation, burning and the like are also frequently produced through inattention or defective technique.

Conscientious and careful treatment of each use gives the physician a unique opportunity to avoid professional error and to protect himself from great trouble and damages. Also, he is always to consider that careless and negligent actions damage his reputation as a physician and hands him over to the Professional Court of Justice which is responsible for punishing offences of the kind which are against the spirit of the high calling of the physician.

The physician must not forget to purchase for himself, his representative and his associates, personal liability insurance. It insures him from material loss or even from financial ruin in case he were to be actually liable for a professional offence.

Exceeding the regulated amount of insurance is expressly prohibited.

Licensure for Fund Practice and Physicians' Responsibility in Social Insurance

Social insurance is based on the idea of community help for individual members of certain occupational groups in times of sickness, premature infirmity and in old age. Before this was actually transferred to a large part of the workers community, there were already health insurance funds for miners during sickness and in old age, and there were guild health insurance funds which served the same purpose in the trades. Today's social insurance covers, in addition to body organs which have been insured against sickness, also accidents and their consequences. There is other insurance which insures in the case of infirmity and for old age.

In *Sickness Insurance* we distinguish Reich legalized and compulsory sickness funds which include general local sickness funds, territorial sickness funds, industry sickness funds, trade or craft sickness funds, Reich miners insurance and merchant marine funds. The circle of insured will in general determine the description chosen. The *general local sickness funds* cover a particular area. The *Rural Sickness Fund* is designated the insurance carrier in the rural economy, in the itinerant trade and occasionally also the domestic economy. This could be constructed in concert with the general health insurance fund. The *Industrial Sickness Fund* encompasses the obligatory insurance of one or more particular occupations and the *Trade Sickness Fund* covers that of one or more trades or crafts.

In addition there are *private health insurance funds* that have been carried forward out of the earlier insurance associations. There are private health insurance funds for salaried employees and such for workers. The private health insurance of the worker is subordinate, like the obligatory sickness fund, to the supervision of the Insurance Office of its district; the salaried employee private sickness fund is subordinate to the Reich Insurance Institution for salaried employees. The carriers of sickness insurance are Reich associations which are recognized according to public law to be a corporation. The circle of insured comes from those workers and employees covered by obligatory insurance. The limit of the insurance will be determined by the income. In addition to the obligatorily insured members of the sickness fund there are also those who are voluntarily self-insured. Fundamentally, assistance during illness also extends to non-self-sufficient family members.

On the grounds of the laws covering the construction of social insurance of 3.7.1934, there must be a physician appointed to the advisory committee which serves as an advisory organ to the leader of individual insurance funds. The responsibility of these advisory members is not to represent the circumstances of the physician in his special relationship to social insurance, but rather to be adviser for the protection of the general health interests of the insured. Through these measures the influence of the medical profession on social insurance is strengthened; at the same time, a part of the requirements for the introduction of social insurance is thereby carried out.

The *function of insurance* of the sickness funds consists in help during an illness, which is understood to mean nursing, medical treatment with the provision of medications and means of healing, as well as the granting of sickness benefits. To exclude trifling cases, sickness benefit is granted by the obligatory health funds only after 4 days of inability to work. *Sickness benefits* end as a rule at the end of 26 weeks after the beginning of the illness. Arrangements have been made during the war for this period to be extended. After completion of the course of sickness benefits, the insured is considered to have ended his entitlement to help; he must from then on trust his fate to the general welfare. The ending of the entitlement does not occur if the insured has not been required to make claims for either physician's help or medications. Also, knowing this, it is absolutely understandable if the insured utilizes preventive medicine to prevent the discontinuation of the entitlement. The war has also brought new regulations which favor the insured.[38]

Further belonging to the functions of insurance include help during lying in, support for breast feeding for married insured, death benefit at the death of an insured person, and family help, which is introduced after a certain duration of being insured and will be granted in general for 13 weeks.

The medical benefit for sickness funds and their entitled family members is provided in normal times only by those physicians who have been expressly licensed to practice in fund practice by the licensing committee established by the Territorial Divisions of the KVD. During the course of the war fund practice is also carried out by a helping fund physician who has been designated to represent the fund physician who has been summoned to military service. The provision of physicians for the insured is no longer to be guaranteed through contract with the individual physi-

[38] If a person is sick and unable to work beyond 26 weeks, then his/her fate is left to the public welfare. The National Socialist welfare system was "to promote the 'living, healthy forces of the German people'". Assistance was not to be extended to alcoholics, tramps, homosexuals, prostitutes, the "work-shy" or the "asocial," habitual criminals, the hereditarily ill and members of races other than the Aryan. For those for whom the program applied, it was quite supportive. Evans reports that by 1939, it was running 8000 day-nurseries and was providing holiday homes for mothers, and extra food for large families (Evans 2005, 491).

cian but rather through contracts between the Fund Physicians' Union of Germany as the representative of the medical profession and the Reich associations of sickness funds.

The practicing of an activity in the sickness fund is – except for emergencies – dependent on the *licensure of the physician for sickness fund practice.* Limited licensure in a specific kind of fund is discontinued; today there is only licensure for the entire fund, which consists of the obligatory and private funds, as well as the general welfare association. Exclusion from one practice fund ends one's licensure to practice in all the sickness funds. As a rule, the number of insured members in a sickness fund will be allowed to be 600 for one doctor, whereby fundamentally the ratio between the primary physician to the specialist should be from 6 to 4. To practice in fund practice is no longer left to the discretion of the individual physician but rather is subject to the planning of the KVD. In earlier times there was licensure for partial practice in the private fund, which led to relaxed conditions and ensured a minimal existence for the young physician who was dependent on the income from his private patients. Then if a fund doctor position in the obligatory insurance fund became vacant this not yet licensed physician could be transferred in to that position. Licensure to engage in sickness fund activities must precede entrance into the physician registry that is administered by the district or the Territorial District of the KVD. The applicant is allowed to apply to at most two physician registries at the same time in whose appropriate field he can apply for a fund practice. The *licensed* physician can be permitted to enter into only *one* additional fund practice. The licensure committee established by the KVD in each Territorial District adjudicates the licensure of each applicant. Up to the time of the war, presumption of licensure consisted of an at least 2 year long preparation in fund practice after successful appointment, of which there had to be proven at least a quarter year as an assistant or substitute for a fund physician who predominantly emphasized rural practice. Further, the applicant must have taken part in an introductory course on fund practice. There is preferred licensure for those candidates who have performed special service in the Main Office for Volks' Health and those who have performed war service or work service, as well as those who have suffered serious war injuries or otherwise have taken part in the war, additionally, married physicians, and among these, those who have a large number of children. It is further anticipated that physicians who have served at least 5 years as a rural physician or in a small city will receive preferential licensure for the appointment for places with better educational opportunities for their children and where they want to overtake a parent's fund practice.[39] It is possible for the Reich Licensure Committee to overrule the Licensure Committee. Members of the Reich Licensure Committee are named by the Leader of the German Fund Physicians' Union; there is also a committee member, named by the Reich Workers Minister, who must have the qualifications for the office of

[39] Ramm lists situations whereby a physician receives preferential treatment for fund practice. The control of fund practice was an important means of controlling doctors and their movements. Other workers were forbidden to move without permission of the local labor exchange (Schoenbaum, 92). Presumably the same held for physicians.

judge. The Reich Licensure Committee adjudicates appeals against the ruling of the Licensure Committee; it makes the ultimate decision if the appeal or a revision to the Reich arbitration office is not entered by the representative of the Reich Workers Ministry within a specific time. The appeal leads to a postponement of the application of the initial judgment. Licensure for fund practice covers specialty areas (whether general or Specialty practice) as well as the place or subdivision to which the licensure has been authorized. In case the license is granted, the licensed physician must within 2 weeks deliver to the Department Leader of the District Department of the KVD his written declaration if he chooses to not accept the licensure. The declaration is irrevocable.

There exists for the insured *free choice of physician*[40] so that the fund physician is committed to advise and treat each fund-insured patient in his office hours. Home visits can be refused if the home of the sick person lies outside of the practice district. Inside of 2 km, the visit of a fund physician is likewise free. For a distance of over 2 km the insured is obliged to change to the closest living fund physician if he is not prepared to declare that he will himself bear the extra expense for the greater distance of the physician to visit.

Here it should be emphasized once again that each fund physician is obligated to undertake the treatment of each insured who comes to him for help. *Refusal* of treatment may be allowed by a fund physician only in the situation of treatment at home in the above mentioned circumstances, if in *non pressing* cases the health insurance certificate is not presented as proof of membership in the sickness fund and is not to be supplied later, and if some treatment is not or no longer necessary.

But also in individual cases, there must be allowed the right of refusal for the fund physician if some more important reason lays before him and the medical care of the patient is not endangered. Certainly there is for the fund physician less latitude to refuse than with the treatment of private patients, where merely the duty of emergency help and the conception of professionalization determines the latitude. In overtaking the treatment of a fund patient there exists for the physician the same obligation and the same personal responsibilities as that in regards to private patients. By entering into treatment the insured is obligated to supply to the physician the required certificate of health insurance. A physician is obligated to treat the patient who does not present a health insurance card only in extreme circumstances. The physician must work industriously towards complete economy in the treatment of the insured. In particular he is obligated to proceed thoroughly and conscientiously when *establishing the inability* to work. He must treat the patient sufficiently and appropriately and thereby not exceed the measure of bare essentials. Above all, if he has a treatment that is not or no longer necessary, he must refuse to give it, he must order the means of treatment economically and completely, especially medications, as well as healing and strengthening measures, so as to protect responsibly the fund as a social institution, as long as it is possible to bring no harm to the insured.

[40] The "free choice of physician" was another major problem physicians had with the funds during the Weimar period.

Reimbursement for proven avoidable violations can be demanded by the fund. Likewise, the fund physician is duty bound to report if he has exceeded *regulations* regarding the ordering of medications. Under the concept of *regulations* is understood the amount that is the average cost of a prescription of medications and remedies, in which one is generally to take care not to exceed by prescribing economic medications and remedies. The regulated charge is universally established for the Reich, but certainly there are differences for general practitioners and representatives of the individual specialties. For the general practitioner, it amounts to RM 4.50. The lowest regulation charge is for the specialist of diseases of the eyes who is allowed RM 2.[41]

In general it is possible for the physician to make ends meet with the relevant rates of the regulated charge. In specially difficult and well grounded cases the regulated charge can be exceeded with the certification of the KVD and sickness fund. *If the physician can finally free himself from the bad habit of just prescribing artificially produced specialties and further turn back to the good old habit of formulating his own medications, whereby one prescribes a sensible skillful prescription,* then, on the grounds of current experience, the belief of the patient in doctoring would at once be greatly strengthened to a great extent, and at the same time, the physician would rarely exceed the regulation charge. If one undertakes an examination of the prescribing of physicians who are in the habit of very often exceeding the regulated charge, then it can be established that ignorance about the price of medications or otherwise ignorance of the individual special preparations and those similar which could be ordered instead, are the causes for most occurrences of exceeding the regulated charge.

As previously mentioned, there is a direct legal relationship between the KVD and the sickness funds. The individual fund physician is, as a member of the *German Fund Physicians' Union,* solely responsible for his work. Complaints and grievances against the behavior of a fund physician are to be directed to the responsible department of the KVD.

Payment for medical activities will be given in a whole lump sum paid from the sickness fund and transferred centrally to the KVD. According to a distribution list certified by the Reich Leader of the KVD,[42] the distribution of the fund honorarium is administered through the responsible clearing house after the withdrawal of administrative costs and a contribution to the Family Burden Compensation Fund.

Non fund physicians who have treated sickness fund members in pressing emergencies will be reimbursed by the responsible clearing house of the KVD, according

---

[41] The National Socialists strictly controlled the charge for medications. Ramm recommends that the physician formulate his own medications in order to keep the cost down.

[42] Payment for medical activities was paid in a lump sum and transferred to the KVD. The Reich Leader of the KVD had a considerable amount of power and control over these funds. Evans reports that, due to the removal of so many Jewish doctors, the economic recovery and people's willingness to contribute to health insurance funds, doctors' pay increased sharply after 1937. The average gross earnings rose from just over 9000 Reichmarks in 1933 to nearly 14,000 4 years later and by 1939 it was in the region of 20,000 (Evans 2006, 445–6).

to the lowest certified rate of the Prussian reimbursement. Payment to the patient himself is permissible only in those cases where membership in a sickness fund cannot be established.

Consultation and support of the sickness fund in the ascertainment and establishment of the presumption of a duty to work and the area of work, especially in determining the ability to work and the prescription of the nature of performance of the insured, is furnished by the *Advisory Examining Physicians Service*. The regulation of this service is a general responsibility of the Sickness Insurance Department of the Territorial Insurance Institution.

The *Advisory Examining Physician* is an official employee of the Land Insurance Institution and has thereby no relationship to any individual sickness fund. The Advisory Examining Physician operates in harmony with the Reich Leader of the KVD. His responsibilities consist in performing a follow-up examination regarding the inability to work, examination of applicants on admission to a hospital or a medical institution, further in the supervision of the course of treatment in the hospital and medical institution, then in the examination of applicants for allied health positions, and finally to participate in the promotion of Volks' health in the areas of tuberculosis and the fight against sexually transmitted diseases.

The Advisory Examining Physician[43] is directed to provide, for these purposes, written or oral information to the treating physician and to plan, in the presence of the treating physician, an examination of patients in the hospital or medical institution. The Advisory Examining Physician must however conscientiously pay attention that the authority of the treating physician is not thereby adversely influenced, and that he does not distract from the main business of service of the hospital. In case of an objection by the attending physician against the expert report of the Advisory Examining Physician, one must turn to a superior-expert-opinion by a Specialty physician named for this purpose or to consultation from the Territorial Advisory Examining Physician with the Department Leader of the responsible department of the KVD or its representative.

With a commercial private health insurance firm each industrial physician produces his bill according to the rules of the general German order of reimbursement and submits it through the responsible department of the KVD. In general these apply to the same or similar regulations of the KVD.

The KVD also stands with the Reich Student Work Service, the Reich Workers Service and the Welfare Union in a similar contractual relationship as with the sickness fund. The fund physician is obligated to recognize the regulations of these contracts as being binding.

The regulation states that all sickness fund patients, during the same case of sickness, if they expect to ask for further treatment afterwards from the sickness fund, are allowed to change their physician only with the agreement of or on the wish of the treating physician. The transfer of a patient by the treating physician to a fund Specialty physician is permissible without collaboration of the sickness fund.

[43] Another level of oversight over the practicing physician was provided by this official physician.

The medical benefit for the Reich Miners Guild was as a rule formerly carried out by the parish physicians, between which there was free choice of physician for the Miners Guild members within a designated area. There were aspirations to set aside the parish system in the interest of unification of the physician system so as to help achieve the breakthrough of free choice for every individual.

Right at the beginning of the war there was decreed from the Reich Leader of the KVD to the Reich Miners Guild that the medical benefit for insured miners and their family was to be strictly established by the KVD.[44]

In *accident insurance* the medical benefit is secured by contracts with the Reich Leader of the KVD. As a rule, in the case of an accident, one can claim help from the sickness fund for the first 13 weeks. The professional/trade association, nevertheless, has the right at the time, from the day of the accident or even later, to take over to itself the process of treatment. In these cases it has the legal right to insist to be allowed to decide on choice of physician and means of treatment. The so-called "*Transitional Physician System*" is in the service of this right. This system has at no time met with the approval of the German medical community; it is in need of amendments in the interest of individual physicians in the treatment of accident cases. It is important for the treating physician to know that, on the demand of a professional comrade association, a special notice of an accident with the appropriate information is to be immediately reported and is to be regularly supplied in the future. The reimbursement of the treating physician takes place through the professional comrade association itself; it has to occur only where this association has been granted a contract for treatment.

The *supply of medical care for the war disabled* is to take place on the basis of a contract with the responsible authorities according to the reimbursement rates of the medical Reich tariff for the maintenance of such provisioning. Recently this special regulation was raised for the war disabled. They have now become obligatory members of the sickness funds; also family help is provided.

Just as the physician is bound to provide non-political expert testimony according to his best knowledge and conscience, there is likewise the same duty for testimony and witness for oral testimony for social security. Each physician must act according to the rule that each expert opinion and testimony is reported from an objective viewpoint, whereby all people involved are best served. Also, certification of the inability to work, invalidization, the inability to work professionally, or reduction in the ability to work because of accident, must be planned with great care and conscientiousness.[45] A too favorable judgment by the pre-expert examiner makes the expert unhappy and brings the correct thinking post-expert examination under suspicion of having a too strenuous or even unsocial position. It is to be emphasized

[44] This paragraph was added to the 1942 edition.

[45] The determination of inability to work was a very serious matter, involving a pre-expert examiner, an expert examiner and a post-expert examiner. If a physician gave testimony which could be judged to be "against his better judgment," he could be held civilly liable, could be imprisoned and lose his civil rights. It is unknown how often this punishment was actually carried out but the threat would have been taken very seriously.

that each advantage which falls to one without justification redounds to the disadvantage of all.

Negligence in the delivery of medical testimony and expert opinions can occasionally lead the physician to civil liabilities and make him obligated to pay damages. Testimony *against his better judgment* has the punishment according to & 278 of the penal code of the following, which says, "A physician or other licensed medical personnel who gives out incorrect testimony against his better judgment about the health situation of a person to be used by an authority or insurance company, will be confined in prison from a month up to two years." In addition to that he is to be recognized to have lost his civil rights.[46] One can also expect the introduction of a proceeding before the professional court.

The Physician as Caretaker of Race and Preserver of the Volk Population[47]

Even though the ultimate responsibility of the physician goes to the healing of patients and the perpetuation of life, this responsibility has experienced an essential expansion through coming to grips with biological thinking in the National Socialist state. For our Volk there existed the same danger of decline that led to the present death of the older volkish cultures. Extensive mixing with other mostly minority races, shocking decline in the birthrate, above all among the high class of the Volk, and an unrestrained increase in the lower classes of our population were the alarming signs of the beginning of degeneration and with that, racial collapse.

The causes were to be found in the inattention to natural law which progressively achieved its dominance through church dogma and through extension of the material ideology of liberalism and Marxism. The great advances in the area of biological knowledge were well regarded scientifically and favorably admired by the educated laity; however the practical application necessary for maintenance and promotion of race and genetics of the Volk was hindered by the leading political parties of the time.

[46]To "lose civil rights" in Nazi Germany meant that you would be confined in a concentration camp. This has been referred to as "government by concentration camp."

[47]This section goes to the very heart of the National Socialist philosophical viewpoint for the physician. As has been mentioned previously, the National Socialist state was essentially a racial state constructed with the central focus on Racial Hygiene. The first paragraph is a succinct review of the founding justification for the National Socialist medical National Socialist philosophical viewpoint. The National Socialists believed that they were responding to natural law in fighting against the "liberal-Marxist" non-biological political policies which had caused a decline, and almost collapse, of the higher creating race, the Aryan Volk. In this context, the National Socialist physician had a moral duty to reassert the application of this natural law and reestablish these Volk into their rightful place as the foundation of the culture. This process was known as "Bevolkerungspolitiks." (R. Mackensen *Bevolkerungslehre und Bevolkerungspolitik im "Dritten Reich"* (Leske + Budrich: Opladen 2004).

A fundamental turnaround in the interpretation and employment of biological research results occurred directly after the victory of the National Socialist revolution. The law for the reestablishment of professional authority and the law for the re-establishment of German blood and German honor (*Law for Defense of the Blood* or *Nuremberg laws*), as well as the Law for Prevention of Genetically Ill Offspring (*Sterilization law*), the Law Against Dangerous Habitual Criminals and the Law for the Defense of the Genetic Health of the German Volk (*Genetic Health Law*) were energetically pursued and are the milestones on the way towards re-winning racial unity and the promoting of the genetic health of the German people.[48] Of these laws, the first two especially work against the influence which the Jews had won in the state and in the body politic. The Law for the Re-establishment of Professional Authority had as its goal, in addition to other responsibilities, the exclusion of Jews and Jewish mixed races from the state, and other public places and out of the leading professions. As one of the most important professions in the life of our Volk, there came to be the purging of medical authority according to the same distinctions followed in the other professions. The Law for the Protection of Blood prohibits for all time a further mixing of pure-blooded German people with the Jewish lower races and with the Jewish mixed races of the First grade.

The three remaining laws serve to improve the health and higher development of the genotype of our Volk through extermination and selection.

The Sterilization Law and *the Law Against Dangerous Habitual Criminals* preclude a certain circle of genetically ill and morally inferior people from transmitting their genes to future generations.[49]

The *Marriage Health Law* serves on the one hand to prohibit the coupling of sick, inferior or endangered genes to superior ones, and on the other hand, promotes the correct choice of spouse for the German people through marriage counselling and genetic-biological principles.[50]

---

[48] Hitler announced the Nuremberg Race Laws in a public speech on September 15, 1935, at the climax of the annual Reich party rally in Nuremberg. The legislation defined who was a Jew right down to one of the four grandparents, but only full Jews, those persons identified as having four Jewish grandparents, were immediately affected. They lost their citizenships and were classified merely as "residents" of German (Kater, *Doctors Under Hitler*, 192–3). Many in the medical profession had demanded the passage of such a law "to prevent all further Jewish racial poisoning and contamination of German blood" (Mueller, 96).

A "full Jew" was one who had three Jewish grandparents. Those who had smaller fractions of Jewishness were labeled as *Mischlinge* or half-breeds, divided into half-breeds first degree (two Jewish grandparents) and second degree (one Jewish grandparent). Those who were classified as half-breed first degree could still be considered full Jews if they (1) belonged to a Jewish religious community, (2) were married to a Jew, (3) were offspring of marriages contracted with Jews after June 15, 1935, or (4) were born out of wedlock to Jews (Fischer, 386). Such criteria produced a bureaucratic nightmare because it involved scores of "family researchers" hunting down uncertain records which would mean life or death.

[49] This law was passed on July 14, 1933. It provided for mandatory sterilization in cases of genetic disorders. More about this law will be presented later in Ramm.

[50] Following the establishment of this law in October, 1935, the right to marry became conditional upon receipt of a certificate of 'fitness to marry' issued by the local health authorities. Marriage

All of these laws, most of which were decreed on the initiative of the Reich Physicians' Leader, serve to improve our Volk.

The laws, aimed at forcing back and excluding Jewdom[51] have found great resonance, and partial imitation in many European states, especially in those, like Germany, which were brought to the brink of the abyss by the Jew. The radical resolution of the Jewish question becomes in this way a European problem; the faster and the more fundamentally it is carried out, the earlier and better will the development of the European continent attain racial principles, leading to a successful future for its Volk.[52]

In the implementation of the Law for the Prevention of Genetically Ill Offspring and the Marriage Health Law, the physician is to take part authoritatively and determinedly. He has become through this law the responsible bearer of the future of his Volk because the genetic health of the coming generation depends on his conscientious application of this law.

The Law for the Prevention of Genetically Ill Offspring was placed in force on 1.1.1934. It provided for the sterilization of the bearers of certain genetic sicknesses, but only after prior Hereditary Health Court proceedings.

The genetic sicknesses which fall under this law are:

1. Those born mentally deficient.
2. Schizophrenia
3. Manic-Depressive Illness

---

loans, tax rebates, and family allowances thus became conditional upon racial criteria. If you were of the right racial makeup you could receive substantial benefits. Newlyweds initially received loans of up to 1000 marks and the birth of each of the first four children converted one-quarter of that loan into an outright gift. The loan – minus deductions resulting from births – was repayable at 3% per month if both parents went to work, and at 1% if only the father did so (Grunberger, 235).

Burleigh reports that it could be dangerous to apply for these benefits. "In 1934 a couple who applied for a marriage loan found that the racial examination resulted in a recommendation that the wife be sterilized for 'feeble-mindedness'. She had apparently had to resit two classes at school" (Burleigh 1991, 252). A new Marriage Law in 1938 made it possible for a fertile husband or wife to file for divorce on grounds of 'premature infertility' or the refusal of the other partner to procreate. By 1941, 3838 divorces had been granted for premature infertility and 1771 because of refusal to procreate (Evans 2005, 520).

[51] *Judentum* – a word of the *"LTI."* V. Klemperer, The Language of the Third Reich: LTI – Lingua Tertii Imperii. A Philologist's Notebook (London: Athlone Press, 1975). Ramm declares that the laws against Jews found great resonance in other European states. He does not give any examples, but it is well known that Germany was not the only European country with a strong anti-Semitic history (Evans 2004, 186). Goldhagen reports that "The medieval European hatred of Jews was so intense and so divorced from reality that all calamites in society could be and were attributed to the Jews' Malfeasance" (Goldhagen, 53).

[52] In view of the fact that, as noted above, it was widely known that the Jews of Germany were being forcefully transported "to the east," and the meaning of the term, *Sonderbehandlung,* "special treatment," was also well known, this sentence seems to implicate Ramm (and possibly the entire medical community) in the medical Holocaust. There is hardly any room for doubt about the meaning of the sentence, **"The radical resolution of the Jewish question becomes in this way a European problem."** He goes even further in implicating the European continent in the responsibility to resolve the "Jewish question."

4. Hereditary Falling Sickness
5. Hereditary Vitus Dance (Huntington's Chorea)
6. Hereditary Blindness
7. Hereditary Deafness
8. Extreme Hereditary physical deformity

Further, one who suffers from extreme alcoholism can be sterilized.[53]

In each case an application is necessary in order to bring the process before a Hereditary Health Court. So that voluntariness is given ample room in the implementation of the law, an application can be placed at first by those with soundness of mind who fall under one of the designations of this law.[54] In cases of incompetence or incapacity from feeble-mindedness or before the completion of 18 years of age, the legal representative can, with the certification of the guardian, submit the application. The written confirmation of a German physician that it was made clear to the genetically sick and the applicant about the essence and consequence of sterilization is to be included with these voluntary applications.[55] The cancellation of this application is possible at any time without cause.

Additionally, the application for sterilization can also be placed by the Civil Service Physician as well for the inmates of State Hospitals and Nursing Homes. Family members of a patient are not authorized to make a direct application. They must follow the course through the official physician or the institution leader. But also each licensed physician who in his professional activities knows of a person who suffers from genetic illness or severe alcoholism has *the duty* to report of this to the responsible Civil Service Physician. The name of the reporting physician will be kept secret. Furthermore, everyone who is concerned with the treatment, investigation and advice to the sick individual is under the same sort of strict obligation. Disregard of this notification is punishable.

---

[53] Ramm lists the diseases which warrant sterilization. Note that extreme alcoholism is included among the genetic illnesses. Grunberger reports that throughout the 1930s there was an overall disparate increase in alcohol consumption. The death rate from alcoholism in Germany was five times as high as in England. Estimates put the number of habitual drunkards in the country at 300,000 (Grunberger, 228). A common local saying was "water is for horses" (Renderle, 35). There were old people in villages who hardly knew the taste of water. During National Socialism, beer consumption rose by a third, wine consumption by a half. Grunberger reports that the wartime situation was characterized by the gradual adulteration of beer – nicknamed 'bladder irrigation a la Conti [the Reich Health Leader] (Grunberger, 208).

[54] Ramm is saying that one can "volunteer" to be sterilized.

[55] The application for sterilization could be made by the Civil Service Physician. In fact, it was his duty to make the application when he identified an appropriate case. Each licensed physician had a duty to report all appropriate cases to the Civil Service Physician. A family member, if not the legal representative of the patient, could not make the application. The identity of the one making the application for sterilization was kept secret. The sick person or guardian was to be told of the consequence of the sterilization. The individual or the guardian is not asked to give consent, for there is no freedom of choice. But the individual (who may be mentally ill) or guardian is to be informed.

The examination of individual cases and the decision about forwarding the application to the Hereditary Health Court lies ultimately with the Civil Service Physician.

Negotiations over an application placed before the Civil Service Physician takes place before the *Hereditary Health Court*[56] in whose district the subject resides. The

[56]These courts, of which there were 220, were attached to local petty courts; they consisted of a judge from the petty court and two physicians, one of whom was to be "particularly familiar with eugenics." It frequently happened that the doctor or psychiatrist who instigated the proceedings also sat on the court (Burleigh 2000, 357). Sessions were closed to the public; physicians appearing as expert witnesses before the court could not insist on professional secrecy and could not refuse to testify (Mueller, 121).

The judgment in a case before a Hereditary Health Court could be appealed to a Hereditary Health Court of Appeals, of which there were 18. This court were attached to every Court of appeals and consisted once again of a judge and two physicians. They reached a final decision on the application, after which no further appeals were possible. If the decision was in favor of sterilization, the person concerned was granted 2 weeks' time to have the operation performed voluntarily. Otherwise the sterilization would be performed "with the aid of the police, and if necessary with the use of direct force" (Mueller, 121). Evans reports that in 1934, the 1st year of the law's operation, nearly 4000 people appealed against the decisions of the sterilization authorities and 3559 of these appeals failed, meaning that the application from a doctor, social worker or other legitimate source for sterilization was successful in over 90 per cent of the cases (Evans 2005, 508).

Mueller reports that there were approximately 350,000 sterilizations and that the "mortality coefficient" (a term used by a Professor Gaus of the University Hospital in Wuerzburg) of 5%, leading to the estimate that 17,500 victims succumbed to the operation, (Mueller, 121) although Burleigh reports the lower number of "5000" who actually died (Burleigh 2000, 358) The operations were carried out by about 140 designated doctors working on a *pro rata* basis. These involved ligation of the fallopian tubes for women, and vasectomy for men (called the "Hitler cut") (Fischer, 385).

Mueller reports that half of all cases heard were initiated on grounds of "congenital feeblemindedness"; in another 27% the diagnosis was "schizophrenia" (Mueller, 121–2). Evidence for the former was merely the attendance at special schools for learning disabilities. The latter diagnosis was on particularly shaky grounds. But the issue of whether a condition was actually hereditary appeared to be of little consequence. Mueller reports of the sterilization of a young woman whose deaf-mutism had resulted from two accidents and a severe ear infection. Even though she had given birth to a normal baby the court declared on the basis of the medical specialist's opinion that this must be a case of hereditary deafness (Mueller, 123). Mueller reports that many other cases were decided on dubious testimony. A worker in Saxony who had lost a leg in an industrial accident was forcibly sterilized on the grounds that his diminished earning capacity precluded him from raising a family. One group which welcomed sterilization was part-time prostitutes (Grunberger, 225).

The proceedings before the court were very brief, each defendant received from 10 to 15 min' deliberation, with the decision being largely determined on the testimony of the doctor expert (Burleigh 2000, 357).

The "Intelligence Test Form" used to determine the subject's intelligence is also interesting. In addition to the standard questions of name, place and time, etc., the following were also asked:

1. Why does one build houses higher in towns than in the countryside?
2. What does it mean to boil water?
3. What is the difference between a mistake and a lie?
4. What is the difference between a loan and a gift?
5. What is the difference between parsimony and saving?

Hereditary Health Court is connected to an Official Court and has an Official Judge as Chairman and two physicians as members, of which one must be official and the other must be an especially trusted physician with the Genetic Health faculty. The Hereditary Health Court can hear physicians and experts as witnesses; all authorities and health institutions are obligated to give information to it and to produce the illness history of the sick person.

The affected can put in a complaint against the decision of the Hereditary Health Court to the *Hereditary Health Court of Appeals*, which is a department of the responsible Superior Territorial Court, which has one member of the College of Judges as chairman and two medical members. The decision of the Hereditary Health Court of Appeals is final.

Since the law lacks some simple formula and only the most severe of the great number of those genetically ill are to be selected, it is felt by all enlightened Volk comrades to be a befriending act and is seen as the appropriate means to limit much outstanding pain and misery.[57]

In order to prevent any discomfort in the population as a consequence of this law and to be sure of an understanding acceptance in all Volk circles, it is the high responsibility of the physician to put himself in the position where he can clarify and advise the Volk regarding the goal of this law.[58]

If the physician intends to apply the sterilization law carefully and scientifically and wants to hold the responsible position that the legislator has given him, he must acquire exemplary knowledge in the areas of genetics and genetic pathology. The demand which is placed in this regard on each physician reads: *Each Physician must become a Genetic Doctor;* he must possess the necessary capabilities and knowledge in order to carry through the protection of the genotype of our Volk.

With the application of the laws we must, with great circumspection and special consideration to the feelings of the Volk, give clarification especially to the sense that the law is not demanding expiation for some guilt, but that the one affected has a tragic fate to thank for his genetic sickness and that his elimination as a link in the chain of genetics represents a sacrifice in the interests of the Volk community.

Just as this work of clarification is important, so is the psychological comfort to be given to one in a generally high valued family, to relieve them of their anxiety and cares, if the family has a genetically sick member – for example a case of Schizophrenia – through being a carrier of a recessive gene. Here the genetic physi-

---

6. What is the difference between a lawyer and a public prosecutor?
7. What is the difference between stairs and a ladder?
8. What is the difference between a pond and a stream? (Burleigh 1991, 139).

[57] Ramm does not specify whose pain and misery will be relieved. As Burleigh comments, "Scientists and doctors were frequently used to lend eugenic claims an element of irrefutable authority, in a society where academics and professionals still basked in uncritical public esteem towards the 'Herr Doktor' or 'Herr Professor'" (Burleigh 2000, 360–1).

[58] It is another of the physician's responsibilities to be the government's front man to explain and justify this law to the population. I take it that this is what Ramm means in the title of this chapter by the term, "politician of the population."

cian can give comfort and advice in his capacity as house physician by using empirical genetic prognosis and again establish trust in the value of the genetic constitution of the affected family.[59]

The law has, out of the large number of existing sick genetic carriers in the body politic, designated groups which have manifest themselves phenotypically with a clear-cut clinical picture and determined these as having priority for elimination. The clinically flawless cases cause no difficulty for the judgment by the Genetic Physician. In contrast, there are many borderline cases which are extraordinarily difficult to judge and put a high demand on the knowledge and responsibility of the genetic health judge. An example is the *genetic idiocy of light grade,* in which there is neither asocial adjustment nor otherwise amoral behavior. Since intelligence tests, in consideration of the environmental conditions under which the proband has grown up – bad education, lack of instruction because of irregular school attendance – do not always make a sharp separation from *common stupidity*, there has come to be employed in the Hereditary Health Court the concept of *probationary life,* in which in most cases a correct and just judgment is ultimately carried out. An employment of this concept by the Hereditary Health Court to this difficult problem corresponds entirely to the conception of the broadest class of the Volk and authoritative party circles.[60] Nevertheless the Hereditary Health Court must distinguish for example in the judgment about probationary life between mechanically performed work and that which requires a certain degree of thought. In cases of probationary life, proof can be considered to be brought only if it is proven that the thoughts and decisions are personally grasped. Besides, it should really not be forgotten that in the judgment of idiocy, the light form of this genetic sickness frequently conceals completely within itself the signs of the bad form of idiocy.[61]

---

[59] In this paragraph Ramm reports how to deal with the clash between two National Socialist philosophical values – that of designating a family as being of "high-value," but has had an individual in it which has been targeted to be one who should be sterilized. Ramm attempts to resolve the anxiety by calling on genetic theory. If the affected person is homozygous for recessive genes, then each parent would be a carrier and unaffected. But this carrier state would have carried an enormous taint for the entire clan. Ramm's reassurances notwithstanding, a family involved in such scientific hockus-pokus would have in the future been in a very vulnerable position in the National Socialist racial state.

[60] By the assurance that the conception "**corresponds to the …authoritative party circles…**" Ramm is stating that the Reich Physicians' Leader agrees with this statement. Burleigh reports that the prevailing precept which drove the court was: 'The judge must always bear in mind Hitler's words that "the right to personal freedom always gives way to the duty of preserving the race" (M. Burleigh, *The Third Reich: A New History* (New York: Hill & Wang, 2000), 357–8).

[61] This paragraph reveals much about the method and reasoning of a National Socialist genetic physician. Ramm starts from the premise that the determination of some genetic groups is a "clear-cut clinical picture," and proceeds to the acknowledgement that there are grey areas which have to be resolved. The example he uses – *genetic idiocy of light grade* – which he acknowledges might just be a case of *common stupidity,* is illustrative of the problem the National Socialist genetic National Socialist philosophical viewpoint created for itself. He states that the Hereditary Health Court has come up with the concept of "*probationary life*" for such immediately unresolved cases. This concept obviously did not allow a resolution. He states, "**In cases of probationary life, proof**

The actual tactical application of the law is important in order to not make it unpopular. I understand this to be the correct choice of the cases to be sterilized at the correct time. Preferably each genetically sick person who is found to be at the age of being capable of reproduction and presents, through unrestrained reproduction of their sick genomes, a direct danger for the coming generation, must be committed for sterilization. It would be senseless and purposeless to give preference in the physician's genetic activities to the not yet sexually mature adolescent or at the beginning of menopause in a female. In these there is either no longer or hardly any possibility of fecundity. Likewise, it would be a misjudgment of the real responsibilities of Hereditary Health Court capacities if there were brought to its notice only those mental illnesses whose effects produce decay of mental personality – epilepsy, schizophrenia or severe physical derangements – which, according to experience, are rarely in danger of being propagated.[62]

I probably don't need to say expressly that the choice of cases must take place with great conscientiousness, with simultaneous consideration of the highest principles of all the physician's activities so as to cause no injury, keeping in mind the many secret and public opponents of this law who, under a cover of a false humanity, seek to sabotage our racial hygiene measures or bring them into discredit in public opinion.

A further word should yet be said concerning the meaning of the physician's testimony which plays a great role in the introduction and implementation of this process. The Reich Physicians' Leader has forbidden transferring into private hands the writing of the certificate of genetic health or genetic sickness. Only on the request of the Civil Service Physician or of the Hereditary Health Court is the house physician authorized and required to give testimony. On the other hand, in order to avoid economic damage to the physician, which can affect his representation as house physician of the affected family, the contents of the testimonies regarding the sterilization of the reported Volk comrade or his members given by a physician in free practice are to be revealed neither by the Civil Service Physician nor by the Hereditary Health Court.

The *act of making someone sterile* is, as a rule, carried out through surgical means, however it can, in women what are over 38 years of age, be accomplished

---

can be considered to be brought only if it is proven that the thoughts and decisions are personally grasped." Ramm gives no clue how this is to be done. Ramm is stating that the Reich Physicians' Leader agrees with this statement.

[62] In this paragraph Ramm gives some insight into the "tactical application" of the law so as to not make it make it unpopular. Even though the National Socialist state was a totalitarian state, it did find that it had to respond to public pressure at times. Burleigh describes the response of the regime when the public became aware of the 'euthanasia' program of patients in asylums in the 1940s (Burleigh 1994, 175–180). When there came to be active public condemnation of the program – in the form of a sermon by the bishop of Muenster, Clemens August Graf von Galen (1878–1946) – the government quietly halted the gassing. Reportedly, Hitler instructed Brandt to 'halt' the program as it affected adults, but not children. However, there is no agreement as to whether the program was stopped because of public criticism or if the T-4 was needed to carry out the infinitely vaster project of extermination of the Jews.

also through the use of x-ray. In women who are pregnant at the time of the commencement of sterilization, the pregnancy can be terminated with the certification of the pregnant person or her legal representative, if at the time fertility is already in jeopardy or otherwise the interruption of the pregnancy would create a serious danger for the life or the health of the woman. If possible, the production of infertility and termination of the ability to be pregnant should be carried out in a hospital *at the same time*.[63]

Sterilization can be forcefully carried out in cases of refusal, but can be avoided through prolonged placement of the genetically ill person in a closed institution, if the family can bear the resulting cost. In so far as the house physician can bear the influence of the decision on the involved family, he should set the plans in place for the operation.

In the "*Law for the Protection of the Genetic Health of the German Volk*" (Marriage Health Law) it is determined that a marriage may not be allowed to take place if:

(a) One of the betrothed suffers from an infectious disease which leads to fear of increased danger to the health of the other betrothed or the offspring.
(b) One of the betrothed is incapacitated or is under temporary guardianship.
(c) One of the betrothed, without being incapacitated, suffers from a mental disturbance which makes the marriage appear undesirable for Volk health.
(d) One of the betrothed suffers from a genetic illness according to the Law for the Prevention from Genetic Illness of the Offspring; however, this does not stand in the way of the completion of the marriage if the other betrothed is infertile.[64]

---

[63] Ramm gives some specifics on how the sterilization was to be carried out. Nazi doctors were never satisfied with their techniques for sterilization and continued experimenting on newer techniques almost up until the end of the war. Lifton documents many of the experiments undertaken in "Block 10" at Auschwitz (Lifton, 268–302) and Gene Church writes of the personal experience of Yakoff Skurnik, who was sterilized while an inmate at Auschwitz (G. Church, *80,629′: A Mengele Experiment* (Richardson, Texas: Sharon Kimberly Damon, 1986). Sterilization was carried out in women by injection of a caustic substance into the cervix in order to obstruct the fallopian tubes, x-ray to the genitals and surgical castration. On March 28, 1942, Dr. Victor Brack reported to Himmler that experimental results showed that mass x-ray sterilization could be carried out without difficulty. He estimated that with 20 x-ray installations, 3–4000 victims could be sterilized daily (V. Spitz, *Doctors from Hell: The Horrific Account of Nazi Experiments on Humans* (Boulder, Co.: Sentient Publications, 2005), 194). He suggested:

One practical way of proceeding [with the x-ray sterilization] would be, for instance, to let the persons to be treated approach a counter, where they could be asked to answer some questions or to fill informs, which would take them two or three minutes. The official sitting behind the counter could operate the installation in such a way as to turn a switch which would activate the two valves simultaneously (since the irradiation has to operate from both sides). With a two-valve installation about one hundred'fifty to two hundred persons could then be sterilized per day, and therefore, with twenty such installations as many as three to four thousand persons per day. (In Spitz, 195–6)

[64] This is the "Marriage Health Law" which is discussed in the Commentary of Ramm's page 128. The various conditions which would prohibit a marriage are listed. Common to all the prohibitions

These marriage prohibitions are meant to prevent the completion of a marriage from the standpoint of promotion of Volk health. If the incapacitation occurs because of overindulgence or alcoholism, it will be cited as grounds for prohibition of the marriage because this situation indicates a sick mental constitution. Among the outstanding illnesses we must reckon with are above all tuberculosis and venereal disease, but also with a bacillus excreter, which puts the marriage as well as the offspring in a high degree of danger.

If despite one of these prohibited conditions a marriage is completed, it is to be viewed null and void because a violation has been committed against & 3 of these laws, meaning that it was carried out through deception of the Health Office or the professional official or by going around the law in a foreign country. The contestable nature of a marriage of this kind is a given.

The prohibition of marriage between a genetically ill person and one healthy is intended, on the one hand, to prevent the generation of a genetically ill offspring and, on the other, *not* bind people with a healthy capacity for reproduction to a genetically ill partner.

& 2 of the law demands that the betrothed produce before the marriage ceremony a certificate from the Public Health Office (certificate of clearance to marry),[65] that shows that no prohibition is present on the basis of & 1 of this law. Since the prohibition of marriage has essentially to do with the medical sphere, this is the responsibility of the Public Health Office. For this purpose each Public Health Office is compartmentalized into an advisory department for care of genetics and race. This department is required to advise the population in all questions of racial hygiene and, through the establishment of a genetic biological index file, lead gradually to an increase in the continued genetic biological existence of the entire Volk. In addition to the registration of genetically ill families, the responsibility of the advisory department should also consist in the establishment of a wider index card file, which designates the valuable families and the healthy genetic lines of the Districts.

In order to acquire the clearance to marry certificate, each betrothed is required to allow the responsible Public Health Office to investigate the genetic health of the applicant. It has however also been determined that the betrothed can be allowed to seek a licensed physician in private practice to do the investigation for the Office for

---

is the proposition that the reason to prohibit a marriage is to prevent the procreation of genetically ill offspring. This point is illustrated by, for example, the fact that the genetically sick can be allowed to marry if one of the individuals is infertile.

Note that alcoholism is to be a warrant against permission to marry. We will see later how Ramm admonishes a woman from drinking alcohol during pregnancy. Proctor reports that, after 1933, the possibility of harm to the "German germ plasm" was used to justify the decision to sterilize "chronic alcoholics in accordance with the Sterilization Law (R. Proctor, *The Nazi War on Cancer* (Princeton: Princeton University Press, 1999), 142).

[65] In this and the following page Ramm presents the application of the Marriage Health Law. It can be seen that, consistent with the totalitarian nature of the regime and its foundational construction on genetics, this law was very important. Essentially, the application of this law was meant to artificially increase what was considered to be the genetic wealth of the Aryan Volk. It was constructed on the ideal of an artificial breeding program, just as one might see on a breeding farm.

Volks' Health. This physician reports the results of his investigation to the responsible Public Health Office which has to base its judgment on this finding. It can be obviously seen that each physician, if he does not know the family well enough, must base his determination about the genetic health on an examination of the betrothed, since the statements of the betrothed, can, out of ignorance or out of intention, not always be taken to be true. The clearance to marry certificate becomes invalid if the marriage is not completed within 6 months of its issuance, however the Public Health Office can extend the period.

Since the & 2 of this law has not yet been put into full force, owing to an overburdening of the Public Health Offices, an interim rule was put into place whereby the clearance to marry certificate is to be produced only in doubtful cases. It is to be left up to the judgment of the professional official to decide if a doubtful case is present. The professional official is neither entitled to practice marriage counseling nor does he possess his own right of testing. Both are the responsibilities of the Public Health Office or more precisely of the physician in general practice. The point in time in which it will become obligatory for all the betrothed to produce clearance certificates for marriage is determined by the Reich Minister of the Interior. Since the law fulfills only the lowest demands of the genetic physician and there are numerous other causes that make many marriages appear undesirable, it will require the complete implementation of this law before normal relationships are achieved. The fact that today the professional official who is installed as a security factor for the purification of our life's blood is only superficially instructed in genetic biological questions is, from a genetic physician's viewpoint, to be permitted only as an emergency measure.

Through a decree seeking wider application of the Marriage Health Law it was determined that from December1941 on, each Volk comrade living in the country on the publishing of the banns or at the latest at the time of the marriage had a responsibility to present to the professional official a certificate, which is given out free of charge from the responsible Public Health Office, on which it is declared that the Public Health Office has no knowledge of facts which would lead to the prohibition of a marriage from the standpoint of the Marriage Health Law, and according to the implemented ordinance for the Law for Protection of the Blood. Exceptions from these declarations are members of the army during the war and male foreigners.

The legal requirement to present this *certificate for a marriage-giving no cause for concern* (certificate of clearance to marry) was permitted because it represented an initial means of help during the war, while letting it be known that it was the firm intention of the legislature to demand as soon as possible before marriage from each Volk comrade his proof of the suitability of the marriage.

For the physician, the completion of the clearance for marriage certificate does not exhaust his acts as caretaker of our Volk. Being knowledgeable of the genetic predispositions of the family entrusted to him, and given his knowledge and experience *on the occasion of each consultation and each visit,* during which questions of marriage and reproduction are brought up, he is to advise and clarify and, where he sees danger, effect limitation and hindrance. By the close contacts with which he cultivates his charges and by which he is in the position to practice great influence, there exists for him the high duty to recommend to one or the other Volk comrade that they only go into a marriage in which there is to be expected no genetic damage to the offspring, but, in addition, above all that there is also to be hoped an increase in the genetic value through the joining together of high valued marriage partners.

The annihilation of sick genotypes paralleled with the limitation of their transmission must be accompanied with the *increase and extension* of the healthy genotype. To be involved in these areas of our Volk life at this re-awakening of the will for reproduction and admonition for conscientious processes regarding the future generations is the most important, and thereby most pleasant side, of the genetic physician's general medical activities.

What Was the Form of the Political Preservation of Our Volk Before the Overtaking of Power?

Even to those who have only superficially followed population statistics during the last decade, the facts must be conspicuous, that the German Volk had been driven to the point of a serious biological crisis. At the end of this process there would ultimately have been a drop off of the number of Volk, collapse of the race and finally the death of the Volk, if appropriate measures had not led to a complete psychological change of mind in the German Volk, leading to a reawakening, hardening and a strengthening of their will to live (Burgdoerfer).

The following facts throw a glaring spotlight on the dangerous biological situation of our Volk: In the year 1900, we had, with 56 million inhabitants, around 2 million births and an excess of births over deaths of around 900,000; in the year 1932, there were, with 62 million inhabitants, only 978,000 births. The excess of births over deaths amounted to just 278,000, and with that, we had not only ceased being a healthy growing Volk, but rather the Volk situation was already thereby in danger; indeed, with the continuation of the crisis of this dimension, we could predict the disappearance of the Volk and that we would sink from 65 million Volk in the year 1932 to 47 million Volk in the year 2000. It appeared as though the German Volk had been encumbered with an un-removable burden of death.

Even though a declining birth rate was evident in Western European countries, and we can also see a decline in the German birth rate after 1900, the process of decline accelerated at the beginning of the world war, exacerbated by the terrible political and economic conditions that Germany suffered as a consequence of the Versailles Dictat. There were many other grounds for this process, which lay partly in the Volk or was planted through foreign ideas which had as their end the destruction of our Volk, marching towards a development which would secure in the foreseeable future the destruction or at least the desired weakening of the enemy, Germany (according to the opinion of the French Prime Minister Clemenceau, 20 million Germans was considered to be too many).

If we seek the causes of this catastrophic decline in birthrate in Germany, we find that "the rationalization of sex life" and "overambitiousness,"[66] leading to pure economic thinking and selfish focusing on life (the price of individual pleasure of life!), were allowed to lead to a decline in reproduction in the well-off classes of the population;

There were for the German Volk, however, even deeper causes. Inflation and unemployment, hunger, need and unlimited hopelessness, in regards to the improvement of the political and economic conditions in Germany, led to the decline of idealism, and all anticipations for a happy future; all led to a gradual weakening of the will to live and in a belief in a better future, so much so that the high quality people could no longer let it be on their conscience to possess a horde of children to which only a gloomy future beckoned and for whom there then could only be wandering about in foreign lands in order to become the fertilizer for the culture of the possessing people of this world.

Especially dominant was the fall in births in the urban population in which not only was there a shrinking of births but also a generalized decay of morality, which produced the grounds for venereal disease and, above all, unlimited abortion. But also, in this general development of things, the country turned gradually towards a negative viewpoint of life and in those places where there was still a surplus of births over deaths, it was not the high-valued inhabitants who produced the surplus, but rather very often it was the lower valued people, racially speaking.

The cities could no longer preserve their population out of their own strength; instead they lived or grew only from the influx from rural regions, which naturally forfeited its character through this everlasting bleeding and lost its characteristics as the source of life of the nation. Since today only just a quarter of our Volk can be spoken of as being a pure rural population, and, according to the experiences of National Socialist Volk populational statistics, 75% of the processes of urbanization have been exposed as having damaging influences, we must give up the old belief that the rural population is inexhaustible and instead construct conditions in the future for not only the maintenance of our Volk, but must also take special custody and protection of that part of the body politic which lives in the cities.

---

[66] Ramm here is primarily criticizing the women's movement for the decline in the birthrate of the upper class, but the decline in the lower class was due to the economic conditions produced by the world-wide financial crisis.

The entire National Socialist philosophical view was essentially anti-feminist. The Nazis closed down Germany's large and active feminist movement soon after the *Machtuebergreifung*. But they were strongly pro-woman as a biologically necessary part of their racial ambitions. "Woman's place is in the home" – or in the family shop – was the natural corollary of their ideology. Shoenbaum wrote:

> The war on the department store or the chain store was at once a war on the economic liberation of thousands of women sales clerks; the war on the university, a campaign against an ever increasing contingent of women doctors, lawyers, judges, and social workers. The campaign against the big city, industrial society, the twentieth century, was at the same time a campaign against social forces that had brought – or forced – thousands of women into shops, offices, and professions in competition with men. The campaign against the democratic republic was a repudiation of the equality of women. (Schoenbaum, 178)

Gradually the breakdown of births intervenes directly into the substance of the body politic and places the life, the circumstances and the future of our Volk into question.

Even though the medical art had greatly limited the mortality rate and the number of Volk as a whole did not at first sink, the senescence of the Volk continued: The death of the Volk marched on!

With the political breakthrough in the year 1933 this biological re-birth of our Volk began what had never been demonstrated in the world and, despite the war, has still progressed in the years of 1939 and 1940. Even though the year 1933 as well brought a small decline in the number of births to 971,000, which corresponds to a birth frequency of 14:7 per thousand, in the next years the number grew in correspondence to our political and economic progress and to the re-strengthening of the belief in a German future to such a pleasant degree that we had almost achieved in 1938, with 1,347,000 births, the total number of births of England (736,6000) and France (612,000) with 1,348,000, and it had exceeded them in 1940 by nearly 300,000 with a birth number of 1,645,000. Here one can demonstrate with children the trust the village citizen has in the political leadership and in the German future and show the re-awakening of the will to live as the greatest accomplishment of National Socialism.

It has been reckoned that,[67] for the maintenance of our Volk, each genetically healthy family must produce *at least four children*. The opening up of the room in the east which the German sword of our Volk has conquered for the security of our nutritional foundation will demand a rise in this number. The National Socialist state has made it it's duty to stand up for the genetically healthy family and to protect it by its power and might. The purpose of marriage and family consists in the responsibility to produce healthy children for the maintenance of the Volk and to enable them to be educated as decent German people. "In the lap of the family the life of the family is decided. If the family remains healthy, striving for the future, the life of the family takes up the fight for Being and then the German Volk will live" (Staemmler).[68]

In the family, the physician can be, in an ideal sense, a caretaker of the race and the preserver of the Volk population. He must induce the genetically healthy high valued family to have as many children as possible and tell the less valuable family or family with endangering biology that they, in the interests of the maintenance of the racial worth of our Volk, must remain child-poor or childless. Here, in the family, the physician is also able to practice a beneficial activity as adviser of the mature youth in whom genetic health is secured for all time in a great part of our Volk.

---

[67] In this paragraph we see the ambitions of the National Socialists to not only acquire the "*Lebensraum*" in the east for the current German Volk, but also to actually increase the population of these Volk. It would require land and the removal of the indigenous population to achieve this ambition. Goetz Aly has described this long and tortuous process in *'Final Solution'* (G. Aly, *Final Solution: Nazi Population Policy and the Murder of the European Jew* (London: Arnold, 1999).

[68] Ramm gives "Staemmler" as the source of this quote but the reference is not listed at the end of the text.

The one thing recommended to the genetic physician and political preserver of the Volk population as the superior principle of his work and action is: *Quantity contains only the visible features of the Volk population. If care is not thereby taken that the good and best genetic worth of a Volk is again present to an extensive degree in the next generation, then the Volk will decline from a high cultural place through the flagging of its creative strength and will be degraded from a leading master race to a Volk of Helots.*

While we have been able to establish in the German Volk an increase in the number of children in many high valued families, there are indeed extraordinarily many families which even now seek to shirk their duty to the whole Volk, out of material considerations. *Compensation for the burden of family,* with legally determined distribution of taxes, preference for the child-rich father with equal qualifications in the acquisition of positions, preferred allotment of apartments, homes and similar means, are all appropriate measures to be used to give these Volk comrades another moral incentive to address the vital questions of the whole Volk, as they are transitioned out of the sick individualist epoch into the time of the Volk community.[69]

For the terribly great responsibilities which are at present demanded of the German people for the securing of our living space, for which our armies are fighting in this enormous struggle of the Volk, we need an ever growing mass of more people to solve the accumulating challenges to build a living border for the defense of our volkish existence.

The breaking up of the humanity-closing and hostile-to-birth great cities and the creation of new and strong farming communities in the enlarged living spaces will create the basics for the maintenance and increase of our volkish strength. This will promote the reputation and the welfare of our Volk in political and economic areas and thereby lead to a constantly higher development of our culture in intellectual and psychological areas.

In this connection, it is especially to be mentioned that the state takes on itself to fight effectively all dangers which threaten the Volk population through venereal diseases, contraception and threatened abortion. The *Decree of the Law for Fighting Venereal Disease* with its most recent implementation ordinances, further the *Police*

---

[69] Ramm lists several measures used to induce the "high-valued" families to have more children. Grunberger calls the mood "philoprogenitive," meaning that there were multiple manipulations of language, rituals and social pressures to encourage the "high-value" families to have more children. The term 'family' was reserved for families with four or more children and the highly emotive phrase *Kindersegen* (blessed with children) was used constantly (Grunberger, 235).

The social pressure for "high-value" Aryan families to procreate was enormous. When the Dresdner Bank – Germany's largest – published its annual balance sheet, it included data about the incidence of marriage and fertility among its staff (Grunberger, 237). Childless Aryan citizens would sometimes resort to newspaper advertisements to attract a suitable mate with whom they could start a family. One such ad reads:

> Fifty-two-year-old pure Aryan doctor, veteran of the battle of Tannenberg, who intends to settle on the land, desires male progeny through a registry-office marriage with a healthy Aryan, virginal, young, unassuming, economy-minded woman, adapted to hard work, broad-hipped, flat-heeled and earring-less – if possible also property-less. (Grunberger, 237)

Ordinance Covering Proceedings, Means and Objects for Interruption and Prevention of Pregnancy, represent, in addition to promoting the will to have children and the intensive fight against infant death, appropriate means for making the Volk situation secure.

In so far as it is practicable during the war it should be possible to achieve decreased infant and child mortality through the arrangements made by the Reich Health Leader for *Departments of Infants and Children* in the general hospitals.[70, 71]

Also the Newborn wards of Obstetrics Institutions and Obstetrics Departments of the general hospitals must now be staffed with infant specialists.

For infants and children in surgical departments, infant and child nurses should be provided. For the care of the newborn and the prematurely born, there are correspondingly established midwives or infant child nurses in the appropriate institutions.[72]

For the unification of preventive medicine and general care for the infant and the small child in all advising and general departments, the Reich Health Leader has declared that a unified "*Health Sheet for the Care of Infants and Small Children*" is obligatory.[73]

The storage of these records takes place in the Health Office or in the counseling center of the NSV. The Health Sheet accompanies the child on a change in residence of the parents and serves later as the basis for the adolescent health index file.[74]

Pregnancy counseling and instruction and general care for mother and child will, in union with a better education of medical trainees in obstetrics and infant health science, contribute their good part in rescuing many a child who would have in earlier times died during birth or infancy.

It is to be expected that there will be regular attendance of a midwife at each birth as is firmly prescribed by the new midwife law of 21.12.1938, which also demands that there be more extensive success in obstetrical areas. Also, if a birth is medically attended, the physician has to pay strict attention that a midwife is called in to consult. This regulation is valid also for births in the family of the physician.[75]

---

[70] Consistent with their National Socialist Philosophical Worldview, the National Socialists were pioneers in pediatric care. Heavily preoccupied with population increase, the Nazi health authorities placed great emphasis on reducing infant mortality, making some definite advances in this field. Starting from a rate of 77 per 1000, they managed to reduce this to 60 just before the outbreak of the war (Grunberger, 225) This rate was not as good as the English figure (53 in 1939) or the American (51 in 1938), but the improvement was nonetheless impressive.

[71] This paragraph was added to the 1942 text.

[72] This paragraph was added to the 1942 text.

[73] The "Health Sheet for Infants and Small Children" (*Gesundheitsbogen)* consisted of a record of immunizations and medical illnesses. It served as another means of keeping track of the population, in this case the most important segment, the children.

[74] This paragraph was added to the 1942 text.

[75] Midwifery had a long history in the German states. A midwifery ordinance had been passed in1757 making professors of obstetrics and gynecology responsible for their education (Lindemann, 199). The encouragement of the practice, with male supervision, was consistent with the National Socialist Philosophical Worldview, in which the woman's role, as bearer of the genetic heritage, is

The Reich Health Leader has in 1942, on grounds of political preservation of the Volk, founded the work community, "*Assistance with childlessness in marriage*," from which we hope that many marriages which have been sterile up to now will have the good fortune to be blessed with children.

The Physician as Health Educator

Medical research and the medical community have succeeded in the course of the nineteenth century in limiting the threat to the Volk condition of the great epidemics, like plague, small pox, diarrhea and cholera, so much that they practically never appear today in cultured countries. One must simply note that in times of war these devastating diseases flicker up here and there; however in the present war we have so far been spared. There have been further successes in improving the outlook for life through appropriate hygienic measures: maternal and child mortality during and after birth have been greatly decreased by the fight against puerperal fever and by the development of scientific and practical obstetrics, and in the last decade, through progress in the medical arts, mortality in infancy has been decreased more than half. Life expectancy has climbed in the last century from an average of around 40–61 years of age, whereas the health circumstances of our Volk have not climbed to the same degree, so that we today are faced by the fact that the German people, especially the working people, are worn out long before they achieve the average age and thus can no longer deliver full-valued working power.

This is the essential point where the activities of the physician as health educator are to begin; here the important responsibilities arise so as to maintain the health and the capability of humans in physiologically given dimensions as much as possible up to the borders of life expectancy.[76]

Health Leadership is part of human leadership and represents one of its most important areas of responsibility within the overall responsibilities of the NSDAP.

The National Socialist movement, as the dynamic principle for all areas of our volkish life, is, on the grounds of its firm anchoring in the soul of the whole Volk, in a position to place moral demands on the individuals or the community in areas of life where laws and regulations of the states would not meet with a wide response or

---

supported. It can be seen that the National Socialists required that midwives attend each birth, even if a physician is present. Even births within the family of a physician required a midwife in attendance. Mary Lindemann's comment about the midwife of the eighteenth century appears to be pertinent to National Socialist times as well. "Midwifes were rooted in their communities inasmuch as the women of the village had chosen them, and their selection to fill what was, after all, a minor civic post was often the handiest and cheapest way to provide for them" (Lindemann, 214).

[76] Ramm is going to argue that one of the most important responsibilities of the National Socialist physician is to educate the Volk of their *moral* responsibility to practice Racial Hygiene. It is this connection between public health – physician education of the Volk – Racial Hygiene which captures the sense of the National Socialist philosophical Worldview and is what makes Ramm's text a text of medical ethics (Aly 1994, 22–98).

would have only a minimal influence. All achievements which have been voluntarily accomplished since the overtaking of power of our Volk once and for all validate the National Socialist movement as a success to such a never anticipated and therefore astounding degree. And it is precisely in health areas where it is required that the free will of each individual is to be fully employed, if the remaining benefits are to be achieved for the present and the future.[77]

It is to the continuing merit of the Party that it re-shapes the "Right to one's own body," that comes out of crass individualism, into a moral "Duty for Health," and designates this to be a demand of the National Socialist philosophical viewpoint.[78]

The party has given its political will a form of organic health through the erection of the Main Office for Volks' Health.[79] Individual Regions report to the Regional office and Districts to the District office for Volks' Health.

The Main Office for Volks' Health supports and extends the public health efforts of the state, hurrying on ahead however in many areas. The intensive attention to physical education, the assistance of "Mother and Child," the dispatching of children to the country for health reasons, "Tuberculosis" assistance, the Organization for the "prevention of injuries," and the "defense and the maintenance of the workforce of working Volk comrades," as well as "youth health assistance" are, just to name a few, state developments which were complementary creations of the Party. The success achieved through the close connection of party and state is a striking proof that it doesn't have to do with just one or the other contradictory dualism or an energy wasting parallelism but rather that the Being of the Party and state is necessary for the validation and welfare of the German Volk which leads through harmonic synthesis to a higher unfolding of power.[80]

---

[77] Following Hitler's lead, the National Socialists preached that all matters were just a matter of the "will."

[78] A fundamental change in the metaphysical view of medicine and the human body was that it was no longer considered to be one's own body, but was a body of the whole Volk. Thus, the crass individualism of the liberal-Marxist era was supposed to be supplanted by the concept of the National Socialist Philosophical Worldview.

[79] This sentence was added to the 1942 text.

[80] The term Ramm uses for "being" is *Dasein*. This is a favorite word of Martin Heidegger, a German philosopher who was famous at the time for his 1927 book *Being and Time*. After Hitler's takeover of Germany in 1933, Heidegger joined the Nazi party and for a time at least he was an active member of the party. Heidegger is reported to have said in 1933: "The Fuehrer himself is the only present embodiment and future embodiment of German nation and its law…To oppose him would be treason against Being." There has been considerable scholarly conjecture on whether Heidegger's philosophy is somehow tainted and must contain elements of Nazi thinking. At present, the issue does not appear to be resolved (J. Young, *Heidegger, Philosophy, Nazism* (Cambridge: University Press, 1997); T. Rockmore and J. Margolis, *The Heidegger Case. On Philosophy and Politics* (Philadelphia: Temple University Press, 1992); H. Sluga, *Heidegger's Crisis: Philosophy and Politics in Nazi Germany* (Cambridge, Mass.: Harvard University Press, 1992); R. Wolin, *The Heidegger Controversy: A critical Reader* (Cambridge, Mass.: MIT Press, 1992); V. Farias, *Heidegger and Nazism* (Philadelphia: Temple University Press, 1987); H. Ott, *Martin Heidegger: A Political Life* (New York: Basic Books, 1993); C. R. Bambach, *Heidegger, Dilthey, And The Crisis of Historicism* (Ithaca: Cornell University Press, 1995); J. Fritsche, *Historical Destiny And*

The sense of National Socialist Health Leadership does not just lie in the protection of the German Volk from illness but rather in the awakening and absolute promotion in it of its preexisting capacities to its highest possible achievement. For that, it requires, on the one hand, keeping one away from damaging attractions which limit optimal development, because one's own capacity to resist is not sufficient to neutralize their effect. On the other hand, the person must, not only in the age of growth but rather during his whole life, resist certain influential stimulations and oppositions in order to conserve his strength which is needed first for development and then for growth and finally for maintenance.

If we take from this knowledge the practical result that the responsibility of the Main Office of Volks' Health of the NSDAP is essentially to develop *in the German Volk the individual's given genetic makeup, which constitutes him but also creates the limits of the extent of his health and protects him until old age.* In all people, this education must develop the capacity to adapt to the always changing life conditions and sharpen their instinct and reason to the extent that they recognize early enough the ever changing forms of confronting world dangers (injuries from civilization) and are able to resist them.

Health leadership is constituted thereby *specifically* to bring a pure educational experience to each individual person, culminating in the facilitation of undisturbed natural development and an order of life which fits his nature. The resolution will be much easier the better the understanding of our efforts is aroused and the more willing the German people are to adjust themselves to this demand for health education. *For this change* the Health leadership must create, in parallel with the progress of health education, the preconditions for success, and must decrease or set aside all dangerous influences which are the consequences of the citification of our life, which results in the devastation of living places and which has produced the perilous situation of the lack of births, the altered nutrition, the one-sided professional activities, the over-achieving labor and general life tempo, with its increase in pure intellectual work and the neglect of physical activity, together with its false free-time and formulated vacations.[81]

Above all, implementation of a truly generous lodging and settlement policy is necessary, whereby the people are again given a healthy and natural foundation for life; especially belonging to that is a reasonable provision of nutrition and a supply

---

National Socialism In Heidegger's Being and Time (Berkeley: University of California Press, 1999); C. Bambach, *Heidegger's Roots: Nietzsche, National Socialism, and the Greeks* (Ithaca: Cornell University Press, 2003).

[81] This long sentence articulates clearly the National Socialists' viewpoint about the effects of urbanization. Despite their rhetoric about the primacy of the farm and the ill effects of urbanization, the agricultural population declined from 20.8% to 18%. All of the metropolises increased substantially in population (Schoenbaum, 175–6).

Nazi propaganda presented the romantic image of an idealized peasant, "the free man on free land." The peasant became the key figure in the ideology of the radical right as elaborated by the Nazis. "A firm stock of small and middle peasants," said Hitler in *Mein Kampf,* "has still been at all times the best protection against social evils as we have them now" (B. Moore, Jr. *Social Origins of Dictatorship and Democracy* (Boston: Beacon Press, 1966), 450).

in moderation of things of pleasure, but also a harmonic life style which will be achieved through correct choice of profession and spouse.[82] The German man so led and promoted will again recognize the sense of his Being through the awakening of an elevated feeling of life, and will react with even greater achievement within the Volk community. This increased achievement will arise out of a joyful practice of his calling and will come to expression with a greater number of children which he sends to and raises for his Volk.[83]

Thus, in regards to that, it is the responsibility of the health leadership to make the Volk healthy, strong, and capable as a whole; then it must, to grasp the whole, distribute its preventive medicine to each individual member of the body politic from the cradle to high old age. The organization which is supposed to introduce these political health responsibilities must consequently be so established that, through a ceaseless grasp of the individual person in his varied development and life phases, it arranges regularly a complete overview of the health situation of each age class in the individual callings of our Volk, in order to register at each desired time the most exact evaluation of the whole health situation.

Preventive Medicine[84] *for Mother and Child*

The health care of the German people comes into play with preventive medicine for mother and child. This applies not just at birth but even from the beginning of pregnancy. To guarantee a normal course of pregnancy and to hinder the introduction of

---

[82] This sentence is another ringing National Socialist slogan-like statement. It represents the Nazis viewpoint of *socialism.* Schoenbaum reports that, in fact, "socialism" in its conventional sense was difficult, if not impossible, to locate in Nazi practice. "But as an effective concept it had a very real meaning in Nazi attitudes. It was hortatory and defined a state of mind" (Schoenbaum, 52).

[83] Children are to be *sent to* and *raised for* the Volk. This represents the National Socialists' politics of population. It underscores the attitude which was consistent with Hitler's thinking in terms of divisions of soldiers, rather than individuals (A. Beevor, *Stalingrad* (London: Penguin Books, 1999)).

[84] *Vorsorge* – The National Socialist Philosophical Worldview considered the ideal of medicine to be for *Vorsorge* (preventive medicine), rather than for *Fuersorge* (treatment or curative medicine). Such an attitude was consistent with the National Socialist philosophical Worldview which encouraged "natural" healing, midwifery and demanded that the doctor formulate his own medical treatments. Warren Reich reports of the profound change in emphasis from *Fuersorge* to *Vorsorge.* He shows how socio-cultural factors shaped this transition and accomplished a betrayal of care in three senses:

First, they radically altered the very idea of care that constitutes the goal of medicine, in this way betraying the meaning that professional care has in the human community and subverting the moral standards of care in medicine. Second, they betrayed the actual care of tens of thousands of individual patients by violating the patients' trust in caregivers and by causing immeasurable physical, mental, and spiritual harm in them…And third, they betrayed the moral integrity of many physicians, nurses, and medical and nursing students by violating their sense of commitment to the interests, lives, and health of their patients. (W. Reich, "The Care-Based Ethic of Nazi Medicine and the Moral Importance of What We Care About," in *Muse* 2001 1: 64–74)

pathological disturbances, especially from miscarriage, the pregnant mother must be made to undertake examinations and nursing care by the midwife and to request pregnancy advice and help, beginning from the first months and at certain intervals thereafter. If the pregnant mother is working, special care must be demanded during the period of gravidity, since work in industry places an entirely different demand on a woman than does household activities. It is self-evident that not all jobs which come into usual consideration for women are appropriate, especially during the pregnancy; to that belongs above all, prolonged sitting and prolonged standing, work requiring quick movement, ceaseless jobs on the conveyor belt and the like, and also activities which require extreme stretching or extreme pressure on the body. From the 6th month of the pregnancy on, and up to the third month after confinement, a working woman, without exception, is not to be allowed to perform either piece work or night work. Six weeks before confinement and up to, at the earliest, 6 weeks thereafter, work activities must be completely put away. During this time she is to receive her full income, since the industry contributes the difference between weekly pay and weekly earnings from free pieces. In case it is necessary during the pregnancy to take instruction in another appropriate occupation, no reduction in income is to occur.[85]

During the week of giving birth there is the possibility of placement of weekly nurses who are to care not just for the woman having the child, but also for the whole household.

Each woman should be allowed, if possible, to breast feed her baby and thereby give to it what is the best natural nutrition. The working mother is to be granted a respite from work for breast feeding where she can nourish her child in a permanent breast feeding manger under the care of an infant or child nurse connected with the firm. Breastfeeding by the mother lays the basis for the health of the child and avoids many dangers which threaten the artificially fed child. To awaken the willingness of all women to breast feed is a very important responsibility of the physician, and the possibility of breast feeding of most women – except for a few exceptions – will be the consequence of this effort.

Proper care of the suckling child in union with natural nutrition prevents the introduction of illness and averts infant death, which today in Germany hovers always around 6%. If our efforts were to succeed in reducing this percentage a hundredfold, then, with a yearly birth rate of 160,000, we would have brought 16,000 infants to life, and, if we were to really succeed in matching the infant mortality of the Netherlands, which is slightly over 4%, then this number would come close to doubling.

In addition to the role played by the general weakening of life as a cause for death, rickets plays a great role. We have learned that light, air, sun and proper nutri-

[85]A keystone to the National Socialist health policy was the care of pregnant women and nursing child. Regular examinations by a midwife and oversight by the health authorities were required. One can see from this narrative the care and attention the National Socialists put into the oversight and management of the central individual of their program to enhance the genetic wealth of the Aryan Volk – the mother.

tion prevent this illness from occurring, if it does not occur because of special genetic factors. Vitamin D in union with ultraviolet light are the means which prevent this sickness from breaking out. We should not turn to this treatment only when a florid case of rickets has occurred, but rather give it in a preventive sense. Through the rickets prophylaxis program established by the Reich Health Leader, which has shown an extraordinary success, nearly every German child has been prevented from the danger of the illness of rickets, which means for the whole Volk a strong reduction in crippling, and means a decline in the number of women who are incapable of bearing children due to a pelvis narrowed by rickets.

Not just the infant but also the small child requires especially careful observation and consideration. Enlightenment must be introduced to the elders about the correct nutrition and care of the children of this age, among which the hardening of one's self should stand in the foreground.

The counseling of mothers by the Health Office, together with the great social work "Mother and Child" of the NSV, interact with each other in the advising and assisting, and attend to the erection of long-term kindergartens in the city and in the country, harvest kindergartens for the protection and care of children whose mother cannot take care of them themselves because of their responsibilities in work and activities of the harvest. For the prevention of damaging environmental influences, childhood dangers are to be avoided by free transport to the country or to climatically healthy regions. Certainly the children in infant and toddler ages should be looked after specially by the house physician, because not all families are able to give those of this age the necessary healthy conditions. Above all the environmental needs of children of this age in the large cities must be fulfilled so that it becomes possible for them to play on green surfaces, and in sand boxes in open air.

The Education of Young People for Health

At the time of entrance into school the child becomes subject to regular examinations by the school and child physician; through this his healthy development is ensured. This is dependent, within genetic biological boundaries, on inner or hormonal and outer influencing stimulations, the most important of which are light, air, nutrition (Vitamins!) and activity. Especially in the beginning school ages, there must be attention paid to the use of too strong or too weak stimulation; the strength of the stimulation must correspond to the age and the constitution of the individual child. Above all, attention must be paid to the avoidance of bad posture which can be caused while sitting in school and through inappropriate school benches. Regularly carried out breathing exercises, stretching and strengthening exercises and frequently repeated posture correction are the methods and means required to avoid this defect. Also, *foot weakness* requires special attention because in the military inspection of the recent years it was established that a great number of those examined suffered from foot deformities, like fallen arches, clubfoot and flat feet. If he is to be declared fully fit, the soldier must have strong capable feet, since the increased appearance of these foot maladies means a weakening of the military strength. The care of the nails on the feet must be especially attended to, following definite prescriptions; likewise the shoe should correspond to our hygienic standards. It should also not be forgotten that foot deformities, above all toe-crippling, are frequently caused by too small and tight fitting stockings.[86]

The health conditions of the child's set of teeth are to be carefully attended to because tooth decay and its consequences have been shown to have detrimental effects on the whole Volk. The cause for this decay lies in incorrect nutrition and terrible care of teeth and mouth. We must come to take regular care of the teeth as early as the milk teeth and carry this through during the entire life, since otherwise caries, which stand in the foreground of teeth illnesses, will assume terrible dimensions. All damages to a tooth, even of the smallest extent, must be repaired as soon as possible, so as not to be allowed to lead to danger to or loss of all the teeth. It is to be hoped that the more vitamin rich nutrition, which has been introduced through whole wheat bread and through strengthened vegetables and raw fruits, will soon bring a change for the better.

Finally a word should be said about the meaning of the pleasant things – alcohol, coffee, tea and especially nicotine.[87] Whenever we today in increasing measures

---

[86] The lives of children were regimented from an early age. There was strong pressure for boys to join the Hitler Youth, while girls were members of the *Bund des Maedels*. All were being prepared for service to the state. One can see how the medical needs of children were carefully attended to. Omer Bartov reports that:

> The Hitler Youth insisted on rigid regimentation, "blind" obedience, and unquestioning faith in the supreme value of action, while teaching profound contempt and distrust for contemplation and discussion; it worshipped the united strength of the group and the "iron" will of the individual, and it despised any manifestation of physical or psychological weakness. (Bartov, 26)

Johnson reports that many youths enjoyed the holidays and hiking outings organized by the HJ and the sporting and leisure-time activities that it sponsored. Likewise, girls even enjoyed the activities, perhaps even more than the boys because of the opportunities it gave to escape from the restrictions and duties that typified female socialization and to shake off the bonds of omnipresent maternal authority (Johnson, 265).

According to Schoenbaum, a girl in the Bund des Maedels would be a "pink-scrubbed non-smoker, comradely, up to date, anti-bourgeois, a hiker and a reader of Rilke" (Schoenbaum, 191).

[87] The National Socialists had a contradictory policy in regards to tobacco. Robert Proctor has reported how, by the late 1930s, German scientists had scientifically confirmed an association between smoking and lung cancer. Afterwards a very active propaganda campaign was waged against tobacco (R. Proctor, "The Nazi Campaign Against Tobacco. Science in a Totalitarian State," in Nicosia et. al., 40–58). The air force banned smoking on its premises in 1938. Post offices and offices of the party itself followed suite. There was considerable literature generated warning of the dangers of smoking (Evans 2005, 319). This all was consistent with the regime's larger principle of *Gesundheitsfuehrung* (leadership in health). However, the tobacco forces counterattacked and the battle lines were drawn between the (pro-tobacco) Economics Ministry and the (anti-tobacco) Ministry of the Interior represented by Conti's office (Proctor 1999, 240). The SA manufactured and profited from its own cigarettes until 1934 ("Storm" cigarettes) (Proctor 1999, 235). German tobacco consumption did not decline until 1942. The wartime dearth of consumer goods – especially in the countryside – robbed money of its attraction as an exchange medium, and farmers traded eggs for cigarettes (at the rate of one for one), pounds of butter for packets of pipe tobacco, and pounds of meat for ten cigarettes (Grunberger, 209).

raise our voice warningly against the exaggerated use of these poisonous pleasures, it is in order to control their undoubted continuing misuse. A measured consumption will cause no injury to adults, but the child's and youth's body should be protected in all cases from these poisonous substances, so that the young person is not limited in his development and become inadequate for life's struggle through premature weakening of his nervous and intellectual strength. Likewise women of childbearing age should not smoke because it is proven that nicotine causes damage to cells and delayed development, frequently leading to sterility, as well as producing miscarriages and difficulties in breast feeding.[88]

For better coordination of the efforts of the party and the states in the area of the care of youth health, there were examinations introduced by the Reich Health Leader, *Dr. Conti*, on 6 Mar 1940, in a general decree of the party Chancellery of the Reich Interior Ministry, the Reich Education Ministry and the Youth Leadership of the German Reich, whose purpose was to avoid duplication of the medical care of the HJ and the schools and to introduce examinations at general time periods, which are meaningful for the HJ[89] as well as for the schools. In this way the young people who leave school in the 14th year and undertake their profession come to be subject to wider health attention and are guaranteed the best possible development of their positions and protection from environmental injuries. The mass screenings previously preferred by the HJ are, as far as possible, no longer to be carried out in the context of the school examination, and indeed they are to occur in the future at 6 years = the entrance to school, at 10 years = entrance into the Young Volk, at 14 years = school leaving examination, thereby establishing suitability for the HJ, BdM,[90] profession, duty year, year in the country; the examination at 15 years determines which achievements and developments of the adolescent determines rather than merely influences professional activities. At 18 years, the care of a youth's health ends with a final examination over the suitability for Reich work service, whereby yet once more the influence of labor on the healthy development of young people is to be tested Especially planned are five to six Health Rallies for the years of 6–14 years of age. Further, each year a rally for teeth takes place for maintenance of the set of teeth.

One can show how important for the fitness of young people this correlation of the assigned medical activities is, for example, in the mass screening of the 14 year old, by which four examinations come to be combined into one, and these are:

1. The school completion examination,
2. The examination for the transfer of young people to the HJ, as well as young girls into the BdM

[88] Again, the National Socialists were ahead of other contemporary societies in recognizing the dangers to the child of tobacco smoking in the pregnant or lactating woman. The growing addiction of women to smoking generated considerable controversy and was widely criticized in the popular press (Grunberger, 209).

[89] Hitler Youth.

[90] Bund des Maedels – organization for young girls.

3. The assessment of the fitness for profession and the suitability for assistance at the harvest.
4. Assessment of suitability for the year in the country.

On the entrance to school the first health examination is to be planned by the *youth-physician,* from which the results raised thereby are carried in the Reich – unified *Youth Health Record,*[91] which accompanies the youth from his beginning in school up to military service. For each school child the Youth Health Record is produced in duplicate; one of these remains at the responsible Health Office at the place of birth, while the other accompanies the student to the new Health Department with any change in school or home changes. After completion of the 10th year of life, a new examination takes place on entrance into the HJ and the BdM; the findings are again entered into the Youth Health Record and the youth is given *proof of suitability* if he is fit to compete completely in the HJ service.

After leaving the HJ or the BdM, the young German will be transferred over to labor service which, together with military service the following 2 years, becomes for him a conventional school for the care of health and the strengthening of the will towards health.

The Health Leadership of the youth must set as its goal an increase in the average performance of the whole through the striving of the individual and make him, in physical, intellectual and moral respects, the strongest possible for his struggles in life.

The connection of the health service of the Hitler Youth to the Main Office for Volks' Health was arranged through an agreement of the Reich Youth Leadership with the Reich Health Leadership, whereby the HJ physician of a district is at the same time leader of the Main Department, as "Health Leader for German Youth" of the corresponding office of this district for Volks' Health. Regarding that, the Leader of the office of "Health" is appointed by the Reich Health Leader, in agreement with the Reich Youth Leader, is Leader of this Department in the Main Office for Volks' Health. In the Regional offices for Volks' Health the Regional Physician leads, and in the District office the District physician leads the youth service department.

Care of the Working Population by Industrial Medicine

There was a time in the industrialization process of Germany when the influx of people into industrial work was so strong that the replacement of energy used up could be accomplished effortlessly through the seemingly inexhaustible life stream from the rural population. The feeling of responsibility, in regards to the whole, of most entrepreneurs became smothered through egoism and materialistic exploitation while the social conscience of the responsible circles, because of over-

[91] To keep track of the health condition of each child, the results of each examination were entered into a permanent record, one copy of which was kept at the local Health Department, while another copy accompanied the student if he moved.

solicitation to the sick and the injured or those invalided by old age, came to reside in social insurance, which remedied the gravest threats through recourse to sickness money, accident, invalid and old age pensions.

Very early, the National Socialist movement fundamentally abolished the exploitation and senseless consumption of the strength of the Volk through reckless use and excessive demands in work, and impressed on each industry leader that, if the industrial and defense strength of our Volk is not to decline to an unbearable degree, working Volk comrades must enjoy a special defense, since they are that part of our body politic with the greatest threat to their health.

While the science of the methods of occupational health for workers and for the special protection of actively engaged youths and working women did progress, it did not extend far enough to cover what was needed to protect the strength of the workforce and establish a healthy and pleasant life style for the industrial worker. For this to occur, not just the support of bodily well-being of the person is required, but also the maintenance of psychological vigor which is the source of all joy in work and desire for life.

National Socialism introduced its will for social justice for all, as well as for working Volk comrades and the German Labor Front[92] has earned abiding merit as bearer of this will to the people who are active in industry. The erection of the National Socialist industrial community, in which each individual is validated as of equal worth, has given to the worker and employee a worthy form of Being, which presents a soothing contrast to the liberalistic-Marxist class standpoint. The social rules of work conditions, healthy construction and beautification of work places, industrial medical care during worktime, the introduction of breaks and the guarantee of extensive vacations, as well as the establishment of free time and vacations from work, "Strength through Joy," are unique in the world, and have given the working Volk comrade the recognition that he is an equally worthy and equally entitled member of the Volk community; he has again returned his heart to the fatherland in unshakable trust.

To defend and to maintain the work force and to raise the working capacity, the Main Office for Volks' Health extended its attention to the care of health in all industries; the implementation of this responsibility was transferred to the office "*Health and Volks' Defense*" of the German Labor Front. This office is given the responsibility to see that all industrial facilities such as factory floors, machine shops, work equipment and the working conditions of the working Volk comrades

[92] Soon after the *Machtuebergreifung,* labor unions were *gleichgeschaltet,* their leaders were arrested, assets were seized and members were compulsorily enrolled in the new German Labor Front (DAF) (Burleigh 2000, 156). Burleigh reports that workers were encouraged to overcome a trades union mentality and to think instead in terms of a 'socialism' transcending mere bread and butter issues. The Nazis recognized the workers' need for respect and the pride they took in their work, their skill, their tools and the products of their labor (Burleigh 2000, 248). The DAF organized vacations, cruises, sailing and golfing outings for workers, all subsidized so that they were financially manageable by the workers. The leader of the DAF, Robert Ley, became notorious even by Nazi standards for his womanizing, alcoholism and brutal behavior; although he was frequently warned by Hitler, *Der Fuehrer* stood by him for his loyalty (Evans 2005, 216).

are so constituted that they correspond to all the demands of hygiene and guarantee the protection of the work force in every respect. The office is organized within the German Labor Front from the Region up to the District. The District and Regional departments of the office of "Health and Volks' Defense," while indeed disciplinarily placed under the corresponding Chairman of the German Labor Front, receive however their technical instructions, working assignments, and directions from the Leader of their office in the Reich Central of the DAF.[93]

The Regional Department Leader of the office of "Health and Volks' Defense" is either centrally or secondarily connected. The District Department of the Office of "Health and Volks' Defense" is to be at first led in personal union by the District Department Leader of the office of Volks' Health of the NSDAP; in the future, a central office industrial physician is to be installed, if possible, as District Department Leader.

Each form of industrial labor contributes an environmental danger to the worker, who frequently has as a consequence premature reduction in performance. We know that many of these injuries, for example, loud noises of the street, the stench of combustible gases of motors, and climatic disturbances, are to a large degree, as yet not avoidable. Nevertheless, with appropriate attention, many of the usual injuries to health could be limited.

The capacities of performance of individuals are as varied as the demands of the work and are dependent on the conditions at the time of the execution, which likewise develop, as previously asserted, out of the hereditary conditions under the effect of favorable and unfavorable environmental influences. This corresponds more or less to the concept of constitution.

We know that work in an appropriate balance of productivity and ability represents a truly healthy appeal of life and that under or over burdening can lead in equal measures to injuries and sicknesses. As a rule, the impairment of capacities occurs as a result of temporary or prolonged over-burdening of individual organs or whole organ systems by the kind or the tempo of the work, by inadequate adaptation as a consequence of unfavorable work conditions (light, air, temperature, dust, poisons), or through other environmental conditions like nutrition, clothing, living quarters, stimulants dangerous to health, free time organizations, sleep. Avoiding these injuries – that means putting off to high old age – can be done if we see to it, through a physician's advice, that the situation of performance corresponds to the correct choice of occupation, and introduce strengent medical oversight of the work of the male and female youth in the industries, with special care of the industry active woman and mother, and take care that a good health situation of the individual is accomplished through appropriate advice and care during work and that health is impaired only as a consequence of the physiological wear and tear of old age.

This process does not begin at any definite year of age, however we can and must push it up beyond 40 years of age. With the woman, the beginning of physiological old age is the beginning of the climacteric phase. With men, we cannot avail our-

[93] German Labor Front.

selves of any such similar sign of this process; here we must satisfy ourselves with the establishment of general symptoms. The working person is especially strongly *disposed* to premature aging if the means whereby he is to perform his work creates a disparity in the physiologically determined decline of his performance strength or if the kind of work performed by him up to that time has not been adjusted to his gradually declining capacities. This work-conditioned-prematurely-threatened decline of strength leads to a situation which we designate with the concept, "*Early Damage.*" Early Damage is regarded to be the function of an organ or organ system somewhere between normal and the sick condition, in which there is decline in function without there being a pathological cause demonstrable. The manifestation of Early Damage occurs for that reason at first less through specific organ failure than much more through a gradual reaction of the body which comes to expression in light tiredness, nervous irritability, abatement of capacities, un-restful non-refreshing sleep, decline in the joy of work and other symptoms. To avoid Early Damage one must apply extensive safeguards by adjusting demanded work to the capacities of aging workers.

We must confess that it will be necessary for science and experience to make dramatic progress in this area to promote the development of imaginable and applicable situations, which now still consist mainly only of supposed hypotheses and theories. As long as no new knowledge is to be won through exact scientific research in these areas, we must support ourselves on the experiences which are to be won at the front, meaning the industrial physician in the industry.

The only fitting activity for the industrial physician is that which brings a certain amount of technical understanding to a fundamental scientific and practical education in the medical field, making it possible for him to fulfill his responsibilities. Great knowledge of life and life experiences must be brought to that responsibility, otherwise the leadership and instruction of the people remain only piece-work. He must especially be given a gift of sharp observation and be in the position to derive from his impressions the correct conclusion concerning the effect of a particular action, allowing him to serve the welfare of the people entrusted to him. This intellectual capacity must be supported by a firm character and a conscientious National Socialist attitude, if he wants to be successful as an educator and taken to be a leader of men.

Oversight of the health-related condition of the industry consists moreover in occasional *industry inspections* by physicians and by *prolonged observation by central and peripheral industrial physicians.* The industry inspection is to be seen as a means to achieve a general overview over the work and health conditions in an industry; it serves more for the education of the physician participating therein, regarding the oversight of health-related conditions of the industry and of its allegiance, and can in fact only be completed by the industry-connected physician. Certainly only really large industries should be supervised by central office industrial physicians. The industrial activities of the industrial physician will make a demand on only a part of the knowledge and ability of the completely educated physician and will thereby not completely satisfy him. Out of this ground and further out of the dearth of physicians, industrial medical activities will have to be performed within the general practice of the current physician in the existing offices.

The industry physician's allegiance is to the industry, having the same duties and rights as these, answering directly to the industry leader. Technical instructions are detailed to him from the office, "Health and Volks' Defense." He is the adviser to the industry leader in all questions which are connected with hygiene within the industry and preventive medicine for the health of the staff. The decision lies however always with the industry leader if he chooses expressly not to order the industry physician to be his representative in the area of health leadership.

The departmental and economic relationships of the industry physician to the industry are regulated by a contract which is subject to certification by the office of "Health and Volks' Defense."

The aim of the industry physician activity lies in the intentions and the efforts to correspondingly collect and analyze all events and occurrences of the working life which wield influence in whatever way on the health and capacity of the workers. For this work, the card index file of each individual serves as the basis for a Reich-unified industry card index file in which all developments, health and performance conditions, are entered, even from the 1st day of employment in the industry. Further, each file card is to be continued and is to be continuously provided with remarks which show the essential illnesses, accidents, deviations in performance, and the like which enable the industry physician always to have an immediate overview of the performance situation of the individual.

It is self-evident that each industry active person must undergo at definite intervals a complete examination, to avoid Early Damage and the attendant progressive decline in function. From the first investigation, these results are entered into the *Health cards*, thereby grounding scientifically the health and performance situation of the working Volk comrades. It enables special statistical evaluation of the results of the performance situation in the various life periods of the individual members and in the various professions.

It is self-evident that the sole responsibility of the industrial physician is to prevent and treat occupational sicknesses and accidents in the factory, with the view that detecting the specific conditions which cause these are to be prevented. Further, the industrial physician will have to see to it that throughout the factory there is immediate delivery of first aid in accidents.

The concept "Industrial Medicine" has not yet achieved its complete and essential content, because the study of the work conditions and their effects on people still stands entirely at its beginning. It will be an interesting responsibility for the industry physician to make an accurate determination of how far certain manifold multifarious methods of work, like machine work, assembly line work, uniform work, monotonous activity as well as the duration and intensity of the demand of the work, each have on the well-being of the worker and how one can come to have injuries. Here is where work shifts, work processes, transportation to work, also nutrition during work, encouragement for hydration and the like, all play a great roll. Also, the industry physician must pay attention to the establishment of free time, with compensation for the burden of work through sports activity, or rest, the spending of vacation and the general life style of the member. His activities must at the *same time* be directed to the avoidance of damaging influences from the work environment, which may be accompanied by attending to the work room, workplace, as well as work clothes, changing, washing, and bathrooms and lavatory, stopping and rest rooms, furnishings for nutrition in the factory, like canteens, and eating rooms, and such things for sports activities, like places for play, playing fields, breast feeding room, nursery and play room for children.

Additionally, the industry physician must reckon among his pressing responsibilities to be the prevention of industrial illness and the prevention of accidents and must *fundamentally* seek to avoid the injuries which come to occur at work through the disparity of demand and the ability to perform.

Above all must he attend to the defense and the promotion of the juvenile worker, in order to protect him from over burdening and otherwise damaging his health. The 1st year of occupation conceals many dangers for the young worker that should be avoided. It is to be noted that the later health and performance of the young worker depends on the developmental stimulations that are permitted during the 1st years of his occupational activity, and that each failure of development correspondingly weakens the Volk strength.

Just as important is the care of the health of the industry active woman. Previously, the woman carried out her position as a housewife and mother or as just a worker based at home, which corresponded to her predisposition and established her purpose as bearer of the coming generation. With growing industrialization, the woman was – mostly just at the end of the school day– introduced into business processes and used there willingly as a cheap and skilled workforce. The performance expected of the woman frequently exceeded her strength; overburdening through heavy work had as a consequence a weakening or slackening of the lower abdominal organs or of the nervous system, occurrences which devastated disastrously our Volk through reduction of fertility and fecundity of women. Today we must sharply distinguish work which a woman is allowed to perform, so as not to injure her biological function; and in no case can she be allowed to perform what is effectively a man's job. It is thereby to be considered that it is not always bodily strength which the woman lacks for certain work, but that it is much more her physical and psychological structure which leads to injury in the performance of certain work.

For the young worker as well as for the working woman the legislature has decreed special regulations over type, duration, etc. of work in industry. We know however from experience that this is by far inadequate to fulfill the demands of the Health Leadership in this regard. With the great dearth of work force which already existed before the war and will continue to an even greater degree after the war, we will have to inject the youth as well as women into the business workforce.[94] Out of the demand that no damage is to be permitted whatsoever with activities in industry,

[94] Attention was paid to the role of women in industry. Legislation was passed prohibiting women workers from having to lift objects heavier than 15 kg in weight. Some plants gave married women – a category forming 40% of the female labor force in 1942 – a choice of shifts while others allowed them to work 5-day instead of 6-day weeks (Grunberger, 257).

grows the obligation of the industry physician and the office of "Health and Volks' Defense" of the German Labor Front to provide all conditions and all means for the establishment of healthy factory work for this essential part of our Volk.

Health Promotion of the Rural Population and the Common Volk Circle

Even if we are able to regard the oversight of health as secured from the viewpoint of consciously responsible health education through leadership and education and, even if we have provided for the young and the employed woman through providing for the mother and child and strengthening the health of a large part of our Volk, large groups of the Volk still stand outside of our health promotion efforts, to which these efforts likewise must be extended. I am thinking here especially of the farmer, the civil servant, the country worker and the freelance man, further of the farm wife with her helpers and the common women who are not engaged in business. The attention of Health leadership must also be directed at them.

Even though there is presently no organization which enables the oversight of health matters for these Volk comrades, I still believe firmly that they also have need for our measures, even if just to a small extent, such as when the house physician of the family gives advice and provides medical help in the sense of our efforts. It is however to be demanded that especially the rural population should experience more intensive attention to their health needs than would normally occur or has occurred. We must not overlook how severely tuberculosis, cancer, rheumatism and other illnesses consume the marrow of our rural populations. And for that reason, by seizing the means of the fight against the devastating Volk illnesses of city dwellers and working people, we must not forget to extend special measures to the rural population if we want to strengthen and maintain this population as the one important source of our Volk strength.

Unfortunately, in general, the farmer calls on the physician only in pressing cases of sickness and injury and rarely requests any regular house physician advice. In the future, he must be placed under preventive health care so that immense damage to this valuable genotype of our Volk is not produced. It is to be the responsibility of the nurturing profession of the Reich and of the states to bring in and prepare the necessary conditions for this purpose, in order to prepare the steps for the Reich Health Leader to achieve the goal of security and promotion of the health of our rural Volk comrades.

The other Volk Comrades still existing outside of healthy preventive medicine represent likewise a valuable part of our Volk. To grasp them effectively in the sense of health leadership is only a question of organization. I hold this Volk group to be developed enough that it is ready and willing to be educated and led health-wise and become responsible for preventive medical checkups to avoid health injuries.

Finally we must recognize that we stand only at the beginning of a work which will be subject to many difficulties, hindrances and fallacies and will be confronted by many critics. This knowledge does not discourage us. It fills us only with so much greater eagerness to achieve the established goal: "*the great health of the German people*"(Nietzsche).[95]

[95] There is an entire historical tradition which finds that National Socialism is a natural consequence of the philosophy of Friederich Nietzsche. This is a complex topic and worthy of several books. Golomb and Wistrich wrote:

Without its biological racism and anti-Semitism, the Nazi worldview had no real cohesion and Nietzsche was as fierce a critic of these aberrations as one can imagine. Moreover, his so-called immoralism, with its questioning of all dogmas and established values, was hardly the basis on which fascist, Nazi, or other totalitarian regimes consolidated their support. On the contrary, such regimes, however radical their intentions, were careful to appeal to conventional morality and nationalist feelings in order to broaden their following, just as they often paid lip service to democratic values in order better to destroy them. (J. Golomb and R. Wistrich, *Nietzsche, Godfather of Fascism?: On the Uses and Abuses of a Philosophy* (Princeton: Princeton University Press, 2002), 14.)

Part VI: The Physician and the Criminal Law

The physician stands like all other Volk comrades under the law. Concerning that, there have been special professional and state laws decreed in consideration of the importance of the physician's activities for the Volk community, whose non-observance or infringement means that he has committed a criminal offense.

The Reich Physicians' Chamber imposes *punishment* on a physician for failure to follow one of its enacted regulations, likewise disciplinary punishment on the grounds of & 53 Abs. 2 of the Reich Physicians' Ordinance for violations against the Professional Ordinance. Also the German Fund Physicians' Union can pronounce disciplinary punishment against him for negligence of his duty as a fund physician. Extreme transgressions set into force the disciplinary punishment of the medical district court or the German Medical Court of Justice. Additionally, the state administration can move against the physician, and this may extend to the point of revocation of his license. If the physician is a member of the Party and the National Socialist Physicians' Association then he should understand that there are special possibilities in the *penal code* for punishment, even the possibility of disciplinary court, in which he can be found guilty in the practice of his profession. Independent of these punishments, there is the duty of compensation for damages, if the physician is found to be guilty.

In case of the raising of a public complaint through the regular court, as a rule, there is opened at the same time a professional judicial proceeding against the accused physician, the implementation of which is postponed however until the judgment of the public court is passed.

With the difficulties associated with the judging of criminality of a physician by non-physicians, several courts in recent years have given a judicial finding whereby

---

As can be seen, the physician was under the jurisdiction of multiple laws and regulations, some of which were so vague that the physician would likely have rightly believed that he was constantly under suspicion. A new Criminal Code had been established in 1933 with the express aim of constructing a policy for 'the elimination from the racial community of elements which damage the people and the race,' (E. Mezger, in Evans 2005, 80) so if the physician failed to do his duty in regards to Racial Hygiene he would become subject to the jurisdiction of this code.

R. Ramm, *Medical Jurisprudence and Rules of the Medical Profession*, Philosophy and Medicine 135, https://doi.org/10.1007/978-3-030-25245-8_6

they are to await the professional court judgment of the Physicians' District Court, in order to find a basis for the judgment of the public court from the charge and judgment rendered thereby.

Prosecutable by the ordering court are *actions* which the law declares to be punishable and *omissions* which lead to a punishable consequence; further unlawful actions and faults are understood to be the deliberate or negligent implementation of an action in the presence of a sound mind.

There is also the concept of a *negligent manner of acting* in the criminal law sense, which relates, in the physician, to when he has permitted medical care outside of his attention to which he was committed and capable of doing in the circumstances and according to his special knowledge and capabilities. One differentiates voluntary and involuntary in criminal law.

In addition to the main sentences (especially prison sentences, jails and fines) there can be *associated punishment* and reprimands for the purpose of security and improvement. For example, in addition to prison sentences, or in some cases in addition to a jail sentence, civil rights can be revoked for up to 5 years, and in some cases for up to 10 years. If the civil rights are revoked the administrative authorities have the duty to revoke the license of the convicted physician & 5 of Reich Physicians' Ordinance] or, if the convicted has not yet been established as a physician, to reject any possible application. After completion of this punishment, the conferring or re-granting of the license comes under the Reich Physicians' Ordinance on the grounds of & 3, number 2.

The & 42 Abs I of the Penal law code presents for all professions and also for the physician the possibility that the practice of the profession can be prohibited[1] for up to a period of 5 years, if one has been declared guilty of a breach or action leading to injury of one under his professional care, and sentenced to a probation of at least 3 months. The prohibition of the practice of the profession can not extend to only parts of the physician's activity, which means, for example, the object of the prohibition can not be made for the treatment of certain body parts, organs or persons, for example women.

The licensure as a physician is an indivisible whole, thus punishment must be either declared completely or completely denied.

Of the actions which the law declares to be punishable, several have already been mentioned. In addition to these are:

Homicide: We distinguish between *premeditated* homicide and homicide by *negligence*. *Premeditated* homicide means assistance in dying in the sense of

[1] Since National Socialist Germany was a "workers" society the prohibition of the practice of one's profession would have been a very serious sentence. One would have been left to the public welfare for subsistence. Welfare assistance was not extended to alcoholics, tramps, homosexuals, prostitutes, the 'work-shy' or the 'asocial,' habitual criminals, the hereditarily ill and members of races other than the Aryan (Evans 2005, 489). Further, the loss of one's civil rights in National Socialist Germany could mean confinement to a work camp. (U. Herbert, K. Orth and C. Dieckmann, *Die nationalsozialistischen Konzentrationslager: Entwicklund und Struktur* (Goettingen: Walstein Verlag, 1998), 822)'

Euthanasia in which the life is shortened with the help of the physician, because of unbearable pain or failing life. It is not customary for the court to consider true assisted suicide to be homicide. If however homicide occurs, even if it occurs with the willingness of the patient, then punishment is given to the physician. The expressed and earnest demands of the person killed will be regarded as mitigating the punishment. With *negligent homicide* a prison sentence of up to 3 years can be assessed on the basis of (*) 222 of the Criminal Law Code. If however the perpetrator has neglected an important duty for which he was especially responsible because of his office or profession, then the punishment can be raised up to 5 years. The omission of a treatment by a physician can lead to a charge of *negligent* homicide.

Abortion [(*) 218 of the Criminal Law Code]

The interruption of a pregnancy is punishable for all people involved, including the woman who aborts her own fetus or allows it to die through abortion or kills it in other ways.[2] Also the attempt to have an abortion is punishable. The commercial involvement in the practice of abortion without the willing participation of the pregnant person is punishable by disciplinary confinement. Also the commercial delivery of a means or device to a pregnant person for the sake of aborting a fetus is punishable. Likewise the public announcement of means, circumstances and processes which lead to abortion is punishable.

In this connection it is worth mentioning an ordinance of the Council of Ministers for the Reich Defense for the protection of honor, family and motherhood of 9 March, 1943. Article II of this ordinance states[3]:

(*) 5 "A women who permits her fetus to die or permits its death through other means will be punished with imprisonment and, in especially egregious cases, with disciplinary confinement.[4]

[2] Abortion in the case of an Aryan woman was prohibited. The physician *as well as the woman seeking the abortion* would be punished.

[3] This paragraph was added to the 1942 text.

[4] Ramm makes a distinction between *Gefangnis* (imprisonment) and *Zuchthaus* (disciplinary confinement). The former consisted of arrest which, in the totalitarian state, could be equivalent to imprisement for an indefinite period of time and associated with interrogations, which themselves could be considered to be a punishing experience.

Regarding disciplinary confinement, Detlev Peukert has reported that since the nineteenth century, there was the conviction that all social problems could be resolved by state intervention (in Herbert, 89). &71 of the German Penal Code of 1871 states: "If punishment by deprivation of liberty and a fine have both been imposed, or is a measure of safety and rehabilitation connected with deprivation of liberty has been imposed in addition to a punishment, the execution of one punishment or measure shall not be barred rior to the bar of the other (Mueller, GOW and Buergenthal T, transl. *The German Penal Code of 1871. (*London: Sweet & Maxwell, 1961). The Nazis often confined people in concentration campes for "protective custody.

The attempt of such an action is punishable.

Whoever destroys the fetus of a pregnant woman by any means will be punished with disciplinary confinement and in milder cases with prison. If the perpetrator has continuously thereby impaired the viability of the German Volk, then this will be recognized as punishable by the death penalty.

Whoever provides a pregnant person with means or conditions for the destruction of a fetus will be subject to punishment and imprisonment and in egregious cases with disciplinary confinement."[5]

(∗) 6 "Whoever destroys negligently in any other than the legally allowed cases the ability to procreate or ability to bear children with another willing person or by oneself alone, or destroys this ability permanently by radiation or hormone treatment will be punished in severe cases with disciplinary confinement, as long as the act is not covered in another regulation with more severe punishment."[6][7]

(∗)7 "Whoever, contrary to a regulation, deliberately or negligently produces, announces or brings into traffic, means or circumstances which are meant to terminate or prevent pregnancy or promote venereal disease, will be punished with imprisonment up to 2 years or with fines."[8]

Obviously the production of an artificial premature birth is not viewed as an abortion, even less so when there exists in the pregnancy a danger for the life or health of the mother.[9] The interruption of a pregnancy on the same grounds may be permitted only through the legally constituted arrangement of an expert.[10]

The physician is guilty of a *physical* damage if he influences the physical wellbeing or disfigures the physical appearance as a consequence of a treatment. Also, worsening of a sickness not introduced from nature can be interpreted to be physical damage. Disturbance of mental health also falls under damage to health. The illegality will however be determined and nonpunishment thereby granted if the physician is authorized through legal determinations to carry out the interventions, like vaccination, sterilization, etc., or if there is the willingness on the part of the patient and if there is danger in delay or if there is an outstanding public interest.

[5] This paragraph was added to the 1942 text.

[6] This paragraph was added to the 1942 text.

[7] The production of sterility was a punishable offense. This particular action was just the sort of sterilization carried out on prisoners by some doctors in the concentration camps did.

[8] This paragraph was added to the 1942 text.

[9] For the sake of the life or health of the mother an "artificial premature birth" could be produced. This would mean the use of artificial means of inducing labor. An abortion was prohibited, but if a doctor could produce an "artificial premature birth," then this was allowed. It would appear that this situation would apply only at term when the pregnancy presented a threat to the health of the mother. Then labor could be induced, for example, with a pitocin drip. It is unclear if a Caeserian section would have been considered to be an acceptable "artificial premature birth." The use of the term "birth" suggests that the fetus would have to survive. It is unclear what it would mean if the fetus did not survive and whether this would constitute an abortion.

[10] This paragraph was added to the 1942 text.

Violation of Professional Secrets

(∗) 13 of the Reich Physicians' Ordinance reads: "A physician who publishes unauthorized an unknown secret which has been entrusted to him in the practice of his profession or has been gathered in the course of his practice, will be punished with imprisonment up to a year and/or fined. The perpetrator goes punishment-free if he makes public such a secret to fulfill a legal duty or moral duty or otherwise for an authorized purpose in a healthy volk sense and if the interests of the law predominate. The act will be pursued only on the application of the injured party. The former President of the Reich Court, Ebermeryer, grounded the entitlement of the criminal offence in this area according to the following: "The trust of the sick person rests in the first line on the fact that the sick can firmly depend that the physician will hold strictly secret all that is told to him regarding the patient's health situation or what the physician himself determines by his treatment, and he will not allow any communication to a third person without or against the will of the patient. Only if the sick person can be able to be certain that the physician remains unalterably silent will he entrust himself unreservedly to the physician. Only then will the physician be able to develop his objective medical activities. So the silence of the physician will become the principle assumption of each fruitful treatment."

The duty of silence lasts throughout the entire life of the physician, and also when he is no longer professionally employed.

It is to be demanded from the professional-ethical standpoint that a physician who in the practice of his profession commits a *moral crime* must suffer an especially harsh penalty.

The physician also commits a crime if he commits a breach against the ordinance which covers the prescribing of medications which contain *narcotics*, just as if he has not followed his duty to report in the *fight against infectious diseases*, or on the *prevention of genetically ill offspring* or *on the abortion of pregnancy*.

Part VII: The Medical Press of the Profession and the Press Organs of the Reich Health Leadership

For the development of a busy professional life and as an informational organ for the whole medical profession and a wider public, the establishment of a medical professional press was of great importance. Before the National Socialist revolution there were two medical newspapers; one entitled the "*Aerztliche Vereinblatt*," which was the organ of the German Physicians' Association and served the professional and ethical concerns of the medical profession; the other, by the name of the "*Aerztliche Mitteilungen*," was produced by the Hartmannbund; it represented the economic professional interests of the medical community. In addition to these there was a long list of local and provincial medical papers.

When in 1933 both medical organizations came under one unified leadership, the two newspapers were consolidated under the name, "*Deutsches Aerzteblatt*" and the entire professional press, if it survived the critical vetting process after the revolution, was put under a unified organization.

The "Deutsches Aerztesblatt" serves to represent the ideal and material interests of the German medical community; it is at the same time the official paper of the Reich Physicians' Chamber and the German Fund Physicians' Union.

Next to the "Deutsches Aerzteblatt" there existed up to the war other medical papers in many medical chamber districts of the Reich, which carried issues on special relationships in the individual territorial divisions and territories of Germany and essentially promoted the lively creation of a regional professional life. It is to be wished that all of these papers will reawaken to life again after the war.

In the recently conquered Regions special physician's papers have also appeared in order to serve the different relationships there. On the grounds of the unification of work these Regions no longer as a rule receive the "Deutsches Aerzteblatt."[1]

[1] This sentence was added to the 1942 text.

R. Ramm, *Medical Jurisprudence and Rules of the Medical Profession*, Philosophy and Medicine 135, https://doi.org/10.1007/978-3-030-25245-8_7

The Health Chambers in the Generalgouvermont[2] *and in the protectorate of Bohemia and Moravia* have their own official papers, which are directed according to the fundamental thinking of the Reich medical press.

Additionally, there is the periodical of the German female physician "*Die Aerztin*," which appears with the report, "Aerztinnen" of the Reich Physicians' Chamber.

The Reich Committee of the *Volk Health Service* produces, in cooperation with the State Academy of the Public Health Service of Berlin and with the Scientific Society of the German Physicians of the Public Health Service, a periodical "*Der Oeffentliche Gesundheitdienst.*"

Also all the usual important health professions produce their own professional periodical.

As in the medical community, there arose for the Party the necessity to create its own press in the area of health politics. *Der Nationalsozialistiche Deutsche Aerztebund* (National Socialist Physicians' Association) founded its own periodical in the year 1932, "*Ziel und Weg,*" which serves as a fighting paper for the expansion of the National Socialist philosophical viewpoint in the health professions; questions over Racial Hygiene, Care of Genetic Health, population politics and general Volk health make up its essential content. After the establishment of the Main Office of Volks' Health in1934, "Ziel und Weg" became the press organ of this office.

It should be mentioned that in individual Gaue of Germany, even before the establishment of "Ziel und Weg," similar fighting periodicals had already come into being, like the "NS-Gesundheitdienst" in the Region of Berlin, to which there followed others very soon in various German Regions.

In addition to "Ziel und Weg" there has been from the time of the overtaking of power a further new establishment, *"Die Volksgesundheit Wacht*, which dealt with the shortcomings of the methods used for promoting health and treatment. Shortly before the death of Dr. Wagner there was established by the Main Office for Volks' Health, "Die Gesundheitsfuhrung des deutschen Volks," which deals with questions of Volks' Health. On 1 Oct 1939, Reich Health Leader Dr. Conti ordered it to join the periodical "Ziel und Weg" and "Die Volksgesundheits Wacht" to become the monthly periodical "*Die Gesundheitsfuhrung-ziel und Weg*." This is now the general organ of the Main Office for Volks' Health of the NSDAP, of the Expert Advisory Committee and of the National Socialist German Physicians' Association.

On 1.11.1942 there appeared in the framework of NS correspondence of the Eher-Verlages in half-monthly issues, "Die Volksgesundheit" as the official press service of the Reich Health Leader and of the Main Office for Volks' Health of the NSDAP. It serves to inject the daily and periodical press with the ideas of preventive healthcare.[3]

---

[2] This term refers to the former country of Poland.

[3] This paragraph was added to the 1942 text.

The *Political Racial Office of the NSDAP* decrees since 1933 have produced, through the monthly periodical "Neues Volk," challenges for the extension of racial and genetic biological thinking.

List of Literature

1. Berger, H.: Kulturspiegel des heutigen Arzttums. G. Fischer, Jena, 1940.
2. Bewer, C.: Die Pflicht zur Hilfeleistung bei Ungluecksfaellen, D.A. Bl 15/141.
3. Beyer, G.: Das Kassenaerzterecht von heute. Noske, Borna 1940.
4. Blome, K.: Die Neuordnung der aerztlichen Fortbildung. D. A. Bl. 1936 – Der aerztliche Nachwuchs. Gesundheitsfuehrung Mai 1940.
5. Coermann und Wagner: Deutsches Aerzterecht. Hippokrates-Verlag 1938.
6. Conti, L.: Jugendgesundheitspflege. D.A. Bl. 18/1940 – Volksgesundheit – Volksschicksal – Die Gesundheitsfuehrung 1/1939. redden. D. A. Bl. u.a. – Die Brudngedanken des neuen Hebammengesetzes. D. A. Bl. 3/1939.
7. Diepgen, P.: Geschichte der Medizin. Walter de Gruyter & Co., Berlin.
8. Grote, H.: Die Entwicklung des Berufs-und Standeslebens der deutschen Aerzteschaft – Die Stellung des Arztes in der deutschen Sozialversicherung. Die Sozialversicherung 1938. – Grundsatzliches zum aerztlichen Versorgungs- und Fuersorgewesen. D. A. Bl. 9/1937.
9. Guett: Der offentliche Gesundheitsdienst. Carl Heymanns Vlg Berlin, 1939. Guett, Conti u. andere: Der Amtsarzt. Gustav Fischer, Jena, 1937.
10. Gruber, G. B.: Einfuehrung in Geist und Studium der Medizin. Georg thieme, Leipzig, 1934. – Von aerztlicher Ethik. Hippokrates-Vlg, St.
11. Hadrich, J.: A-Z der aerztl. Organisationskunde. G. Thieme, Leipzig.
12. Haeser, H.: Geschicht der Medizin. Gustav Fischer, Jena 1882.
13. Hebestreit, Hoffmann, Teitge: Schutz und Erhaltung der Arbeitskraft. Verlag Otto Elsner, Berlin, 1939.
14. Hoerdemann-Joppich: Die Gesundheitsfuehrung der Jugend. J.F. Lehmann, Muenchen-Berlin, 1939.
15. Kitzing, E.: Erziehung zur Geundheit. Reichsgesundheitsverlag, Berlin-Wien, 1941.
16. Klare, K.: Soll ich Medizin studieren? Georg Thime, Leipzig 1941.
17. Krehl, L.: Der Arzt, Hippokrates-Verlag, Stuttgart, 1938.
18. Kraus, H.: Die Verpflichtung des Aerztefuehrers. Hippokrates-Verlag, Stuttgart, 1941.
19. Liek, E.: Der Arzt und seine Sendung. J. F. Lehmann, Muenchen, 1936.
20. Liertz und Paffrath: Handbuch des Arztrechtes. L. Schwann, Duesseldorf, 1938.
21. Meyer-Steinegg u. Sudhoff: Geschichte der Medizin im Ueberblick. Gustav Fischer, Jena, 1938.
22. Mrugowsky, J.: Das aerztliche Ethos. J. F. Lehmann, Muenchen, 1939.
23. Organisationsbuch der NSDAP. Verlag Franz Eher Nf., Muenchen 1938.
24. Ramm, R. u.a.: Der Fruehschaden. 1937.

25. Schuett?Wollenweber: Der Arzt des oeffentlichen Gesundheitsdienstes 1941. Georg Thieme, Leipzig.
26. Stuckart-Globke: Kommentare zur deutschen Rassengesetzbebung. Verlag C. H. Beck, Muenchen, 1936.
27. Wagner, g.: Die Ziele der nationalsozialistischen Gesundheitspolitik. Ziel und Weg 1937.
28. Wege zur Gesundheitsfuehrung in den Betrieben. Verlag der DAF, 1941.
29. Zeis-Pintschowius: Zivilisationsschaeden am Menschen. J. F. Lehmann, Muenchen, 1940.

Appendix

Laws, Ordinances and Decrees Appointment and Testing Ordinance for Physicians

Of 17 July, 1939 (RGBl I S. 1273)

On the grounds of && 3 and 92 of the Reich Physicians' Ordinance of 13 December, 1935 (Reich Law Code I P. 1433) it is ordered:

First Part

Responsibility for the Appointment as a Physician

& 1

Second Part

Preconditions for the Appointment as a Physician

& 2

The appointment as a physician is to occur, as long as there are no disqualifying grounds (& 3 Abs. 2 to 4 of the Reich Physicians Ordinance), if according to the judgment of the Authorities of the German State, the physician examination has been passed. Exceptions to this are to occur only on special grounds after a hearing by the Reich Physicians' Chamber (& 80).

R. Ramm, *Medical Jurisprudence and Rules of the Medical Profession*,
Philosophy and Medicine 135, https://doi.org/10.1007/978-3-030-25245-8

Third Part

Physician Education

& 3

The goal of physician education is herein shown to be preparation for his Specialty by fulfilling the obligatory responsibilities of a capable physician according to the Reich Physicians' Ordinance.

& 4

1. The education is scientific and practical.
2. The course of the scientific education is directed by decrees of medical ordinance studies enacted by the Reich Minister of Science, Education and Volks' Education in agreement with the Reich Minister of the Interior.
3. Scientific education is to consist of university study of a duration of 10 half-years, of which there are 4 half-years of preclinical study and 6 half-years of clinical study.
4. Practical education is to be engaged in before, during and after the scientific education.
5. Practical education is to consist of:

   (a) Clinical service of at least 6 months (& 5)
   (b) Factory or rural Service of 6 weeks (& 6)
   (c) Activity as an intern altogether of 6 months (& 7)

& 5

1. Those fit for military service carry out their obligation for training in a health care institution as a rule before the beginning of studies in the Sanitary Service of the Army or of the Waffen SS. They obtain thereby a certification from these departments of service.
2. Those unfit for military service and female students undertake 6 months of nursing service before the beginning of studies under the oversight of the German Red Cross in a university clinic or one of the hospitals deemed appropriate. The supervision in the clinic or hospital is to take place by agreements between the German Red Cross and the Specialty Groups for Volks' Health of the Leadership of Students of the university to which the studies are anticipated to begin. They produce proof of the training in nursing by a medical leader of this training and from the Specialty Group Leader for Volks' Health of the Leadership of Students of a university of the German Reich before and after the completion of the training with a witnessed notarized document exhibited according to pattern 1.
3. During their student time, those who are unfit for military service and female students are on standby to the German Red Cross or the Health Service of the Hitler Youth. They are to carry out the previously described service mission of external and continued training according to the service manual Nr. 1 of the German Red Cross or according to the regulations on Health Service of the Hitler Youth. Mission and external and continued training are to proceed in

harmony with the Reich Students' Leadership. These are to be proven by a notarized certified copy from Reich Specialty Group for Volks' Health of the Leadership of Reich Students of the Presidium of the German Red Cross or of the Youth Leader of the German Reich.

4. Exceptions to the conditions of Abs. 1, 2 and 3 can be granted only on special grounds. (& 80).

& 6

1. The factory or rural service is to be served as a rule in the pre-term free time at the end of the third student half-year. It is to be proven through a certification exhibited according to pattern 2 from the Specialty Group Leader for Volks' Health of the Leadership of Students of a university of the German Reich. Exceptions can be granted only on special grounds (& 80).
2. Active Sanitation Officials of the Army and the SS are relieved from factory and rural service.

& 7

1. The training as an intern is to take place during the clinical study time, as a rule in the pre-lecture free time at the end of the seventh and ninth student half-years in university clinics or polyclinics of the German Reich or in affiliated institutions certified thereby by the Reich Minister of the Interior, such as hospitals or affiliated institutions or in hospitals of the Army or the SS or with free standing active physicians, who are named by the Reich Physicians' Chamber.
2. The training has to be done in general for each half in two different areas of medicine.
3. At least 4 weeks of the training are to occur in an affiliated institution or in a university clinic for obstetrics or in a Specialty physician led obstetrics department or in some other departments of a hospital which is deemed appropriate by the Reich Minister of the Interior, with approval by the Reich Physicians' Chamber for practical training for the studying of medicine in obstetrics, or with an independent active physician who has been empowered by the Reich Physicians' Chamber for practical training for the study of obstetrics. Whoever during the student time finds no opportunity for this practical training in obstetrics must gain it during the time of being an obligated assistant. (& 77).
4. Supervision as an intern in the university clinic and polyclinic, which takes place at health care and affiliated institutions and independent active physicians empowered by the Reich Minister of the Interior (& 7 Abs.1), is covered by the Specialty Group for Volks' Health of the university in which the training occurs. The training as an intern is to be proven by a certificate according to pattern 3, which has been produced by the physician who provided the training or under whose leadership the training was undertaken, as long as the training has not occurred in a military hospital; a notarized statement is to be provided before and after the completion of the training by the Specialty Group Leader for Volks' Health of the Leadership of Students of a university of the German Reich.

5. Exception to the conditions of Abs. 1 to 4 can be granted only on special grounds (& 80)

Fourth Part

Preparation for Independent Practice in the Medical Profession
& 8

Immediately after the appointment as a physician, activity of a year's duration as an obligatory assistant (& 77) and a three-month-long rural medical activity are to commence. (& 78)

Fifth Part

Conditions of Examinations
General Conditions
& 9

The examination year goes from 1 October to the 30th of September

& 10

1. The examinations are to be taken before an examination committee.
2. Committees for physician medical pre-examinations are established at each university of the German Reich, committees for physician examinations, at each university of the German Reich and at the Academy of Medicine in Dusseldorf. They are convened for each examination year by the highest Territorial authorities after consultation with the medical faculty – in Dusseldorf of the Academic Council of the Academy of Medicine.
3. As a rule, the Chairman and his Vice-Chairman of the regular professors of the medical faculty, as well as the members of the university subject of the Specialty are to produce the subject matter of the examination.

& 11

The Chairman formulates the examination and establishes the sequence in which the individual Specialties or sections are to be taken up. He sees to it therefore that the conditions of the Ordinance of Appointment are followed exactly. In the case of temporary incapacity of a member of the examination committee, he assigns a substitute. He reports immediately after the completion of the examination year to the established authorities of the activity of the committee and reports the calculation of the fees.

& 12

Each examiner is allowed to test as a rule no more than four examinees at the same time.

& 13

The Reich Minister of the Interior, the Reich Minister for Science, Education and Volks' Training and the highest Territorial authorities may dispatch a representative to the examinations.

& 14

1. The application for licensure for examination is to be directed to the Chairman of the Examination Committee.
2. Application for licensure for the examination of foreigners and applications for licensure which require approval of an exception have to be submitted to the Chairman of the highest Territorial Authorities.

& 15

1. To the application is to be attached the school leaving certificate from a public or recognized private college in foundational or established form or some other from the Reich Minister for Science, Education and Volks' Training of equally recognized pre-training. Exceptionally, the school leaving certificate of a corresponding school outside of the German Reich can be deemed satisfactory.
2. With school leaving certificates in which one is unable to prove knowledge of Latin, the contestant must at the latest at the time of pretesting produce proof that he possesses knowledge in Latin equivalent to that required in the school leaving certificate of high school. The proof is to be gained through a witnessed examination which is taken before a special state committee.
3. To the application is further to be attached a state certified proof of the birth certificate and a completed questionnaire according to pattern 4. German state citizens have to produce in addition the marriage certificate of their parents as well the birth certificate of the parents and the grandparents or in place of these certificates, the proof of ancestry (*Ahnenpass*. The documents must prove the date of birth, the ancestry and the religion. A married candidate must also produce necessary documents for the spouse for the proof of ancestry as well as the marriage certificate.
4. In addition, proofs of the studies which are appropriate for the Ordinance of medicine are to be attached to the application, with the record of registration or the certificate of graduation from a university.

& 16

(1) Licensure for examination is to be denied if the student cannot prove training appropriate to the Ordinance or the necessary documents and witnesses relevant to & 15 cannot be produced. Exceptions can be granted only on special grounds. (& 80)

(2) The licensure for examination is further denied,

   1. if the application does not possess civil rights,
   2. if the facts are present which charge that the applicant lacks political or moral reliability, especially if severe criminal or moral failings are charged;

3. if the applicant, as a consequence of a physical defect or because of weakness of his intellectual powers or because of an addiction, lacks the required qualification or reliability;
4. if the applicant or his spouse, because of their ancestry, cannot be a public official. Exceptions from this can be granted only on special grounds (& 80).

(3) Foreigners who are licensed for the examination are to be notified that they have no claim to the Apppointment as a physician.

& 17

The proofs and documents which are required for licensure for the examination are to be submitted in the original. Only notarized copies can be recognized as adequate except in exceptional circumstance.

& 18

The examination may only be postponed or repeated with the committee with which it was begun. Exceptions can only be granted on special grounds (& 80). With the application for approval of exception there is to be likewise produced a declaration by the Chairman of the previous examination committee on whether consideration is opposed by the committee.

& 19

For each Specialty examination of each examination section there is to come from each of the participating examiners a judgment produced using the exclusive designations: very good (1), good (2), adequate (3), not adequate (4), and bad (5).

& 20

For the examination of each examinee there is to be produced a record with a heading in which the name of the examiner, the examination Specialty or examination section, the examination day, the judgment and the entire result of the examination are produced. The examiner must personally sign the given judgment, the Chairman must personally sign the record with the completed result. A judgment of "not adequate" or "bad" must be briefly reported. To establish a time period of repetition the Chairmen is to take into account the period of time and the conditions of whose fulfillment the licensure for a repeat examination depends.

& 21

The rulings from the Chairman of an Examination Committee covering the result of an examination are binding for all Examination Committees.

& 22

1. The examination fees are established by the Reich Minister of the Interior
2. The employment of relevant savings as well as accrued fees regarding the distribution of the fees for actual and administrative costs is decided by the highest Territorial authority.

& 23

The medical pre-examination has to be taken before the examination committee of the university of the German Reich in which the student pursued medical studies. Exceptions can be granted only on special grounds (& 80).

& 24

Examinations take place in the period from 10 February until 30 April and in the period from 10 July until 31 October. The deadline of the application for the examination is to be established by the Chairman in agreement with the examiners.

& 25

1. The application for licensure for medical pre-examination is provided by the Chairman of the examination committee until the 25th of January or until the 25th of June. Tardy applications can be considered only on adequate grounds.
2. At the time of reporting for the examination, the student must prove that he has studied medicine which conforms to the Ordinance (& 15 Abs. 4), has completed according to the school leaving certificate at least four half-years at universities of the German Reich, as well as completed the nursing service (& 5) and factory or rural service (& 6). Those unfit for military service and female students have in addition to prove that since the beginning of their studies they have belonged to the Readiness Reserve of the German Red Cross or to the Health Service of the Hitler Youth (&5 Abs. 3).
3. To the application is to be attached in addition the documents designated in & 15 Abs. 1 to 3.
4. To the application are furthermore to be attached the documents that the student
   (a) has taken the following courses:
   During the course of a half-year, one course each in zoology, botany with excursions for healing herbs, histology, theory of heredity and racial science, preservation of the Volk population, history of medicine, embryology, physiological chemistry encompassing military chemistry and work-, sport- and defense physiology encompassing flight medicine, during two half-year, one full course in chemistry, physics and general physiology and during three half-years, a complete course in anatomy.
   (b) has regularly and with success taken part in the following practical activities:
   During the period of a half-year, a physical, a chemical, a general-physiological and a physiological-chemical practicum, as well as a microscopic-anatomy course and during two half-years in practice, preparation for anatomical studies.
5. To the document covering the attendance at courses, there is to be produced, according to pattern 5, the registration books or the school-leaving certificate of the university; the document covering the participation at the practical activities is to be produced with witnesses. (& 80)

& 26

Exceptionally, the study time of the preclinical study time can be entirely or partly credited (& 80), which according to the completion of the school leaving certificate

(a) it has been attended at one of the medically related university or college studies,
(b) it has been covered in a foreign university.

& 27

1. If the student has been approved, then he will, after the payment of the examination fee, be invited to examination by the Chairman, after the declaration of the examination time established for the individual Specialty.
2. The examination day established by the Chairmen serves as the beginning of the examination (& 33 Abs. 3)

& 28

1. If a student appears at the incorrect time or not at all without adequate excuse, this is to result in the sacrifice of the relevant portion of the fees for the affected Specialty.
2. Whoever appears after the beginning of the examination with an adequate excuse is reimbursed the portion of the fees for the yet incompletely begun Specialty. The yet unused portion of the fees are to be thereby forfeited for actual costs and administrative costs. If an adequate excuse for the withdrawal is not produced, then the half of the portion of the fees for the not yet begun Specialties is likewise forfeited.
3. If a student is hindered from concluding the examination by an unexcused absence from an established examination period or unexcused withdrawal, the Chairman can, in agreement with the examiners, declare a non-pass for all or individual Specialties; he has then to establish if necessary a time for a repeat examination (& 32). The portion of the fee for the Specialty declared a non-pass is entirely forfeited. One may appeal the ruling of the Chairman within 2 weeks to the highest Territorial authority.

& 29

The medical pre-examination encompasses the following specialties:

I. Anatomy
II. General Physiology and Physiological Chemistry
III. Physics
IV. Chemistry
V. Zoology and Botany.

& 30

1. The examination is to be seen as a unified whole. It is as a rule to be finished in 4 week days, one after the other, so that the anatomy examination takes place

over 2 days while 1 day is taken for general physiology and physiological chemistry and 1 day for the remaining examination subjects.

2. The two parts of subjects II (a. general physiology and b. physiological chemistry) and V (a. zoology and b. botany) may be specially examined.
3. In the anatomy examination, the student must

   (a) elucidate the addressed part in the main portion of the body or a region of the phylogeny or the limb in the body according to form, place and relationship (Situs).
   (b) prepare properly a simple anatomical preparation and elucidate and prove by an oral examination his familiarity with the various parts of the described anatomy;
   (c) prepare two microscopic-anatomical preparations and elucidate and show by an oral examination his fundamental knowledge of the theory of tissue and that he knows the foundations of the history of its development.

4. In the examination in General Physiology and in Physiological Chemistry, the student must show that he is familiar with general physiology as well as acquainted with the more important investigational apparatuses and methods.
5. The examination in Chemistry and in Physics is assumed to produce and especially to take into consideration the demands on the future physician. In Zoology and Botany the examination is to extend to the foundations of general Biology with special consideration of the theory of heredity.
6. Whoever has achieved a doctorate at a university of the German Reich on the grounds of an examination in science will then be examined in Physics, Chemistry, Zoology and Botany only if these subjects have not been present on the graduation examination.
7. Some other examinations in natural science subjects which were taken entirely at universities or colleges of the German Reich can as an exception be counted as the medical pre-examination.

& 31

1. If an examination subject has been judged as "not adequate" or "bad," then it is considered to have not been passed.
2. If in the Specialty II one or the other part has been judged as "not adequate" or "bad," then the entire examination subject "General Physiology and Physiological Chemistry" is considered to have not been passed.
3. Furthermore, in Specialties II and V the judgment for the entire subject will be dealt with in the following way: The sum of the numerical value (& 19) of the two individual judgments is divided by 2, which leads to the total grade for the examination subject; the grade fraction which is remaining of the distribution will thereby be calculated as a whole.

& 32

1. The student must repeat the examination in the subject in which he has not passed.

2. The earliest period, after which the repetition of the examination can be earliest taken, after the student has completed the examination in all subjects, is determined by the Chairman, after consulting with the upcoming examiners. It may be from 2 to 9 months, depending on the judgments rendered and the number of not passed subjects.
3. If the student has failed subject I or II, then the Chairman can, after consulting the subject examiner, make the licensure for a repeat of the examination dependent upon the student studying another half-year, with this additional study conducted under the direction of the Chairman. One may appeal the decision of the Chairman within 2 weeks to the highest Territorial authority.

& 33

1. The Chairman determines the point in time up to the latest that the notification of a repeat examination is permitted.
2. If the student reports at the wrong time for the repeat of the examination without an adequate excuse, then the Chairman, after consultation with the examination committee, can rule that the medical pre-examinations in all the subjects are to be repeated. The already completed subjects are then considered to have not been passed. The unused remaining fees are forfeited. One may appeal the ruling of the Chairman within 2 weeks to the highest Territorial authority.
3. If an examination has not been completed in a period of 12 months after the beginning of the examination (& 27 Ab 2), then, as in all subjects, it is considered to have not been passed. It may not be repeated. The unused remaining fees are forfeited. Exceptions can be granted only on special grounds. (& 80)

& 34

The repeat examination takes place in the presence of the Chairman. If the examiner or the student requests, a holder (of documents) is to be consulted. The holder (of documents) will be designated by the Chairman from the membership of the examination committee. The registrations of the supervision of the repeat examination are to be specifically signed by the examiner as well as by the Chairman and the holder of documents.

& 35

Whoever also does not pass the repeat examination has not passed the medical pre-examination. He will not be admitted to another examination. Exceptions can be granted only on special grounds. (& 80)

& 36

After the completion of each examination and repeat examination, the supervision of the examination by the examiner of the last subject is immediately transmitted to the Chairman.

& 37

If the student has been given in all five of the subjects at least the grade of "adequate" and with that, passed the medical pre-examination, then the Chairman is to designate the entire result of the medical pre-examination in the following way:

For the subjects I and II it will be every fifth subject, for the subjects III and IV every second subject and for subject V the simple number is reported, which of the grades for each subject come up according to the gradations in & 19. The sum of the numbers gained thereby give to the entire judgment that if the sum is up to 22 it is considered to be "very good," from 23 to 37 "good" and from 38 as "adequate."

& 38

1. For the result of the medical pre-examination there is to be produced for the student a document according to pattern 6. If a repeat examination is to be entered, then the document is to bear the intervals according to && 32 and 33. After the completion of a repeat examination, the student receives a document according to pattern 7.
2. If the result of the examination is established according to & 28 Abs. 3 or & 33 Abs. 2, then no judgment is given to the examination document for the relevant subjects or the entire judgment (&19), but rather the relevant assessment is briefly given.
3. The documents produced with the application for licensure (& 25) are, after the ultimate settlement of the medical pre-examination of the student, again produced, afterwards an endorsement concerning the result of the medical pre-examination is to be entered in the registration book or the school leaving certificate.

& 39

After the conclusion of each examination and repeat examination, the Chairman must within 3 days distribute the results of the examination and the rulings according to & 28 Abs. 3 and &33 Abs. 2 to the university authorities. If the student leaves the university before passing the entire examination, then the university authorities are to enter a corresponding endorsement in the school leaving certificate.

& 40

C. Medical Examination

The medical examination is to be seen as a unified whole. The candidate must have at the beginning of the examination concluded the preparation for the entire medical examination, so that he is the position to complete the examination in the shortest amount of time without pauses between the individual sections. As a rule, the medical examination should take up in its entirety not more than 6 weeks.

& 41

The medical examination can be taken before each committee for the medical examination at any university of the German Reich or before the examination committee at the Medical Academy in Duesseldorf.

& 42

1. The examination periods begin on 10 February and on 10 July each year.
2. The applications for licensure for the examination are to be submitted to the Chairman of the examination committee before which the examination is to be taken, from 25 January or 25 Jun; late applications can only be considered on adequate grounds.

& 43

1. To the registration are to be attached the certificate which is required according to & 25 for licensure for the medical pre-examination as well as the document covering the completely passed medical pre-examination.
2. The exceptions which are accepted for the licensure for medical pre-examination are valid also for the medical examination.
3. An examination completely passed outside of the German Reich can only in exceptional circumstances be recognized as a substitute for the medical pre-examination.

& 44

1. To the registration is further to be attached the School Leaving Certificates of the universities or of the Medical Academy in Duesseldorf or the registration book which adduces proof that the candidate has studied medicine according to the ordinance after the attainment of the School Leaving Certificate, which itself attests to the medical pre-examination, including at least 10 half-years at a university of the German Reich or the Medical Academy at Duesseldorf.
2. Of the study time which is documented, there must be reserved at least 6 half-years, after the completely passed pre-examination. The half-year in which the medical pre-examination has been passed will only be credited if the medical pre-examination has been completely passed by 30 April or 31 October. Exceptions can be granted only on special grounds. (& 80)

& 45

1. To the registration is further to be attached proof that the candidate after the completely passed medical pre-examination, at least

   (a) has attended a course covering medical preparation, surgical preparation, obstetrical preparation, general pathology and pathological anatomy, special pathology, topographical anatomy, military pathology, pathological physiology, pharmacology and toxicology of inorganic substances, military pharmacology and military toxicology, natural healing methods, medical radiology, orthopedics, diseases of the teeth and gums, occupationl diseases, expertise in social insurance and accident medicine, legal medicine and medical jurisprudence and rules of the profession, human genetic theory, racial hygiene and hygiene with the special consideration of industry and the military.

(b) has regularly, and with success, participated in a pathological-anatomical demonstration course, a pathological-histological course, a sectioning course, a course on auscultation and percussion, a course of clinical chemistry, an obstetric and gynecological investigation course, a medical house-call course, a surgical house-call course, an obstetrical-gynecological house-call course, an obstetrical operations course, an ophthalmology course, an ear, nose and throat course, a course on prescribing, a bacteriological-serological course and an immunization course.

(c) has regularly participated with success two half-years each as a practitioner in the medical, surgical, obstetrics-gynecological clinics and pediatric clinic or polyclinic and has delivered three presentations as an assistant physician in the presence of the teacher.

(d) has visited regularly and with success a half-year as practitioner of a medical polyclinic, a surgical polyclinic, a polyclinic for tooth, mouth and mandible diseases, a psychiatric clinic (with discussion of military psychiatry and psychology), a polyclinic for throat, nose and ear diseases, a clinic and polyclinic for eye diseases, a clinic and polyclinic for skin diseases and venereal diseases and a surgical practicum and has observed and contributed to the carrying on of business.

(e) was active 6 months as an intern according to the relevant conditions which are in & 7.

2. The proof of the visits to the lectures (Abs. 1 Book a) is to be entered into the record of registration or graduation certificate. The proof of participation in the courses and clinics (Abs. 1 Books b, c and d) are provided by the medical leaders of the clinics, polyclinics, hospitals or institutes on documents issued according to pattern 8. Concerning participation in the immunization course, there is to be a document produced from a teacher charged by the authorities to give the training in immunization technique, the document is produced according to pattern 9. The activity as an intern is to be proven according to & 7 Abs. 4
3. Exceptions to the conditions of Abs. 1, 2 and 3 can be granted only on special grounds. (& 80)

& 46

Additionally to be attached to the application:

(a) A personally written autobiographical statement in which the course of the university studies is represented.

(b) In case the applicant has not applied soon after leaving the university, a certificate of good conduct from the police for the intervening time.

& 47

Within 3 days after receiving the disposition of licensure, the candidate must report personally to the Chairman of the Examination Committee without special request and thereby show the disposition of licensure as well as the voucher of receipt for the submitted fees (& 22).

& 48

1. The examination encompasses the following sections:

    I. Pathological Anatomy and general Pathology,
    II. Topographical Anatomy,
    III. Pathological Physiology,
    IV. Pharmacology,
    V. Internal Medicine
    VI. Pediatrics,
    VII. Natural Healing Methods,
    VIII. Surgery,
    IX. Obstetrics and Gynecology,
    X. Ophthalmology,
    XI. Ear, Throat and Nose Diseases,
    XII. Dermatology and Venereal Disease,
    XIII. Mental Illness
    XIV. Diseases of Teeth and the Gums,
    XV. Industrial Diseases,
    XVI. Expertise in Social Insurance and Trauma Medicine,
    XVII. Legal Medicine,
    XVIII. Hygiene,
    XIX. Racial Hygiene,

2. The examiner in the individual examination sections must determine if the candidate has grasped the knowledge offered in the pre-clinical study time in Anatomy and Physiology and has learned to deepen this during his clinical studies. In so far as the candidate has been given the opportunity, they are to consider whether the candidate is also familiar with the various areas of military medicine. He also directs his attention to determine that the candidate knows how to take into account economic matters. At the same time, the history of the individual candidate under examination and his relationship to the practically important area of the theory of genetics and social hygiene are to be taken into consideration. Finally, it is also to be noted if the candidate possesses verbal understanding for medical technical terms.

& 49

1. In the clinical examination, the student of medicine is given access to the clinic where he may participate in the auscultation practice in the relevant clinic.

Students who have completely passed the medical pre-examination are allowed to attend the standard examinations.

2. In addition, admittance is left at the discretion of each teacher of medicine at a university of the German Reich and the Medical Academy in Duesseldorf.

& 50

The examination in pathological Anatomy and general Pathology (I) encompasses two parts. It is to be picked up from an examiner and completed in 1 day. The candidate must be prepared:

(a) to point to the complete section of at least one of the three main cavities of the body and immediately write down the findings.
(b) to do two to three pathological-anatomical preparations, of which in each case one should be a microscopic one, to thereby elucidate in a thorough oral examination his knowledge of pathological anatomy and general pathology.

& 51

The examination in Topographical Anatomy (II) is to be completed in a single day. It is to be given in general by two examiners and specifically from the Specialty representative and the representative of Internal Medicine or the Surgical Clinic or the Woman's Clinic. The candidate must demonstrate in an oral examination his familiarity with the topographical part of anatomy under consideration on the living subject. The examination must be confined as a rule to one body region.

& 52

The examination in Pathological Physiology (III) is oral and is to be completed in 1 day. It is to be developed in general by two examiners and specifically by the Specialty representative and the representative of Internal Medicine. The candidate has to prove that he is familiar with the most important physiological principles of disease signs.

& 53

The examination in Pharmacology (IV) is to be taken in a single day from a single examiner. The candidate has to complete several assignments consisting of prescribing of medication and orally showing that he possesses the knowledge required for a practicing physician in pharmacology and toxicology, including military toxicology, and that he has also become familiar with the economical manner of prescribing.

& 54

1. The examination in Internal Medicine (V) is to be completed in three consecutive days and developed by two examiners in a university clinic or university polyclinic or in the medical department of a large hospital. The candidate must

   (a) on two consecutive days, each in the presence of the examiners, investigate a disease, its anamnesis, diagnosis and prognosis in the given case, as well as give a treatment plan, write down his findings immediately with the endorsement of the examiner and, on the same day, prepare at home a critical report of the disease case, which, with date and signature provided, is delivered the next morning to the examiner.

(b) visit the patient who is assigned to him on the first examination day on the second and third days, visit the patient who is assigned to him on the second day at least once on the third day, visit more often on the demand of the examiner, describe on the report submitted by the examiner given to him the interconnections of the course of the disease, with the information of the treatment in the form of a disease sheet, and if the patient dies before the completion of the examination, give a written judgment of the case, as well as taking into account as much as possible the findings of each section. If one of the patients assigned to the candidate leaves treatment before the completion of the examination, then the examiner has to determine if the candidate is to have another patient assigned.

2. Each examiner must attend the patients' visits (Abs. 1 Book b) at least once, so as to go through the disease report with the candidate and induce him if necessary to supplement it.
3. On the occasion of the visit of the patients (Abs. 1 Book a and b) the candidate must prove at the patients' visits' (Abs. 1 Book a and b) his capability in the diagnosis and prognosis of the internal diseases and his familiarity with the entire theory of the means of healing, in so far as it is not the object of the examination in Pharmacology.

& 55

1. The examination in pediatrics (VI) is to be developed by one examiner in a university clinic or a university polyclinic or in the pediatrics department of a large hospital, and is to be completed in 2 days.
2. In the presence of the examiners, the candidate must investigate a disease of a child, its anamnesis, diagnosis and prognosis in the given case as well as give a treatment plan, write down his findings immediately with the of the examiner, and still on the same day prepare at home a critical report of the disease case, which, with date and signature provided, deliver it the next morning to the examiner. Then he has to treat the child on the next day under the supervision of the examiner and prove in an oral examination as well as in other cases, that he possesses the knowledge required in pediatrics to be a practicing physician.

& 56

1. The examination in the natural methods of healing (VII) is oral. It is to be completed in 1 day.
2. The candidate must prove that he possess the knowledge in the methods of natural healing required for a practicing physician.

& 57

1. The examination in surgery (VIII) is as a rule to be completed in four consecutive week days. It is developed by two examiners, who must examine generally in the theory of operations (Abs. 5), in the theory of fractures and dislocations (Abs. 6) and in orthopedics (Abs. 7), in a university clinic or university polyclinic or in the surgical department of a large hospital, or, in requisite cases, in an anatomical institute.
2. The candidate must

   (a) on two consecutive days each in the presence of the examiners, investigate a disease, its anamnesis, diagnosis and prognosis in the given case as well as give a treatment plan, write down his findings immediately with the endorsement of the examiner and, still on the same day, prepare at home a critical report of the disease case, which, with date and signature provided, is delivered the next morning to the examiner;
   (b) visit on each of the next 2 days the two patients assigned to him, on the demand of the examiner visit more often, describe the connection of the course of the disease on the report submitted by the examiner given to him with the information of the treatment in the form of a disease sheet, and if the patient dies before the completion of the examination, give a written judgment of the case, taking into account as much as possible the findings of each section. If one of the patients assigned to the candidate leaves treatment before the completion of the examination, then the examiner must determine if the candidate is to have another patient assigned.

3. Each examiner must attend the patients' visits (Abs. 1 Book b) at least once, so as to go through the disease report with the candidate and induce him if necessary to supplement it.
4. On the occasion of the visit to the patients (Abs. 1 Book a and b), the candidate must prove at the patients' visits' (Abs. 1 Book a and b) his capability in the diagnosis and prognosis of surgical diseases, injuries and wounds, his familiarity with the various methods of their treatment with special regard to asepsis and antisepsis as well as his capability in carrying out small surgical operations.
5. The candidate must undergo an oral examination in the theory of the operation, perform two operations on the body, one of which represents an arterial ligation, one which represents the required knowledge in the theory of instruments for a practicing physician.
6. In addition, the candidate must give information in another oral examination on questions from the theory of fractures and dislocations, in one case to lay out skillfully the advised course and bandaging on a manikin or on a patient.
7. The candidate must prove also his familiarity with the theory of orthopedics as well as the knowledge which is required for the practicing physician.

& 58

1. The examination in obstetrics and gynecology (IX) is given by two examiners in a university clinic or in a public hospital or connected institution in which there is a preexisting gynecological department and is as a rule to be completed in three consecutive week days.
2. The Candidate must

    (a) investigate a birthing in the presence of the examiner or one of the assistant physicians of the institution charged with that, determine the time of birth and the lay of the child, the prognosis and processes being entered into and participate as necessary in the measures taken to assist the birth as well as also in the course of the next 24 h, prepare at home a critical report of the disease case, which, with date and signature provided, is delivered the next morning to the examiner;
    (b) visit the maternity case twice in each of the next 2 days, to complete thereby the report in relation to the care of the maternity case and the newborn as well as on the possible diseases of both and in the case of death ensuing on the confined before the course of 2 days, give a written judgment of the case, taking into account as much as possible the findings of each section. If the maternity case assigned to the candidate leaves treatment before the completion of the 2 days of treatment, the examiner is to determine if the candidate is to have another patient assigned.

3. During this time, the candidate must demonstrate before both examiners his capability in the diagnosis, prognosis and treatment of pregnancy and the maternity bed and in an oral examination the next day under the supervision of the examiner and prove in an oral examination as well as in other cases, that he possesses the knowledge required for a practicing physician in the recognition and treatment of diseases of women.
4. At a specially appointed time the candidate has to prove in the presence of both examiners his familiarity with operations which are scientifically recognized; Also, he must show on a manikin the diagnosis of various irregular positions of the child, demonstrating the delivery by turning, as well as show his dexterity in the use of the forceps.
5. Where there is a lack of maternity cases or patients in the institution, it is left up to the directing physician to take these examinations from a polyclinical practice. The assignment of the same maternity cases for examination for two or more candidates is in no situation permitted.

& 59

1. The examination in ophthalmology (X) is to be given by one examiner in a university clinic or university polyclinic or in the eye department of a large hospital, and is to be completed in 1 day.
2. In the presence of the examiner, the candidate must investigate an eye disease, its anamnesis, diagnosis and prognosis in the given case as well as give a treatment

plan, and briefly write down the findings and his treatment plan. Then he must prove in an oral examination as well as in other patients, that he possesses the knowledge required in ophthalmology to be a practicing physician and that he has familiarity with the use of the ophthalmoscope.

& 60

1. The examination over ear, throat and nose diseases (XI) is to be given in 1 day, by one examiner in a university clinic or in a university polyclinic or in the department for ear, throat and nose diseases of a large hospital.
2. The candidate must examine a patient in the presence of the examiner, briefly writing down the findings and the healing plan, and then show that he possesses the knowledge of and treatment for ear, throat and nose diseases required for a practicing physician.

& 61

1. The examination over skin and venereal diseases (XII) is to take place in 1 day from one examiner in a university clinic or a university polyclinic or in the department of skin and venereal diseases of a large hospital.
2. The candidate must examine a patient in the presence of the examiner, briefly writing down the findings and the healing plan and then show orally that he possesses the knowledge of skin and venereal diseases required for a practicing physician.

& 62

1. The examination in Mental Illness (XIII) is to be given by one examiner in a university clinic or in the Mental Illness department of a large hospital and is to be completed in 1 day.
2. In the presence of the examiner, the candidate must examine a mentally ill person, establishing the findings immediately with the endorsement of the examiner and prove in an oral examination as well as in other patients that he possesses the knowledge of mental illness required of a practicing physician.

& 63

1. The examination over the diseases of the teeth and gums (XIV) is oral. It is given by one examiner and is completed in 1 day.
2. The candidate must prove that he possesses the knowledge of diseases of the teeth and the gums that are required for a practicing physician.

& 64

1. The examination over industrial diseases (XV) is oral. It is given by one examiner and is to be completed in 1 day.
2. The candidate must prove that he possesses the knowledge of the recognition and treatment of industrial diseases required for a practicing physician.

& 65

1. The examination in expertise in social insurance and accident health care (XVI) is oral. It is given by a single examiner and is completed in 1 day.
2. The candidate has to prove that he is competent to reimburse experts in the area of social insurance and possesses the knowledge of social insurance and accident health care required for the practicing physician.

& 66

1. The examination in legal medicine (XVII) is oral. It is given by a single examiner and is to be completed in 1 day.
2. The candidate must prove that he is acquainted with the important theories of legal medicine and the fundamental rules for reimbursement of experts as well as with the law and duties of the physician which are required for a practicing physician.

& 67

1. The examination in Hygiene (XVIII) is oral. It is given by a single examiner and is to be completed in a single day.
2. The candidate must prove that he has acquired the knowledge required for a practicing physician, has become acquainted with the important hygienic and especially also bacteriological methods of investigation, as well with the principles and techniques of small pox immunization, also that he possesses the knowledge required for extraction and maintenance of the lymph.
3. On the examination in general hygiene, the practically important areas of Social Hygiene as well as Military and Industrial Hygiene are to be especially attended to.

& 68

1. The examination in Racial Hygiene (XIX) is oral.
2. The candidate must prove that he understands how to think genetic-biologically and racial-hygienically, that he has command of the principles of the theories of genetics, genetic change and selection, that he knows the most important facts of human genetic and racial theories, genetic pathology and the movement for preservation of the Volk population according to their quantitative and qualitative sides, and that he has received instruction over the most important means and demands of practical racial hygiene, especially over the prevention of hereditarily sick offspring, advising regarding marriage and racially hygienic protection of the Volk population.

& 69

In the sections in which he is only tested orally, only two or three as a rule are to be completed in a single day.

& 70

1. Immediately after the completion of one examination section the examiner must send the recorded examination to the Chairman.
2. He reports, if two examiners have participated in a single section, that the examination results for this section are tabulated in the following way:

The sum of the numerical values (& 19) of the two individual parts divided by 2 gives the whole result for the examination subject; any fraction remaining thereof will then be counted as a whole. If one of the two examiners gives a "not sufficient" or "bad," then his judgment counts as the whole section.

3. The candidate reports in person within 2 days after the completion of the section for the acceptance of the notification of the result if there has been no special challenge by the Chairman of the Examination Committee or, according to these conditions, no relevant challenge by the business office of the Committee and, within 24 h schedule with the examiner (or the examiners) the next following examination section, until completion. Concerning this, it is to be noted that as a rule at most 3 days lie between the individual examination sections.

& 71

1. If an examination section has been judged to be "not satisfactory" or "bad," then it is considered to not have been passed.
2. It the candidate has not passed more than four of the examination sections of V (Internal Medicine), VI (Pediatrics), VIII (Surgery) and IX (Obstetrics and Gynecology) or not passed more than five of the whole lot of examination sections then he is considered to have not passed the entire examination. All of the sections must be repeated.
3. Fees for sections in which in the case of Abs. 2 have not been examined will be applied to the fees for the repeat examination.

& 72

1. The Chairman establishes the period for the repetition of the non-passed examination sections, after which the candidate must undertake the examination in all the sections.
2. He determines a period during which the examination in the un-passed sections may be repeated at the earliest, which, according to his judgment, can vary from 2 to 6 months. He determines at the same time under consideration of & 73 Abs. 6 the point in time up to the latest that the notification for repeat examination must occur.
3. The repetition of the entire examination (& 71 Abs. 2) is to take place according to the discretion of the Chairman at the earliest, six and at the latest, 9 months after the completion of the examination.
4. During this period, according to the discretion of the Chairman and his instruction, the candidate must either study medicine at least a half-year or be engaged

at least 3 months as an intern. One may appeal the ruling of the Chairman within 2 weeks to the highest Territorial authority.

5. The repetition of an examination section takes place as a rule in the presence of the Chairman. The Chairman must attend if the examiner or the candidate requests it. He can recruit some other member of the examination committee to attend the repeat examination.
6. Whoever does not pass the repeat test has not passed the physician examination. He will not be permitted to take yet another examination. Exceptions can be granted only on special grounds (& 80).

& 73

1. Whoever does not report personally at the right time according to & 47 and & 70, can be transferred by the Chairman to the following examination period. In this case, the portion of the fees which is not used becomes forfeited for the actual and administrative costs. One may appeal the ruling of the Chairman within 2 weeks to the highest Territorial authority.
2. Whoever does not appear in an examination period at the correct time or does not appear at all, loses that portion of the fees which are applicable for the relevant examination section.
3. Whoever withdraws with adequate justification from an examination which has been undertaken will receive back that portion of the fees for the examination sections which have not yet been commenced. The yet unused portion of the fees are forfeited thereby for actual costs and administrative costs.
4. If the candidate withdraws without an adequate excuse, the Chairman can declare that the examination in totality or in individual sections has not been passed. The portion of the fees for the examination sections which were begun and the unused portion of the fees are forfeited for actual costs and administrative costs. One may appeal the ruling of the Chairman within 2 weeks to the highest Territorial authority.
5. Whoever reports to the repeat examination at the wrong time without adequate excuse must, according to the discretion of the Chairman, repeat the examination from the beginning, whereby the already passed sections are also considered to have not been passed. One may appeal the ruling of the Chairman to the highest Territorial authority.
6. If a period of time of 18 months after the beginning of the period of the examination has occurred, and the candidate has not completed an examination for which he has been approved, then all sections are considered to have not been passed. It may not be repeated. The unused portion of the fees is forfeited. Exceptions from this can be granted only on special grounds (& 80).

& 74

1. The documents which have been directed for the application for licensure are given back to the candidate only after the completion of the examination. If he demands it back earlier, then the highest Territorial authorities in a body are to be notified through intercession of the Reich Ministry of the Interior that the candidate began

the examination but did not complete it and that the documents of his application have been returned to him. In the original certificate of his university school-leaving certificate or in the documents produced otherwise in its place a notice is to be entered over the deficiency of the respective examination.

2. If the examination is ultimately not passed (& 72 Abs. 6 and & 73 Abs. 6), then the return of the documents from the office can be done according to Ab. 1.

& 75

1. If the candidate has achieved in the entire examination section the judgment of at least "satisfactory" and with that having passed the examination, then the Chairman communicates the entire result of the examination in the following way:

   It is to be set out that the sections V, VIII and IX are six-fold each, the section I threefold, the sections VI, XIII, XVIII and XIX each twofold and for the remaining each a single-fold of the number, which will come to the judgment for each section according to the gradation in & 19. The sum of the numbers thus gathered results in the whole, which with the sum up to 59 means "very good," from 60 to 99 "good," and from 100 up "adequate."

2. After the establishment of the examination result, the Chairman gives to the candidate a certificate covering the passed examination according to pattern 10.
3. Thus he delivers within 3 days after the completion of the examination the document of the examination and, if the candidate so desires to be appointed as a physician, the submission of the appointment to the highest Territorial authorities (& 76).

Sixth Part

Conferring the Appointment as a Physician

1. After the candidate has passed the physician examination, he has to submit the application for appointment as a physician to the responsible highest Territorial authorities through the hands of the Chairman of the examination committee (& 75 Ab. 3). The highest Territorial authorities transmit the application with their endorsement to the Reich Minister of the Interior.
2. If he is married, the candidate must include on the application the marriage certificate and the supporting documents required (& 15 Ab. 3) for the proof of ancestry of the spouse, in case these supporting documents and the questionnaire concerning the ancestry of the spouse are not yet present in the examination file.
3. The Reich Minister of the Interior presents the appointment according to pattern 11.
4. This appointment entitles the physician to practice the medical profession in his own practice only in the case where the Reich Minister of the Interior has verified on the Appointment Certificate that he has complied with the conditions of

the Ordinance of Appointment for physicians concerning the required period as an assistant and the rural quarter year.

5. The fee for the appointment is established by the Reich Minister of the Interior.

& 77

1. The physician has to certify – as a rule in direct connection to the appointment – a year's period as a required assistant (& 8) at a hospital, healing or connected institution or in a university clinic or as a helper of a solo practitioner inside the German Reich, which have been certified as an enterprise for assistants by the Reich Physicians' Chamber. The activity as a physician in the sanitary service of the army or the Waffen SS is qualified to be the required time as an assistant.
2. During the time required to be an assistant, the physician must participate at least twice in public immunizations and re-immunization periods as well as the accompanying observation periods, in case this has not already taken place during the student time after the completion of the immunization course (& 45 Abs. 1).
3. If the physician was not practically instructed during his clinical student time according to & 7 Abs. 3 in obstetrics, then he must be active as least 4 weeks as a required assistant in one of the institutions designated in & 7 Abs. 3 or with a physician who has been designated by the Reich Physicians' Chamber for practical instruction of physicians in obstetrics.
4. Exceptions to the conditions of Abs. 1, to 3 can be granted only on special grounds (& 80).

& 78

1. After or also before the completion of the required time as an assistant the physician must be active 3 months as an assistant or representative of a Fund physician with emphasis on general practice in the rural setting. Exceptions from the regulation can be granted only on special grounds. (& 80).
2. The Reich Physicians' Chamber decrees similar regulations concerning the implementation of this rural quarter year which require the approval of the Reich Ministry of the Interior.
3. For the active sanitary officers of the army and the Waffen SS there is to occur in place of the rural quarter year an additional three-month time of required assistance (& 77 Abs. 2).

& 79

1. After the completion of the time as a required assistant and the performance of the rural quarter year, the physician must submit the certification to the Reich Minister of the Interior (& 76 Abs. 4).
2. To the application the following documents must be attached:
   (a) the appointment certificate (& 76 Abs. 3),
   (b) from the physician under whose leadership he has been active as a required assistant, a document according to pattern 12, elaborating on his work as a required assistant (& 77 Abs 1),

(c) the certification produced by an immunization physician of the participation of at least twice in public immunizations and re-immunization periods, as well as at the accompanying observation periods (& 77 Abs 3),
(d) the document covering the situation in which he had not been practically active in obstetrics for at least 4 weeks according to & 77 Abs. 4, and one that he has not been practically instructed at least 4 weeks as an intern according to & 7 Abs. 3,
(e) A certificate from the Reich Chamber concerning the performance of the rural quarter year or, if he has been active as a sanitation officer of the army or the Waffen SS, the document concerning an additional 3 month-long period as a required assistant,
(f) documents of political conduct for the period of time since the appointment as a physician.

3. If the Reich Minister of the Interior has established on the grounds of the documents presented to him that the physician has lived up to the conditions of the Ordinance of Appointment for Physicians, of the required time as an assistant and the rural quarter year, then he completes the appointment document by a certificate according to & 76 Abs. 4.

Seventh Part

Exceptions

& 80

1. Concerning the licensure for the exceptions foreseen in & 2, & 5 Abs. 4, & 6 Abs. 1, & 7 Abs. 5, & 15 Abs 1, & 16 Abs. 1 and 2, & 18, & 23, & 25 Abs. 6, & 26, & 30 Abs. 7, & 33 Abs. 3, & 35, & 43 Abs. 3, & 44 Abs. 2, & 45 Abs. 3, & 72 Abs. 6, & 73 Abs. 6 and & 77 Abs. 5, the Reich Minister of the Interior rules after consulting the responsible highest authorities of the Territories. Concerning the exceptions from the conditions of & 78 Abs. 1, he rules after a hearing of the Reich Physicians' Chamber.
2. The Reich Minister of the Interior can, in agreement with the highest authorities of the Territory in specially determined cases after a hearing of the Reich Physicians' Chamber give exceptions of other kinds.

Eighth Part

Conclusions and Transitional Conditions

& 81

1. This Ordinance comes into force with exceptions of the First and Sixth parts on 1 August 1939; The First and the Sixth parts (& 1 and & & 76–79) come into force on 1 April 1940.

2. The Ordinance of Appointment for Physicians of 25 March 1936 in the version of the 21 July 1938 (Reich Ministerial Page, p. 549) went out of force on 31 July 1939 with the exceptions of & & 63–66, which are still valid until March 31, 1940.
3. Students who began the study of medicine before April 1, 1939 and had reported for medical pre-examination up to February 5, 1942 need to bring, for the medical pre-examination, in place of the documents mentioned in & 25 Abs. 2 and 4 mentioned in the decree of July 21, 1938, only the documents mentioned in & 7 of the Ordinance of Appointment for Physicians of March 25, 1936.
4. Up until October 31, 1939, one can still find medical pre-examinations in the natural science section according to the conditions of the Ordinance of Appointment for Physicians of March 25, 1936 in the decree of July 21. Students who have taken the natural science section of the physician's medical pre-examination according to the previously valid conditions are credited with the passage of this section on the physician's examination.
5. Students who have passed completely the medical pre-examination before November 1, 1939 may take the physician examination according to the previously valid conditions, as long as they report to the examination before February 1, 1942. They have however to prove at their appearance at the examination that they have been active as an intern for at least 6 months during their clinical time in accordance with the Ordinance (& 7). In the previously mentioned special circumstances, for students who report to the physician's examination up to February 1, 1941, a short practical activity of this kind can be recognized as adequate, if the period has not dropped below 3 months.
6. The candidates of medicine who on the day of the publication of the Ordinance have already begun the practical year or are beginning after this day will be credited with proven activity as an intern of at least 3 months for the yet to be accomplished part of the practical year, documented by an official with a detailed document by the instructing physician (leader of a hospital or connected institution).
7. For the required assistant time (& 77) the time of the practical year which is spent according to the Ordinance will be credited according to & & 63 to 66 of the Ordinance of Appointment for physicians of March 25, 1936 in the Decree of July 21, 1938.
8. The enactment of this Ordinance is reserved for the Ostmark.

Berlin July 17, 1939
Reich Minister of the Interior
Representative
Pfundtner

[II]

Addendums for Ordinance of Appointment for Physicians

Circular of the Reich Ministry of the Interior of 17.8. 1939 –
IV d 4376/39 – 3561

In accordance with & 80 of the Fifth Ordinance concerning the implementation and completion of the Reich Physicians' Ordinance (Ordinance of Appointment for Physicians) of 7. 17. 1939, I empower – in my name – the administration of colleges to independently rule regarding licensure with the following exceptions foreseen in & 5 Abs. 4, & 6 Abs. 1, & 7 Abs. 5, & 15 Abs. 1, & 18, & 23, & 25 Abs. 6, & 26, & 39 Abs. 7, & 33 Abs. 3, & 45 Abs. 3 und & 73 Abs. 6, in the cases of & 45 Abs. 3, however, only in so far as it regards the recognitions of a single subject which have been covered and heard before the previously passed medical pre-examination.

Where the conditions demand the presence of special grounds for the approval of an exception a strong standard is to be applied to the decision so that the exception does not become the rule.

The Chairmen of the committees for physician medical pre-examination in Prussia may independently rule regarding the acceptance of an ongoing course (& 26) which has been passed (consisting of the previously described examination) up to a half year, if and in so far as this does not put into question the attainment of the certificate, according to & 25 Abs. 2 and 4.

Regarding individual exceptions, I determine the following:

To & 1. From 1.4. 1940 onwards, the administration of the colleges submit to me the Appointment applications with the attached examination files. Up to this point in time the responsibility in regards to the granting of Appointment remains with the highest Territorial authorities and consists in the raising of the statutory fees.

To & 5 Abs. 2 and & 7 Abs. 1. The announcements of the hospitals and connecting institutions and physicians who have been appropriately determined and empowered are to be published yearly in the Reich Ministry Publication for interior administration.

To & 14 Abs. 2. Before submission of the application for licensure to the highest Territorial authorities, the Chairman of the examination committee must examine the application especially for correctness and completeness of the contents, to facilitate where necessary its completeness, and render his judgment. The contents must be completed whenever practicable on time so that the decision of the highest Territorial authorities can be issued before the beginning of the examination period.

To & 15 Abs. 3. The ancestral descent questionnaires (pattern 4) are to be completed by the student clearly and carefully. The supporting documents for the ancestry of examinees who can not produce proof of ancestry without a gap, is presented to the highest Territorial authorities, who transfer it promptly for consideration of verification of ancestry, according to the notice of July 6, 1936 of the Reich Department of Ancestral Research. The proof of ancestry must be completed before the time of reporting for the physician examination. In case *no reason* exists for doubt of German blooded ancestry, the affected examinee is to be admitted by the Chairmen of the Examination Committees to the medical pre-examination as well as the examination, with reservation.

On the circular of 4.4. 1939 it was advised.

To & 25 Abs. 1 concerning the acceptance of a late application for licensure, the Chairman of the examination committee rules.

To & 28, & 32 Abs. 2, & 33 and & 38 Abs. 2 The circular of February 23, 1937 also validates the given elucidations according to the sense of the new conditions.

To & 33 Abs. 3. A second licensure for the physician medical pre-examination is only allowed after repeated medical-preclinical studies.

To & 35. The notation in the registration book or the school leaving certificate in this case is: Physician medical pre-examination ultimately not passed; a repeat licensure for medical studies is excluded.

The examinee is, with the restoration of his documents (& 38 Ab.3), notified in writing that he can no longer be admitted to the physician medical pre-examination only after taking new pre-clinical studies.

To & 42. Concerning the acceptance of a late application for licensure, the Chairman of the Examination Committee rules.

To & 43 Abs. 3. The passed first medicine Rigorosum in the German University in Prag in all subjects is to be recognized.

To& 44 Abs. 2 and & 45 Abs. 2. For the student clinical time a study at the State Academy for Practical Medicine in Danzig up to 2 half-years will be credited. The documents for this study concerning the attendance at lectures and the participation in courses encompassing the immunization course and clinics will be recognized. (The Danzig Academy has meanwhile become recognized to be of equivalent value to the others in the medical faculty. The author.)

To & 81 Abs. 3 and 5. Not to demand of students who had begun the study of medicine before April 1, 1940, if they have proof, that they have performed before the beginning of the study, 6 months of nursing. For students who had served or are serving at least 1 year's service in the army, after the taking up of studies, as well as after the completion of the physician medical pre-examination, extend the period of military service to a duration of 18 months.

To & 81 Abs. 6. The activity of intern must be performed after completely passing the physician medical pre-examination. Activity in a laboratory, in a pathological, hygienic or bacteriological institute or in a similar department of a hospital, of a health department or of another not immediately devoted to medical treatment or obstetrics, can not be accepted to prove activity as an intern for the licensure for examination.

Ordinance of Appointment for Physicians

Circular of the Reich Ministry of the Interior of May 14, 1940 –
IV d 2053/40 – 3561

On June 30, 1940 the period expired, in which on the grounds of & 81 Abs. 5 of the Ordinance of Appointment for Physicians in connection with the circular of February 9, 1940 concerning the activity as intern of the candidates for medicine for licensure for the physician examination, one needed proof of an only three-month long practical experience as an intern. Candidates, who only after June 30, 1940 have fulfilled the prerequisites for the licensure for the physician examination must, for the registration for the physician examination, prove fundamentally a practical experience of 6 months duration This education time, under exceptional circumstances, can however be taken up to 3 months after the transitional condition in the last sentence of & 81 & Abs. 5 Ordinance of Appointment, if the registration for the examination is accomplished up to February 1, 1941 (therefore the arrangement of the student year which was temporarily in effect in the trimesters up to November 30, 1940). A special circumstance which justifies an application for shortening of the practical educational time may be allowed, especially if the educational course of the candidate is disturbed by his deployment for army service. The Minister empowers the highest Territorial authorities, in Prussia the Chairmen of the Committee for Physician Examination, to rule regarding the application for curtailment of the educational time as intern on the grounds of & 81 Abs. 5 of the Ordinance of Appointment.

According to Abs. 4 of the Circular of 17.8.1939, the period of time which was established in & 81 Abs. 3 and 5 of the Ordinance of Appointment regarding the duration of the army service may be prolonged up to a period of 18 months, if the student has served at least 1 year service in the army after taking up of the studies or after the ending of the medical pre-examination. The same privilege can also be granted to that student who as a consequence of the war has been deployed for military service of a shorter period that 1 year.

According to & 30 of the Ordinance of Appointment, students of medicine, who on the grounds of an examination in the natural sciences, have attained a doctorate in physics, chemistry, zoology and botany will only then be tested, if these subjects in the physician medical pre-examination have not been the object of the graduate examination. If the condition for the entire result of the medical pre-examination for the valuation of the subject in the medical pre-examination has not been met, the judgment of the of the graduate examination is to be inserted proportionally so that the graduate examination judgment of "outstanding" or "very good" are to be valued as a (1).

The duration of factory or rural service in the year 1940 is to be 4 weeks instead of 6. (Vgl. Abs, 5 d. RdEl. V. 11.1. 1940).

Ordinance of Appointment for Physicians

Circular of the Reich Ministry of the Interior of August, 22, 1941 –
IV d 5855/41 – 3561

The permission for warranting the studying of medicine according to the propositions of Abs. 2 of the circular of May 14, 1940 which is determined by the highest Territorial authorities as well as the Chairmen of the Examination Committees, to permit the physician examination to take place according to the previous instructions, will be extended to those candidates who served work or war service *before* taking up the study of medicine, taking up the study at the latest in the summer half-year of 1938 and had completely passed the physician medical pre-examination at the latest up to May 15, 1940. Registration for the physician examination must take place in these cases at the latest up to June 25, 1942. Students at the Universities of Vienna, Graz or Innsbruck who fulfill the same prerequisites, may take the physician examination still in the form of the second and third medical Rigorosum according to the conditions of the Austrian medical Rigorosum Ordinance of April, 14, 1903.

Female students of medicine, who have been drafted for nursing service on the grounds of the emergency service ordinance, will be credited for this activity for the prescribed nursing service as well as the factory and rural service for the Ordinance of Appointment for Physicians according to & 4 Abs. 5 Books a and b.

In Abs. 3 part 5 of the Circular of June 20, 1941[1] there is to be placed the following words in parenthesis: (e.g. Sanitary service with the Army, unless he served as an assistant at the bedside under the oversight of a permanent physician, activity during the semester, etc.)

Concerning the accreditation of practical educational time of medical studies, only the highest Territorial authorizes as well as the Chairmen of the Examination Committee are to make the determination. The responsibility of the Specialty Groups for Volks' Health of the Leadership of Students is confined to the students in hospitals, etc., as provided in the conditions of & & 5,6 and 7 of the Ordinance of Appointment for Physicians.

Authorities Responsible for Appointment

According to & 1 of the Ordinance for Decentralization of the Department of Licensure of March 19, 1942, the granting of the KGV (license to practice) as physician, dentist, apothecary, foodstuff chemist devolves to the intermediate administrative authorities unless there was a responsible higher Reich authority or higher Prussian Territorial authority, In accordance with & 2 of the Ordinance, the Reich

[1] Not published (footnote in original).

Minister of the Interior determines the intermediate authorities and their areas of responsibility as follows:

Authorities	Area of responsibility (University, Medical Academy, College)
State Ministry of the Interior in Munich	Erlangen, Munich, Wuerzburg
Minister for Volks' Education in Dresden	Leipzig
Minister of the Interior in Karlsruhe	Freiburg i. Br., Heidelberg
Minister for Volks' Education in Weimar	Jena
Reich Governor in Hessen – Territorial Government in Darmstadt	Giessen
State Ministry of the Interior in Schwerin (Meckl.)	Rostock
Minister of the Interior in Braunschweig	Braunschweig
The Responsible Reich Governor	Hamburg, Danzig, Graz,
	Innsbruck, Posen, Wien
Reich Protector in Bohemia and Prague	Moravia

For the Appointment (license to practice) of persons who do not possess a German citizenship, who are not of German or a blood related category, or who have not passed the previously prescribed examinations in a German college, as well as the ruling for the application and conferring of the revoked permission to practice the profession of physician, dentist, apothecary or food stuffs chemist, as well as the conferring of permission for the practice of healing science without Appointment (Physician for Natural Healing Science), the Reich Minister of the Interior reserves for himself the conferring of permission, according to & 2 Abs. 1 of the Healing Practitioner Law of February 17, 1939 in connection with & 8 paragraph 3 and & 9 of the First Implementation of the Ordinance for the Healing Practitioner Law of February 18, 1939.

The fees to be raised for the conferring of Appointment (license to practice) belong to the effected Territories *(Laender)*, as long as the conferring is implemented by Territorial authorities.

Sixth Regulation for Implementation and Completion of the Reich Physicians' Ordinance

(Ordinance of Appointment for Physicians)
Of December 28, 1942

On the grounds of & 92 of the Reich Physicians' Ordinance of December 13, 1935 it is determined:

Article I

The Fifth Regulation for Implementation and Completion of the Reich Physicians' Ordinance (Ordinance of Appointment for Physicians of July 17, 1939 (p. 178) is to be changed according to the following:

1. In & 4 Abs. 5 there is to be under letter a instead of "six" to be a "four."
2. In the first paragraph of & 5 Abs. 1 the words "before the beginning of studies" is to be struck.
3. In & 5 Abs. 2 the first paragraph is to contain the following wording:

"(2) Those unfit for military service and female students serve four months nursing service before the beginning of the studies or in lecture free times of the pre-clinical student time in a university clinic or in an hospital found to be appropriate by the Reich Minister of the Interior under the oversight of the German Red Cross."

4. In & 6 Abs. 1 there is to be inserted as a second paragraph:

"It may be served also in establishments and enterprises which serve the Health Department directly or indirectly."

5. In & 47 Abs. 1 Nr. XIII is to contain the following wording:

"XIII, Psychiatry and Neurology."

6. & 62 is to contain the following wording:

& 62

1. The examination in Psychiatry and Neurology will be given by an examiner in a university clinic or in a mental illness department of a large hospital and is to be completed in 1 day.
2. In the presence of the examiner the candidate is to examine a mentally ill person to establish the anamnesis, diagnosis and prognosis of the case as well as the healing plan, to write down the findings immediately with the endorsement of the examiners signature and prove in an oral examination as well as in other patients that he possesses the knowledge of Psychiatry required of a practicing physician. In addition, he must bring the proof that he commands the methods of investigation in clinical neurology, is capable of explaining their results and has the necessary knowledge of nerve diseases required of a practicing physician."
7. & 75 is to contain the following wording:

"(1) If the candidate has achieved in the collected examination parts at least the judgment of "satisfactory" and thereby has passed the physician examination, then the Chairman is to communicate the entire result of the examination in the following way:

The number to be established for the sections V, VI, VIII and IX is six fold each, for the section I three fold, for the sections XII, XVIII and XIX two fold each and for the remaining subjects as single, which comes to the distribution of each section according to the arrangement in & 19. The total of the numbers so achieved results in the whole judgments, which with the total up to 65 means "very good," from 66 to 109 "good," and from 110 on as "satisfactory."

Article II

This Ordinance is valid also in the integrated eastern territories and for the German state citizens in the Protectorate of Bohemia and Moravia.

Article III

This Ordinance goes into effect April 1, 1943. It does not apply for physician examinations which were begun in an examination period before this Ordinance goes into effect.

Practical Education of Students of Medicine in Nursing Service, Rural and Factory Service and as Intern

Circular of the Reich Ministry of the Interior of January 1, 1940 –
IV d 6865/39 – 3563

The RMfWEuV has established through the hereinafter set forth expressed circular of prerequisites which the students of medicine have to undergo, so long as they are not prohibited from doing military duty, in the period from the end of March to the end of August 1940, the practical education previously described in && 3 up to 7, 25 Abs. 2 and 45 Abs. 1 Book e of the Ordinance of Appointment for Physicians of July 17, 1939, according to the following guidelines, which are to bring the students the required knowledge.

The admittance into educational institutions and service places is carried out by the Reich Specialty Group for Volks' Health of the Leadership of Reich Students. Those obligated for practical education according to Ordinance of Appointment have to report immediately, at the latest up to February 5, 1940, to the Specialty Group Leader for Volks' Health of the university in which they intend to begin studying.

As long as the designation of the empowered hospitals or connected institutions for studying medicine in nursing and as intern has not yet been published, all well led and directed hospitals and connected institutions outside of the university clinic can be seen as adequate institutions for education.

At the most, *Nursing Service* needs to be of only 3 months duration.

All those unfit for military service, girls and women who want to begin the study of medicine in the 2nd semester of 1940 and have not yet served any nursing service, are obligated to participate in the nursing service. Students of medicine who began the study of medicine before April 1, 1940, after the Ordinance of Appointment for Physicians came into force (8.1. 1939) need especially, according to the circular of August 17, 1939 regarding & 81 Abs. 3 and 5 concerning the documentation, to participate in the service of nursing in the interest of their better education, so that they care to perform the nursing service willingly, by urging, or by being forcefully suggested.

All medical students who began the study after April 1, 1939 have to participate in rural or factory service. The employment in rural and factory service is to take place in the time from July 29 to September 7, 1940. The time of the employment for the help during harvest in the year 1939 is credited to cover the obligation for the performance of rural or factory service.

For the practical education as an *intern,* all medical students who have completed after the completion of the 1. Trimester of 1940 two clinical student semesters or more must participate in the internship, if they have not already participated in a 6 month long period as an intern according to the Ordinance. I must make it expressly noted that in performing the obligatory activity as an intern only the education in a clinical department of a hospital, not however the activities in an institution, laboratory and other nonclinical departments of a hospital, can be credited.

Obligatory Internship

The implementation of an obligatory internship, prescribed according to the Ordinance of Appointment for Physicians of July 17, 1939, is the responsibility of the Reich Specialty Groups for Volks' Health of the Leadership of Reich Students. The conditions hereby decreed by the Reich Specialty Groups for Volks' Health emanate out of the following expressed "Guidelines for the Implementation of the Student Nursing Service" and the "Pamphlet for the Intern."

Guidelines for the Implementation of the Student Nursing Service.

With the Ordinance of Appointment for Physicians of July 17, 1939 (RGBl. Nr. 130) the Nursing Service in practical education of students of medicine was decreed by the Reich Minister of the Interior. Originally 6 months was foreseen to be the time, then it was shortened by the circular of January 11, 1940 to 3 months, but was pushed back by the circular of April 3, 1941 to the originally foreseen time of 6 months and then through a Ministerial Decree of December 28, 1942 finally established at 4 months. In & 5 of the Ordinance of Appointment it says:

> "Those fit for military service carry out their obligation for training in a health care institution as a rule before the beginning of studies in the sanitary service of the Army or of the Waffen SS." They receive from this place of service a certificate.
>
> Those unfit for military service and female students serve 6 months of nursing service before the beginning of studies in a university clinic under the supervisions of the German Red Cross. The transfer to the clinic or the hospital is to be undertaken in agreement with the German Red Cross by the Specialty Group of Volks' Health of the Student Leadership of the university in which they intend to begin study. They produce the proof of education in nursing through a document provided with an endorsement provided by the physician leader of this education according to pattern 1 and by the Specialty Group Leader for Volks' Health of the Leadership of Students of a university of the German Reich and after the completion of the education."

For the implementation of the nursing service one is to convey to the leading physician of the institution's relevant department as well as to the responsible nurse and the one required to perform the nursing service herself the following instructions:

1. *The Process of Instruction*

is regulated according to paragraph 2 of the agreement between the Reich Students' Leadership and the German Red Cross covering the entrance of medical students and military unfit medical students in the DRK from 7 until 20 November, 1940. Therein it says:

> "During the work service time, female medical students report to the Specialty Groups for Volks' Health of the Leadership of Students of the university in which they are to begin their studies. It grants to the students the admission card to the hospital and gives information concerning the Territorial department, personnel and the hospital in which the involved person would report. The student admitted for education is to be informed by the DRK-Territorial Department of the responsible inspector, who has to grant the approval for the course of lectures according to &14 of the Law covering the German Red Cross. The DRK-Territorial Departments communicate further the names of the students to the District Departments in whose District the students undertake their practical-clinical education as nursing assistant, and arrange for their acceptance in a DRK-squad.

2. *Position in the Hospital*

The students of medicine who are in the position of pre-studies of education have the position in the hospital as helper of the DRK and undertake those duties and rights. They must follow the chain of command of the hospital.

3. *Dress of Service*

Regarding dress, they wear, during the period of education, the traditional attire of the DRK...e.g. stripped dress, white pinafore and white personal scarf. During the service a white smock is to be worn over the dress.

4. *Accommodations, Board and Benefits*

The accommodation and board as well as the cleaning of the wash take place in most cases in the hospital, for free. Since the service as a nurse is to be seen as education, the involved students, in contrast to the employed nurse, after completion of the first quarter year, have no claim on benefits. In the second quarter year, on special application, which is submitted to the relevant Specialty Group with the Territorial Department of the DRK, she can be paid spending money by the DRK for vouched for economic emergencies and necessities.

5. *Time of Service*

The service of the active students will be regulated according to the general usual service regulations and conduct themselves according to the proper care of the hospital. As a norm, there is a service time of 10 h, in which the time for meals is worked in. Each week they should have a free afternoon and each month two free days. Depending on need, the service time is extended if the early service is too overwhelming. For night service the active students are likewise employed.

6. *Organization of the Service*

The student nurses are to be employed in all the daily work which is necessary to learn nursing. They are directed to the individual stations according to the character of the hospital (surgery, eye, pediatrics, etc.), as well as according to the coinciding stations. In order to develop the most possible all-round education they should be directed every half year to different stations. The participation in visitation should then only ensue if it has to do thereby with the taking over of nursing services according to the Ordinance. The female medical students attending are to assume no special position.

7. *Judgment*

At the completion of the half-year, there is to be produced by the physician Leader of the institution as well as the department, a record exhibited according to pattern 1 of the Ordinance of Appointment about the nursing students, which takes into account a judgment about the personality and special characteristics such as taking pleasure in responsibility, conscientiousness, the ability to put aside one's own interests and the desire to be included in situations involving illness as well as achievements. This document is to be produced by that Specialty Group in which the assignment has taken place.

8. *Protection from Illness and Accident*

With the approval of the course of lectures by the Inspector for voluntary nursing, the student gains the right for insurance protection according to the conditions for care of the DRK. The precondition for that is that she serves in the Ready Reserve. The acknowledgement of Ready Reserve service is only then possible if the Specialty Groups of the Territorial Departments of the DRK have reported the inclusive students. In regards to Ready Reserve, each nursing student must take personal responsibility to enroll in the Ready Reserve. In case of sickness, one is to demand a sickness card for the relevant District Department. The question of accident insurance in the student nursing service has already been decided with a ruling of the Reich Labor Minister of 7 January, 1940 II a Nr. 17,739/39, "that the future students of medicine who are already engaged in professional education serving as a practical nurse in a hospital recognized by the Reich Minister for science, education and Volks' education, stand under the protection of the statutory Reich Accident Insurance."

9. *Service with the Ready Reserve*

Service with the Ready Reserve is to take place during the education in the hospital. It must however be continued during the theoretical nursing course at the time of nursing service, so that the education with the DRK is completed before the beginning of the studies.

10. *Conditions of Exceptions*

Mixed blooded people, foreigners, and stateless people cannot be members of the DRK. They perform the nursing service under the auspices of the Specialty

Groups for Volks' Health in medical institutions, which are independent of the DRK and are excluded from participating in the DRK course of lectures and the Ready Reserve. Since they also can not be admitted into the insurance scheme of the DRK, it is to their advantage to insure themselves privately against sickness.

To complete the circular of the Reich Ministry of the Interior, of March 25, 1943, the following words are to be attached verbatim:

In order to execute the sixth Ordinance for Implementation and Completion of the Reich Physicians' Ordinance (Ordinance of Appointment for Physicians) v. December 28, 1942 (RGBI. I p. 745), I decree in agreement with the Reich Health Leader the following:

The performance of nursing service is from the beginning of the summer half-year of 1942 on for those unfit for military duty and women as well as for non-members of the Reich no longer a prerequisite for registering with the medical faculty of the universities and medical academies. Nursing service may no longer be served in segments, of at least one monthly duration, during college vacation or during the creditable semesters of study before the physician medical pre-examination. Proof of the completed 4 month practical education in nursing (& 5 Abs. 1 and 2 of the Ordinance of Appointment for Physicians) must therefore to be produced from the end of the summer half- year of 1943, in general only at the time of reporting for physician medical pre-examination.

By the shortening of the nursing service to 4 months it has become possible for a great portion of the students to perform this service during the college vacation. Also it can be reckoned that the nursing service from summer 1943 on will be included in the employment of the arming of the German student community. It remains to the students however further to be at liberty to perform the nursing service *before* taking up the study of medicine. This is especially recommended for those boys and girls who still up to the physician medical pre-examination have to take the comprehensive examination in Latin (&15 92/a.a.O.) or for whom, out of fundamental grounds, a consolidation of scientific and practical education is not advisable. Also to be considered is that the college vacation, especially the second summer vacation after the completion of the fourth semester, is necessarily required for the completion of student material and for preparation for the physicians medical pre-examination. Those therefore who reckon that they will not really be able to manage the nursing service and the medical pre-clinical study in 2 years, had best take the nursing service beforehand, particularly as an interruption of studies during the pre-clinical study time or certainly directly before the physician medical pre-examination, which works to his disadvantage experience-wise.

The former prerequisites for the nursing service remain unaffected. Especially also further, the licensure for the physician medical pre-examination is fundamentally dependent, according to the Ordinance, on the previously completed nursing service. Exceptions for the militarily fit students to stand for the test just before their taking up of active military service are in effect only according to the terms of Abs. 2 des RdErl. v. 19.3.1942 – IV d 3844/42–3572 (not published).

The obligation for the militarily unfit and female students of medicine according to & 5 (3) of the Ordinance of Appointment for physicians, to belong to the German

Red Cross from the beginning of the student time, remains a firmly established guideline according to Abs. 2 of RdErl. v. 19.9.1941 (MBliv.S. 1707). Female students who have taken up studies without previously performing the nursing service will not yet have obtained the education as a nursing assistant at the time of the taking up of studies; they may even lack the fundamental education, if this has not been gathered during labor service or comparable student service. The Specialty Groups of Volks' Health of the Leadership of Reich Students have to make sure that the occasional education lacking is made up for as soon as possible.

The Leadership of Reich Students *exclusively* will arrange for and manage the factory or rural service, which serves the health system dependently or independently. The local Specialty Groups for Volks' Health of the Leadership of Students of the university will introduce the students accordingly to the health offices, to the chemistry laboratories, assistance for lecture hours with practicing physicians in work area rooms or medical plant gardens, etc.

In the Abschn, XII of the physician's examination, neurology has been incorporated, which corresponds to its factual development. Irrespective of this, the examiners for the Abschn. V. (Internal Medicine) are again directed, as before, to test in the area of their Specialty in Neurology.

Granting equal status in the assessment of Abschn. VI (Pediatrics) with Abschn. V(Internal Medicine),VIII (Surgery) and IX (Obstetrics and Gynecology), it follows that the candidates of medicine must acquire likewise especially penetrating knowledge in these three central Specialties in the future as well as in pediatrics. The higher assessment of pediatrics is to take effect from the summer period on (Examination beginning October 7, 1943). The preexisting examination reviews must be brought up: they are to be changed on p. 2 under Abschn. VI and on p. 3 under Abschn XIII as well as in the handwritten footnotes. With the examinations after the Ordinance of Appointment for Physicians of 1936/1938 the assessment of Abschn. X (Pediatrics) does not change.

Pamphlet for the Intern

A. *Legal Foundation*

According to the Ordinance of Appointment for Physicians of July 17, 1939, Reich Law Sheet Nr. 130 will require for the state examination, proof of the performance of an obligatory internship of 6 months.

Activity as an intern can only be credited if the entire performance of the student is taken into consideration. Activities which require only a few hours a day are not creditable.

Creditable is only the activity as intern in the lecture free times (vacation or for non-related study and in semester of non-creditable study time, post-appointment). The internship should, whenever possible, be taken in three periods of 2 months.

In no case are educational periods of less than 4 weeks duration creditable. The education should preferably cover the Specialties of Surgery, Internal Medicine, Pediatrics and Obstetrics. The Ordinance of Appointment does not however prohibit the education to take place also in other *clinical* departments. Activity in the non-clinical departments (Pathology, Legal Medicine, Pharmacology and Hygiene) is not creditable. The activity in the Polyclinic is certainly creditable according to the VO, it should however not cover more than a third of the educational time required for the licensure for the physician examination. Assistant physician activity with the Army of 6 months is creditable for the internship.

The internship may be taken only at hospitals as well with physicians who have been empowered for education of interns by the Reich Minister of the Interior. A corresponding list for inspection is published by the Specialty Groups for Volks' Health.

Information regarding the internship in the Warthegau and in the General Government is administered by the Specialty Groups for Volks' Health.

B. *Implementation of the Internship*

Each internship position is to be applied for with the responsible Specialty Group for Volks' Health at the place of study. An application to the Chief physicians, physicians or non-responsible Specialty Groups is purposeless since the application is to be processed only by the responsible Specialty Group for Volks' Health and the positions are to be distributed only through these in the frame of the unified Reich implementation.

The period of registration for the internship will be announced at the time.

The expense charge for the internship is 1.5 RM; The ticket of the proof of the contribution is distributed by the Specialty Group of Volks' Health.

Each internship position that cannot be filled must immediately be reported back to the Specialty Group which has distributed the internship card, who returns the same. Also the return of the reported position is reported to the responsible Specialty Group.

After receiving the internship card the intern is to make himself known personally or in writing to the Chief Physician before his entrance into the internship. It is to be emphasized that the approval, according to the Ordinance, is presented to the responsible Specialty Group for Volks' Health for the Hospital District. During the internship the intern must be subordinate to the orders of the Chief Physician.

After the completion of the internship, there is to be produced during the appointment period of the new semester an internship certificate with endorsement of the Part III of the place of study of the responsible Specialty Group for Volks' Health.

A short written report about the course of the internship is to be submitted to the Specialty Group of the Hospital District.

Reich Physicians' Ordinance

Of December 13, 1935 (RGB1 I P. 1433)

The Reich Government has decreed the following law, which is herewith proclaimed:

2. SECTION

The Physician

& 1

1. The physician is called to the service of the health of the individual person and of the whole Volk. He fulfills a public responsibility regulated by this law.
2. The medical profession is not a business.

& 2

1. Only those authorized by the responsible German authorities are to be appointed for the practice of the medical profession in the German Reich. The Appointment is directed to the practice of health care in the relationship as a physician. The Appointment is valid for the entire area of the Reich.
2. The fulfillment of the responsibilities in the areas of health care or medical science, the public rights which are transferred or taken over from an authority or a corporation, can, in so far as it is not otherwise legally determined, only be applied to whomever is installed as a physician. This does not apply to persons who are active in the leadership or oversight of a physician.

& 3

(1) The Appointment as a physician applies to whomever fulfills the prerequisites of the Ordinance of Appointment, which are decreed after a hearing of the Reich Physicians' Chamber of the Reich Minister of the Interior.

(2) The Appointment is to be denied,

   1. if the applicant does not possess civil rights;
   2. if there comes to be evidence that the applicant lacks national or moral reliability, especially if serious criminal or moral failings are presented;
   3. if the applicant is declared to be unworthy to practice the medical profession by a professional judicial judgment;
   4. if the applicant lacks the required inclination or reliability for the practice of the medical profession as a consequence of physical handicap or because of weakness of his mental or physical strength or because of an addiction;
   5. if the applicant or his spouse cannot become an official because of ancestral origin. The Reich Minister of the Interior can permit exceptions in difficult cases in agreement with the Reich Physicians' Chamber.[2]

(3) In the cases of the paragraphs 2 number 2 and 4, the Reich Physicians' Chamber is to be heard before the ruling.

(4) If there was raised in a criminal proceeding a public complaint of the sort which was designated in Abs. 2 Nr. 2 or if a professional judicial proceeding is opened,

[2] Changed according to the notification of June 12, 1939 (RGB1. I 1041) (footnote in original).

then the decision on the application of Appointment is to be suspended until after the completion of the judicial or professional judicial proceeding.

& 4

If the physician loses state citizenship through a judgment or through cancellation of naturalization then the Appointment is terminated at the same time.

& 5

(1) The Appointment is rescinded,

1. if essential prerequisites for the Appointment have been shown to the contrary to that presented.
2. if the physician has lost his civil rights.
3. if it is shown, through a major criminal or moral failing of the physician, that he lacks the inclination or reliability to practice the medical profession.
4. if the physician is declared by a professional judicial judgment to be unworthy to practice the medical profession.

(2) The Appointment can be rescinded if, apart from the grounds in Abs. 1 Nrn 2 to 4, facts are produced which would justify a rejection of the Appointment according to & 3 Abs. 2 Nm. 2 or 4.
(3) In the cases of paragraphs I Nrm. 1 and 3 and of the paragraphs 2, the Reich Physicians' Chamber is to hear the case before a ruling is made.
(4) If there is a judicial or professional judicial proceeding against a physician pending, his Appointment on the grounds of the named facts cannot be rescinded.
(5) If a physician is specifically suspected of commiting a serious violation of his professional duty, there can be imposed against him, after a hearing of the Reich Physicians' Chamber, a preliminary prohibition of the practice of the medical profession, until the ultimate ruling.

& 6

The Reich Minister of the Interior reinstates an Appointment, which on the grounds of & 5 Abs. I Nm. 2 to 4 or Abs. 2 has been rescinded, after a hearing of the Reich Physicians' Chamber, if additional facts are introduced which allow a resumption of the medical practice to be unobjectionable.

& 7

1. The authority to practice the medical profession is suspended if the responsible authorities establish that the physician, as a consequence of physical disability or as a consequence of weakness of his physical or mental strength or as a consequence of an addiction, lacks the required inclination or reliability for the practice of the medical profession. The authority is again restored as soon as the authorities cancel their declaration.
2. Before the declaration or its cancellation the Reich Physicians' Chamber is to have a hearing.

3. The Reich Minister of the Interior can determine whether to suspend the authority to practice the medical profession in the case of double earnings.

& 8

1. A renunciation of the Appointment is permissible. It requires the agreement of the Reich Physicians' Chamber. If there is denial of agreement, the Reich Minister of the Interior can be called upon.
2. A renunciation of the practice of the medical profession is directed to the Reich Physicians' Chamber. The latter determines how much such a renunciation liberates one from professional duties. The renunciation can be revoked with the approval of the Reich Physicians' Chamber.

& 9

1. It is forbidden to practice health care as a business or as a hobby if the Appointment has expired, been rescinded or has been renounced, while the practice of the medical profession is renounced. The same holds, while the practice of the medical professional is temporarily prohibited (& 5 Abs. 5, & 74 Abs. 1) or while the authority to practice the medical profession has been renounced, if the Appointment has been rescinded or has been renounced, while the practice of the medical profession is renounced. The same occurs while the practice of the medical profession is temporarily prohibited (& 5 Abs. 5,& 74 Abs. I) or while the authority to practice the medical profession is suspended (& 7)
2. Whoever practices the medical science counter to the conditions in Abs. I will be punished with prison up to 1 year and with a fine, or with one of these penalties.

& 10

The Reich Minister of the Interior determines the authorities who are responsible for the approval and revocation of the Appointment, the temporary prohibition (& 5 Abs. 5) and the establishment of the suspension of the authority to practice the medical profession. He also directs the proceedings.

& 11

1. The Reich Minister of the Interior can allow on probation, after a hearing by the Reich Physicians' Chamber, to practice the medical profession in the German Reich, persons who have not been appointed as a physician (& 2 Abs. I), but prove that they possess an independent education for the medical profession.
2. For the authority to practice the medical profession in the border Districts of the German Reich by a physician who was licensed in a foreign country, who in the interior would have no appointment (border physician), the negotiated agreement between states is hereby valid.
3. Persons who are permitted to practice the medical profession inside the German Reich according to Abs. I, as long as a there is not a conflicting regulation, have the same duties and rights as those installed physicians according to & 2.

& 12

The physician is required to practice his profession scientifically and to worthily display through his behavior inside and outside of the profession the attention and trust which the medical profession requires.

& 13

1. A physician who makes public an unknown secret which has been made available or entrusted to him as a consequence of his practice of the profession with be punished with a prison sentence of up to 1 year and a fine or one of these.
2. Assistants who are professionally active and the persons who participate in the professional activities for the preparation for the profession stand equal to the physician. Likewise, one will be punished if, after the death of the one obligated to, he publishes, without authority, protected secrets according to Abs. I, specifically a secret acquired from the deceased or from his estate.
3. The perpetrator goes penalty free if he publishes such a secret to fulfill a legal duty or moral duty or otherwise for a purpose directed according to healthy Volk interests and if the threatened public interest predominates.
4. The act will be pursued only on application of the injured.

& 14

1. The Reich Physicians' Chamber regulates in a professional Ordinance the medical professional duties and provides therein conditions for the protections of professional honor. Especially it can therein decree regulations concerning improper extensions of the medical activity.
2. The Professional Ordinance requires the approval of the Reich Minister of the Interior.

& 15

1. The Reich Minister of the Interior decrees after a hearing of thc Reich Physicians' Chamber an Ordinance of Fees for physicians.
2. The highest official rate of the fees may be exceeded only with the approval of the Reich Physicians' Chamber, such that an agreement covering the compensation of the performance of the physician is reached in writing.
3. The Reich Physicians' Chamber is alone responsible for the opinion regarding the suitability of a proposed fee for an expert witness to the court. Its opinion is binding, such that special grounds are required for a diverging judgment.
4. The Reich Physicians' Chamber can decree general regulations concerning how much the physician may raise the compensation for the performance of a person who is not in the position of employee.

& 16

1. Whoever, without being appointed as a physician, produces the designation through which it appears that he practices the healing arts under the designation

as a physician, will be punished with prison up to a year and with a fine or with one of these penalties.

2. The Reich Minister of the Interior can decree, after a hearing of the Reich Physicians' Chamber, regulations covering the introduction of such designations.

&17

A physician may make no designations (e.g. on signs, on placards, decrees), referring to a previously practiced activity. Exceptions can be permitted by the Reich Minister of the Interior with the agreement of the Reich Physicians' Chamber.

& 18

Physician officials in the sense of this law are those officials to whom their office is transferred to them by virtue of their education as a physician.

2. Section

The German Medical Profession

2. *The Reich Physicians' Chamber*

& 19

The German medical profession is called to work for the welfare of the Volk and Reich, for the maintenance and improvement of the health, the genetic wealth and the race of the German Volk.

& 20

The Reich Physicians' Chamber is the representative of the German medical profession. It is a corporation of the public law. Its headquarters is determined by the Reich Minister of the Interior, after the consultation with the Reich Physicians' Leader (& 21).

& 21

1. The Leader of the Reich Physicians' Chamber (Reich Physicians' Leader) assumes the authority of the Reich Physicians' Chamber and represents the Reich Physicians' Chamber legally and extra-legally. He has a permanent Vice-Chairman. He can also entrust other persons with his representation in individual areas of responsibility or with the observation of specific powers.
2. The Leader of the Reich Physicians' Chamber is called and dismissed by *der Fuehrer* and Reich Chancellor. The assignment and dismissal ensues from a recommendation of the Reich Minister of the Interior in agreement with the Party Chancellors.

3. The permanent Vice-Chairman is assigned and dismissed by the Leader of the Reich Physicians' Chamber with the agreement of the Reich Minister of the Interior and the Party Chancellors.

& 22

1. The Leader of the Reich Physicians' Chamber works with an advisory committee, whose members are assigned and dismissed by him.
2. The Advisory Committee is to advise and support the Leader of the Reich Physicians' Chamber.

& 23

1. The members of the Reich Physicians' Chamber are the Leader of the Reich Physicians' Chamber and his permanent Vice-Chairman, the permanent Vice-Chairman of the Reich Leader of the Fund Physicians' Union of Germany, the members of the Advisory Committee as well as a representative of each Physicians' Chamber (& 28). The Reich Physicians' Chamber has at least one Civil Service Physician as a member and another Civil Service Physician who is the Vice-Chairman. They are assigned in an emergency by the Leader of the Reich Physicians' Chamber.
2. Each Physicians' Chamber proposes from its membership five representatives.
3. The membership of the representatives of the Physicians' Chamber and the Civil Service Physician is valid for a period of 4 years. One may resign before completion of this time for important reasons or be removed by the Leader of the Reich Physicians' Chamber. The latter also regulates the details of the Vice-Chairmanship.
4. The conventions of the Reich Physicians' Chamber are arranged by their leaders.

& 24

The Leader of the Reich Physicians' Chamber can call together the members of the Reich Physicians' Chamber and Physicians' Chamber to a Reich Physicians' convention.

& 25

1. All physicians in the German Reich are subjects of the Reich Physicians' Chamber.
2. Exceptions to this are the active sanitary officers of the army. For other physicians who are in service in the army, their assignment under the Reich Physicians' Chamber is suspended for the duration of the performance of their service.

& 26

1. The regulations of the Reich Physicians' Chamber are binding for the physician. These regulations are not to interfere with the service activity of the medical officials or medical employees of the Reich, the Territories, the community (community associations) and the carrier of the Reich insurance or in the service

of the independent examining physician in Reich insurance. The medical officials and the previously named medical personnel are exempt from participation in the organizations of the Reich Physicians' Chamber and their departments and administrative offices, if this hinders them from carrying out their official duties.
2. The Reich Physicians' Chambers can require that physicians follow its regulations through forced penalty up to a thousand Reich Marks. The penalty of a designated physician in Abs. 1 sentence 2 is only permitted after his appropriate department has decided that the physician has deviated from an official activity of the regulations of the Reich Physicians' Chamber. Furthermore, the proceeding is regulated by the Reich Physicians' Chamber with the approval of the Reich Minister of the Interior.

& 27

The Reich Physicians' Chamber is to produce a Business Ordinance which requires the approval of the Reich Minister of the Interior.

Departments and Administrative Departments of the Reich Physicians' Chamber
& 28

1. The Reich Physicians' Chamber erects as its departments, Physicians' Chambers and District Medical Unions.
2. The Regulations of the Reich Physicians' Chamber regarding the erection of the Physicians' Chambers and the District Medical Unions as well as the borders of their Districts require the approval of the Reich Minister of the Interior.

& 29

1. The Leaders of the Physicians' Chambers are assigned and dismissed by the Reich Physicians' Chamber. The assignment and dismissal is contributed to on a case by case basis by the Reich Minister of the Interior.
2. The Leaders of the Physicians' Chambers have permanent Vice-Chairmen. Regarding their assignment and dismissal Abs. I correspondingly finds use. The Leaders of the Physicians' Chambers can also entrust other persons with their representation in individual areas of responsibility or with acting on behalf of a specific responsibility.

& 30

The Leader of the Physicians' Chamber works with an advisory committee whose members are assigned and dismissed by the Reich Physicians' Chamber. & 22 Abs. 2 is likewise valid.

& 31

1. The members of the Physicians' Chambers are the Leader of the Physicians' Chamber, his permanent Vice-Chairman, members of the Advisory Board as well as one representative each of the subordinate District Medical Unions and the university medical faculties of the Chamber District. Each Physicians' Chamber has at least one Civil Service Physician as a member and another Civil

Service Physician to consult as Vice-Chairman; they will be assigned in emergencies by the Reich Physicians' Chamber.

2. Each District Medical Union communicates to the Reich Physicians' Chamber, as a suggestion, the names of five physicians, who are chosen from within the membership of the District Union. Each university medical faculty of the District Chamber proposes to the Reich Physicians' Chamber five members of the faculty. The Reich Physicians' Chamber determines from these the membership of the Physicians' Chamber and a Vice-Chairman. It can deviate thereby from the suggestions of the District Medical Unions, but must communicate the deviation to the Reich Minister of the Interior.
3. The membership of the representatives of the District Medical Unions and the university medical faculties as well as the Civil Service Physician is valid for the duration of 4 years. Furthermore, one finds & 24 Abs. 3 and 4 correspondingly to be of use.

& 32

All physicians who belong to one of the District Medical Unions of the Chamber District (& 35) are subjects of the Physicians' Chamber.

& 33

The Leaders of the District Medical Unions and their permanent Vice-Chairmen are assigned and dismissed by the Reich Physicians' Chamber. The assignments come from the suggested lists. This must contain the names of five physicians who are chosen by the members of the District Medical Union from out of their membership. The Reich Physicians' Chamber can deviate from the suggestions, but must communicate the deviation to the Reich Minister of the Interior. & 23 Abs. 4 and & 29 Abs. 2 sentence 3 are likewise valid.

& 34

The Leader of the District Medical Union works with an advisory committee, whose members are assigned and dismissed by him. & 22 Abs. 2 is likewise valid.

& 35

Each physician belongs to that District Medical Union which represents his place of residence. The Reich Physicians' Chamber can effect a deviation from this regulation.

& 36

1. The Reich Physicians' Chamber can in certain circumstances construct special departments as administrative departments.
2. Within the Reich Physicians' Chamber, the Fund Physicians' Union of Germany exists as a corporation of public law. The Reich Physicians' Leader is at the same time Leader of the Fund Physicians' Union. The prescriptions of the Ordinance covering the Fund Physicians' Union of Germany of August 2, 1933 (Reich Law Sheet I. P. 567) remain.

& 37

The Reich Physicians' Chamber decrees the distribution of the responsibilities to the under-departments and administrative departments. It regulates their authorities and oversees their activities. The Regulations of the Reich Physicians' Chamber are issued irrespective of the validating prescriptions of the Fund Physicians' Union of Germany.

2. *Special Conditions*

& 38

1. The Leader of the Reich Physicians' Chamber and the Leaders of the Physicians' Chamber and the District Medical Unions practice their office in the frame of the legal conditions, to their best estimate of their duties.
2. The Leader of the Reich Physicians' Chamber and the Leader of the Physicians' Chamber are not bound by the opinion of the Chamber, the Leader of the District Medical Union is not bound by the opinion of the District Medical Union. They have to however support their deviating interpretation in the records.
3. If the Leader of a Physicians' Chamber deviates from the opinion of the Physicians' Chamber he must report thereby to the Reich Physicians' Chamber forthwith. This goes likewise for the Leader of the District Medical Union; the commentary in this case is to report to the higher Physicians' Chamber.

& 39

The activity of the advisory committee is honorary.

& 40

For the members of the Reich Physicians' Chamber and the Physicians' Chamber as well as for the Leader of the District Medical Union, the prescriptions covering the ancestry of an official and his spouse are likewise valid; the Leader of the Reich Physicians' Chamber can permit exceptions.

& 41

1. Each physician must report to the District Union in which he is a member. Additionally, if a physician practices the medical profession in a district of the medical District Union in which he is not a member, he must report this.
2. The District Medical Union must communicate reports promptly principally to the Physicians' Chamber, the Reich Physicians' Chamber and to the Public Health Office.
3. Physician registrations are be made to the Physicians' Chambers and District Medical Unions, the Reich Physicians' registration to the Reich Physicians' Chamber.
4. The Reich Physicians' Chamber decrees the more detailed conditions for the reporting and carrying out of physician's registrations.
5. For an offense against the duty to report, & 26 Abs. 2 sentence 1 and 3 are likewise valid.

& 42

The Reich Physicians' Chamber collects physicians' contributions on the basis of a contribution ordinance decreed by it. There are foreseen likewise for medical officials, contributions which are related to the extent of their participation. The contribution ordinance requires approval by the Reich Minister of the Interior, who decrees it in agreement with the Reich Minister of Finance.

& 43

Non-voluntarily paid contributions and forced penalty will be enforced, according to regulations regarding the enforcement of payment as a public duty.

& 44

The Reich Physicians' Chamber establishes its official publications and the official publications of the subordinate departments and administrative departments. The regulation covering this will be published in the Reich Notice.

& 45

1. The Reich Physicians' Chamber has a legal department at its place of residence.
2. In the case of a disagreement between the Reich Physicians' Chamber and a third party over matters which concern the responsibility of a subordinate department or administrative unit, the legal department decides concerning the position of this department.

D. *The Responsibilities of the Reich Physicians' Chamber*

& 46

(1) The Reich Physicians' Chamber brings the physicians together for general work in order to provide for the fulfillment of the responsibilities of the German medical system (&& 1, 19). It attends to the interests of the physicians. Especially it has the responsibility,

   1. to see to the existence of a moral and scientifically high standing medical profession;
   2. to watch over the protection of the physicians' professional honor and the fulfillment of professional duties (professional viewpoint);
   3. to promote physician education;
   4. to see to the education and continuing education of physicians and create the necessary conditions for this; the Reich Physicians' Chamber can establish regulations covering this, which are binding for the physician, with the exception of physician officials.
   5. to generate an extended relationship of physicians with each other.
   6. to work on the interests of the preservation of the Volk or the medical profession's corresponding participation by the physicians in the whole area of the Reich. It can arrange that the laying down of a practice of physicians in

individual Districts or sub-District is allowed only with their approval. The arrangement requires the approval of the Reich Minister of the Interior;

7. to create the conditions for medical treatment of physicians.

(2) The Reich Physicians' Chamber can enact regulations regarding insurance for the physician in order to protect the physicians and their survivors from pressing emergencies. The regulations require the approval of the Reich Economics Minister. The implementation of the insurance does not require the creation of any new insurance enterprises.

(3) It can decree special regulations regarding the participation of physicians in the responsibilities of maintenance and raising the genotype and the race of the German Volk.

(4) It can further be active, while conferring with the Reich Health Office and the Statistical Reich Office in oversight and instructions, in matters which have meaning for the care of health of the genotype and race of the German Volk.

(5) The Reich Physicians' Chamber can be given special responsibilities from the Reich Minister of the Interior.

& 47

1. The Reich Physicians' Chamber must support the departments of the Reich, of the Territories and of the community (Community Associations) and the other public organizations as well as the National Socialist German Workers Party and its organizations in all the questions affection Volks' health and the medical system, especially also through the establishment of experts and through the naming of Specialists.
2. The departments of the Reich, the Territories and the community (Community Associations) and the other public departments should work on the issues designated in Abs 1 together with the Reich Physicians' Chamber and their subordinate departments and administrative departments and consult them before ruling on health related questions of general interest.
3. The Reich Physicians' Chamber, and, with their consent, also their subordinate departments and administrative departments, can give encouragement to the departments of the Reich, Territories and the community (Community Associations) and incorporate them in their propositions. These departments should share information on demand as long as there are no official grounds against this.

& 48

1. Medical therapy in public welfare is, aside from treatment in an institution, reserved for professionally free physician activity. The Reich Physicians' Chamber is alone authorized to conclude contracts concerning the activity of physicians with the carrier of public general care. It determines the conditions under which physicians are permitted to treat, and regulates the process of licensure. It can effect reorganization of the activity of physicians, especially determine the conditions which are binding for the physician, since it is mandatory

that their methods of treatment and prescriptions protect that economy which is in the interests of public health care, since the demonstration of that economy has been proven. It can further regulate the distribution of all reimbursement.

2. The general guidelines which are established by the Reich Physicians' Chamber and the conveyor of public general care require for their agreement the approval of the Reich Minister of the Interior.

& 49

1. Where the Reich Physicians' Chamber overtakes medical care in public health or in departments which serve public welfare, it can require physicians to participate.
2. The Reich Physicians' Chamber can decree for physicians, with the approval of the Reich Minister of the Interior, binding regulations concerning contracts regarding the overtaking of medical treatment by one individual physician or several physicians in public health care or with non-public departments; it can agree to deviations from these regulations in an individual case. It deals promptly with medical activities in institutions of the Reich, the Territories, the community (community associations) or the insurance carrier in Reich insurance, and decrees the relevant regulations of the Reich Minister of the Interior after consultation with the Reich Physicians' Chamber; the Reich War Minister administers the institutions of the army.
3. The regulations in Ab. 2 Sentence 1 are valid also for the contracts covering the taking up or overtaking of a practice.

& 50

1. With each District Medical Union, there will be constructed a permanent mediation committee. It is required to mediate in disagreements between physicians, on the request of one of the participants or from the departments. With disagreements which arise from the medical professional relationship between a physician and a third party, an attempt at mediation should occur only on the application or agreement of the third party. Under special conditions, there can be in an individual case a special Mediation Committee established.
2. The Mediation Committee of the District Medical Union to which the affected physician belongs is responsible. If the affected physician belongs to more than a single District Medical Union, then the first to be called for mediation is responsible, or otherwise the Mediation Committee connected to the Specialty of one of these District Unions.
3. On request of the Mediation Committee, the physicians are required to appear and bound by the outcome. In the case of unwarranted refusal of acceptance of the outcome, there can be, according to the former Ordinance, a fine of up to a thousand Reich Marks, which can be challenged within 2 weeks by appeal to the Reich Physicians' Chamber. Requests to a medical official are to proceed through official channels. If there is an objection for legitimate reasons to the decision regarding the outcome or the personal appearance of the official, then the first two sentences of this paragraph are not applicable to these officials.

4. If the effort at mediation fails, if the affected parties have already declared a renunciation of wider pursuit of rights, then as the occasion arises, the Leader of the District Medical Union himself is permitted to propose an arbitration policy over which the parties are directed to make a response. The regulations of civil proceedings find corresponding use in the proceeding.
5. The Reich Physicians' Chamber can set up the Physicians' Chamber Mediation Committee on its own, for which the paragraphs 1 to 4 are likewise valid.
6. The Reich Physicians' Chamber decrees more detailed conditions covering the medical mediation and arbitration systems. It can thereby regulate jurisdiction of the Mediation Committee in specific cases which deviate from paragraphs 2 and 5.

3. Section

Penalty for Professional Violations

& 51

A physician who violates a professional duty, especially infringing against the Professional Ordinance (Professional violation) is subject to penalty according to the following conditions.

& 52

(1) The penalties for professional violations are:

1. Warning
2. Censure
3. Fine, up to 10,000 Reich Marks.
4. Exclusion from further clinical activity in the public general care for a period or permanently.
5. The establishment that the guilty party is unworthy to practice the medical profession.

(2) The penalties outlined in Abs. 1 number 2 and 3 can be applied successively.
(3) In special cases the ruling can be made public.

& 53

1. Fines of over 1000 Reich Marks and the penalty designated in & 52 Abs. 1 Nr. 5 can only be imposed by the Medical Professional Court (medical professional jurisdiction).
2. Warning, reprimand and fines up to a thousand Reich Marks as well as exclusion can also be imposed by the Reich Physicians' Chamber according to & 52 Abs. 1 Nr. 4. The Reich Physicians' Chamber regulates the proceeding with approval of the Reich Minister of the Interior. In the proceeding, && 63, 78 and 79 likewise find use.

& 54

The responsibility of the Medical Professional Court and the authority to punish of the Reich Physicians' Chamber extends to all the physicians who are subjects of the Reich Physicians' Chamber with the following exceptions:

1. The Medical Professional Courts are not responsible for physicians who are involved in a state ordained criminal proceeding;
2. the authority of the Reich Physicians' Chamber to assign penalty is confined to the physicians designated in Nr. 1, so that the Reich Physicians' Chamber medical officials who practice outside of their office an activity in public general care, according to & 52 Abs. 1 Nr. 4 and & 53 Abs. 2, can be excluded from this activity.

& 55

If & 54, Nr. 1 is applied against a physician who has been accused of committing a civil offence as a consequence of a professional infraction, then the Reich Physicians' Chamber, on petition, is given the opportunity to give an expert opinion from the standpoint of the medical profession in the matter and be granted the right of inspection of the preliminary and investigational proceedings.

& 56

1. If a public complaint in a judicial proceeding is raised against the accused for the same facts which led to a professional proceeding, then a professional judicial proceeding can still be opened, however it must be suspended until after the completion of the judicial proceeding. Likewise, an already existing professional judicial proceeding must be suspended if during its course the public complaint was rescinded. The professional judicial proceeding can be resumed if the judicial proceeding has been discontinued or has not been undertaken because the accused has escaped.
2. If the accused is acquitted in the judicial proceeding, then a professional judicial proceeding is to begin or proceed, if the facts, without fulfilling the requirements for judicial case, involve a professional infraction.
3. For the ruling in the professional judicial proceeding, the factual establishments of the criminal judgments are binding, if the Medical Professional unanimously verifies this.

& 57

1. The professional judicial proceeding is opened on the application of the supervisory authorities or the Reich Physicians' Chamber.
2. A physician can undertake the opening of a professional judicial proceeding against himself in order to clear himself of suspicion of a professional infraction.

& 58

For a professional court of the German medical profession, there is to be opened a District Medical Court (*aerztliches Bezirksgericht*), and for the Reich area, a Medical Court of Justice (*Aerztegerichtsfhof*). The District Medical Courts have their residence in the residence of the Physicians' Chamber. The place of residence of the Medical Court of Justice will be determined after consultation with the Leader of the Reich Physicians' Chamber by the Reich Minister of the Interior.

& 59

The District Medical Court is composed of a Chairman who is qualified to be an official judge and two physicians as Associate Judges. The Medical Court of Justice is composed of a Chairman who is qualified to be an official judge and two physicians as Associate Judges.

& 60

1. The jurisprudential members of the Medical Professional Courts are to be named by the Reich Minister of Justice with approval by the Reich Minister of the Interior after a hearing with the Reich Physicians' Chamber, the medical members by the Reich Physician Chamber. A deputy is to be assigned to each member. The members of the professional Courts and their deputies are not allowed to hold a leading office in the Reich Physicians' Chamber or in one of its subordinate departments or in administrative offices.
2. & 40 likewise holds for the members of the Medical Professional Court and their deputies.

& 61

1. The members of the Medical Professional Courts and their deputies are to serve for a period of 5 years.
2. The Associate Judges are obligated in their offices to render service to the Presiding Judges for an impartial and conscientious fulfillment of their obligations.

& 62

The District Court of the Physicians' Chamber in which the accused physician is a member at the time of the opening of the proceeding is responsible for the ruling.

& 63

The public authorities, especially the courts, and the corporations of public law are required to provide clerical official and legal help for the Medical Professional Courts. The Medical Professional Courts have the same obligations regarding the previously named authorities and corporations and with each other.

& 64

The actual and personal costs of the Medical Professional Court are born by the Reich Physicians' Chamber. It establishes the reimbursement for the members of the Medical Professional Court.

& 65

1. Prescriptions covering disciplinary penalty of Reich officials in a professional judicial proceeding and review proceeding apply, as long as there are no deviations from the following conditions.
2. A representative of the complaint does not participate.

& 66

The accused can employ in each case of the proceeding a lawyer of a German court or an official qualified as a legal official or a physician as Associate Judge. The Medical Professional Court can also exceptionally decree other appropriate persons to be Associate Judges.

& 67

The proceeding before the District Medical Court consists of the preliminary proceedings and the main trial.

& 68

1. The professional judicial proceeding is to be opened by a decision of the District Court in which the offences which have been laid as charges on the accused are introduced. At the same time there is to be named in the decision a member of the District Court who is to lead the preliminary proceedings (investigation leader).
2. The Chairman of the District Court can dismiss the application for the opening of the professional judicial proceeding as being ungrounded. With the dismissal of the application, the supervisory authorities can apply for a ruling by the District Court, the Reich Physicians' Chamber and in the case of & 57 Abs. 2, the applicant can make a request, following the legal process, seeking a dismissal in a ruling by the District Court.
3. If the facts of the case are clear enough, then the District Court refrains from introducing the preliminary proceedings and immediately orders the main trial.

& 69

1. In the preliminary proceeding, the accused is notified of the point of accusation. The supervisory authorities and the Reich Physicians' Chamber are to advise. The accused as well as the representative of the supervisory authorities and the Reich Physicians' Chamber, if they appear, are to be heard with their applications. The witnesses and facts are to be taken up and the other factual matters are to be raised. The investigative leader can exclude the accused from the presence of the proceeding if he considers this to be necessary for the purpose of the investigation; the accused is however, as soon as he is again admitted, to be informed of the contents of the negotiations. The investigative leader can make the official court aware of witnesses and expert witnesses.
2. The swearing in of witnesses and expert witnesses is only permissible if there is imminent danger or if the oath is required for the production of a true statement over a point raised for a wider proceeding; regarding the swearing in, the official

court makes the determination, based on terms of the undertaking which is sought. The swearing in takes place after the interrogation. At the swearing in of witnesses and expert witnesses there must be a transcriptionist called in.

& 70

After the conclusion of the preliminary proceeding, the investigative leader transmits the file to the District Court. The Chairman of the District Court can if necessary order or undertake himself a completion of the investigation.

& 71

1. If the Chairman of the District Court delivers in a decision a warning, a reprimand or a fine of up to 500 Reichmarks, then he can declare an order of the District Court without a trial. In the declaratory proceeding only a warning, reprimand or fine up to 500 Reichmarks can be recognized. The accused is to be heard before the ruling. The accused as well as the oversight authorities and the Reich Physicians' Chamber can raise objections against the decision within 2 weeks after this citation in writing or by record of the office of the District Court.
2. A punctual objection before the District Court is to be directed at the trial as long as the objection is not rejected at the outset.
3. If the Chairman of the District Court or the District Court in the declaratory proceeding determines that a warning, a reprimand or a fine up to 500 Reichmarks is not adequate, then the Chairman must schedule an appointed time for a trial before the District Court.

& 72

The District Court determines the extent of the evidence to be considered, without being bound by prior applications, renunciations or decisions. It can on application order that witnesses and expert witnesses be examined under oath and allow the consideration of other types of proof as well. The Court can reject the acceptance of witnesses and expert witnesses which were used in the preliminary proceeding. The trial is not public. The Court rules at its discretion on the grounds of the result of an oral hearing.

& 73

1. The accused, his counsel, the Reich Physicians' Chamber and the supervisory authorities are summoned to attend.
2. The Reich Physicians' Chamber and the supervisory authorities have the right to send a representative to the trial, who are authorized to produce motions.

& 74

1. If a professional judicial proceeding is opened against a physician, then there can be imposed against him, by a ruling of the District Court, a temporary prohibition of medical practice, if it is to be expected that he will be declared in a professional judicial proceeding to be unworthy to practice the medical profession.

2. The ruling can only proceed on the grounds of an oral hearing to which the accused, his counsel, the supervisory authorities and the Reich Physicians' Chamber have been summoned. The summons is to designate the breach of duty which is charged, provided that the court order covering the opening of the professional judicial proceeding has not already been carried out.
3. In the oral hearing, the participants are to attend. & 72 is likewise applicable.
4. The District Court can negotiate and rule in direct connection to the trial, regarding temporary prohibition of medical activity, if it has been recognized on the declaration that the physician is unworthy to practice the medical profession. This is also valid if the accused is not to appear at the trial.
5. The ruling is to be signed and delivered to the accused.
6. The physician's appeal of the ruling is directed to the Medical Court of Justice. It does not postpone the process. The Medical Court of Justice rules on the appeal on the basis of an oral hearing. & 72 is applicable.

&75

1. The provisional prohibition of medical activity lapses if in the professional judicial proceeding it is not determined at the declaration that the accused is unworthy to practice the medical profession or if the process is discontinued.
2. The prohibition is taken up by the District Court or, as long as the professional judicial proceeding in the professional instance is suspended, by the Medical Court of Justice, if it is established that the presupposition for its imposition is not or is no longer in effect.
3. If the accused applies for the provisional prohibition to be lifted, then the court can order a new oral hearing. The denial of the application is not related to the appeal.

& 76

1. The Reich Physicians' Chamber can lodge an appeal against the judgment of the District Medical Court, the oversight authorities and the accused.
2. The appeal is to be placed within 2 weeks after the announcement of the judgment with the District Medical Court in writing or by filing with the office of the District Court. It has the effect of postponement of the judgment.
3. The appeal is to be made in writing. The period for the grounding is 2 weeks. This begins with the completion of the time of the filing of the appeal.

& 77

1. The appeal is decided by the Medical Court of Justice. This court is not bound by the ruling of the District Court. If the Medical Court of Justice overturns the appealed ruling, then it can itself rule or send the issue back for a ruling from the District Medical Court or to some other District Medical Court. The District Medical Court is bound by the legal ruling of the Medical Court of Justice.
2. & 70 Sentence 2 and & 71 are relevant for the proceeding of the Medical Court of Justice.

& 78

1. The expense of the professional judicial proceeding can be imposed in its entirety or in part in the ruling. Only a direct payment is valid for the expenses of the proceeding.
2. If the proceeding has come about because of the reporting of something which goes against better judgment of information resting on carelessness, then the expense and the outlays which necessarily arise for the accused are to be laid on the informant. The informant is to be heard first. The appeal to the Medical Court of Justice against the ruling of the District Medical Court is directed to it. & 74 Abs. 6 Sentence 2 is likewise valid.

& 79

1. & 43 is likewise valid for the execution of a fine including expenses.
2. The contribution coming from the fine accrues to the Reich Physicians' Chamber.

4. Section

State Supervision

& 80

1. The Reich Minister of the Interior conducts the supervision of the Reich Physicians' Chamber and the general State supervision over the commercial enterprise of the Medical Professional Court. He can transfer his supervisory authority regarding the subordinate departments and administrative departments and the District Medical Court to other authorities.
2. The supervisory authority can at that time demand from the Reich Physicians' Chamber information concerning those matters. It can take up and demand, considering those rulings or regulations which violate the existing law or run counter to the goals of state leadership,that measures, which on the grounds of such rulings or regulations have been enacted, are to be rescinded. If the supervisory authority is one of the authorities subordinate to the Reich Minister of the Interior, then the Reich Minister of the Interior ultimately rules on the appeal to the Reich Physicians' Chamber.

& 81

The supervisory authority is punctually invited to the Conventions of the Reich Physicians' Chamber, the Physicians' Chamber and the District Medical Union. Their representatives are to listen to each of the presentations. A convention is to be held, if the supervisory authority demands it.

& 82

The Leader of the Reich Physicians' Chamber is to submit to the Reich Minister of the Interior yearly a report covering the business of the out-going year.

5. Section

Conclusions and Transitional Conditions

& 83

1. Persons, who have passed the medical exaimination, but have not yet been appointed a physician, being in all cases subjects of the Reich Physicians' Chamber, are to declare in writing that they are going to continue their education as a physician. Physicians of the army however are not subjects of the Reich Physicians' Chamber. For persons designated in statement 1, assignments during the period of service rests with the army.
2. The conditions valid for the physicians find analogous use on the persons named in Abs. 1 statement 1. They are under medical professional jurisdiction. Furthermore, the Reich Physicians' Chamber regulates the details.

& 84

On the grounds of the previous laws, the license to practice as a physician is valid for the Appointment in the sense of this law.

& 85

The prescriptions of the Reich Business Ordinance as well as those of & 300 of the Penal Code are not applicable insofar as they refer to the medical profession in the sense of these laws.

& 86

1. The statutory conditions covering the medical profession and the Medical Court of Honor are to be rescinded. The prescriptions of implementation cover the transition of suspended proceedings.
2. The professional[3] medical representations previously prescribed by state law are to be abolished. The Reich Physicians' Chamber is the legal descendant. For the transition of business affairs the Reich Physician Leader is to establish trustees.

& 87

1. With the implementation of this law, the German Physicians' Association (Potsdam) and Association of Physicians of Germany (Hartmannbund)(Leipzig) as well as their subordinate departments are to be dissolved. This is not a liquidation. The legal successor to the German Physicians' Association, and its subordinate departments, is the Reich Physicians' Chamber, the legal successor of the Association of Physicians' of Germany (Hartmannbund), and its subordinate departments, is the Fund Physicians' Union of Germany. The Reich Physicians' Chamber and Fund Physicians' Union of Germany adhere to the commitments

[3] *Standes*.

of both Associations and their subordinate departments as general debtors; the Reich Physicians' Leader decides what areas of commitment of the two Associations in the internal relationships of the Reich Physicians' Chamber to the Fund Physicians Union, are to be established. The Reich Physicians' Leader can decree that individual objects of the assets transferred from the Reich Physicians' Chamber are transferred to the Fund Physicians' Union of Germany.

2. Contributions and taxes are not levied for the registrations of changes in the law in the title registry book and other public registries which are permitted on the grounds of Abs. 1, as well as for the management of laws and legal enterprises connected therewith.
3. Unions of physicians, which have responsibilities important for the oversight of professional matters or of economic importance for physicians, can change their bylaws only with the approval of the Reich Physicians' Chamber. If there are doubts on whether the union is to be regarded in this way, the question is decided by the Reich Minister of the Interior. The Reich Physicians' Chamber can dissolve unions of this kind and establish conditions thereby so that after the implementation of the liquidation the remaining assets of the union are retained. The Reich Physicians' Chamber can also pronounce that the liquidation of a union of this kind has not occurred and it itself or the Fund Physicians' Union of Germany is the legal successor. In this case one finds Abs. 1 statements 4 and 5 under Abs. 2 likewise of use. The establishment of new unions of this kind require the approval of the Reich Physicians' Chamber.
4. The Reich Minister of the Interior can liquidate unions in agreement with the Reich Minister for Science, Education and Volks' Education, which have the responsibility to care for medical science, after a hearing with the Reich Physicians' Chamber. He can thereby make regulations covering the use of the union's remaining assets after the implementation of the liquidation.

& 88

1. When a contract of medical unions or professional[4] representation of group insurance for physicians or those having to do with recognized insurers has been closed, then the Reich Physicians' Chamber can enter into the place of the union or professional representation in the contract.
2. Whenever insurance or arrangement for benefits for physicians or their survivors directly involve the insurance or benefit, the Reich Physicians' Chamber can overtake that part that has to do with legally dependent arrangements. For legally independent arrangements, however not for public limited companies or interdependent insurance unions, the Reich Physicians' Chamber can order a change of the business structure or change the union with some other arrangement; when an affected arrangement is regarded as being in effect by this law by some insurance supervisory authority, if the Reich Physicians' Chamber requires this for its arrangements of the licensure of the supervisory authorities, then there should be

[4] *Standes.*

only a change in the possession of the organs of arrangement. & 87 Abs. 2 likewise finds use.

& 89

1. The Reich Physicians' Chamber is to be established initially by its Leader.
2. Until the Leader of the Reich Physicians' Chamber has appointed (& 23 Abs. 2) each representative of the Physicians' Chamber erected according to && 28ff to membership of the Reich Physicians' Chamber, 15 physicians which belong to the Reich Physicians' Chamber are called by the Leader of the Reich Physicians' Chamber to take the place of representing the Physicians' Chamber.

& 90

The Reich Physicians' Leader can establish the permissible regulations for oversight according to && 86 to 88 and for the erection of the Reich Physicians' Chamber.

& 91

Existing or future tax laws will not be suspended by the regulations of this law.

& 92

The Reich Minister of the Interior decrees the implementation and completion of this law or permissible laws and administrative prescriptions.

& 93

1. This law is to go into effect on 1 April, 1936.
2. The Reich Minister of the Interior can determine that individual regulations of this law can already come into effect before this time.

Berlin, December 13, 1935
The Leader and Reich Chancellor
Adolf Hitler
The Reich Minister of the Interior
Frick

Membership of the Reich Physicians' Chamber

(& 35 RAO) Regulation Nr. 2 of 27 March, 1936 (DAB1. 26 S. 379) On the grounds of & 35 of the Reich Physicians' Ordinance of 13 December 1935 I herewith decree the following:

1. Each physician belongs to the District Medical Union in which his place of residence exists, as long as none of the following conditions determine otherwise.
2. If some other place of residence is established by the physician then he belongs to the District Medical Union of the District where he was licensed.

3. Physicians who are predominantly active as a ship's physician belong to the District Medical Union of the city of Hamburg.
4. Physicians who have no place of residence and physicians who have not established a place of residence, for the purpose of representation, belong to the District Medical Union of Berlin 4 (Tiergargen-Schoeneber). Physicians who need only transitional representation are not included hereunder.
5. Employed physicians, especially also leading hospital physicians, senior and assistant physicians, voluntary and medicinal practitioners belong to the District Medical Union in whose District they are predominantly active.
6. In case of doubt, the Leader of the Reich Physicians' Chamber determines to which District Medical Union a physician belongs.

Berlin March 27, 1936
Reich Physicians' Leader
Dr. Wagner
[VI]

Reporting to the Reich Physicians' Chamber

(& 41 RAO) Regulation Nr. 3 from March 27, 1936 (DAB1. 36 P. 379)
On the grounds of &41 of the Reich Physicians Ordinance I decree the following:
1

(a) Each physician is to report to the District Medical Union to which he belongs. This does not apply for border-physicians in the sense of & 11 Abs. 2 of the Reich Physicians' Ordinance.
(b) If a physician practices his profession longer than a week in the district of another District Medical Union to which he does not belong, then he must in addition report to that District Medical Union.
(c) A questionnaire according to *Design 1*) and a questionnaire regarding his ancestry according to *Design 2*) are to be included in the initial report. The completion of the ancestry questionnaire is required only for those physicians who have not already completed it for the Fund Physicians' Union of Germany or the responsible Physicians' Chamber. The physician must request the forms from the place of business of the Reich Physicians' Chamber or its subordinate department, if they has not been sent to him from the office. If the physician has made the report once, and changes his District Medical Union, then he uses, subject to the following conditions, for all further reports, the notification of his name and the place of practice, bzw., place of work, the declaration of the District Medical Union to which he previously belonged.
(d) On the demand of the Reich Physicians' Chamber and the responsible subordinate departments, each physician must answer such questions which are not contained in Design 1. For the questionnaire of Design 2, the physician must ultimately produce on demand the birth certificates back to the grandparents.

2

(a) If the physician holds recognition as a Specialty physician or if he is changing his Specialty, then he must so state this in his District Medical Union report.
(b) If the physician marries, then he must without delay present to his District Medical Union the documents concerning the ancestry of his spouse.
(c) If a physician establishes or changes his place of practice or changes his state of work, then he must give notice to his District Medical Union.

3

(a) For the construction of a card-index file according to the ordinance, all physicians are to present their initial report to the responsible District Medical Union by May 31, 1936, according to subparagraph 1 of Abs. c.
(b) Medicinal practitioners are also required to report. For this there is in place of the questionnaire according to Design 1[5]), a special questionnaire (*Design 3*[6])). Furthermore, the conditions found valid for the physicians are similarly used for the medicinal practitioner.

4

The responsibility of reporting belongs to the duties of each physician and medicinal practitioner. The Physicians' Chamber and the District Medical Union supervise the compliance with the duty to report. The Reich Physicians' Chamber can force compliance to the duty to report with a fine of up to 1000 Reich Marks.

Berlin, March 27, 1936

First Regulation for the Implementation and Completion of the Reich Physicians' Ordinance

From 31 March, 1936 (RGB1. I. P. 338)

On the grounds of & 92 of the Reich Physicians' Ordinance of 13 December, 1933 (Reich Law Code I P. 1433) – in the following named "law" – it is decreed:

I. Validation of the Reich Physicians' Ordinance for Dentists and Veterinarians

&1

I. Validation of the Reich Physicians' Ordinance for Dentists and Veterinarians

The Reich Physicians' Ordinance finds application for dentists and veterinarians if they are installed as a doctor, so long as other conditions do not apply.

2. Proceeding in the case of && 5 and 7 of the Reich Physicians' Ordinance

(a) Revocation of the Appointment

---

[5] Design not printed (footnote in original).

[6] Design not printed (footnote in original).

&2

1. The following are responsible for the revocation of Appointment:

   in Prussia: the government President (in Berlin: the police President),
   in Bavaria: the government President,
   in Saxony: the District Chief,
   in the Saarland: the Reich Commissar for the re-integration of the Saarland,
   in the remaining Territories: the state government.

2. The local jurisdiction is determined according to the residence of the District Medical Union in which the physician belongs (& 35 of the Law). If the physician lives in a foreign country, then the Police President in Berlin is responsible for the revocation of the Appointment.

& 3

1. If facts become known which would justify the revocation of the Appointment of a physician on the grounds of & 5 Abs. 1 Nr. 3 or of paragraph 2 of the law, then the authorities designated in & 2 must arrange for the investigation which is required to clarify the facts. A record is to be taken of the interrogation of witnesses or experts.
2. The physician, against whom the investigation is directed, is to attend. The hearing can be discontinued if the physician is not found, if he is in a foreign country, or if the hearing is impossible because of the sickness of the physician.
3. After the completion of the investigation, the files are to be transmitted for comment to the Reich Physicians' Chamber (& 5 Abs. 3 of the Law).

& 4

The Appointment will be revoked in the cases of & 5 Abs. 1 Nrn. 2 and 4 of the Law, on the basis of a certified copy of the judgment which is administered with the declaration of the force of the law.

& 5

1. The Appointment can also be revoked on the grounds of facts which occurred before the effective date of the Law.
2. A license to practice medicine which had been legally revoked at a time before the effective date of the Law on account of the denial of civil rights can because of this loss of civil rights be once more revoked on the grounds of & 5 Abs. 1 Nr. 2 of the Law.

& 6

1. The revocation decree is to proceed on these grounds and delivered to the physician.
2. It can, except for the case of & 4, be contested, within 2 weeks after the delivery, in an administrative judicial proceeding. Its disposition is determined therein. If

the place of residence of the physician is in a foreign country, then the decree of the period of the contestation is extended.
3. The contestation has a suspensive effect.

& 7

1. If a criminal or professional judicial judgment upon which the Appointment was revoked is changed in a retrial, then the authorities who had carried out the revocation of the Appointment are to test on application if the disposition is to be continued or suspended. The one whose Appointment had been revoked is entitled to apply. & 3 is likewise applicable.
2. If the disposition is maintained, reasons must be provided and delivered to the applicant. & 6 Ab. 2 is applicable for his appeal.

(b) Provisional Prohibition on the Grounds of & 5 Abs. 5 of the Law

& 8

1. && 2,3 and & 6 Abs. 1 are likewise valid for the responsibility to decree a provisional prohibition on the grounds of & 5 Abs. 5 of the Law and for the proceeding.
2. The decree of a provisional prohibition will not be hindered such that against the physician the same facts are entered into a judicial proceeding or a proceeding for the revocation of the Appointment. If there is, because of the same facts, a professional judicial proceeding opened, then a provisional prohibition can only be decreed as long as the professional judicial proceeding is separated from the public complaint in the judicial proceeding (& 56 Abs. Paragraph 1 and 2 of the Law).

& 9

1. The decree, in which a provisional prohibition is declared can be appealed within 2 weeks after the filing of the complaint to the highest state authority and, if the latter has declared the prohibition, to the Reich Minister of the Interior. This is to be indicated in the decree. The appeal is to be brought up to the authorities who have declared the provisional prohibition. The period for appeal is also guaranteed if the appeal is brought in promptly to the authorities, who have to rule on the complaint.
2. The complaint has no suspendive effect.

& 10

(1) The provisional prohibition is revoked,

    1. if the presuppositions of its decree (& 5 Abs. 5 of the Law) are dropped.
    2. if a ruling according to & 7 of the Law has been met.

(2) The provisional prohibition goes out of effect,

1. if in a professional judicial proceeding of the decree opened because of the same facts, a provisional prohibition is declined (& 74 of the Law) or in a professional judicial proceeding, a provisional prohibition is excluded.
2. if in a judicial proceeding, a legally inforceable judgment is rendered that the physician is forbidden to practice the profession.
3. if in the proceeding the Appointment is declared to go into effect instead of being revoked.

(c) Determination on the grounds of & 7 of the Law

& 11

1. For the responsibility of a ruling on the grounds of & 7 of the Law and for the proceeding && 2, 3 and 6 Abs. 1 are likewise valid.
2. As long as a criminal or professional judicial proceeding against a physician is pending, a determination should only occur according to & 7 if there is danger in delay.

& 12

The decree, in which a ruling according to & 7 of the Law has been delivered, can be appealed in an administrative judicial proceeding within 2 weeks after its delivery. & 6 Abs. 2 and 3 likewise are applicable. The delaying effect of the appeal can be excluded in the decree if there are overwhelming reasons relative to the general welfare.

(d) The Serving of Legal Process

& 13

(1) The serving of the legal process according to & 6 Abs. 1, & 8 Abs. 1 and& 11 Abs. 2 are to be presented:

    1. by transfer to the recipient with a receipt or, if there is refused acceptance or the presentation of the receipt is refused through return of the paperwork, to be delivered to the place of origin, with preparation of a document in which the denial and the return of the paperwork is reported, or
    2. by registered letter, or
    3. as a consequence of the prescribed civil process covering office delivery.

(2) The serving according to Abs.1 Nr.3 can be executed by each official. Public delivery will be carried out by the authorities who are responsible for the ruling. The certified copy which is delivered is attached to the tablet of the authority; the decree according to & 6 Abs. 1, & 8 and & 11 are to be attached without a statement of reasons. If the document contains a charge, then an extract is in addition to be published one time in the official periodical of the Reich Physicians' Chamber.

& 14

3. Refusal of the Appointment of the Practice of the Medical Profession

1. A refusal of the Appointment of the practice of the medical profession cannot be declared under a proviso or under a condition.
2. A refusal of the Appointment is only legally in force if the physician informs the Reich Minister of the Interior in writing. With the notification of the refusal, the written declaration is forwarded to the Reich Physicians' Chamber. The notification should be attached to the Appointment document.

& 15

4. A Physician in a Foreign Country

Permission for a physician who was licensed in a foreign country to practice his profession as a physician inside the German Reich is granted according to & 11 Abs. 1 of the Law. The authorization of the medical designation which is contained in a foreign medical license document or a supplement showing a license to practice has occurred in a foreign country is not allowed.

& 16

A physician who was licensed in a foreign country, but has not established a practice in this country, may in an isolated case, in which he has been called for medical advice or treatment, practice the medical profession in this country without the permission foreseen by & 11 Abs. 1 of the Law, if he has not already been entitled for this on the grounds of & 11 Abs. 1 of the Law.

& 17

Physician licensed to practice in a foreign country, who have not established a practice in this country, but are allowed to practice the medical profession in the border Districts of the German Reich on the grounds of contracts between the states, have duties and rights of a licensed physician given by the Reich Physicians' Ordinance, which according to & 2 of the Law, are valid only in so far as this comes from valid contracts between the states.

5. Business Residence of the Reich Physicians' Chamber

& 18

1. The Reich Physicians' Chamber can, with approval of the Reich Minister of the Interior, also erect an office at another locality as the seat of its business residence. Its Court of Law is at the place of residence of the place of business.
2. Erection or termination of a place of business is to be announced in the official periodical of the Reich Physicians' Chamber and in the ministerial periodical of the Reich and Prussian Ministry of the Interior.

6. Advisers

& 19

The Leader of the Reich Physicians' Chamber must give an expert opinion in the cases given in the law:

1. on the proposal of the budget and with the establishment of the contributions of the Reich Physicians' Chamber,
2. at the yearly rendering of accounts

& 20

The Reich Physicians' Chamber can grant the members of the Advisory Board a specified reimbursement for participation in the Advisory Board.

10. Sanitation officers, medical officials and employees, contracted employed physicians

& 21

1. & 25 Abs. 2 Paragraph 1 of the Law is valid also for uniformed physicians of the Reich Police, the physicians of the Waffen SS and physicians of the Reich Labor service belonging to the Reich Labor Service.[7]
2. For physicians who are required through contract to perform medical activity for the army & 25 Abs. 2 Paragraph 2 of the Law is not applicable, as long as they are otherwise medically active.

& 22

1. & 26 Abs. 1 Paragraph 2 of the Law is also valid for medical officials and medical employees of the German Reich Railway Service.
2. Each physician who is a medical employee in the sense of & 26 Abs. 1 of the Law is required by contract to be medically active.

& 23

The regulations which are decreed in & 50 Abs. 3 of the Law for medical officials are valid for the medical employees designated in & 26 Abs. 1 Paragraph of the Law and in & 22 of this ordinance, with the limitation that the settlement boards which direct their petitions directly to these physicians, at the same time have to submit evidence to those proposed departments of the petition.

8. Regulations of the Reich Physicians' Chamber and its Subordinate Departments

& 24

General regulations of the Reich Physicians' Chamber, its subordinate departments and departments of administration are to be published in determined official periodicals according to & 44 of the Law.

9. Enforcement of Contributions, Enforcements or Decrees of Penalty

& 25

---

[7] Changed according to the 4th Decree for the implementation and completion of the RAO of 31 March, 1939(RGB1. I S. 978) (footnote in original).

The enforcement of involuntary contributions, enforcements or decrees of penalty are to be carried out by petition by the responsible communities. The subject is required to answer this petition.

10. Conclusion and Transitional Conditions

& 26

Proceedings which are suspended on account of revocation of a medical license with the coming into force of the Law are not reinitiated. The proceedings which concern the state of affairs are passed on to the responsible administrative authority according to & 2, which rules according to & 5 of the Law.

& 27

The authority of penalty of the Reich Physicians' Chamber (& 53 Abs. 2 of the Law) extends to the persons named in & 83 Abs. 1 Statement 1 of the Law.

& 28

Up until the decree of a Reich Fee Ordinance for Physicians the Fee Ordinance for Physicians established by the highest state authorities remains in effect.

& 29

Up until the decree of a Contribution Ordinance (& 42 of the Law) the Reich Physicians' Leader can raise a contribution from physicians. & 42 Statement 2 and 3 and &43 of the Law find corresponding use.

& 30

To the certified copy and notification of rulings of the medical professional tribunal as well as at the introduction of legal measures against such rulings and on their execution, the previous statutory conditions are to be in use, however with the exception of the execution of fines and court costs. The medical professional tribunal continues to exist.

& 31

The Ordinance comes into effect 1 April, 1936.
Berlin, March 31, 1936
Reich Minister of the Interior
Frick

Raising Contributions for the Reich Physicians' Chamber

Of 25 June, 1936 (DAB1 36 P. 685)

Up until the decree of a final contributions ordinance, I declare the following for the raising of the contributions for the Reich Physicians' Chamber for the second and third quarter year of 1936:

I

The contribution for the Reich Physicians' Chamber including their subordinate departments (Physicians' Chamber and District Medical Unions) are brought together from a fundamental contribution and a supplement to the fundamental contribution expressly for insurance or accommodations of benefits for physicians and their survivors.

A

The Fundamental Contribution is of a fixed composition. It is collected every calendar quarter-year.

I. *for established physician*..20.-RM

The established physician stands in the same circumstance as medical officials or employed physicians, who in addition to their fixed salary have incomes from clinical activity.

II. *for employed physicians,* as long as they are not in the same circumstance as the established physician (e.g., Assistant physician, permanent administrator)..7.50 RM
III. *for medical officials*, as long as they are not at the same time physicians who are in practice..6, – RM
IV. *for voluntary physicians*, medicinal practitioners, as well as for physicians who have revoked the practice of the medical profession without taking up an activity elsewhere..3, – RM

B

The surcharge to the fundamental contribution is established by the Physicians' Chamber. The amount is determined according to the presumed need of the physician and his survivors for support and emergency. The contribution is not to exceed the amount raised previously for this purpose. The Reich Physicians' Chamber reserves for itself the right to determine the fixed contribution other than that envisioned by the Physicians' Chamber.

Physician officials and employed physicians who are at least 60 years of age and are steadily employed and have a demand on retirement and survivor's benefits are allowed to be excused from the surcharge to the fixed contribution only in so far as they have in addition to their fixed salary income from clinical activity.

C

The raising of contributions for insurance or arrangements for benefits for physicians or their survivors remains unaffected according to the conditions which have been validated for that.

2

If the relationship used for the calculation of the contribution changes (e.g. a practicing physicians becomes an employed physician, a previous medical practitioner becomes an assistant physician), then the Physicians' Chamber establishes and coordinates the contribution for the next calendar quarter year. If a physician expires, then the duty of contribution ends in the course of the calendar quarter year in which the physician has died.

3

The collection of not freely paid contributions is to occur according to the regulations for the enforcement of payment (& 43 RAO). Corresponding petitions are to be directed to the responsible community (& 25 of the First Regulation for the Implementation and Completion of the Reich Physicians' Ordinance of 31 March, 1936 in the "German Medical Periodical" p. 110). This is valid also for the contributions for insurance policies or arrangements for benefits for physicians or their survivors, as long as the participation thereof is made a duty by the Reich Physicians' Chamber.

4

The collection of the contribution is carried out by the Physicians' Chamber and continued every quarter year. To avoid hardship, the Reich Physicians' Chamber reserves for itself the right to decree, lower, or to delay contributions.

Berlin, 25 June, 1936
The Reich Physicians' Leader
I.V. Dr.Joh.Hartmann

Regulation Regarding the Raising of Contributions for the Reich Physicians' Chamber

Of 17 August, 1936 (DAB1. 36 P. 885)

There have been many doubts raised concerning the implementation of my Regulation over the raising of contributions for the Reich Physicians' Chamber of 25 June, 1936 ("German Medical Periodical" 1936 P. 885).

I

Each physician who stands under the Reich Physicians' Chamber (& 25 RAO) is required to make the payment. Regarding that, physicians who do not practice any kind of medical activity are also required to contribute.

A

If they practice some other activity, then it is to be determined if they are an official, if they are employed or if they are self-standing.

If they are predominantly employed (e.g. anatomist, pathologist, physiological chemist, bacteriologist, hygienist, physicians as a business leader with organizations with industrial or other sorts of enterprises), then they have to arrange for the contribution as an employed physician, in the case where they are an official, then for a physician official.

If they are self-employed, for example as bacteriologist, hygienist, writer, then they pay the contribution of the physician in practice. It is presumed that they practice an activity which has been validated by their education or position as a physician. If they are active in some other area which is not validated by their education or position as a physician, for example as a merchant, landlord, settler of a fox farm, then they pay each calendar year 3 RM.

B

If the physician generally practices no activity, then they bear the contribution each quarter calendar year of 3 RM.

C

Whether or not the physician has renounced the practice of medicine has no relevance to the amount of the contribution.

2

My Regulation of 25 June, 1936 states that physicians in practice as a medical official or employed physician are equivalent to those who have their steady course of income from clinical activity.

Expert witness activity is not to be understood as clinical activity.

Whoever, for example, is employed as a central office independent examining physician, is not considered to be the same as the physician in practice, but rather pays the contribution of the employed physician.

If there is doubt on whether or not an activity is seen to be a clinical activity, the Reich Physicians' Chamber is to rule.

3

What is to be decided is the distinction between medical officials and employed physicians. A document must be produced which reveals their status as an official. Physicians who are employed, but who do not possess such a document, are considered to be an employed physicians.

4

Physicians, over which a provisional prohibition of the practice of the medical profession hangs or with whom privileges for the practice of the medical profession is suspended, pay a contribution in the calendar quarter year of 3 RM. If the activity is carried out by a substitute, then that contribution is valid which would be paid without regard to the prohibition or the suspension.

5

Contributions to the NSD-Physicians' Association are to extend over and above the contribution to the Reich Physicians' Chamber. The negotiations regarding what form the contributions to the NSD-Physicians' Association are to be credited to the contributions for the Reich Physicians' Chamber are not yet completed. In the contributions to the Reich Physicians' Chamber there is included the subscription for the periodical "Volks' Health-Watch" of the Specialty Advisory for Volks' Health for the leadership of the NSDAP, as well as the collective contribution, which the medical community pays over to the DAF and "Strength through Joy" ("German Physicians' Paper 1934 p, 253), but not the contribution, which the physicians who are individual members of the DAF pay to their administrative departments.

6

The contributions are to be raised by the Physicians' Chamber in which the physician is a member on the 10th of the month of the calendar quarter year. The Physicians' Chamber raises the contribution for the entire calendar quarter year, even if the physician withdraws in the course of the calendar quarter year.

Deviations are valid only for the regulation of the contribution of the II quarter year of 1936. Since the reports are completed only at the end of the calendar quarter year, the Physicians' Chamber collects the contribution for the II quarter year of 1936, of which the physician is a member on 10 July, 1936.

7

The Fund Physicians' Union of Germany assists the Reich Physicians' Chamber with the collection of the contributions. It is directed to withhold the contributions of honoraria which are directed to the Fund Physicians' Union of Germany (Fund physicians' income, income from medical preventive care activity) and to transfer the contribution to the Reich Physicians' Chamber. The physician is to be thereby notified.

8

It is not possible to regulate with general regulations all the special circumstances which arise. Where there is doubt over where the classification is to be placed, the ruling of the Reich Physicians' Chamber is solicited.

9

The creation of hardship must be avoided. In order to compensate for this, it is possible to decree partial rather than full contribution. The invalid physician who already receives benefits is especially to be taken into account. Also cases in which a physician is at the same time a dentist and is expressly confined to dental practice will especially need the documentation.

The Reich Physicians' Chamber assigns directly to each Physicians' Chamber a specialty worker or a committee which rules regarding requests and delays. These are directly responsible to the Reich Physicians' Chamber. I reserve for myself the right to examine the relevant rulingss and to rule otherwise in certain cases. Decree requests and requests for a delay are directed from the physicians to their District Medical Union which pass on the request, with its opinion, to their Physicians' Chamber.

Berlin, 17 August, 1936
The Reich Physicians' Leader
Dr. Wagner

Professional Ordinance for German Physicians

November 5, 1937 (DAB1. 37 P. 1031)

On the grounds of & 14 of the Reich Physicians' Ordinance (RAO) with the approval of the Reich Minister of the Interior of 27 October, 1937 – IV B 16287/37/3121- I decree the following:

"The Professional Ordinance for German Physicians"

The Professional Ordinance comes into effect on the day of its publication in the "Deutschen Aerzteblatt" under the condition that the changes of the description of the physician according to & 36 and the notes, receipt notices, stamp, etc. according to & 38 up to April, 1938 are introduced.

The approval of the Reich Physicians' Chamber foreseen in && 23 Abs. 1 and 2 and 28 is, so long as special applications are not forthcoming, only to be sought if the official valuation (&23 Abs. 1) according to the Professional Ordinance in force is undertaken or contracts or other agreements (& 23 Abs. 2 and & 28) according to the Professional Ordinance in force are concluded.

Munich, November 5, 1937
Reich Physician Leader
Dr. Wagner

Professional Ordinance for German Physicians

"The physician is called to the service of the health of the individual person and the whole Volk, and the German medical profession is called with him to work for the welfare of the Volk and the Reich, for the maintenance and elevation of the health, the genotype and the race of the German Volk. The physician fulfills a public responsibility regulated by the Reich Physicians' Ordinance. The medical profession is not a business.

The medical profession demands that the physician become familiar with the validating regulations contained herein and fulfill his responsibility in the sense of the National Socialist Comprehensive Worldview and Health Leadership. He must adapt himself to the professional constitution of his profession, of the Reich Physicians' Chamber and the Fund Physicians' Union of Germany and their instructions, meet their expectations which are authorized on the grounds of their validating regulations. A professional ordinance cannot treat exhaustively the professional duties of the physician. The physician will only complete his duties regarding the Volks' community and the profession if he feels himself to be the servant of his Volk.

A. General Professional Regulations

& 1. *General Professional Duties*

The physician is obligated to practice his profession scientifically and to be worthy, in his behavior, inside and outside of his profession, of the attention and trust which the medical profession requires. (& 12 RAO).

& 2. *Duty of Silence*

The physician has the obligation to protect the secrecy of an unknown secret that has been entrusted to him from the practice of his profession or been made accessible to him, which means to be silent or to not make it public unauthorized.

The publication of an unknown secret is not prohibited if the physician is relieved of the duty of silence for the single case or if he publishes such a secret to fulfill a legal duty or moral duty or otherwise for the purpose of the health for the Volk and if it is outweighed by an interest protected by law. The physician must attend to the duty of silence of his family members. He should see to it that his professionally active helpers and the people who take part in the preparation of the practice and professionally related activities maintain silence. The latter are likewise obligated to remain silent like the physician (& 13 RAO).

& 3. *Protection and Termination of Pregnancy, Sterilization*

The physician must resist all efforts which are inclined to go against the Volks' strength and the Volks' number. He should strengthen the will to have children and in his medical activity undertake no measure without overwhelming reasons which serve to encourage contraception. The performance of abortions and the production of infertility are allowed of the physician only under certain legal conditions.

& 4. *Continuing Education, Clinical Treatment*

The physician has the duty to improve professionally and to familiarize himself with all important clinical methods without presuppositions either for or against a certain direction in the healing science. With each case of illness the physician must strive to achieve in the simplest way the most successful healing.

& 5. *Office Hours and The Conduct of Visits*

The establishment of office hours at several locations is permissible only with the approval of the District Medical Union.

Another general practitioner is not allowed to establish a practice in a building in which a general practitioner has already established a practice. The same applies for a Specialty physician or with a sub-Specialty practitioner. Exceptions can be allowed by the District Medical Union.

If a physician moves within his practice District, then no other physician of the same Specialty is allowed to establish in the building of the prior practice for a duration of a half-year, unless the previous inhabitant or the District Medical Union agrees to it.

The District Medical Union can, where it is permissible for the benefit of the population, determine that with general practitioners, gynecologists and surgeons, the site of practice and residence cannot be separated.

Seasonal change of a practice place is permissible only with the approval of the Reich Physicians' Chamber.

Outside of his place of practice the physician should carry out a regular activity of visits only if there is no question that another physician practices there. If visits come to be carried out in a locality in which only one other physician has laid down a practice, then as a rule this should be considered to be reasonable.

& 6. *Treatment From A Distance and Itinerant Practice*

Patients may not be treated only in writing or only from a distance or in any other way only from a distance. The practice of the medical profession as an itinerate is prohibited. As a rule, travels to cultivate the delivery of medical care are allowed only in special cases and only with the agreement of the District Medical Union.

& 7. *Physician's Records, Patient's Histories and Roentgen Pictures*

The physician must make records of important findings and methods of treatment, especially of accidents, operations and x-ray treatment. This is valid likewise for private practice as well as for service in Reich insurance, Reich Benefit and public welfare. These records as well as patient histories and Roentgen pictures are to be preserved for at least 5 years after the completion of the treatment. One is to take notice of the regulations covering the medical duty of silence regarding their disclosure. The records as well as the patient records and Roentgen pictures should be produced irrespective of special regulations only with a demand of a medical expert witness at the time as a supporting document or as part of the same.

& 8. *Presentations As An Expert and Witness*

When appearing as a medical expert and witness the physician must proceed with the greatest of care and speak his medical conviction according his best knowledge. Appearance as a witness as a favor is prohibited. The purpose of a written document and its receiver are to be emphasized.

The physician is not allowed, without contract from the Reich Physicians' Chamber to appear as an expert witness before a court concerning the appropriateness of demand of a medical charge. Expert witnesses and witnesses for which the physician is obligated to appear must be delivered in a reasonable period of time.

& 9. *Consideration of Medical Readers' Questions and House Physicians' Books*

The consideration of so-called medical readers' questions and the like require the approval of the Reich Physicians' Chamber. The same goes for the production of so-called Home Physician Books or collaboration on these.

& 10. *Instruction and Testing by Physicians*

The training and testing of persons who are active or want to be active in the areas of predominantly professional health care is established only with the agreement of the Reich Physicians' Chamber, it being then that a physician is to participate in an official capacity or with an official contract.

& 11. *Physicians' Fees*

Regarding the collection of the fees, the physician is to comply with the fee ordinances decreed from the Reich Minister of the Interior according to & 15 of the Reich Physicians' Ordinance. The highest rate of fees of the Ordinance can be exceeded only with the approval of the Reich Physicians' Chamber, it being then that its coherence with reimbursement for this occurrence is effected in writing to the physician.

It is left up to the physician to excuse payment entirely or in part for direct patients as well as relatives, near friends, professional comrades and their members. Furthermore, this is not to be reported in the usual manner.

The calculation of fees should be done in general at least each quarter year. On demand the physician must split up the reckoning among those noted in the fee ordinance. He can designate it to the sickness category, if not contradicted by dominant medical grounds; attention to physician's duty of silence should be noted.

& 12. *Collegial Relationships*

The physician must show the same attention to his professional comrades that he himself demands for remarkable and collegial relationships. Each unauthorized expression about the means of treatment or the professional knowledge of another physician is to be worthy of the profession.

& 13. *The Treatment of Patients of Some Other Physician*

If a physician has knowledge that a patient has called in some other physician for the same illness, or he is forced to assume this from circumstances, then he should treat the patient in this circumstance only if he has ascertained that the patient or member renounces the former treatment by the up to now called in physician. He must see to it that the previously called in physician is informed by the patient or this member.

If a physician is called to an emergency of a patient of a physician who is not available, then he should deal with the situation promptly and inform the physician about the treatment. If in urgent cases several physicians are called, then the first arriving physician undertakes the treatment in the absence of any other understanding.

The physician is permitted to treat each patient in his office hours.

& 14. *Consultation and Supervision*

The physician is not permitted to refuse offered assistance from some other physician without extreme reasons.

The treating physician cannot decline a consultation of another physician requested by a patient or his family. The conditions which are valid for Fund practice remain hereby in effect.

A Physician should refer back a patient who was transferred to him from some other physician after the conclusion of his treatment, if further treatment is required.

A general practitioner should as a rule only assume supervision of another general practitioner, if a Specialty physician is not available.

& 15. *Representatives and Assistants*

Physicians should fundamentally be ready for mutual representation.

Patients who are overtaken representationally must be given back again to their physician.

Physicians whose right to practice the medical profession is removed or against whom a provisional prohibition of medical activity is imposed, may only with the approval of the Physicians' Chamber be represented.

Physicians who have been prohibited from the practice of the medical professions are not allowed to the represented.

The practice of deceased physicians can be continued for their widows or children for the duration of a quarter year with the approval of the District Medical Union. The District Medical Union can extend the period of time in special cases.

Physicians are allowed to employ assistants for their free practice only with the approval of the Physicians' Chamber.

Representatives and assistants of a physician active in free practice are not allowed to establish a practice in the same District for the course of a year after the ending of a practice, without the approval of the physician as well as the Physicians' Chamber.

& 16. *Welfare Physician Activity*

Physicians engaged in health related welfare must limit each treatment to the frame of an emergency and are not to allow this to estrange the persons entrusted to them from their house physician.

& 17. *Physicians in Cure or Bath Resorts*

Physicians in Cure or Bath resorts must discontinue the treatment of non-resident patients after the completion of treatment. The measures used by physicians active in Cure and Bath resorts should not be anticipated by non-resident physicians, so that patients do not bring along a healing plan.

During his own cure or recovery stay a physician is not allowed to carry on his own practice.

& 18. *Allocation of Compensation*

It is impermissible for patients to allocate compensation to some other physician or a medical facility, even in disguised form.

& 19. *Group Practice*

The establishment of a group practice is not permissible.

Larger medical equipment (e.g. Roentgen equipment) can be generally employed only with approval of the Physicians' Chamber.

& 20. *Advertising and Boostering*

All forms of advertising and boosting is prohibited to the physician. The following are expressly forbidden:

1. Commentary about methods of healing or procedures of healing in public or in other ways, such as in contracts, in radios or film, in connection with an advertisement for one's own practice,
2. To make known histories of patients and operations in anything other than in Specialty scientific writings,
3. To announce gratuitous or written treatment,
4. To announce private polyclinics or other gratuitous office hours

& 21. *Physician and Non-Physician*

The physician is allowed to treat patients together with non-physicians and support their treatments, if the permission prescribed in the law of 17. February, 1939 (covering the professional practice of the healing arts without Appointment) is followed. Cooperation with members of the medical helping professions are not affected by these conditions. Likewise the duty of physicians to deliver help in emergencies is not affected by this.

The physician is allowed to permit non-physicians to be an observer of operations, hypnosis and similar demonstrations if it has to do with cooperative work according to Abs. 1.[8]

The establishment of offices in the lay associations for health care and life reform or similar unions is permitted of the physician only with the approval of the Reich Physicians' Chamber.

& 22. *The Essence of the Means of Healing*

The physician must cooperate in the struggle for healing and methods of healing.

With the choice of his methods of healing the physician must attend to the calculation of the prerequisites of Volks' economy, which are published by the Reich Physicians' Chamber.

& 23. *The Physician and Trade in Methods of Healing*

The business exploitation of discoveries or inventions in the area of methods of healing is permitted to the physician if there is written approval the Reich Physicians' Chamber, according to Abs. 2. The Reichs Physicians' Chamber can revoke the approval subsequently if it is established that the exploitation brings the physician into conflict with his professional duties.

Contracts or other agreements through which the physician is required to participate in the trade of the health methods, or in methods of advertising require in each case the approval of the Reich Physicians' Chamber. The approval can be prohibited or revoked under the same presuppositions as those in Abs. 1. The Reich Physicians'

[8] Changed according to the Decree of 18 July 1939 (DABl. 39 S. 530) (footnote in original).

Chamber will contact the Reich Economic Chamber if a prohibition or revocation of the approval arises. If there is no agreement on these issues, then the Reich Minister of the Interior rules.

It is forbidden for the physician to give out his name in connection with a medical professional designation for proposed advertising, e.g. for a title of a firm or for designation of a method of treatment (also not in the form "According to Prof. XY"). The physician must notify and communicate all existing obligations to the Reich Physicians' Chamber, as conditions allow. If there are doubts or difficulties in the relationships regarding trade in the methods of healing, the physician should turn to the Reich Physicians' Chamber.

& 24. *Prescription of Methods of Treatment*

It is forbidden for the physician to prescribe or recommend methods of treatment in any way so as to demand or to allow himself compensation or other privileges (benefits, licenses or likewise). Any existing relationships are to be dissolved.

Medical samples may be promoted and used only in a circumstance necessary for knowledge or testing of the methods. They may not be returned for compensation.

It is forbidden for the physician to let be delivered for his prescriptions anything other than the prescribed substance, or to apply an improper use of a prescription.

One is not allowed to banish certain apothecaries or medical specialty businesses without adequate grounds, or to unite with apothecaries so that methods of treatment which are under a cover-name or designation not understandable by an apothecary are ordered.

& 25. *Testing and Evaluation of Methods of Treatment*

The physician is not allowed to promote or let be warranted, even in disguised form, any unofficial contract or contract outside of & 23 Abs. 2, for expenses or any form of compensation, for testing or examination of methods of treatment. Abstracts of the determination of expenses and the expert opinion are to be sent promptly to the Reich Physicians' Chamber. The physician is allowed to use a public expert opinion only after the Reich Physicians' Chamber has determined that this is in agreement with the regulation covering expenses.

The physician is prohibited from using the display of expert opinions or witnesses for methods of healing for the use of advertising to the lay public. The physician must refuse to use such expert opinions or witnesses. This is valid also for physicians who are in a contract relationship approved according to & 23 Abs. 2. The Reich Physicians' Chamber can agree to exceptions in specially considered cases.

The physician is not allowed to use in any way papers or reports in which methods of treatment have been recommended, in writing or in surreptitious form, to demand or agree for an honorarium over and above what is standard. He is allowed to reference only publications which are scientifically convincing.

& 26. *The Conception of the Methods of Treatment*

All other objects of the needs of health as well as health procedures are also valid as methods of treatment in the sense of the professional ordinance.

& 27. *Granting of Advantages*

The physician is forbidden to grant advantages of any sort or to make an exhibition in order to procure for himself professional employment.

& 28. *Contracts*

The physician must present to the Reichs Physicians' Chamber for approval contracts covering any medical activity which is covered by decreed prescriptions in the RAO according to & 49 Abs. 2.

B. Specialty Ordinance
& 29 *Specialty Designations*

Physicians are allowed to designate themselves as a Specialty physician if they are recognized according to & 32 as a Specialty physician.

The following specialty physicians' designations are approved at the following time:

1. Specialty of Internal Medicine,
2. Specialty of Gastroenterology
3. Specialty of Pulmonary Diseases,
4. Specialty of Pediatrics,
5. Specialty of Surgery,
6. Specialty of Gynecology and Obstetrics,
7. Specialty of Urology,
8. Specialty of Nerve and Mental Illnesses,
9. Specialty of Orthopedics,
10. Specialty of Opthalmology,
11. Specialty of Ear, Nose and Throat,
12. Specialty of Skin and Venereal Diseases,
13. Specialty of Teeth, Mouth and Jaw Diseases,
14. Specialty of Roentgenology and Radiation Therapy,
15. Specialty of Pathology.

Participation in several Specialty physician designations and the connection of a Specialty medicine designation with a general medical designation are not permitted.

& 30. *Period of the Training for Specialty Physician*

For the recognition as a Specialty physician with the Specialties of Internal Medicine, Gastroenterology, Pulmonary diseases, Pediatrics, Surgery, Gynecology and Obstetrics, and Urology, a training of 4 years, and with the other Specialties, 3 years is required. In addition for Specialty physician recognition one has to prove 1 year of general medicine or internal medicine training. The Specialty physician for Internal Medicine must instead of this have been active for a year as a general physician, a surgeon or a gynecologist.

To be recognized as a Specialty physician for teeth, mouth and jaw diseases, in addition, the successful completion of the test as a dentist is required.

Specialty physicians for Gastroenterology and Specialty physicians for Pulmonary diseases must have had 2 years of general medical training, Specialty physicians for Pediatrics must have been in general-internist activity for 1 year. Specialty physicians for Gynecology must prove a 2 year Obstetrics training, Specialty physicians for Nerve and Mental illnesses at least 1 year training each in the areas of Neurology and Psychiatry.

A training time in which one carries out his own practice is as a rule not considered to be adequate. Physicians who during their training time have represented their area as a Specialty physician can count this representative activity up to a quarter year.

Training in related Specialty areas can be counted up to at most 1 year.

& 31. *Type of Training for Specialty Physicians*

The training should take place in a department connected to a Reich German University Clinic or hospital. The training must be led by a Specialty physician. For the training only larger hospitals are appropriate in which patients of various types are entrusted. These must possess all of the scientific credentials which are required for fundamental and encompassing training in the relevant specialty. The training must extend to all areas of the Specialty and is permitted to occur only in Specialty departments. If diseases are also treated in a hospital or a hospital department which belong to some other Specialty, then the training time is calculated only partly, up to at most half of the prescribed education time.

Training in a polyclinic and clinics under the leadership of a Specialty physician is allowed to be counted only up to half and at the most up to a year; training at a University poly-clinic which has available an extensive permanent department can be entirely counted.

The training should take place as a rule in an assistanceship.

The training in a so-called voluntary or helping physician place is counted, if proof is produced that the volunteer has practiced his activity in an equally responsible place as an assistant.

Training acquired in a foreign country can be recognized if it is of the same value of that acquired in the Reich.

If the training deviates from these conditions and prescriptions & 30, in special exceptional cases, the recognition as a Specialty physician can be granted.

& 32. *Recognition of the Specialty Physician*

The recognition as a Specialty physician is carried out by the Physicians' Chamber in which the member belongs. The required documents are to be attached to the application. The Physicians' Chamber rules in the case of a disagreement over the existence or non-existence of a Physician Specialty Community.

The Physicians' Chamber determines the members of a Professional Committee called from its members.

The affected can appeal the ruling within 2 weeks to the Physicians' Chamber which gives the final ruling.

The recognition as a Specialty physician is valid for the entire area of the Reich.

Physicians who are licensed in a foreign country and possesses approval for the practice of medicine within the Reich according to & 11 RAO can likewise be recognized as a Specialty physician. The recognition comes from the Reich Physicians' Chamber.

The recognition as a Specialty physician can be revoked if the physician does not possess the inclination for Specialty physician activity. At a proceeding, the conditions for the recognition as a Specialty physician finds corresponding use.

& 33. *Duties of the Specialty Physician*

The Specialty physician is fundamentally excluded from practice as a general physician or as an independent examing physician. Sunday, night and Ready Reserve Service and Honorary activity are excluded from this.

Specialty physicians must confine themselves essentially to their Specialty and must have available the necessary instrumentation to carry out their Specialty physician activity.

The Specialty physician is not allowed to turn his visiting practice into a general house physician activity. He is not allowed to alienate the family from their house physician.

Specialty physicians, who are leaders of large hospitals or their departments should limit themselves outside of the hospital to general office hours and consultative activity.

Specialty physicians are allowed as a rule to be represented only by Specialty physicians of the same Specialty. If this does not occur, then the represented physician must exercise the proper care in the choice of representative.

& 34. *Transitional Conditions of the Specialty Ordinance*

Physicians who were recognized as a Specialty Physician before the decree of these conditions or were allowed to continue a Specialty physician designation remain subject to the prescriptions of & 32 Abs. Paragraph 3 and Abs. 6 for Specialty Physicians.

For the physicians who were licensed before 1 January, 1935, the training of 1 year duration foreseen in & 30 Abs. I is shortened regarding general physician or intern activities (e.g. surgery or gynecology).

If a Specialty physician who carried a double designation has been previously approved for the continuation of this activity in an entire area by the responsible Department Leader of the KVD, then this may be continued under this regulation, as long as the approval from the Physcians' Chamber is not revoked.

C. Regulations Concerning the Announcement of the Physician in Free Practice

& 35. *Announcements and Registers*

The announcements of the establishment of a practice are allowed to contain outside of the residential quarters only the legend which is established for the sign of the physician and is to be published only three times in the same newspaper.

Furthermore, announcements are permitted only before or after a prolonged absence as a result of illness of 2 weeks or longer. Such an announcement may be published in the same newspaper only once and outside of the commercial section, where the breaking up or re-uptake of practice is presented, containing only the name, the physician or Specialty physician designation and the residence address.

The form and size of the announcement have to conform to the local customs.

The laying down of a practice as well as the breaking up or resumption of a practice is not permitted to be announced in any other way than through announcements in newspapers.

Physicians are not permitted to be included in a special registry other than those of the official registries. The Reich Physicians' Chamber as well as the Physicians' Chamber or the District Medical Union can make exceptions for local designations.

& 36. *The Inscription of the Sign*

The sign of the physician is allowed to contain only the name of the physician, the title "Dr. med." and "Medical Adviser" or "Private Medical," the designation as physician or a Specialty designation, the report of office hours and the telephone number. Further the following addendums are stated:

1. (a) the addendum "Obstetrics" for general physicians who practice obstetrics.
   (b) the addendum "Natural Healing Procedures" for physician who use these procedures.
2. With the agreement of the Physicians' Chamber:
   (a) the addition "Homoeopathies" for general physicians and internists who can prove sufficient training in Homeopathy and limits himself essentially to the use of this healing procedure.
   (b) the addition "Tropical Diseases" for physicians who can prove a special training of such.
   (c) the addition "Roentgen Institute" for Specialty physicians for Roentgen and radiation therapy for those who possess sufficient Roentgen equipment for diagnostics and therapy.
   (d) the addition "Medical Diagnostic Institute" for physicians who possess the corresponding education and equipment and do not announce or practice some other medical activity.
3. The addition ""State Approved for Serological Blood Investigations" for physicians who possess a state license for this. For the official physicians, the validating regulations of & 37 Abs. 2 of the German Official Law of 26 January, 1937 (Reichsgesetzblatt I S. 39) are to be applied.

& 37 *The Mounting of the Sign*

The sign of the physician should show to the population only the residence or location of the clinic of the physician. It is not permitted to be displayed or attached in an obtrusive form and its size is not permitted to exceed a standard size (app. 35 X 50 cm).

In exceptional cases, especially with a secluded residence and with a corner house, there can be, with the approval of the District Medical Union, an additional physician's sign put up.

Signs at the private residence of the physician, on which the office hours are not noted, must correspond to the standard sign of an otherwise private residence.

With the change of residence, the physician can put on the house out of which he has come a sign with a corresponding inscription for the duration of a half year.

& 38. *Announcement for Letterheads, Printed Receipts, etc.*

For the announcement on letterheads, printed receipts, stamps, etc. the conditions are similar to those covering signs.

& 39

D. Concluding Conditions

The Reich Physicians' Chamber can decree related prescriptions for the implementation of the Professional Ordinance.

The Reich Physicians' Chamber can excuse in special cases physicians from the regulations of & 21 Abs. I Paragraph I. It can decree deviations from the Specialty physician designations approved in & 29 and decree regulations covering the announcement of physicians who work in a clinic or healing institution.

The specially decreed regulations from the Fund Physicians' Union of Germany (KVD) remain in effect. The Reich Leader of the KVD and the Leader of the Territorial and District departments of the KVD designates from the membership of the Physicians' Chamber and District Medical Unions the authorities of the Reich Physicians' Chamber foreseen in && 5,6, 15 Abs. 5–7 and 19. In the case of & 28, the Reich Leader of the KVD gives, instead of the Reich Physicians' Chamber, the approval, as long as it has to do with contracts which fall in the area of responsibility of the KVD.

Physicians can file an appeal against the rulings of the Medical District Union as well as the Leader of the District Places of the KVD to the responsible Physicians' Chamber as well as to the Leader of the Territorial Department of the KVD. Appeals may be filed with the Reich Physicians' Chamber as well as to the Reich Leader of the KVD against the rulings of the Physicians' Chamber as well as the Leader of the Territorial Department of the KVD. The Reich Physicians' Chamber as well as the Reich Leader of the KVD can revoke or abandon a ruling of the Physicians' Chamber and the District Medical Union as well as the Leader of the Territorial and District Departments of the KVD as well as cases where there is doubt as to which is the responsible department. The proceeding regarding the recognition of the Specialty Physician (& 32) remains unchanged by this.

The authorities of the Reich Physicians' Chamber, the Physicians' Chamber and the District Medical Union are to be appointed by the Leader or an authorized representative thereof.

Regulation Concerning the Taking Up or Overtaking of a Practice

From 5 November, 1937 (DABI, 1937 P. 1037)

On the grounds of & 49 Abs. 2 Paragraph I and Abs. 3 of the Reich Physicians Ordinance, I decree with the approval of the Reich Minister of the Interior from 30 October, 1937 – IV B 15287 II/37/3121 – the following

"Supplement Concerning the Taking Up or Overtaking of a Practice":

Contracts concerning the taking up or overtaking of a practice require the approval of the District Medical Union. If a member of the Fund Physicians' Union of Germany participates, then the Leader of the District department of the Fund Physicians' Union of Germany is responsible for the approval.

As a rule, a reimbursement is allowed to be agreed upon only for overwhelming circumstances and for the overtaking of a physician's house or a physician's residence.

In particular cases, especially when survivors are in distress, and the nature of the practice consisted of the taking over the life work of a deceased physician, a special compensation can be paid.

Munich, 5 November, 1937
The Reich Physicians' Leader
Dr. Wagner

Disciplinary Ordinance of the Reich Physicians' Chamber According to and 53 Paragraph 2 of the Reich Physicians' Ordinance

The Reich Physicians' Ordinance in & 53 paragraph 2 gives to the Reich Physicians' Chamber the right to mediate disagreements in a comradely way on unapproved therapies, as long as there are no serious consequences and to levy a warning, a reprimand or a fine. It has therefore not to do with a new professional judicial proceeding in which the physician is subjected, but much more to do with the fact that the Reich Physicians' Chamber has now the opportunity to deal in those closely related matters for which in the past there was a lack of regulations, and these matters came before the professional court.

Consequently, on 11 July, 1940 the Reich Minister of the Interior gave his agreement to the Disciplinary Ordinance & 53 Abs. 2 of the Reich Physicians' Ordinance. The text of the Disciplinary Ordinance is published as follows.

The Disciplinary Ordinance furthermore does not revoke the right of the physician according to & 57 Abs. 2 of the Reich Physicians' Ordinance to take recourse in the professional court. The & 14 of the Second Regulation for the Implementation and Completion of the Reich Physicians' Ordinance simply brings a necessary legal limitation relating to the fact that a physician can no longer submit an application for the opening of a professional judicial proceding, if he has already followed the legal procedure in appealing an initial ruling of the Reich Physicians' Chamber according to & 53 Abs. 2 RAO, making it such that an appeal according to & 5 of the Disciplinary Ordinance was filed or if the period of time for the introduction of a appeal has expired.

The publication of the Disciplinary Ordinance could take place only now, after the revisions of the statutes of the Fund Physicians' Union of Germany of 27 January, 1941 were published in January 1941 (in the Deutsches Aerzteblatt", Issue No. 8 of February 22, 1941, page 95); because the Reich Minister of the Interior has made his approval of the Disciplinary Ordinance of the Reich Physicians' Chamber dependent upon the penalty authority of the Fund Physicians' Union of Germany in the first instance being transferred over to the Leader of the Territory – meaning the Territorial Department Leader of the Fund Physicians' Union of Germany – so that collected disciplinary measures in the underlying instances reside no longer in a single hand.

Disciplinary Ordinance

& 1

1. If the Physicians' Chamber comes to know facts about a physician which warrant the suspicion of a professional violation, then it must first clarify the factual matter.
2. The Physicians' Chamber must give the accused the opportunity to express himself concerning the professional violation complaint. It is to communicate not only the charge, but in addition, the extenuating circumstances including those meaningful to the determination of penalty.
3. The manner of investigation remains at the discretion of the Physicians' Chamber. It can also task the Leader of a District Medical Union with the undertaking of an investigation, seeking public authorities in the process for legal assistance according to & 63 of the Reich Physicians' Ordinance in order to request the employment of investigations or it may limit itself to written expressions and information.

& 2

If the investigation results in the conclusion of no professional violation or the investigation result does not warrant a penalty, then the Physicians' Chamber must dismiss the proceeding and report this to the accused, if he has heard the facts.

& 3

1. If as the result of the investigation, a serious professional violation has been found, that a professional judicial penalty according to & 53 Abs. 1 of the Reich Physicians' Ordinance is warranted, or that the matter appears to be professionally-legally worthy on other grounds, then the Physicians' Chamber must open a professional judicial proceeding, according to & 57 Abs. 1 of the Reich Physicians' Ordinance.

& 4

1. If the penalty after the investigation leads to a warning, a reprimand or a fine up to 1000 Reich Marks or exclusion from further clinical activity in public welfare for a period or indefinitely by the Physicians' Chamber and if the professional judicial worthiness is not prohibited from other grounds, then the Physicians' Chamber must declare such an order. The order establishing penalty is also to give a ruling regarding the expenses of the proceeding. The regulations of & 78 of the Reich Physicians' Ordinance are likewise valid and specifically & 78 Abs. 2, with the instructions that in place of the German Medical Court of Justice, the Reich Physicians' Chamber is to rule concerning the charges for the notifications.
2. The penalty is to be made known with grounds, and transmitted to the accused.
3. The legal process must correspondingly follow the conditions of & 13 of the First Implementation of the Ordinance for the Reich Physicians' Ordinance.

& 5

1. The legal process of the appeal of the accused to the Reich Physicians' Chamber against the ruling of a penalty is directed to the Physicians' Chamber.
2. The appeal is to be submitted in writing within 2 weeks after the ruling of the penalty to the Physicians' Chamber or in a notification to the Business Department of the Physicians' Chamber and is to be grounded in an additional 2 weeks after the filing of the appeal.
3. The appeal for costs by the accused is to be rejected as inadmissible if there is non-compliance as to the form and period of time of the appeal.
4. The regulations of the Ordinance covering the penalty process in regard to reintroduction into the previous profession are likewise valid if the period of time has been neglected.

& 6

The Reich Physicians' Chamber is not bound by the rulings of the Physicians' Chamber. Its ruling is final.

& 7

1. In & 14 of the Second Implementation Regulation of the Reich Physicians' Ordinance containing this qualification the accused is still at liberty to bring against himself the opening of a professional judicial proceeding according to & 57 of the Reich Physicians' Ordinance in order to clear himself of the suspicion of a professional violation.
2. With a correctly timed placement of application, the Physicians' Chamber must discontinue its pending proceedings and transfer its files to the responsible Medical District Court for investigation and further proceedings.

& 8

Regarding the establishment of the expenditures and the execution of penalty, the regulations of & 13 of the Second Implementation Regulation of the Ordinance for the Reich Physicians' Ordinance find corresponding use, which is declared by the Leader of the Physicians' Chamber instead of the Chairman of the District Medical Court.

Munich, 20 June, 1940
The Reich Physicians' Leader
Dr. L. Conti

The Reich Minister of the Interior Berlin, July 11, 1940
IV d 3434/40
3400 Bay. 1.

Regarding *Disciplinary Ordinance of the Reich Physicians' Chamber according to & 53 Abs. 2 of the Reich Physicians' Ordinance.*

Herewith I distribute on the grounds of the RAO, & 53 Abs. 2, my agreement to the forelying proposals to the Disciplinary Ordinance of the Reich Physicians' Chamber.

Dr. Frick

Regulation of the Reich Physicians' Leader to the Reich Physicians' Ordinance and 53 Paragraph 2

On the grounds of the RAO & 37, I decree the following

Conditions for the Introduction of & 53 Paragraph 2 of the RAO
Part I. General

& 1. *Duties of the Members of the Reich Physicians' Chamber and Authority of the Reich Physician Chamber according to the RAO & 53 Paragraph 2*

1. The physician is required to practice his profession scientifically and to show himself worthy with his behavior, inside and outside of his profession, of the attention and the trust which the medical profession demands. According to the Ordinance, among his duties is to be in an interactive relationship between the Departments of the Reich Physicians' Chamber, the Fund Physicians' Union of Germany, with the authorities as well as with other state institutions.
2. A physician, who violates the professional duties, especially offending against the Professional Ordinance (professional offence), is subject to the penalty of the Reich Physicians' Chamber according to the RAO & 53 Paragraph 2.

& 2. *Responsibility of the Reich Physicians' Chamber*

1. All physicians in the German Reich are subject to the Reich Physicians' Chamber with the following exceptions:

   (a) Active Sanitation Officers of the Army,
   (b) Sanitation Officers of the police,
   (c) The physicians of the Waffen-SS,
   (d) Reich Labor Service Physicians who are employees of the Reich Labor Service.

2. The assignment in the Reich Physicians' Chamber is suspended

   (a) for other physicians who are in the service of the Army for the duration of their service performance,
   (b) for physicians who are required to be active in the Army and are not medically active in any other way.

3. The penalty authority of the Reich Physicians' Chamber according to the RAO & 53 Abs. 2 is limited regarding medical officials, for which there exists a state regulated procedure of penalty, which excludes further clinical activity in public welfare for a time or indefinitely, in so far as one practices such activity outside of his office.

& 3. *Relationship to Other Proceedings*

1. If a violation becomes public knowledge and is to be examined, if a proceeding according to the RAO & 53 Abs. 2 is initiated, or if one becomes recognized in a professional judicial proceeding (RAO & 57 Abs. 1) or it is to be expressly pursued, then it should be referred to the Fund Physicians' Union of Germany. With the introduction of a proceeding according to the RAO & 53 Abs. 2 or an application for the opening of a professional judicial proceeding is to be examined, a communication to the Fund Physicians' Union of Germany for the purpose of exercising their authority is still necessary.
2. The Reich Physicians' Chamber is not bound by other courts in it rulings. If there is a judgment involving the same violation by a court, then the foundation can be laid for the factual establishment of a legally enforced judgment without further evidence for the ruling according to the RAO & 53 Abs. 2. With regard to other pending proceedings one can wait for the introduction of a proceeding

according to RAO & 53 Abs. 2 up to the time when the other proceeding has achieved legal force. A continuing proceeding can be suspended on the same grounds.

Part II. Penalty
& 4. *General*

1. The penalties which can be imposed, are

    (a) Warning
    (b) Reprimand
    (c) Fine up to 1000 RM
    (d) Exclusion from further clinical activity in public welfare for time or for a prolonged period.

    Other penalties are not to be declared.

& 5. *Warning and Reprimand*

1. A warning is the mildest form of the disciplinary punishment. It is levied to indicate disapproval of a certain relationship of a physician, with the demand to avoid this in the future.
2. A reprimand is a rebuke for certain behavior of a physician.
3. A warning and reprimand may be pronounced only in the context of this proceeding.
4. Disapproving expressions (complaints, admonishments, reproofs, etc.) which come to be pronounced by the Reich Physicians' Chamber on the grounds of its professional authority (professional oversight), are not penalty in the sense of the RAO & 53 Abs. 2.

& 6. *Fines*

Fines consist of at least 10, and at the most 1000 RM.

& 7. *Exclusion of Wider Clinical Activity in Public Welfare for a Period or for an Indefinite Period*

1. Exclusion from wider clinical activity in public welfare begins at the time the ruling comes into legal force.
2. The period of the exclusion is to be precisely declared. An exclusion for an indefinite period is not permitted. It may also not be pronounced to be for the time up to the ruling of another proceedings, e.g. of a proceeding introduced by a state criminal court.
3. If it is not certain when a ruling will be legally binding, the beginning date of the exclusion is not indicated.
4. For continuing the exclusion the conditions which are valid for a temporary exclusion are applied.

& 8. *Publication*

If there has been a ruling for publication, then this may occur only after prior approval of the Reich Physicians' Chamber. The grounds for the ruling are not publishable. In case the Reich Physicians' Chamber determines that nothing else is relevant, the publication takes place by a single printing in the official periodical of the Physicians' Chamber.

& 9. *Forms of Penalty*

1. For the determination of the severity of a professional violation it is to be above all noted out of what motive the violation has been committed.
2. For the determination of penalty the entire circumstances are to be taken into consideration. Also earlier violations by the physician can thereby be taken into consideration.

Part III. The Proceeding (General)

& 10. *Responsibility for the Practice of Authority According to & 53 Abs. RAO*

1. By practicing the authority according to the RAO & 53 Abs. 2, the Reich Physicians' Chamber assumes a responsible public power. It assumes a high legal power emanating from the state power.
2. The Leader of the Physicians' Chamber assumes the authority according to RAO & 53 Abs. 2. Collective penalties are to depend on him personally. He can direct others to support him in the consideration of a case, especially with the approval of the accused physician, in taking regard of witnesses and facts. The ruling falls exclusively to the Leader of the Physicians' Chamber.
3. The responsibility to introduce the proceeding falls to the Leader of the Physicians' Chamber in which the physician is a member at the time.
4. In doubtful cases, the Reich Physicians' Chamber decides which is the responsible Physicians' Chamber. It can also in the individual case declare the Leader of another Physicians' Chamber to be responsible.

& 11. *Disability of the Leader of the Physicians' Chamber*

1. If the Leader of the Physicians' Chamber becomes prevented (e.g. through illness or long absence), from practicing the authority according to the RAO & 53 Abs. 2, then his current Vice-Chairman takes up the existing authority. If this one is prevented from practicing the authority, then the Reich Physicians' Chamber determines who is to assume the authority according to the RAO & 53 Abs. 2.
2. The Leader of the Physicians' Chamber as well as his Vice-Chairman are excluded from assuming the authority, if
   (a) the accused physician is or was his spouse,
   (b) he is related in a direct line or related by marriage or is related in a direct line up to the third grade or is related by marriage up to the second grade, even if the marriage, through which the relation by marriage is founded, no longer exists.
   (c) he has been interrogated or had contributed decisively in a professional violation as witness or as an expert witness in this or some other proceeding.

& 12. *Bias of the Leader of the Physicians' Chamber*

1. The Leader of the Physicians' Chamber can be excluded on account of bias, if there are sufficient grounds presented to justify mistrust regarding his impartiality.
2. The accused physician can assert with cause the bias of the Leader of the Physicians' Chamber in which the ruling is under consideration.

& 13. *Ruling Regarding the Grounds of Disability and Bias*

1. If the Leader of the Physicians' Chamber has been excluded from the practice of the authority of penalty or bias has been asserted against him or he holds himself to be biased, then he has to refrain from further activity. He must report the action promptly to the Reich Physicians' Chamber with a statement. The latter ultimately decides.
2. These regulations find corresponding use for the Vice-Chairman of the Leader as well as for other affected persons.

Part IV. Proceeding Before the Leader of the Physicians' Chamber
& 14. *Introduction of the Proceeding*

1. The Leader of the Physicians' Chamber rules regarding the introduction of a proceeding according to RAO & 53 Abs. 2.
2. If a proceeding is introduced according to & 53 Abs. 2 by communication of the Leader of the Physicians' Chamber to the affected physician regarding the professional violation, it becomes his responsibility. From the communication the physician must be made to understand that it has to do with a proceeding according to RAO & 53 Abs. 2.
3. The proceeding can be extended each time that further facts are found in the course of the investigation. The physician must be informed that these additional facts are the object of the proceeding.

& 15. *The Investigation*

1. The introduction of the proceeding follows the investigation. It is extended to all circumstances which serve to clarify the proceeding regarding the physician and his motives. It is to deal with not only the facts which incriminate, but also those which exonerate the physician, and the circumstances which are meaningful for the determination of penalty.
2. The Leader of the Physicians' Chamber determines the course and extent of the investigation. It is not bound by an application. If a demand for a statement of criminal record appears necessary, then the Leader of the Physicins' Chamber is to turn to the Reich Physicians' Chamber.

& 16. *Interrogation of Witnesses and Expert Witnesses.*

1. Witnesses can be heard in writing or orally. The Leader of the Physicians' Chamber can arrange for the personal appearance of the accused physician before him or his representative.

2. As long as there is no special grounds against it, the accused physician should be given the opportunity to be present during the interrogation of witnesses and to place questions regarding the facts.
3. If witnesses can not travel the distance because of great remoteness or there are other grounds against a personal appearance, then the Leader of the Physicians' Chamber, in case the interrogation does not take place by him on the spot, should entrust another with the interrogation. He can also seek the Leader of a Medical District Union to carry out the interrogation.
4. A written record of the interrogation of each witness is to be taken which gives the complete picture of the testimony of witnesses and records, not only the incriminating but also the exonerating facts. The written record is read aloud to the witness. He is to sign it. To be signed, in addition, is that which had led to the testimony of the witness, and any secretary called in is also to sign. If the witness refuses to sign the record, then this should be noted in the record along with the grounds of the refusal of the request.
5. The same conditions are likewise valid for the interrogation of expert witnesses.
6. Witnesses and expert witnesses receive actual travel expenses, as much as allowable, a measured remuneration for the expenditure of time and for the preparation of an opinion. The Reich Physicians' Chamber retains for himself the right to determine the specificity thereof.

& 17. *Due Process for the Physician*

1. Before the ruling is given, the accused physician is given the opportunity to express himself regarding the accusations raised and comment on the essential results of the investigations. The Leader of the Physicians' Chamber has to see that the physician receives knowledge of the essential results of the investigations for the ruling.
2. It suffices if the physician is given the opportunity to express himself in writing. The period of time must be at least a week. Each communication to the physician, as long as it contains no ruling, is at the same time an invitation to him to express himself. The Leader of the Physicians' Chamber can also order the personal appearance of the physician before him or before his subordinates if consideration of the extent and the kind of the interrogation assumes the personal appearance of the physician.
3. If the physician does not make a statement or does not appear for a personal hearing, then the Physicians' Chamber rules regarding the disposition of the file.
4. This opportunity is given for the physician on his demand for a personal hearing before the Leader of the Physicians' Chamber.

& 18. *Counsel*

1. The physician can avail himself of a lawyer licensed by a German court or of an official competent in legal matters or of a physician as an assistant in each part of the proceeding. Exceptionally, other appropriate persons can be approved by the Leader of the Physicians' Chamber.

2. Communications are to occur to the physician and not to the counsel, except for the cases designated in & 22.

& 19. *Legal Help*

Public authorities, especially the court and corporations of the public law, have to provide office and legal help (& 53 Abs. 2, Sentence 3, & 63 RAO).

& 20. *The Ruling*

1. The ruling can lead to a stay of the proceeding or to the penalty of the physician.
2. A proceeding is stayed if a penalty is not presented, especially if a breach of duty is not given. It can be stayed if the guilt of the physician is minimal and the consequence of his violation are meaningless. In the case of a stay, the prior testimony of the physician is not necessary. With each ruling which declares a penalty, only those facts which have been communicated to the physician and for which he has been given the opportunity to comment. Are to be taken into consideration The ruling must contain:

   Date of the ruling, name and residence, and, with large cities, also the home address of the physician, and a statement that refers to a proceeding according to & 53 Abs. 2. It must further express if the proceeding is dismissed or if a penalty is assessed. There is to be a statement concerning clinical activity in public welfare & 7.

3. The ruling is to be communicated furnished with the grounds.
4. With rulings which result in a stay, the accusation is asserted exactly against what the proceeding was introduced. Reference can be made thereby to a cover document. The ruling must report if the proceeding has been dismissed because there has not been a professional violation by the physician or because the guilt of the physician is minimal and the consequence of his violation was so meaningless that a penalty has been rejected.
5. With a ruling in which a penalty is pronounced, the facts are to be clearly given, especially describing the behavior of the physician against whom the penalty occurs. Other documents (court judgments, letters, etc.) are to be included in this way. It is not enough to just declare that the physician has violated his professional duties without discribing his behavior more closely. The penalty notice must also report on how the behavior of the physician was established. The judgment focuses on the establishment of the facts, the establishment of the penalty of the physician and the consideration of the length of the sentence.
6. At the conclusion of the penalty notice, it is further noted that it is permissible within 2 weeks after the decree of the notice of the penalty to lodge a legal appeal to the Reich Physicians' Chamber and that the appeal is to be substantiated in writing within another period of 2 weeks. The methods of legal instruction must further point out that the appeal is introduced in writing or with a note to the business department of the responsible Physicians' Chamber.

7. The ruling is to be signed by those who have decreed it. It is to be transmitted to the physician, furnished with the grounds.

& 21. *Costs*

1. In each ruling it is declared who is to bear the cost of the proceeding. This can be computed on part or the entirety of the judgment (& 53 Abs. 2 Sentence 3, & 78 Abs. 1 RAO).
2. With the staying of the proceedings, the Reich Physicians' Chamber bears the costs with the following exceptions:

   If the proceeding was established by false testimony or because of gross negligence of the accuser, then the costs and the outlays which necessarily resulted on the accused are to be imposed on those making the accusation. The informer is to be heard in advance. For the costs of the proceedings only the bare expenditures are valid.

3. The costs of the proceeding are established by the Leader of the Physicians' Chamber in a decree of notification after the ruling has taken legal force. In so far as there are costs arising in the instance of an appeal, the Reich Physicians' Chamber is to inform the Leader of the Physicians' Chamber what costs result from restitution of the file.
4. The notice of the establishment of costs is to be shared with those who have imposed the costs.

& 22. *Communication in the Case of Unknown Whereabouts of a Physician in a Foreign Country*

1. Is the physician's whereabouts is unknown or if he has his domicile or constant residence in a foreign country, communication can occur to him through public delivery or through communication by an authorized delivery service.
2. The public delivery is arranged by the Leader of the Physicians' Chamber and occurs by a one time publication in the "Deutsche Aerzteblatt." The delivery is considered to be valid for 4 weeks after the publication of the periodical. The date of the publication of the periodical is the date on the title page. In the publication it must be reported that it has to do with a proceeding according to & 53 Abs. 2 RAO whose report (e.g., Introduction to the Proceeding, Ruling of the Leader of the Physicians' Chamber) should be communicated to the physician. It must also contain the invitation to receive this document in the Business Office which is empowered to deliver it.
3. The arrangement of public notification is to be communicated to the counsel of the accused. On demand, an abstract of the reports which are communicated are to be transferred to him. The distribution of this report to the counsel is without meaning for the course of the period in which the counsel is not empowered to receive delivery.
4. If the communication occurs through public delivery by an empowered delivery service, then the communication is authoritative from the period of time when it first appears.

& 23. *Suspension of the Proceeding*

The Leader of the Physicians' Chamber can suspend a pending proceeding.

Part V. Legal Procedures
& 24. *Appeal*

1. The physician can within 2 weeks after the delivery of the ruling introduce an appeal against the ruling to the Leader of the Physicians' Chamber.
2. The appeal can be introduced only if the physician has been charged in the ruling. An independent contestation against the demand of the costs is excluded.
3. The appeal is to be entered in the Physicians' Chamber in which the ruling was decreed in writing or by a report to the Business Office of the Physicians' Chamber.
4. The appeal is to be substantiated in writing within a further period of 2 weeks after the introduction of the appeal. Later directed representations need not be regarded in the examination of the appeal.
5. If the appeal period or the period for the grounding of the appeal is not followed or the appeal is not generally grounded, then it will be returned as unacceptable, at the cost of the accused.
6. The regulations of the Ordinance of the Process of Penalty covering reintroduction to the prior professional position is correspondingly valid.
7. The bearer of the costs can introduce an appeal within 2 weeks after the delivery against the notice of the establishment of costs.

& 25. *Effect of the Appeal*

1. The appeal has the effect that the ruling is contested in its entire extent, even if the appeal covers only part of the ruling.
2. With the appeal, the facts are to be further verified by the Reich Physicians' Chamber. The Leader of the Physicians' Chamber must transmit the appeal without delay to the Reich Physicians' Chamber with the entire file of the proceeding.
3. With the appeal, the implementation of the contested ruling of the Leader of the Physicians' Chamber is suspended.

& 26. *Legal Force of the Ruling of the Leader of the Physicians' Chamber*

If the physician has not introduced an appeal against the ruling of the Leader of the Physicians' Chamber, then the ruling goes into legal force after the expiration of the period of an appeal.

Part VI. Proceedings before the Reich Physicians' Chamber
& 27. *Application of the Conditions from Part IV*

1. The prescriptions which are valid for the proceeding before the Leader of the Physcians' Chamber find corresponding use for the proceeding before the Reich Physicians' Chamber, as long as none of the following conditions determine otherwise.

2. The Reich Physicians' Chamber is not bound by the petitions and the factual determinations of the Leader of the Physicians' Chamber.
3. A renewed interrogation of witnesses and expert witnesses can occur at the discretion of the Reich Physicians' Chamber.
4. Due process of law is to be protected for the physician if the investigations lead to new results which are essential for the ruling. At his demand, the physician however is to be given the opportunity for a personal hearing before the Reich Physicians' Chamber.
5. New violations are not allowed to become the object of the proceeding before the Reich Physicians' Chamber.

& 28. *The Ruling of the Reich Physicians' Chamber*

1. If the appeal is not admissible or not consistent with the ordinance or not filed in the required period of time, then it is directed back as unacceptable without further inspection.
2. If a foundation of the appeal is not introduced within the prescribed period, then the appeal is returned without actual inspection.
3. If the Reich Physicians' Chamber establishes that the Leader of the Physicians' Chamber was biased according to & 12 or acted outside of the authority according to & 11 Abs. 2, then the ruling of the Leader of the Physicians' Chamber is suspended and the matter is returned for a another implementation of the proceeding.
4. The Reich Physicians' Chamber can confirm the ruling of the Leader of the Physicians' Chamber, or modify the proceeding in favor of or not in favor of the physician, or dismiss the proceeding.
5. If the facts are not extensively clarified, then the Reich Physicians' Chamber can send the matter and the ruling back to the Leader of the Physicians' Chamber for a renewed examination, by revocation of the ruling of the Physicians' Chamber. The Reich Physicians' Chamber can pronounce in the grounds of its ruling which viewpoints are to be especially noted.

& 29.*Legal Force of the Ruling of the Reich Physicians' Chamber*

The ruling of the Reich Physicians' Chamber is final. An exclusion from further clinical activity in public welfare begins at the time the ruling takes legal force.

Part VII. Special Conditions
& 30. *Effect of the Application by the Physician According to & 57 Abs. 2 RAO*

1. The physician may apply against himself an application for the opening of a professional judicial proceeding with the responsible Medical District Court up to time that a ruling of the Leader of Physicians' Chamber takes legal force (& 57 Abs. 2 RAO, & 14 of the Second Regulation of Implementation of the RAO).
2. The application is not allowed if the physician has introduced an appeal to the Reich Physicians' Chamber against the ruling of the Leader of the Physicians' Chamber or if the period of the appeal has completed its time period. The appeal can be taken back only with the approval of the Reich Physicians' Chamber.

3. With the timely placement of an application according to & 57 Abs. 2 RAO, the Leader of the Physicians' Chamber must dismiss the pending proceeding and produce his files for the responsible Medical District Court for the implementation of the proceeding.

& 31. *Application of the Leader of the Physicians' Chamber According to & 57 Abs. 1 RAO*

1. If a ruling by the Medical District Court appears to show that a case has a fundamental meaning, then there is to be anticipated from the proceeding according to & 53 Abs. 2 RAO, an application for the introduction of a professional judicial proceeding.
2. If it appears from the investigation that the punishment authority under Section 53 & 2 RAO is not sufficient for the prosecution of discovered infringements, then an application is to be made to initiate a professional judicial proceeding by the Leader of the Physicians' Chamber.

Part VIII. Concluding Conditions
& 32. *Execution*

1. For the prosecution of fines and established costs && 43, 79 of the RAO and & 25 of the First Implementation Regulation of the Ordinance of the RAO are applicable. The prosecution is to be carried out by the Physicians' Chamber. The ongoing contributions flow to the Reich Physicians' Chamber.
2. If it was declared that the ruling was to be published, then this must occur within 4 weeks after the legal force of the ruling.

& 33. *Securing of Medical Benefits in the Case of Exclusion of a Physician from the Welfare Activity*

If through the exclusion of a physician from clinical activity in the public welfare the medical support of the population is endangered, then regulations from the Leader of the Physicians' Chamber which are available for the medical supply for security are to be applied.

& 34. *Supervision*

1. The Reich Physicians' Chamber carries out supervision of the implementation of the proceedings according to & 53 Abs. 2 RAO.
2. The Leader of the Physicians' Chamber must present each ruling verbatim promptly to the Reich Physicians' Chamber.
3. The publication of the rulings or their communication to other departments than the departments of the Reich Physicians' Chamber and the the Fund Physicians' Union of Germany is permissible only with the permission of the Reich Physicians' Chamber.

& 35. *Communication of the Penalty*

The penalty of a physician which has legal force is to be communicated:

to the penalty registry of the Reich Physicians' Chamber with the grounding and statement of legal force.
to the Reich Leadership of the Fund Physicians' Union of Germany with grounding and statement of legal force.

Munich, April 28, 1941
Reich Physician Leader
Dr. L. Conti

Statute of the Fund Physicians' Union of Germany

Revised form of the wording including the Regulation of the Leader of the KVD for & 8 of the Statute. The Statute of the Fund Physicians' Union of Germany has been formulated with a change of several conditions. Hereafter is set the revision with the acknowledged approval of the Herr Reich Labor Minister.

Statute of the Fund Physicians' Union of Germany

& 1. *The Fund Physicians' Union of Germany*

The Fund Physicians' Union of Germany is a legal corporation of public law. It was erected by the Ordinance covering the Fund Physicians' Union of Germany of 2 August, 1933 (RGB1.I P. 567). Its place of residence is Berlin.

& 2. *Responsibilities*

1. The Fund Physicians' Union of Germany is the sole professional representative of the German medical system of Reich Social Insurance and Reich Benefit. It has the responsibility to secure the intended legal or contractual medical benefits. It can also conclude and secure contracts with other departments covering medical benefits.
2. It is incumbent on the Fund Physicians' Union of Germany to implement medical benefits and abide by the relevant conditions of ongoing relationships. It in addition regulates participation in medical benefits which are secured by it and can thereby require its members to participate also without their declaration of preparedness. It is directed to distribute directions for the implementation of medical benefits and determine the coherence of the economics of the method of treatment as well as examine medical performance. It further regulates the distribution of all compensation and other honoraria which are paid to the Fund Physicians' Union of Germany. Thereby it can introduce a comparison of compensation of the physicians within the Reich or in parts of the Reich and use means to secure medical benefits as well as establish measures which serve to

maintain the workforce of physicians and their economic security, while taking into account the family situation of the physicians.

3. The demand for an honorarium is valid only f the honoraria are to be paid for legally empowered medical benefits or on the grounds of a contract with the Fund Physicians' Union of Germany. With the payment of the honorarium to the Fund Physicians' Union of Germany, the carrier of Reich Social Insurance and Reich Benefit as well as other departments are freed of their obligation to pay. The physician can make valid his demand of honorarium only to the Fund Physicians' Union of Germany.
4. It regulates the relationship of its members with each other and with carriers of Reich Social Insurance and Reich Benefit as well as with other departments of its responsible areas.

& 3. *Membership*

Members of the Fund Physicians' Union of Germany are physicians carried in the Reich Physicians' Registry.

& 4. *Constitution and Administration*

1. The Leader of the Fund Physicians' Union of Germany is the Reich Physician Leader. He represents the Fund Physicians' Union of Germany legally and extra-legally. He has a permanent Vice-Representative. The Vice-Representative is assigned and dismissed by the Reich Physicians' Leader, with the agreement of the Reich Minister of Labor.
2. The Reich Physicians' Leader can assume the leadership of the Legal Department of the Reich Physicians' Chamber in the name of the Fund Physicians' Union of Germany.

& 5. *Administrative Departments*

1. The Reich Leadership of the Fund Physicians' Union of Germany is responsible for the implementation of the responsibilities of the Fund Physicians' Union of Germany. The Leader of the Fund Physicians' Union of Germany erects Territorial and District Departments as Administrative Departments, whose area of service he determines. The Leader of the Territorial and District Departments are named and dismissed by the Leader of the Fund Physicians' Union of Germany.
2. The assignment of the responsibilities to the Administrative Departments is regulated by the Leader of the Fund Physicians' Union of Germany. All declarations of the Administrative Departments are sent in the name of the Fund Physicians' Union of Germany. They are binding only for the Fund Physicians' Union of Germany when it is subject to the transactions which have been transferred over to the Administrative Department for independent handling or if it receives the approval of the Leader of the Fund Physicians' Union of Germany.
3. The authority and the activity of the Administrative Departments are carried out according to the directions of the Leader of the Fund Physicians' Union of Germany. He can also decree that the Leader of the Territorial and District

Offices themselves can transfer existing authority to others. The Leader of the Fund Physicians' Union of German can revoke or change measures or rulings of the Administrative Departments.

& 6. *Procuring of Funds*

The Fund Physicians' Union of Germany, for the implementation of their responsibilities, raises contributions which can consist of a definite amount or a hundreths of the reimbursement for medical activity or both. The contributions can be established variously in their form and amount according to various groups of physicians. Correspondingly, there is for the physicians various approved ranges.

& 7. *Publication*

The publication of the Fund Physicians' Union of Germany takes place in the "Deutschen Aerzteblatt" or in the District Physicians' periodical.

& 8. *Special Authority in Regards to Physicians*

1. Physicians are obligated to the Fund Physicians' Union of Germany for the fulfillment of their responsibilities and are to show themselves worthy of the attention and the trust which the fulfillment of these responsibilities require.
2. If a physician does not fulfill or does not fulfill in a proper way the duties for which he is obligated, then he can be prosecuted by a warning or fine up to 1000 RM or prolonged exclusion from clinical activity for a period or for a prolonged period for individual treatment or for all responsibile areas of the Fund Physicians' Union of Germany. All of these penalties can also be imposed together.
3. The disciplinary punishment will be pronounced by the Leader of the Territorial Department of the Fund Physicians' Union of Germany in which the physician is a member at the time of the introduction of the proceedings. The Leader of the Fund Physicians' Union of Germany can also make the Leaders of other Administrative Departments or and any other physician aware of the introduction of a proceeding. Before a disciplinary punishment is pronounced, the physician is given the opportunity to express himself. If there is no need of disciplinary punishment, then the proceeding is to be suspended. The suspension or disciplinary punishment is communicated to the physician in writing, with the grounds explained.
4. Within 2 weeks after the receipt of the communication, the physician can file an appeal against the disciplinary punishment with the Reich Leadership of the Fund Physicians' Union of Germany. It can be withdrawn only with the approval of the Leader of the Fund Physicians' Union of Germany.
5. Through the appeal, the disciplinary punishment in its entirety will be challenged. The Leader of the Fund Physicians' Union of Germany rules regarding the appeal, after consultation with a physician and ultimately a lawyer who is legally qualified. He can uphold the disciplinary punishment or alter or dismiss the proceeding in favor or not in favor of the physician. If the factual basis is not

extensively clarified, then he can direct back the facts for further testing and ruling by rescinding the disciplinary punishment.

6. The appeal has a suspensive effect. In serious cases, the Leader of the Territorial Department can make a temporary order regarding ruling on the facts through which the suspensive effect of the appeal is excluded. The Leader of the Fund Physicians' Union of Germany can revoke this order by his ruling on the facts.
7. The Leader of the Territorial Department must communicate each ruling promptly to the Reich Leadership of the Fund Physicians' Union of Germany. The Leader of the Fund Physicians' Union of Germany can order that the proceeding before him can then proceed, if the physician has not entered an appeal against the disciplinary punishment. This order of the Leader of the Fund Physicians' Union of Germany has the effect that the disciplinary punishment by the Leader of the Territorial Department is not to be revoked if the Leader of the Fund Physicians' Union of Germany does not expressly permit it. He can further order the resumption of a proceeding.
8. Furthermore, the Leader of the Fund Physicians' Union of Germany regulates the specifics of the implementation of these conditions. He can also alter or revoke the relevant rulings.

Berlin, January 27, 1941
The Reich Physician Leader
I.V.: *Dr. Grote*

The Reich Labor Minister Berlin, February 15, 1941
II a 206

Regarding: *Statute of the Fund Physicians' Union of Germany*

On the grounds of & 10 of the Ordinance of the Fund Physicians' Union of Germany of 2 August, 1933 (RGBI. I. P. 567), I declare the fore lying renewal of the statute of the Fund Physicians' Union of Germany of January 27, 1941, subject to the condition that this takes effect on February 15, 1941.

I.V.: *Dr. Syrup*
State Secretary

Regulation of the Leader of the Fund Physicians' Union of Germany Regarding and 8 of the Statute of the Kvd

On the grounds of & 8 Abs. 8 of the Statute of the KVD, I decree the following conditions for the implementation of & 8 of the Statute of the KVD.

I. General

& 1. *Duties of the Membership of the KVD and Authorities of the KVD according to & 8 of its Statute*

1. It is the duty of each member of the KVD to fulfill the responsibilities which according to the Ordinance fall in the area of the KVD and to show themselves in this behavior inside and outside of the responsible areas of the KVD to be worthy of the attention and trust which are required for the fulfillment of the responsibilities in the area of the KVD. To the duties belong also behavior consistent with the Ordinance in the relationship with the Administrative Department of the KVD, the Reich Physicians' Chamber, with the carriers of Reich Social Insurance and Reich Benefit, with authorities as well with other state institutions.
2. If the member of the KVD does not fulfill these duties or does not fulfill them in the proper way, then the KVD can prosecute the physician according to & 8 of the Statute.

& 2. *Practice of the Authority of the KVD. Relationship to Other Proceedings*

1. With the practice of the authority according to & 8 of its Statute, the KVD assumes its dominant public power. It exercises therewith the state power which is directed from the highest legal authorities. The rulings which are issued in this proceeding are actions of administration.
2. The KVD exercises authority according to & 8 independently. It is not bound by the rulings of other Departments. If a court rules on the same violation, then the factual determinations of a jurisdictional judgment without further review of a ruling are to be established.
3. Other proceedings, such as before courts, or state legal investigations, do not exclude the introduction of a proceeding according to & 8. If the behavior of the physician is being judged in another proceeding, then a proceeding can be opened according to & 8 or also the introduction of such a proceeding can be suspended up to the completion of the other proceeding.
4. With the publication of the violation of a physician, it is to be determined if a proceeding according to & 8 of the Statute of the KVD should be introduced or if the facts should be given over to the Physicians' Chamber for the introduction of a professional judicial proceeding or a proceeding covered by the Reich Physicians' Ordinance & 53 Abs. 2.

II. Disciplinary Punishments

& 3. *General*

The disciplinary penalties which can be enacted according to & 8 are:

(a) Warning,
(b) Fine up to 1000 RM,
(c) Temporary exclusion,
(d) Prolonged exclusion.

Several of these disciplinary penalties can be levied together. No other disciplinary penalties are to be levied.

& 4. *Warning*

1. A warning is the mildest form of disciplinary penalty. It may be pronounced only in the frame of this proceeding.
2. Disapproving expressions (Reprimands, admonitions, rebukes, etc) which are pronounced by authorities of the KVD are not disciplinary penalties in the sense of & 8 of the Statute.

& 5. *Fine*

1. Fines consist of at least 20 RM, at most 1000 RM.
2. Fines are computed entirely in Reich Marks; They are not permitted to be in a percentage of the Fund Physicians' honorarium or in other currency.

& 6. *Temporary Exclusion*

1. The temporary exclusion may not exceed a period of 3 years.
2. As a consequence of a violation, a physician can be excluded temporarily from participation in one or more responsibilities which belong to the area of the KVD. The specific activity from which the physician is excluded is always to be noted. In a Reich-sanctioned Sickness Fund the exclusion is not allowed to be limited to the activity of one or individual Fund types but rather must always cover the entirety of these Fund types. Exclusion from Fund Physician activity means an exclusion from these Sickness Funds as well as private health insurance Funds.
3. The duration of the exclusion is to be given exactly. Also, it may not be based on the time of a ruling of some other proceeding, for example, of a professional judicial proceeding, a criminal proceeding or a common court proceeding.
4. If the time at which the ruling is to come into effect is not declared, then the ruling itself is not to stipulate the day on which the exclusion time is to begin. The date of the beginning of the exclusion time is to be established by the Leader of the Territorial Department, if it is not established according to & 26 by the Leader of the KVD, as soon as the ruling has come into effect, especially also if the Leader of the Territorial Department has effected a one-time regulation through which the exclusionary effect of a statement is pronounced. The Leader of the Territorial Department communicates to the physician the date of the beginning of the exclusion time. Regarding the beginning of the exclusion period, regard should be taken that there is a period of time from the notification to implementation, so that patients who seek him can be notified that he will not be allowed to treat them in the future.

& 7. *Prolonged Exclusion*

Prolonged exclusion is only to be used for the worst possible cases. The conditions which are valid for temporary exclusion find analogous use.

& 8. *Degree of Penalty*

1. It is to be noted in the judgment regarding the severity of the violation out of what motive the violation was committed.
2. The entire circumstances are to be taken into account in the degree of penalty. Also earlier violations of the physician can thereby be taken into account. The extent of the fine is to take into account the economic situation of the physician.

III. The Proceeding – General

& 9. *The Jurisdiction for the Practice of Authority*

1. The Leader of the Territorial Department exercises the authority according to & 8. He can establish or consult a disciplinary committee of physicians and legal experts who possess qualifications for higher administrative service or the legal department. He is to especially take into account witnesses or expert witnesses in the interrogation of the accused physician.
2. The Leader of the Territorial Department of the KVD in whose District the physician is licensed at the time of the introduction of the proceeding is responsible for the introduction of the proceeding.
3. The Leader of the KVD can also notify the Leader of any other Department or any other physician of the implementation of the proceeding. For this, the conditions which apply to the Leader of the Territorial Department are correspondingly valid.

& 10. *Disability of the Leader of the Territorial Department*

If the Leader of the Territorial Department is prevented from carrying out his authority according to & 8 or if he is considered to be prejudiced, then his permanent Vice-Chairman is to assume this authority. If the latter is also prevented from assuming this authority, then the Leader of the KVD decides who is to assume the authority under & 8.

IV. Proceedings Before the Leader of the Territorial Department.

& 11. *Introduction of the Proceeding*

1. The Leader of the Territorial Department decides regarding the introduction of a proceeding according to & 8. If the proceeding is introduced in a communication of the Leader of the Territorial Department to the affected physician, the latter is informed of the violation for which he is charged. The communication informs the physician that it has to do with a proceeding according to the Statute of the KVD & 8.
2. The Proceeding can be broadened to investigate further facts which are revealed in the course of the investigations. The physician must be informed that these wider facts are likewise objects of the proceeding.

& 12. *Investigation*

1. The introduction of the proceeding follows the investigation. It is extended to all circumstances which serve to clarify the behavior of the physician and his

motives. It is to communicate not only the incriminating but rather also the non-incriminating facts and the circumstances which are meaningful for determining the penalty.

2. The Leader of the Territorial Department determines the course and extent of the investigation.

& 13. *Interrogation of Witnesses and Expert Witnesses.*

1. Witnesses can testify in writing or orally. The Leader of the Territorial Department can order the personal appearance of members of the KVD.
2. As long as no special grounds contradict, the accused physician should be given the opportunity to be present during the interrogation of witnesses and to place factual questions.
3. If a witness cannot be interrogated because of great distance or if there are other reasons against his personal appearance, then the Leader of the Territorial Department, if the interrogation is not carried out by him personally, is to task another to do the interrogation.
4. A written record of the interrogation of the witness is to be taken, which gives a complete picture of the expressions of the witness and produces not only the incriminating, but the non-incriminating evidence as well. The written record is submitted to the witness. He is required to sign it. In addition, it is to be signed by those who have interrogated the witness and, if a secretary is called in, also by the latter. If the witness refuses to sign the written record, then this should be noted in the written record along with the grounds for the refusal.
5. The conditions are correspondingly valid for the interrogation of the expert witnesses.
6. Witnesses and expert witnesses receive travelling expenses and, as far as required, a calculated reimbursement for the missed time and for the creation of an expert opinion. The details of this remains to be determined.

& 14. *Due Process for the Physician*

1. Before a disciplinary punishment is declared, the physician is given the opportunity to express himself regarding the accusations raised and the essential result of the proceeding. The Leader of the Territorial Department is to make certain that the physician receives knowledge of the essential results of the investigation leading to the ruling.
2. It suffices if the physician is given the opportunity to express himself in writing. The Leader of the Territorial Department can declare a time limit for this. The period of time must be at least a week. He can also order the personal appearance of the physician for a hearing if in regard to the degree and the kind of violation, his personal appearance is required. If the physician does not reply or does not appear for a personal hearing, then the Leader of the Territorial District determines the course of action.
3. At the request of the physician he is given the opportunity for a personal hearing before those who exercise the authority according to & 8.

& 15. *Legal Assistance*

1. The physician can at any level of the proceeding have a legally trained legal assistant or a physician as legal assistant. The legally trained legal assistant must possess the qualifications for higher administrative service for the legal department. Exceptionally, the Leader of the Territorial Department can also permit other appropriate persons to act as legal assistant.
2. Communications are to occur to the physician, not to the legal assistant, except for the cases described in & 17.

& 16. *Ruling*

1. The ruling can lead to a stay of the proceeding or in the disciplinary penalty of the physician.
2. A proceeding is to be stayed if a breach of duty is not shown. It can be stayed if the guilt of the physician is small or the consequences of his violation are insignificant. The prior testimony of the physician is not required for a proceeding to be suspended.
3. In a ruling in which a disciplinary penalty is declared, only facts which are transmitted to the physician and to which he has had the opportunity to respond are to be taken into account.
4. The rulings must contain: Date of the ruling, name and place of residence, and larger cites, also the home residence of the physician and the matter on which a proceeding according to & 8 of the Statute of the KVD deals. It must further state if the proceeding was dismissed or if a disciplinary penalty is declared. With an exclusion, && 6 and 7 are to be followed.
5. The rulings are to be furnished with grounds.
6. With rulings which result in the dismissal of the proceeding, the accused is informed exactly why the proceeding was introduced. This can be accomplished in writing. It must be determined from the ruling if the proceeding was dismissed because a violation of duty by the physician has not occurred or because the guilt of the physician is so minimal and the consequence of his violation were so inconsequential that a disciplinary penalty has been excluded.
7. With a ruling in which a disciplinary penalty is declared, the behavior of the physician is to be given exactly for which the disciplinary penalty of the physician occurs. This can be accomplished in writing (court judgments, letters, etc.). It does not suffice just to declare that the physician would have injured the professional duty without his behavior being more specifically disclosed. The ruling must also disclose upon what the establishment of the behavior of the physician is supported. The judgment for the disciplinary penalty of the physician and the determination of the degree of the penalty is connected to the establishment of the factuality. It is further to be noted that an appeal is permitted against the ruling within 2 weeks after receiving the ruling and that the appeal is to be sent in writing to the Reich Leadership of the Fund Physicians' Union of Germany, Berlin SW 68, Lindenstrasse 42. It should also be pointed out that the appeal can be taken back only with the approval of the Leader of the KVD.

8. The ruling is to be signed by those who are affected by it. It is to be communicated to the physician in writing, furnished with grounds. At the same time, a copy of the ruling is to be sent to the Reich Leadership of the KVD.

& 17. *Communication in the Case of an Unknown Residence of the Physician or of Residence in a Foreign Country*

1. If the physician takes up a place of residence or has his residence for a prolonged period in a fore ign country, then communication can be carried out through public delivery or through communication by an empowered legal delivery service.
2. The public delivery will be arranged by the Leader of the Territorial Department and occurs through a single appearance in the "Deutsche Aerzteblatt." The delivery is considered to be valid for 4 weeks after the edition of the paper. The day of the edition of the paper is the date on the title page. From the publication it must be noted that it has to do with a proceeding according to & 8 of the Statute of the KVD and the kind of written report (e.g. Introduction of a Proceeding, Ruling of the Leader of the Territorial Department) which is supposed to be communicated to the physician. It must further contain the summons to take in receipt or to allow the delivery through an empowered delivery service this document from the business office.
3. The order of the public delivery is to be communicated to the counsel of the accussed. On demand, an abstract of the document which was delivered to him is to be provided. The distribution of the written report to the counsel is without meaning for the period of time in which the counsel is not also fully legally empowered.
4. If the communication occurs through public notification and to a fully empowered legal delivery service, then the communication is authoritative from the beginning of the period of time.

& 18. *Costs*

1. The costs of the proceeding may not be imposed.
2. If the proceeding leads to a suspension of the proceeding because a violation of the duty by the physician has not occurred, then the KVD reimburses the physician the applicable expenses similar to a witness or expert witness.

& 19. *Suspension of the Proceeding*

The Leader of the Territorial Department can suspend a pending proceeding.

The Right of Appeal

& 20. *Appeal*

1. The physician can within 2 weeks after the receipt of the ruling introduce an appeal to the Leader of the Territorial Department against the disciplinary penalty. The day of receipt of the ruling is not counted in the period.
2. An appeal can be introduced only if the physician is charged in the ruling.

3. The appeal is delivered to the Reich Leadership of the KVD. It is considered to have been turned in on time if it is received within the appeal period to a department of the KVD or the Reich Physicians' Chamber.
4. The appeal should be substantiated within 2 weeks after its introduction. Later statements which are made are not required to be taken into account in the examination of the appeal.

& 21. *Effect of the Appeal*

1. The appeal has the effect that the ruling is challenged in its entirety, even if the appeal covers only part of the ruling.
2. With the appeal to the Leader of the KVD, the facts are extended for wider investigation. The appeal can be taken back only with the approval of the Leader of the KVD.
3. With the appeal, the implementation of the contested ruling of the Leader of the Territorial Departments is suspended. Indeed the Leader of the Territorial Department can in serious cases make it such that the suspending effect of the appeal is excluded by an interim order. The interim order should only occur if the violation of the physician is so serious that legal measures are unavoidable. An interim order can only be about facts in the ruling or simultaneous to it.

& 22. *Effectiveness of the Ruling of the Leader of the Territorial Department*

If the physician has not introduced an appeal against the ruling by the Leader of the Territorial Department, then the ruling will become effective with the expiration of the period for an appeal. The implementation of the ruling does not however take effect as long as the Leader of the KVD suspends its implementation.

VI. Proceedings before the Leader of the KVD

& 23. *The Resumption of the Proceeding Before the Leader of the KVD*

1. With the appeal, the matter is extended for further testimony and ruling by the Leader of the KVD.
2. The Leader of the KVD can order that the proceeding before him is also to then be continued if the physician has not introduced any appeal against the disciplinary punishment. Such an order can also be declared if the proceeding was dismissed by the Leader of the Territorial Department. With an order by the Leader of the KVD for the continuation of the proceeding, a disciplinary penalty of the Territorial Department will not be postponed, yet the Leader of the KVD can suspend the implementation of the ruling of the Leader of the Territorial Department.
3. If the Leader of the KVD has taken up the continuation of a proceeding for himself, then the facts in their entirety are considered by him for further testimony and ruling.

& 24. *Application of the Conditions of Part IV*

1. The prescriptions for the proceeding which were validated by the Leader of the Territorial Department find corresponding application for the proceeding before the Leader of the KVD as long as none of the following conditions determine otherwise.
2. The Leader of the KVD is not bound by the declarations and the factual rulings of the Leader of the Territorial Department.
3. Further interrogation of witnesses and expert witnesses is at the deiscretion of the Leader of the KVD.
4. Due process of law is guaranteed to the physician as long as it leads to the investigation of the essential results for the ruling. Furthermore, further testimony by the physician occurs at the discretion of the Leader of the KVD. On the demand of the physician he is given the opportunity for a personal hearing before a representative of the Leader of the KVD.
5. The Leader of the KVD decides regarding advising consultation of a physician and a legal expert who must possess qualifications for legal office.

& 25. *Ruling of the Leader of the KVD*

1. If the appeal has not been introduced according to the Ordinance or the appropriate time then it will be rejected as unauthorized without further consideration.
2. If a foundation for an appeal does not occur in the period prescribed in & 20 Abs. 1, then the appeal can be rejected without actual inspection.
3. If the Leader of the KVD establishes that the Leader of the Territorial Department was prejudiced according to & 9, then the ruling of the Leader of the Territorial Department is rescinded and the facts are sent back for further implementation of the proceeding.
4. The Leader of the KVD can, regarding the ruling of the Leader of the Territorial Department, modify in favor or not in favor of the physician or dismiss the proceeding. If the facts of the case are declared to be insufficient, then he can under revocation of the ruling of the Leader of the Territorial Department return the matter to the Leader of the Territorial Department for further examination and ruling. The Leader of the KVD can express in the reasons for his ruling what directions further clarifications would be considered to be acceptable and which viewpoints are especially to be taken into consideration. The Leader of the Territorial Department is bound therein.
5. The Leader of the KVD can revoke an interim order of the Leader of the Territorial Department, through which he has excluded the delaying effect of an appeal, before a ruling on the facts.

& 26. *Effectiveness of the Ruling of the Leader of the KVD*

A ruling by the Leader of the KVD is final.

VII. Concluding Conditions

& 27. *Execution*

Fines can be withheld from Fund Physicians' honoraria or other claims of the physician on the KVD. The contributions are to go to the KVD.

& 28. *Supervision*

1. The Leader of the KVD provides supervision covering the implementation of the proceeding according to & 8. The Leader of the Territorial Department must communicate promptly each ruling of the Reich Leadership of the KVD verbatim.
2. The Leader of the KVD can order the introduction of a proceeding according to & 8 or the continuation of a suspended proceeding, and can also instigate or suspend an on-going proceeding. He can further order the resumption of a proceeding before himself or before the Leader of the Territorial Department.
3. The publication of rulings or their deliberations to other departments such as to the departments of the KVD and the Reich Physicians' Chamber is permissible only with the approval of the Leader of the KVD. This does not apply if the communication covering the relevant disciplinary penalty is responsible for the implementation of the ruling to other departments, for example, the communication to the carrier of Reich social insurance regarding the exclusion of a physician from Fund physicians' activity.

& 29. *Transitional Conditions*

1. If there is introduced by the Leader of a District Department a proceeding according to & 8 with the coming into effect of the revised version of the statute of the KVD (15 February, 1941), then the Leader of the District Department carries out the proceeding according to the prior conditions of & 8 and communicates his decision to the Leader of the Territorial Department and the Reich Leadership of the KVD. After the decree of the ruling by the Leader of the District Department, further introduction of the proceeding is decided by these conditions so that a complaint which was introduced by the physician to the District Department or Territorial Department is submitted to the Reich leadership of the KVD.
2. If there are proceedings which follow the earlier amendment of & 8 of the statute of the KVD pending with the Leader of the Provinical Department at the time of the coming into effect of the revision of the statute of the KVD (15 February, 1941), then the latter releases the facts to the Reich leadership of the KVD without a ruling.

Berlin, February 20, 1941
The Permanant Vice-Chairman of the Reich Physicians' Leader
For the Fund Physicians' Union of Germany
Dr. Grote

Ordinance of Licenscure

Of May 17, 1934 in the Amendment of the Notification of September 8, 1937 (RGBI. I P. 977)

Ordinance of Licensure

Chapter 1. *General*

& 1

In the sense of this Ordinance of Licensure the designations mean.

(a) Sickness Fund: the Reich legalized Sickness Funds (& 225 of the Reich Insurance Ordinance); Fund associations (& 406 of the Reich Insurance Ordinance) are in the same category as the Sickness Funds.
(b) Physicians: those physicians who are empowered to practice the medical profession within the German Reich;
(c) Licensure: the authorization and obligation of a physician regarding the Fund Physicians' Union of Germany for participation in the Fund Physicians' Benefit;.
(d) Fund Physicians: the physicians whose license is active and who have not refused licensure according to & 42.

& 2

Only Fund Physicians are authorized to practice Fund Practice, except for pressing cases.

.

Chapter 2. *Registry*

I. Registry of Physicians

.

& 3

1. A physician who intends to be licensed must be carried in the Physicians' Registry.
2. A non-licensed physician may at the same time be carried in at most two Physicians' Registries.
3. A Fund physician may be carried only in one other Physicians' Registry..
4. If the Reich Physician Registry establishes that there are more applicants for entrance than that permitted by Abs. 2 or 3, then it is to determine which applicants are to remain and requests the responsible administrative departments to delete the unlicensed applicants.

& 4

1. The Physicians' Registry is to be administered by the administrative departments which are determined by the Reich Leader of the Fund Physicians' Union of Germany.
2. The Reichs Leader also determines the District for which the Physicians' Registry is to be administered.
3. The Department Leader of the Administrative Department decides regarding the applicants (those new, changing or deleted) in the Physicians' Registry, who are to be admitted into the Physicians' Registry.

& 5

1. Entrance is only refused if the physician is not a German state citizen or is found to not be in possession of civil rights.
2. A physician who is not in possession of German citizenship is however entered if he is authorized to participate in the Fund Physicians' Benefit according to & 20 Abs. 2.

& 6

1. Facts which rest on or are meaningful for licensure are officially noted on the application of the physician to the Physicians' Registry.
2. The physician is to be informed before the endorsement in case he himself has not proposed the endorsement.

& 7

In the Physicians' Registry the time of entrance is to be noted. The date of the receipt of the entrance application is considered to be the time of entrance, if thereby the presuppositions for the entrance have been produced, otherwise the day in which these documents have been produced. The time of the entrance determines the place in the list in the Physicians' Registry.

& 8

1. A physician will be stricken out of the Regristy:

   (a) if he requests the deletion;
   (b) if he has died;
   (c) if he has declined the Appointment or the Appointment has expired or has been revoked;
   (d) if the presuppositions for his entrance according to & 5 are not or not longer present. However a licensed physician who is not a German citizen may be stricken only on the grounds that he has lost his citizenship after his licensure;
   (e) if according to & 22 Nr. 2 or 3 his licensure ends;
   (f) if the license has been revoked because of & 25 Abs. 1 Nr. 1,3 or 4.

2. In the cases of the paragraph 1 Nr. 6 the physician may not be again entered into a Physicians' Registry before the point in time which is established in the decision covering the revocation of his license.

& 9

1. The examination of the Physicians' Registry is permitted for physicians and Sickness Funds as well as their associations and unions.
2. The examination of the Registry Files is not permitted. The leading administrative departments of the Fund Physicians' Union of Germany are directed to communicate the contents to the Physicians' Registry, but this is not obligatory.

2. Reich Physicians' Registry
& 10

1. The Fund Physicians' Union of Germany administers the Reich Physicians' Registry in which the entered physicians are carried in a Physicians' Registry.
2. The administrative departments which administer the Physicians' Registry have to communicate entrants in the Physicians' Registry of the Reich Physicians' Registry.
3. The Reich Physicians' Registry has facts which have meaning for another Physicians' Registry which are to be communicated to the leading administrative departments of this Physicians' Registry.
4. The Reich Physicians' Registry passes on to the Licensure Committee and the Reich Licensure Committees without charge the collection of facts which are relevant to them. The Reich Ministries, the Reich Arbitration Office and the Reich Committee for Physicians and Sickness Fund and the top associations of the Sickness Funds are to give information in the same manner and are to grant insight upon demand.

Chapter 3. *Principles of Licensure*
& 11

1. For each six-hundred Fund members there is one physician licensed.
2. The number of physicians which are licensed according to Abs. 1 is established for each Licensure District. Licensure Districts are either the Physicians' Registry District or a part thereof (Sub-District). Whether or not a Sub-District should be constructed is determined by the Reich Leader of the Fund Physicians' Union of Germany.
3. The Licensure Committee (& 31) establishes the relationship of the number of Fund physicians to the number of Fund members for the beginning of each calendar quarter-year and makes known the numerical relationship promptly in the "Deutschen Aerztblatt." This numerical relationship is established up until the next passing of a resolution covering the numerical relationship of licensing.
4. The number of members of the sickness Fund which have their residence in the Licensure District gathered from the sickness Funds or the responsible official departments and the number of Fund physicians who are at the same time

licensed in the District are used for the determination of the numerical relationship. Fund physicians whose License has expired are not counted.

& 12

1. Licenses follow irrespective of & 20 Abs. 1, until the relationship is represented according to & 11 Abs. 1.
2. *If there are in a Licensure District more Fund physicians on hand than the relationship of* & 11 Abs. 1 allows, then it is adjusted irrespective of & 20 Abs. 1 up to the achievement of the relationship, *for each three retired Fund physicians only one physician is to be licensed.* The Reich Leader of the Fund Physicians' Union of Germany can also declare that in especially strongly oversettled Districts, where for more than each three retired Fund physicians only one physician is to be licensed or generally no physician more is to be licensed. If such a condition applies, then the Reich Leader of the Fund Physicians' Union of Germany can establish the licensure proceedings for individual physicians and for places of licensure Districts which are designated by him.
3. If the replacement of a retired Fund physician is required for the security of the medical treatment of those previously insured by him for medical benefits, then an additional physician can be licensed in his District, if licenses according to Abs. 1 and Abs. 2 paragraph 2 or according to & 13 Abs. 2 are not possible or if the presuppositions of these and & 14 Abs. 1 are not present. In such cases correspondingly fewer physicians are to be licensed in the next licensure.

& 13

1. The licensure follows for one of the Districts or Sub-Districts for which the physician has been proposed.
2. *In localities in which the number of Specialty physicians among the Fund physicians amounts to more than four per hundred of all Fund physicians, Specialty physicians can only be licensed for non or non-sufficiently supplied Specialties; furthermore, only general practice physicians are to be licensed.*
3. If in a District or a Sub-District in which no Fund physician has settled, the establishment and licensure of a physician for the securing of medical treatment of the insured and their members being necessary, licensing for the Licensure District can be denied irrespective of & 12 Abs. 2 until a physician is licensed for the District or Sub-District which is more urgently required.
4. If the licensure of a physician seriously endangers the existence of an already licenced physician in a Territory, then the Reich Leader of the Fund Physicians' Union of Germany can determine on application of the Department Leader of the Territorial Department of the Fund Physicians' Union of Germany after consultation with the Vice-Chairmen of the Licensure Committees that within the borders of spaces designated by him no more physicians are to be licensed for the time being.

& 14

(1) Presupposition for licensure is an at least two-year preparation for Fund practice. Existing licenses are not to be affected thereby.
(2) During the preparation, the physician must be active 3 months as the representative or assistant of a Fund physician with a predominantly general practice in the rural regions. Consequently, if rural practice is done in this sense, then on application of the Department Leader of the appropriate Territorial Department and on appeal of the physician, the Reich Leader of the Fund Physicians' Union of Germany will make a binding ruling for the License authorities. The ruling of the Department Leader is to be produced as a rule before the initiation of this procedure. The appeal must be raised within a period of 2 weeks after the serving of the ruling.
(3) In the remaining time there will be credited:

1. practical activity as an Assistant or Voluntary physician in hospitals, private clinics, healing institutions, sanitoriums or polyclinics up to 21 months;
2. medical activity in areas designated by the Reich Leader of the Fund Physicians' Union of Germany up to 12 months;
3. Activity as an Assistant or representative of a Fund Physicians up to 9 months;
4. At least 1 year practical activity up to 6 months as a main official Physician in a Health Department;
5. medical activity as a general practitioner of up to 6 months in a medical-scientific institute.

   If however at the same time an activity according to no. 4 is proven, then only one of these activities are to be credited.
6. Participation in a teaching course recognized by the Reich Leader of the Fund Physicians' Union of Germany

(4) The activity as Assistant of a Fund Physician will be counted if the Fund Physician has the approval of the Department Leader of the Territorial Department of the Fund Physicians' Union of Germany for activity of an Assistant in the Fund practice.
(5) An activity as Assistant or Voluntary physician will not be counted if the physician practices at the same time his own practice.
(6) Physicians who have been licensed longer than since the tenth of January of 1932 and physicians who were active uninterrupted longer than 2 years as a Fund Physician but have however given up this activity, are freed from the preparatory activity for the Fund practice.
(7) Physicians who have had heavy engagement in the war and physicians who were active in the fight for national revival can be excused from the preparatory activity for the Fund practice. In this case there is however a presupposition for the licensure that the physician has been active as a physician for at least 1 year since the day of his Appointment.

(8) The paragraphs 2–4 are not valid for physicians who have fulfilled with the coming into effect of the licensure ordinance of an at least 2 year preparation for the Fund practice according to the previous regulations of licensure.

& 15

Excluded from licensure are:

1. Physicians against whose licensure there exists an important reason lying in their character;
2. Physicians who themselves or their spouse are not of German or related blood. With those of mixed-blood, the Reich Leader of the Fund Physicians' Union of Germany can allow his exception;
3. Physicians who are not certain that they are entirely committed without reservation to the National Socialist State.
4. Married female physicians if the practice as Fund Physician activity does *not* appear to provide economic security of the family.

& 16

1. Physicians who as a consequence of having an official or employed relationship or receives regularly from a medical benefit or social insurance organization at least 400 Reichmarks monthly are as a rule not permitted a Fund practice. Their licensure should only occur if there appears to be a necessary definite Fund Benefit.
2. The sum named in Abs. 1 of 400 Reichsmarks is raised with married physician by 100 Reichsmarks and with physicians who have children, for each child up to a completed 24th year, with daughters the longest up to their marriage, up to 50 Reichsmarks.
3. If there are especially unfavorable economic conditions, then a physician can also then be admitted, if his regular monthy income is not more than 20% of that foreseen in Abs. 1 and 2.
4. Leave and retirement money are valid as income in the sense of paragraph 1, while child allowance is not, and not the compensation allowed for the damage to their medical activity introduced by the office leader of the Reich Leader of the Fund Physicians' Union of Germany.
5. Paragraphs 1–4 also apply to mine physicians. Exceptions are part-time physicians who practice their part-time activity on the grounds of a contract decided by the Fund Physicians' Union of Germany according to the system of the organized free choice of physician.

& 17

(1) If there comes to be a question of the choice of several physicians for licensure, then all circumstances relating to the licensure comes into question and are to be weighed carefully.
(2) In the choice these are to be preferred:

1. Physicians who have been active, with their first licensure, at least 2 years continuously in the Central Office for Volks Health of the NSDAP;
2. Physicians who can prove, with their first licensure, a service time of at least 1 year duration in military service and in the labor service or in one of their service branches;
3. Seriously war-injured, other war participants and war orphans;
4. Displaced and expelled physicians with their first licensure;
5. Married physicians and those among them with a large number of children;
6. Physicians, who have been at least 5 years in the country or in a small city as a Fund Physician who request licensure for a District with better educational possibilities for their children;
7. Physicians who have no regularly recurring income like salary, retirement income or pension.
8. Physicians who intend to overtake a parental practice with the licensure for the District of this practice.

(3) The Reich Leader of the Fund Physicians' Union of Germany can decree further guidelines for the choice, irrespective of the regulations of paragraph 1 and 2.

& 18

1. The physician must before, at the latest however a half year after, his licensure have participated in an introductory course for Fund Practice, which the Fund Physicians'Union of Germany has organized or permitted to be organized. Existing licenses are not affected by this.
2. Physicians who have been active continuously longer than 2 years as a Fund Physician, but have however given up this activity, are freed from the introductory course.
3. If more than 2 years have passed since participation in a course prior to the licensure, then the Department Leader of the District Department of the Fund Physicians' Union of Germany in whose District the physician is licensed is to require a visit to a further course if the licensed physician has not in the meantime continuously stood in for at least a year for a self-standing Fund Physician.

& 19

The Leader of an introductory course has to produce for each participant after the completion of the course a certificate reporting the date and duration of the course as well as the participation of the physician.

& 20

(1) The && 11, 12 Abs. 1 and Abs. 2 sentence 1, & 14 Abs. 1 and && 17, 47 are not valid:

1. for the first License of physicians who acquired special merit in the national renewal and had belonged to and continuously belonged to the National Socialist German Workers Party, a branch of the Steel Helmets on 30 January,

1930. A prerequisite is that the physicians have been active at least a year as a physician since the day of their Appointment. Concerning the presence of the prerequisites named in sentence 1, the authorities of licensure are bound by the decision of the Reich Leader of the Fund Physicians' Union of Germany;
2. for the first license of physicians who have practiced a medical activity at least 3 years in a foreign country which served to promote German culture or German science;
3. for a repeat licensure of seriously war injured physicians who would had given up their last license after 1 September, 1933 if they make it clear that the disturbance to their health by the war injury would have made the practice in which they were licensed impossible.

(2) The Reich Leader of the Fund Physicians' Union of Germany can in exceptional cases, in physicians who on the grounds of & 11 Abs. 1 of the Reich Physicians' Ordinance were established in the practice of the medical profession, and in physicians who have maintained the Appointment as a physician without having German citizenship, allow participation in the Fund Physicians Benefit at places to be designated by him. The approval can be revoked at any time without applications or grounds. During the period of the practice of the Fund Physicians' Activity these physicians have furthermore all the rights and duties of a Fund Physician.

& 21

A Fund Physician who moves out of a District of his previous practice remains licensed if the Department Leader of the responsible Territorial Department of the Fund Physicians' Union of Germany of the new District of establishment or of the new District of residence agrees. The decision of the Department Leader is final.

Chapter 4. *Termination and Suspension of Licensure*

& 22

The License is terminated:

1. with the death of the physician;
2. with the declaration of the physician that he does not accept the license;
3. for a Fund Physician who removed himself to a foreign country or left the District of his former practice without the approval of the responsible Department Leader according to & 21, such that his license was suspended;
4. for a Fund Physician who was stricken from the Physicians' Registry of the District in which he is licensed.

& 23

(1) The License is suspended:

1. as long as the practice by the physician of the medical profession is provisionally forbidden (& 5 Abs. 5 and & 74 Abs. 1 and 4 of the Reich Physicians' Ordinance);

2. as long as the authority to practice the medical profession according to & 7 Abs. 1 of the Reich Physicians' Ordinance is suspended.

(2) The suspension of the license is to be carried out:

1. if circumstances are presented which would exclude licensure according to & 15 Nr. 4 as well as according to & 16 Abs. 1 or 5. If the physicians designated in & 16 Abs. 1 and 5 are married, then the suspensions is to be carried out if their regular income exceeds the monthly contribution of 500 Reich Marks. If these physicians have children, then this threshold is raised for each child who has completed the 24th year, with daughters at the most up to her marriage, of a hundred Reich Marks monthly; In these cases & 16 Abs. 3 finds no application;
2. if a Fund Physician who is required has not taken an Introductory Course within a half year of licensure has not complied.

(3) The suspension of the license can be carried out if and so long as the physician is licensed to be a dentist, in so far as there are no special circumstances for the licensure appear.
(4) Furthermore, a proceeding is carried out over the suspension of the license of an application of the physician.
(5) In the ruling the time of suspension must be established. In the cases of paragraph 2 Nr. 1 the beginning of the time of the suspension is determined after taking into consideration the economic circumstances of the individual case. The end of the time of suspension can be determined also by a statement designated in the decision.
(6) During the period of suspension Fund Physician activity can not be practiced

& 24

(1) The revocation of the license is to be carried out:

1. if the license had not been allowed to occur because of important grounds lying *on the character of the physician*, or if after the *license, such a grounds arise* and in these cases the concern over the character the the physician continues to exist, if the presuppositions of & 15 Nr. 3 occur after the coming into force of this License Ordinance (1. July 1934);
2. if a physician of German or related blood had married a wife of non German or related blood after 1 July, 1933, it being then that this exception was permitted according to & 15 Nr. 2.
3. if a Fund Physicians declines without adequate grounds to participate.in the Fund Physicians' Benefit.
4. if a Fund Physician does not practice in the Fund Practice longer than 3 months without adequate reasons

(2) In the cases of paragraphs 1 Nos. 1, 3 and 4, there is to be established the point of time in which the physician may at the earliest be again readmitted in a Physicians' Registry.

Chapter 5, *Proceedings*

&25

(1) The new entrance in the Physicians' Registry is to occur on written application by the physician in the case owing to the office of & 5 Abs. 2. The application is directed to the Administrative Department of the Fund Physicians' Union of Germany in which the Physicians' Registry is applied.
(2) The application should include the employees of the physicians and also his wife and his children, if applicable, along with his signature.
(3) With the application should be included:

1. The birth information, as well as the document from which this information is derived, if the applicant and, if applicable, also his wife are of German or related blood;
2. The document covering the Appointment;
3. Documents about the medical activity practiced since the Appointment;
4. A police clearance.

(4) If a physician gets married, then he has to communicate it promptly to the Physicians' Registry and produce the documentation which proves that the wife is German or of related blood.

& 26

With the application for a new entrance into a Physicians' Registry a fee of five Reich Marks is assessed, which is used to cover the costs of the processing. The fee will not be refunded on exclusion from the Physicians' Registry. Furthermore, the dismissal of an application to the Physicians' Registry occurs without a fee.

& 27

1. With the injunctions over entrances according to & 4 Abs. 3, communications are to be made by registered letter or with a receipt to the physician and to licensed physicians, also to the Department Leader of the District Department of the Fund Physicians' Union of Germany, in whose District the license lies.
2. Against the injunctions, the physician and, in given cases, the Fund Physicians' Union of Germany can introduce within a month after the licensure an appeal to the Licensure Committee representing the District Department designated by the Department Leader in Abs. 1. The appeals effects a delay.

& 28

Official channels of licensure are the License Committee, the Reich Licensure Committee and the Reich Department of Justice.

& 29

1. The physician or physicians are to participate at the proceeding at which entrances or licensure matters are decided, as well as the Fund Physicians' Union

of Germany, represented on the occasion by the Department Leader designated in & 34 Abs. 2.

2. In a proceeding before the Reich Department of Justice there is contributed an observer from the Reich Licensure Committee who is separate from the the observer (& 36 Abs. 3) named by the Reich Labor Minister.

& 30

The official channels of authority of licensure decide in the frame of the legal prescriptions according to free or obligatory matters. The members of the official channel of licensure are not bound regarding the directions of the decision.

& 31

For each Medical District a Licensure Committee with the Administrative Department of the Fund Physicians' Union of Germany leads the Physicians' Registry.

& 32

The Licensure Committee is expressly responsible for the Physicians' Registry District for which it is directed.

& 33

1. The Licensure Committee consists of the Chairman and two members.
2. The Chairman and the members as well as the Vice-Chairman are called and dismissed in the necessary number by the Reich Leader of the Fund Physicians' Union of Germany. The members as well as the Vice-Chairman are not to be licensed in more than one Physicians' Registry. The Department Leader of the Administrative Department of the Fund Physicians Union of Germany in whose District the Licensure Committee is established proposes appropriate persons to the Reich Leader.
3. In the case of licensure, a non-licensed assessor who is not directly involved in the outcome of the voting must participate in the passing of a resolution of the Licensure Committee.

& 34

1. The Licensure Committee rules concerning the license, its revocation and its continuing revocation as well as in any contention over the existence or non-existence of a license. It rules further on appeals against injunctions over entrances in to the Physicians' Registry.
2. Against the ruling of the Licensure Committee, the affected physician and the Fund Physicians' Union of Germany can introduce within a month after the licensure an appeal to the Reich Licensure Committee represented by the District Leader of the District Department in whose District the license lays. Against a ruling according to Abs. 1 sentence 2, the Fund Physicians' Union of Germany can introduce an appeal which has the effect of challenging the injunction represented by the Distric Leader.

3. The appeal effects a delay.

& 35

The Reich Licensure Committee coexists with the Reich Department of the Fund Physicians' Union of Germany.

& 36

1. The Reich Licensure Committee consists of the Chairman and four members
2. The Chairman and three members as well as the Vice-Chairman are called and dismissed in the necessary number by the Reich Leader of the Fund Physicians' Union of Germany.
3. A member and the Vice-Chairman are appointed by the Reich Labor Minister after consultation with the Reich Leader of the Fund Physicians' Union of Germany. The member and the Vice-Chairman should have the qualifications of a judicial officer and be experienced in the law of licensure.

& 37

(1) The Reich Licensure Committee rules regarding notifications concerning decisions of the Licensure Committee. The notification can be proposed without oral discussion by a decision of the Chairman of the Reich Licensure Committee, of the members appointed by the Reich Labor Minister and an additional member, if these are in agreement over the inappropriateness, the late application, or the unexceptional nature of the notification.
(2) According to the legal procedure of revision and the Reich Arbitration Office, the member appointed by the Reich Labor Minister has only a month to appeal the ruling of the Reich Licensure Committee. The denial of revision is to be declared in writing or recorded orally.
(3) The revision can only be supported if

    1. the contested ruling would rest on the non-use or on the inappropriate use of the existing claim or on an offense contrary to the clear contents of the file.
    2. the proceeding would suffer an essential shortcoming.

(4) the revision causes a delay.

& 39

1. The Reich Justice Department rules on the facts designated in & 38 in a special session, consisting of the Chairman and four members.
2. The Chairman and two members as well as the Vice-Chairman and the President of the Reich Insurance Office constitute the necessary quorum. The Chairman and his Vice-Chairman are to be drawn as a rule from Directors or Senate Presidents of the Reich Insurance Office. The member and the Vice-Chairman should have the qualification of a judicial officer and be experienced in the law of licensure.

3. The two other members and Vice-Chairman are to be called and dismissed in the necessary number by the Reich Leader of the Fund Physicians' Union of Germany.

&40

Conditional Licenses are not allowed. If the license was promised under a condition, then it is to be considered to be unconditional.

& 41

When dealing with licenses, the Specialty Area (general practice or a designated physician's specialty) is required to specify the District or the Sub-District where the license is allowed.

& 42

The physician can declare within 2 weeks after the taking effect of the legal power of his license an expressed decision if he does not intend to take up the license. The declaration is to be presented in writing to the Department Leader of the Administration of the Fund Physicians' Union of Germany in which he is carried in the Physicians' Registry; it is irrevocable.

& 43

1. With the exception of the application for licensure, applications and legal matters are to be grounded with the accompaniment of written proof. With each written document and presentation there to be enclosed four supplements each for the Licensure Committee for the Reich Licensure Committee and the Reich Arbitration Department. If the supplements are lacking then they can be prepared at the expense of the sender. If a legal procedure is introduced, then there is to be included a supplement of the contested ruling.
2. The Chairman transfers each supplement of the documents which are introduced by the participants to the usual participants. If he wishes a counter expression, then there is a period of time to set that and to prove thereof, that also can be dealt with and decided if no counter expression is introduced. As long as it does not have to do with the presupposition of the license, the participants are to communicate the facts individually which have to do with the presence of conflicts and they are to be given an opportunity of a statutorally designated period of time to express thereto in writing.

& 44

1. The passing of a resolution through the channels of licensure authority must precede an oral negotiation irrespective & 37 Abs. 1 and of & 49 Abs. 1, whose point in time is determined by the Chairmen. The participants are summoned by a notification by registered letter or invitation to an oral negotiation where negotiations and decision can also be made in the case of their absence. The written material should be sent at the latest a week before the oral negotiation.
2. The Chairman should produce for the negotiation the requisite previous files.

3. In the oral negotiation informants are to be heard. They are invited by the Chairman through a registered letter or receipt. If an informant stays away or declines to make a statement, then the facts can be determined according to the context. Information and expert opinion can also be taken in writing. The regular courts and the other public authorities are required to give legal assistance.
4. The informants are to be reimbursed on demand for the out-of-pocket expenses for the interrogation as well as for income lost from work, up to the highest that has been proven. The decision regarding this is ultimately up to the Chairman of the Licensure authority.

& 45

The participants can be represented as well by written submissions as well as also in oral testimony certified by a power of attorney. The power of attorney must be in writing. The requirement of a power of attorney can be disregarded if the authority of representation is made appropriately believable.

& 46

1. The hearing begins after the review of the facts with the representation of the expert witness by the Chairman or the member who has proposed him as being a witness. The Chairman leads the hearing, the consultation and the voting. The Chairman has to make it such that the testimony of the expert witness is made extensively clear. Each member of the Licensure Committee can question facts and make inquiries.
2. Consultation and the passing of a resolution, which occur in the absence of the participants are to be consistent with the negotiation. Only a member who has taken part in the hearing may participate.

& 47

In the matter of Licenses by the Licensure Committee, then the Chairman, on application of the District or Sub-District, is to indicate in the "Deutschen Aerzteblatt" of the forthcoming passing of a resolution and likewise set a determined period of time for the reception of applications for licensure and the statements of the participants, so that after a period of time, applications and statements regarding the passing of the resolution are no longer to be taken into account.

& 48

(1) The License is to be applied for in writing.
(2) In the application it is to be noted for which of the known Districts or Sub-Districts the license is desired.
(3) With the application is to be included:

    1. the proof for the supplement which designates a Specialty physician, if the application is entered for a Specialty physician.
    2. a certificate of the Physicians' Chamber concerning the District and duration of the establishment if the physician is established;

3. a certificate of the responsible Physicians' Registry concerning the duration of the license, if the physician is approved;
4. the corresponding documentation with entrances for license according to & 17 or according to & 20;
5. a written declaration by the physician that he is narcotic free and that he was not previously addicted to narcotics.

(4) If doubt exists regarding the political reliability of the physician, then the Chairman of the Licensure Committee is to get from the responsible high ranking authority of the National Socialist German Workers Party a certificate of political approval.

& 49

1. The passing of a resolution concerning the selection of lincenses takes place without oral negotiation. The Chairman of the Licensure Committee can nevertheless invite the participants and the informants. He determines the point in time of the negotiation.
2. If with the passing of a resolution concerning licensure among several applicants there is a choice to be made, then he is generally to advise and to decide among the applications.

& 50

1. The negotiation, advising and passing of a resolution of the license authorities are not public. Silence is to be observed concerning the course of the advising and concerning the relationship of the voting to the vote; the License Authority can make exceptions by unanimous decision. The result of the proceeding is to be noted in a ruling.
2. The License Authorities who participated in the passing of a resolution are to enumerate the date of the passing of the resolution. The ruling is to be made clear with its grounds and is to be signed by the Chairman and onc of the members not appointed by the Reich Labor Minister.
3. The Chairman carries out the preparation or if he is disabled, one of the members not named by the Reich Labor Minister who has worked on the ruling.
4. The Chairman gives to each of the participants a transcript of the ruling with.a registered letter or receipt. He can order that other departments also receive a transcript of the decision.

& 51

A secretary is assigned to the Chairman. He can also decide on a secretary who is not a member of the License authority. A record is prepared for each meeting. It records the course of the proceedings and reports the decisions enacted. It is to be signed by the Chairman and the Secretary. The records are to be kept for 15 years.

& 52

The legal force of the ruling is to be limited if there is a call for the rejection of a license, also in regard to a license which is claimed by another physician in accord with & 49 Abs. 2. In these cases the License Committee can on application, or from the Department on the agreement of the Department Leader of the Territorial Department of the Fund Physicians' Union of Germany which is appropriate for the License District, order temporarily through a special uncontested decision that the licensed physician may practice provisionally as a Fund Physician all together or in part until the ultimate passing of the resolution covering the same condition. The ruling will be published in the "Deutschen Aerzteblatt." On application, each of the physicians introduced in the ruling receive a certified copy of this ruling. After the ultimate passing of the resolution covering a limited license the ruling loses its effect.

& 53

If a contested ruling comes to be legally proceduraly entirely or partly rescinded, then the License Authority can decide himself on the facts or send it back as a whole or in part to the lower court.

& 54

To cover the costs arising from the activity of the License Authorities, fees will be raised according to the measures given in & 55.

& 55

1. Outside of the fee indicated in & 26 each physician who is licensed will pay a further fee of ten Reich Marks to the License Committee which is due when the legal validity of the ruling which declares the licensure takes effect. With the rejection of the license by the License Committee a fee is not collected.
2. As long as it does not have to do with the undertaking or rejection of licenses according to Abs. 1, the fee is, if the facts for a ruling are adequate, to be laid on the underlying participants (of the physician or the Fund Physicians' Union of Germany). It amounts to, with the proceeding before the License Committee, of at least 10 and at the highest 50 Reich Marks, in the proceeding before the Reich Licensure Committee, of at least 50 and at most 150 Reich Marks, and in the proceeding before the Reich Arbitration Office, of at least 20 and at most 200 Reich Marks. The License Authority determines the amount of the fee; it can refrain from assessing a fee. The fee becomes due when the ruling takes legal force.
3. In a proceeding before the Reich Arbitration Office the member of the Reich License Committee appointed by the Reich Labor Minister may order that a fee is not to be imposed in case of dismissal of a revision.
4. If the contested ruling is revoked or changed in essential points, then the rejecting authority has to fairly decide whether after a free evaluation who has to bear the fees arising in the previous proceeding. For this, the amount of the fee established by the lower court is regularly taken as a basis.

& 56

1. The fees are to be discharged in a proceeding before the License Committee and the Administrative Department of the Fund Physicians' Union of Germany on

which the License Committee is established, in a proceeding before the Reich License Committee on the Fund Physicians' Union of Germany, and in a proceeding before the Reich Arbitration Office on the Reich Arbitration Office.

2. The Department Leader of the Administrative Department of the Fund Physicians' Union of Germany, the Reich Leader of the Fund Physicians' Union of Germany and the President of the Reich Social Insurance Office can waive the imposition of a fee, if it would mean for the person obligated to pay an unreasonable hardship, or if it is encumbered by costs or complications out of proportion to the income.
3. The incomes and expenditures of the License Committees and of the Reich License Committees are to be carefully calculated. The assets are to be especially protected. The incoming fees may be used only for the purposes given in & 54.

& 57

The Fund Physicians' Union of Germany distributes information covering the interpretation and use of the License Ordinance. In case of doubt about the explanation of its conception, information can be given from the Chairman of the Reich Arbitration Office (& 39)

Chapter 6. *Assignments and Closing Instructions*

The contents mentioned in && 58 to 65 as well as that in && 60 and 64 are repealed.

& 66

The documents and proceedings of the Office of Oversight of Social Insurance and Arbitration Office are to be preserved.

& 67

The proceedings connected to matters of applications and licensure which are pending with the Arbitration Offices are transferred to the License Committees (& 31), the license proceedings pending before the Reich Arbitration Office go to the Reich Arbitration Office (& 39).

& 68

(has become void.)

& 69

If a physician at the effective date of the License Ordinance has entered into more than two Physicians' Registries, then he must at the latest within 4 weeks after the effective date of this Ordinance notify the Reich Physicians' Registry of the two Physicians' Registries in which the entrance should continue to exist. If this is not done after this passage of time, the Reich Physicians' Registry arranges so that only the first two entrances are to continue. The Reich Physicians' Register requests the responsible Administrative Departments to cancel the entrance of those hereafter unlicensed. If there are more than two entrances in place at the same point in time and if the physician has himself not expressed a preference, then the choice is left up to the Reich Physicians' Registry.

& 70

The license of physicians who are of non-Aryan ancestry or of physicians with a wife who is of non-Aryan ancestry which have not practiced or not resumed practicing free Fund Physicians' activity after an interruption at the the time this License Ordinance takes effect, expires effective 7 April, 1933.

& 71

1. This License Ordinance takes effect with its general announcement on 1 July, 1934, together furthermore with the procedures for its implementation.
2. It finds application with its coming into effect for all proceedings which are pending in matters of applications and licensure.

& 72

With the coming into effect of this License Ordinance the following are repealed:

1. The implementational and transitional conditions covering the Fund Physicians' Service relationship, second part (License Ordinance), in the version published on 5 April, 1933.
2. The Ordinance covering the Offices of Oversight of Social Insurance of the Physicians' Registry of 29 February, 1932 (Reich Legal Code I P. 100);
3. The Ordinance for the Change of the Ordinance covering the Office of Oversight of Social Insurance of the Physicians' Registry of 18 July, 1932 (Reich Legal Code I P. 379);
4. The Ordinance covering the Licensure of Physicians for Activity in the Sickness Funds of 22 April, 1933 (Reich Legal Code I. P. 222) Article II No. 1 to 5;
5. The Ordinance covering the Licensure of war participants in medical activity with the Sickness Funds of 9 May, 1933 (Reich Law Code I P. 260);
6. The Ordinance covering the Licensure of Physicians for activity in the Sickness Funds of 28 September, 1933 (Reich Law Code I P. 696) Article II;
7. The Ordinance covering the Licensure of phsicians, dentists and dental technicians for activity in the Sickness Funds of 20 November, 1933 (Reich Law Code. I P. 983) Article I, in so far as it deals with physicians, as well as Aritcle IV.

Article 2 *of the Third Ordinance*
Over the Licensure of Physicians for Activity in Sickness Funds
Of 8 September, 1937 (RGBI. I P. 973

The Ordinance finds use with its coming into effect for all applications and license matters of pending proceedings. The previous prescriptions of the proceedings pending at the time of its coming into effect concerning the extra-ordinary licensure of war-participants are still to be used.

Bibliography

A. R. Aisenberg, *Contagion: Disease, Government, and the "Social Question" In Nineteenth-Century France* (Stanford: University Press, 1999).
W. S. Allen, *The Nazi Seizure of Power: The Experience of a Single German Town, 1930–1933* (Chicago: Quadrangle Books, 1965).
G. Aly, G, P. Chroust, and C. Pross, *Cleansing the Fatherland: Nazi Medicine and Racial Hygiene* (Baltimore: Johns Hopkins, 1994).
G. Aly, *Final Solution: Nazi Population Policy and the Murder of the European Jew* (London: Arnold, 1999).
G. Aly, *Hitlers Volksstaat: Raub, Rassenkrieg und nationaler Sozialismus* (Frankfurt am Main: S. Fischer, 2005a).
G. Aly, *Endloesung: Voelkerverschiebung und der Mord an den europaeischen Juden* (Frankfurt am Main: Fischer, 2005b).
American Medical Association Code of Medical Ethics (Chicago: American Medical Association, 1997).
G. J. Annas and Grodin, MA, *The Nazi Doctors and the Nuremberg Code* (Oxford: University Press, 1992).
H. Arendt, *The Origins of Totalitarianism* (San Deigo: Harcourt Brace, 1979).
H. Arendt, *Eichmann in Jerusalem: A Report on the Banality of Evil* (New York: Viking Press, 1963).
K. A. Armstrong, *History of God: The 4,000-Year Quest of Judaism, Christianity and Islam* (New York: Ballantine Books, 1993).
P. Aycoberry, *The Social History of the Third Reich: 1933–1945.* (New York: New Press, 1999).
G. Baader, "Rassenhygiene und Eugenik: Vorbedingungen fuer die Vernichtungsstrategien gegen sogenannte "Minderwertige" im Nationalsozialismus," *Deutsches Aerzteblatt,* 85 (1988) : H. 27.
G. Baader and Schultz, U, *Medizin und Nationalsozialismus: Tabuisierte Vergangenheit – Ungebrochene Tradition?* (Berlin, 1989).
G. Baader, *Zur Ideologie des Sozialdarwinismus,* (Berlin: 1989.
R. B. Baker, D. Porter and R. Porter, eds. *The Codification of Medical Morality: Historical and Philosophical Studies of the Formation of Western Medical Morality in the Eighteenth and Nineteenth Century* (Dordrecht: Kluwer Academic Publishers, 1993).
R. B. Baker, ed. *The Codification of Medical Morality: Historical and Philosophical Studies of the Formalization of Western Medical Morality in the Eighteenth and Nineteenth Centuries, Volume Two: Anglo-American Medical Ethics and Medical Jurisprudence in the Nineteenth Century* (Dordrecht: Kluwer Academic Publishers, 1995).

R. Ramm, *Medical Jurisprudence and Rules of the Medical Profession*,
Philosophy and Medicine 135, https://doi.org/10.1007/978-3-030-25245-8

R. B. Baker, et al., *The American Medical Ethics Revolution: How the AMA's Code of Ethics Has Transformed Physicians' Relationship to Patients, Professionals, and Society* (Baltimore: The University of Johns Hopkins Press, 1999).
P. Baldwin, *Contagion and the State in Europe 1830–1930* (Cambridge: University Press, 1999).
C. R. Bambach, *Heidegger's Roots: Nietzsche, National Socialism, and the Greeks.* (Ithaca: Cornell University Press, 2003).
C. R. Bambach, *Heidegger, Dilthey, And The Crisis of Historicism* (Ithaca: Cornell University Press, 1995).
W. Barnstone, *The Poetics of Translation: History, Theory, Practice* (New Haven: Yale University Press, 1993).
O. Bartov, *Germany's War and the Holocaust: Disputed Histories* (Ithaca: Cornell University Press, 2003).
A. Beevor, *Stalingrad.* (London: Penguin, 1998).
W. Benz, W. H. Graml, and Weiss, H, *Enzyklopaedie des Nationalsocialismus* (Stuttgart: Deutscher Taschenbuch Verlag, 2001).
J. Berlant, *Profession and Monopoly: A Study of Medicine in the United States and Great Britain* (Berkeley: University of California Press, 1975).
D. L. Bergen, *Twisted Cross: The German Christian Movement in the Third Reich* (Chapel Hill: University of North Carolina Press, 1996).
C. Berning, *Vom "Abstammungsnachweis" zum "Zuchtwart". Vokabular des nationalsozialismus* (Berlin: de Gruyter, 1964).
K. Binding, and A. Hoche, *Die Freigabe der Vernichtung lebensunwerten Lebens: Ihr Mass und Ihre Form* (Leipzig: Verlag von Felix Meiner, 1920).
P. Blickle, *Obedient Germans? A Rebuttal: A New View of German History* (Charlottesville: University Press of Virginia, 1981).
B. Bodo, "The Medical Examination of Biological Selection of University Students in Nazi Germany," *Bull. Hist. Med* 76 (2002) : 719–748.
D. Bothe, *Neue Deutsche Heilkunde: 1933–1945* (Husum : Matthiesen Verlag, 1991).
B. Brecht, *Die Dreigroschenoper* (Frankfurt am Main: Insel Verlag, 2004).
B. Brecht, *Threepenny Opera,* trans. Eric Bently, (New York: Grove Press, 1949).
B. Brecht, *Threepenny Opera,* trans. Marc Blitzstein, (New York: Decca, 1954).
B. Brecht, *Threepenny Opera,* trans. Michael Feingold, (Frankfurt: Ensemble Modern, 1989).
B. Brecht, *Threepenny Opera,* trans. Ralph Manheim and John Willett, (New York: Arcade Publishing, 1994a).
B. Brecht, *Threepenny Opera,* trans. Robert David MacDonald, (London: Digital Jay, 1994b).
M. Broszat, *The Hitler State* (New York: Longman, 1981).
C. R. Browning, *Ordinary Men: Reserve Police Battalion 101 and the Final Solution in Poland* (New York: Harper Collins, 1992).
F. Bruns and T. Chelouche. "Lectures on Inhumanity: Teaching Medical Ethics in German Medical Schools Under Nazism," in *Annals of Internal Medicine* 2017; 2017;166:591–595. doi: https://doi.org/10.7326/M16-2758.
F. Bruns. Medizine ethics im Nationalsozialismus. Entwicklungen und Protagonisten in Berlin (1939–1945). (Stuttgart, Germany: Steiner; 2009.)
M. Burleigh and W. Wippermann, *The Racial State: Germany 1933–1945* (Cambridge: University Press, 1991)
M. Burleigh, *Death and Deliverance: ‚Euthanasia' in Germany 1900–1945* (Cambridge: Cambridge University Press, 1994).
M. Burleigh, *Ethics and Extermination: Reflections on Nazi Genocide* (Cambridge: University Press, 1997).
M. Burleigh, *The Third Reich: A New History* (New York: Hill & Wang, 2000).
W. E. Bynum, *Science and the Practice of Medicine in the Nineteenth Century* (Cambridge: Universtiy Press, 1994).

A. L. Caplan, "The Meaning of the Holocaust for Bioethics," *The Hastings Center Report* 19 (1989) : N. 4.
A. L. Caplan, ed. *When Medicine Went Mad: Bioethics and the Holocaust* (Towota, NJ: Humana Press, 1992).
J. H. Cassedy, *Medicine & American Growth: 1800–1860* (Madison: University of Wisconsin Press, 1986).
A. F. Chalmers, *What is this thing called Science?* (St. Lucia: U. of Queensland Press, 1982).
T. Childers, *The Formation of the Nazi Constituency, 1919–1933.* (London: Barnes & Nobles Imports, 1986).
G. Church, *'80629': A Mengele Experiment* (Richardson, Texas: Sharon Kimberly Damon, 1986).
M. M. Cohen, *A Stand Against Tyranny: Norway's Physicians and the Nazis* (Detroit: Wayne State University Press, 1997).
N. Cohn, *Warrant for Genocide* (London: Serif, 2001).
R. E. Conot, *Justice at Nuremberg* (New York: Harper & Row, 1983).
J. S. Conway, *The Nazi Persecution of the Churches 1933–1945* (New York: Regent College Publishers, 1968).
G. A. Craig, *Germany, 1866–1945,* (Oxford: University Press, 1978).
L. S. Dawidowicz, *The War Against the Jews: 1933–1945* (New York: Bantam Books, 1986).
A. Doeblin, *Berlin Alexanderplatz* (Dusseldorf and Zuerich: Patmos Verlag, 1996).
A. Doeblin, A, *Berlin Alexanderplatz,* trans. Eugene Jolas (New York: Continuum, 1961.
M. Domarus, *Hitles's Reden 1932 bis 1945: Kommentiert Von Einem Deutschen Zeitgenossen* (Berlin: Loenberg Pamminger & Partner, 1973).
Dreyer-Schmitt, *Lehr und Uebungsbuch der deutschen Grammati.* (Muenchen: Max Hueber Verlag, 2000).
E. Durkheim, *Professional Ethics and Civic Morals* (London: Routledge, 1957).
A. Ebbinghaus and K. Doerner, *Vernichten und Heilen: Der Nuernberger Aerzteprozess und seine Folgen* (Berlin: Aufbau-Verlag, 2001).
U. Eco, *A Theory of Semiotics* (Bloomington: Indiana University Press, 1979).
K Epstein. *The Genesis of German Conservatism.* (Princeton: University Press, 1966).
MA Eisenberg. *The Nature of the Common Law.* (Cambridge, Mass.: Harvard Univ. Press, 1988).
lR. J. Evans, *The Coming of the Third Reich* (New York: Penguin, 2004).
R. J. Evans, *The Third Reich in Power* (London: Penguin, 2005).
V. Farias, *Heidegger and Nazism* (Philadelphia: Temple University Press, 1987).
G. D. Feldman, *The Great Disorder: Politics, Economics, and Society in the German Inflation, 1914–1924* (Oxford: University Press, 1997).
N. G. Finkelstein and R. B. Birn, *A Nation on Trial: The Goldhagen Thesis and Historical Truth* (New York: Henry Holt, 1998).
K. P. Fischer, *Nazi Germany: A New History* (New York: Continuum, 1997).
A. Flexner, *Medical Education in the United States and Canada* (New York: Carnegie Foundation for the Advancement of Teaching, 1910).
C. E. Frewer, *"Euthanasie" Und die Aktuelle Sterbehilfe-Debatte: Die Historischen Hintergruende Medizinischer Ethik* (Frankfurt: Campus Verlag, 2000).
H. H. Freyhofer, *The Nuremberg Medical Trial: The Holocaust and the Origin of the Nuremberg Medical Code* (New York: Peter Lang, 2005).
A. Frewer and C. Eickhoff, *Euthanasie Und die Aktuelle Sterbehilfe-Debatte.* (Frankfurt am Main: Campus Verlag, 2000).
H. Friedlaender, *The Origins of Nazi Genocide: From Euthanasia to the Final Solution* (Chapel Hill: U. of North Carolina Press, 1995).
J. Fritsche, *Historical Destiny And National Socialism In Heidegger's Being and Time* (Berkeley: U. of California Press, 1999).
T. Gerst, *Aerztlich Standesorganisation und Standespolitik in Deutschland 1945–1955* (Stuttgard: Franz Steiner Verlag, 2004).

T. Gerst, "Verschworene Gemeinschaft im Gienste der NS-Gesundheitspolitik," in *Dtsch Aerzteblatt* 92A (1995) : 1588–91.

E. Gibbon, *The History of the Decline and Fall of the Roman Empire. Vol. VII* (London: The Folio Society, 1990).

D. J. Goldhagen, *Hitler's Willing Executioners: Ordinary Germans and the Holocaust* (New York: Vintage Books, 1997).

J. Golomb, and R. S. Wistrich, *Nietzsche, Godfather of Fascism?: On the Abuses of a Philosophy* (Princeton: University Press, 2002).

R. Griffin, ed. *Fascism* (Oxford: University Press, 1995).

R. Grunberger, *The 12-Year Reich: A Social History of Nazi Germany 1933–1945* (New York: Holt, Rinehart and Winston, 1971).

S. Haber, *The Quest for Authority and Honor in the American Professions, 1750–1900* (Chicago: University of Chicago Press, 1991).

S. Haffner, *Geschichte eines Deutschen: Die Erinnerung 1914–1933* (Muenichen: Deutscher Taschenbuch Verlag, 2002).

H. Haller, Jr., *American Medicine in Transition: 1840–1910* (Urbana: University of Illinois Press, 1981).

P. J. Haas, *Morality After Auschwitz: The Radical Challenge of the Nazi Ethic* (Philadelphia: Fortress, 1988).

J. Herf, *Reactinary Modernism: Technology, culture, and politics in Weimar and the Third Reich* (Cambridge: Cambridge University Press, 1984).

S. Hervey, I. Higgins and M. Loughridge, *Thinking German Translation: A Course in Translation Method: German to English* (New York: Routledge, 1995).

E. C. Helmreich, *The German Churches Under Hitler: Background, Struggle, and Epilogue* (Detroit: Wayne State U. Press, 1979)

U. Herbert, Orth, K and C. Dieckmann, *Die nationalsozialistischen Konzentrationslager: Entwicklund und Struktur* (Goettingen: Walstein Verlag, 1998).

L. Heston and R. Heston, *The Medical Casebook of Adolf Hitler: His Illnesses, Doctors and Drugs* (New York: Scarborough, 1979).

C. Huerkamp. *Der Aufsteig der Aerzte im 19 Jahrhundert: Vom gelehrten Stand zum professionellen Experten* (Goettingen, 1985a).

R. Hilberg, *The Destruction of the European Jews* (New York: Holmes & Meier, 1985).

W. Hofer, *Der Nationalsozialismus Dokumente 1933–1945* Frankfurt am Main: Fischer Verlag, 2004.

H. Holborn, *A History of Modern Germany: 1840–1945* (Princeton: University Press, 1969).

C. Huerkamp, *Der Aufstieg der Aerzte im 19 Jahrhundert. Vom gelehrten Stand zum professionellen Experten: Das Beispiel Preussen* (Goettingen: Vandenhoeck & Ruprecht, 1985b).

C. M. Hutton, *Linguistics and the Third Reich: Mother-tongue fascism, race and the science of language* (New York: Routledge, 1999).

S. Jarcho, *The Concept of Contagion: In Medicine, Literature and Religion* (Malabar, Florida: Krieger Publishing, 2000).

E. A. Johnson, *Nazi Terror: The Gestapo, Jews, and Ordinary Germans* (New York: Basic Books, 1999).

S. T. Joshi, ed. *Documents of American Prejudice: An Anthology of Writings on Race From Thomas Jefferson to David Duke* (New York: Basic Books, 1993).

D. Junker, et al., *Die USA und Deutschland im Zeitalter des Kalten Krieges: 1968–1990.* (Stuttgard: Deutsche Verlags-Anstalt, 2001).

H. Kammer and Elisabet Bartsch, *Lexikon Nationalsozialismus* (Hamburg: Rowohlt Taschenbuch, 2002).

M. H. Kater, *The Nazi Party: A Social Profile of Members and Leaders, 1919–1945* (Cambridge: Harvard University Press, 1983).

M. H. Kater, "Doctor Leonardo Conti and His Nemesis: The Failure of Centralized Medicine in the Third Reich," *Central European History* 18 (1985a), 299–325.

M. H. Kater, "Professionalization and Socialization of Physicians in Wilhelmine and Weimar Germany," *Journal of Contemporary History* 20 (1985b), 299–325.

M. H. Kater, "The Burden of the Past: Problems of a Modern Historiography of Physicians and Medicine in Nazi Germany," *German Studies Review* 10 (1987a) : 31–56.

M. H. Kater, "Hitler's Early Doctors: Nazi Physicians in Predepression Germany," *The Jounal of Modern History,* 59 (March 1987b) : 25–52.

M. H. Kater, *Doctors Under Hitler* (Chapel Hill: U. of North Carolina Press, 1989).

R. E. Keller, *Die deutsche Sprache* (Hamburg: Helmut Buske, 1995).

H. K. Kelling, Deutsche Kulturgeschichte (New York: McGraw-Hill, 1999).

J. F. Kett, *The Formation of the American Medical Profession: The Role of Institutions, 1780–1860* (New Haven: Yale University Press, 1968).

C. E. King, *The Nazi State and the New Religions: Five Case Studies in Non-Conformity.* (New York: Edwin Mellen Press, 1982).

E. Klebs, "Zur Behandlung der Tuberkulose. II. Hereditaere Uebertragung und andere Infektionswege," *Muenchener Medizinische Wochenschrift* 48 (1901).

E. Klee, *Das Personenlexikon zum Dritten Reich* (Framkfurt: Fischer Taschenbuch Verlag, 2005).

V. Klemperer, *The Language of the Third Reich: LTI – Lingua Tertii Imperii. A Philologist's Notebook* (London: Athlone Press, 1947).

V. Klemperer, *LTI. Notizbuch eines Philologen* (Leipzig: Reclam, 1980).

W. Kline, *Building A Better Race: Gender, Sexuality, and Eugenics From the Turn of the Century to the Baby Boom* (Berkeley: U. of California Press, 2001).

D. Konold, *A History of American Medical Ethics, 1847–1912* (New York: Book Craftsmen, 1962).

C. Koontz, *The Nazi Conscience* (Cambridge: Belknap Press, 2003).

Claudia Koonz. *Mothers in the Fatherland: Women, the Family, and Nazi Politics.* (New York: St. Martin's Press, 1968).

R. Koselleck, *The Practice of Conceptual History: Timing History, Spacing Concepts,* trans. Todd Samuel Presner (Stanford: Stanford University Press, 2002).

S. Kuehl, *The Nazi Connection: Eugenics, American Racism, and German National Socialism* (Oxford: University Press, 1994).

G. Lakoff and M. Johnson, *Metaphors We Live By* (Chicago: University Press, 1980).

S. Lee, *The Weimar Republic* (London: Routledge, 1988).

F. Lenz, "Zur Erneuerung der Ethick," *Deutschlands Erneuerung, 1* (1917), 56.

G. Lewy, *The Catholic Church and Nazi Germany* (New York: De Capo Press, 1964).

R. J. Lifton *The Nazi Doctors: Medical Killing and the Psychology of Genocide* (New York: Basic Books, 1986).

M. Lindemann, *Health & Healing in Eighteenth-Century Germany* (Baltimore: Johns Hopkins University Press, 1996).

H. J. Lutzhoeft, *Der Nordische Gedanke in Deutschland 1920 bis 1940* (Stuttgart: Klett-Cotta, 1971).

R. Mackensen *Bevolkerungslehre und Bevolkerungspolitik im „Dritten Reich*" (Leske + Budrich :Opladen, 2004).

G. Mann, *The History of Germany Since 1789* (Victoria, Australia: Pimlico, 1958).

G. Mann, "Rassenhygiene-Sozialdarwinismus," *Biologismus im 19. Jahrhundert* (Stuttgart: Klett-Cotta, 1973).

K. Mann, *Mephisto* (Hamburg: Rowohlt Taschenbuch Verlag, 2005).

K. Mann, *Mephisto,* trans. Robyn Smith (New York: Random House, 1977).

E. Margolis and S. Laurence, eds. *Concepts: Core Readings* (Cambridge: MIT Press, 1999).

A. Margoshed, "Schelling," in *The Encyclopedia of Philosophy,* Edwards, P. ed. (New York: MacMillan, 1967), 7–8.

DJ, Marcus, and S. A. Eiceluk, eds. (New Brunswick: Rutgers University Press, 1995).

M. Mazower. *Hitler's Empire: How the Nazis Ruled Europe.* (New York: Penguin Books, 2008), 245–6.

K. Meier, *Kreuz und Hakenkreuz: Die evangelische Kirche im Dritten Reich* (Munich: Dtv, 1992).

J. J. Michalczyk, *Medicine Ethics and the Third Reich* (Kansas City, Mo.: Sheed & Ward, 1994).

A. Mitscherlich and F. Mielke, eds. *Das Diktat der Menschenverachtung* (Heidelberg: Verlag Lambert Schneider, 1947).
H. Mommsen, *From Weimar to Auschwitz* (Princeton: University Press, 1991).
H. Mommsen, *Von Weimar nach Auschwitz. Sur Geschichte Deutschlands in der Weltkriegsepoche* (Berlin: Ullstein Tb, 2001).
B. Moore, Jr., *Social Origins of Dictatorship and Democracy* (Boston: Beacon Press, 1966).
Mueller, GOW and Buergenthal T, transl. *The German Penal Code of 1871.* (London: Sweet & Maxwell, 1961).
I. Mueller, *Hitler's Justice: The Courts of the Third Reich* (Cambridge: Harvard University Press, 1991).
R. Neuhaus, *Arbeitskaempfe, Aerztestreiks, Sozialreformer, Sozialpolitische Konfliktregegung: 1900 bis 1914* (Berlin: Duncker & Humblot, 1986).
F. R. Nicosia and J. Huener, eds. *Medicine and Medical Ethics in Nazi Germany* (New York: Berghahn Books, 2002).
D. Nowak, "Doctors on Strike – The Crisis in German Health Care Delivery," *N Engl J Med 355* (2006) *: 15.*
M. Nyiszli, *Auschwitz: A Doctor's Eyewitness Account* (New York: Arcade Pbl, 1960).
H. Ott, *Martin Heidegger: A Political Life* (New York: Basic Books, 1993).
S. G. Payne, *A History of Fascism: 1914–1945* (Madison: University of Wisconsin Press, 1995).
G. E. Pence, *Classic Cases in Medical Ethics: Accounts of Cases That Have Shaped Medical Ethics, with Philosophical, Legal and Historical Backgrounds* (Boston: McGraw-Hill, 2000).
J. Peter, *Der Einbruch der Rassenhygiene in die Medizin: Auswirkung rassenhygienischen Denkesn auf Denkkollektive und medizinische Fachgebiete von 1918 bis 1934* (Frankfurt am Main: Mabuse-Verlag, 1995).
W. Poller, *Medical Block Buchenwald* (New York: Lyle Stuart, 1960).
K. Popper, *The Open Society and its Enemies* (London: Routledge and Kegan Paul, 1945).
R. Proctor, *Racial Hygiene: Medicine Under the Nazis* (Cambridge, Mass.: Harvard University Press, 1988).
R. Proctor, *The Nazi War on Cancer* (Princeton: Princeton University Press, 1999).
P. Pulzer, *The Rise of Political Anti-Semitism in Germany and Austria* (Cambridge, Mass: Harvard University Press, 1988).
P. Pulzer, *Germany, 1870–1945: Politics, State Formation, and War* (Oxford: University Press, 1997).
F. Redlich, *Hitler: Diagnosis of a Destructive Prophet* (Oxford: Oxford University Press, 1999).
W. Reich, "The Care-Based Ethic of Nazi Medicine and the Moral Importance of What We Care About," in *Muse* 2001 1: 64–74).
J. Remak, ed. *The Nazi Years: A Documentary History* (New York: Touchstone, 1986).
W. Rinderle and B. Norling, *The Nazi Impact on a German Village* (Lexington, Ky: University of Kentucky Press, 1993).
T. Rockmore, and J. Margolis, *The Heidegger Case. On Philosophy and Politics* (Philadelphia: Temple University Press, 1992).
E. Rodin, *War And Mahem: Reflections of a Viennese Physician* (Victoria, B.C.: Trafford, 1999).
N. Rosenstand, *The Moral of the Story: An Introduction to Ethics* (Boston: McGraw-Hill, 2005).
J. K. Roth, L. Grob, and P. J. Haas, eds. *Ethics After The Holocaust: Perspectives, Critiques, and Responses* (St. Paul, Minn.: Paragon House, 1999).
W. G. Rothstein, *American Physicians in the Nineteenth Century: From Sects to Science* (Baltimore: Johns Hopkins Press, 1972).
R. L. Rubenstein and J. K. Roth, *Approaches to Auschwitz: The Holocaust and Its legacy* (Atlanta: John Knox Press, 1987).
B. Sax, and D. Kuntz, *Inside Hitler's Germany: A Documentary of Life in the Third Reich* (Lexington, Mass.: D.C. Heath, 1992).
U. Schmidt, *Justice at Nuremberg: Leo Alexander and the Nazi Doctors' Trial* (New York: Palgrave Macmillan, 2004a).

U. Schmidt, *Karl Brandt: The Nazi Doctor* (New York: Continuum, 2007).
W. Schmidt, *Geschicht der deutschen Sprache: Ein Lehrbuch fuer das germanistische Studium* (Stuttgart: S. Hirzel Verlag Stuttgart, 2004b).
C. Schmitz-Berning, *Vokabular Des National-Sozialismus* Berlin: Walter de Gruyter, 2000).
D. Schoenbaum, *Hitler's Social Revolution: Class and Status in Nazi Germany, 1933–1939* (Garden City, NY: WW Norton, 1980).
R. Shandley, ed. *Unwilling Germans?: The Goldhagen Debate* (Minneapolis: University of Minnesota Press, 1998).
H. Sluga, *Heidegger's Crisis: Philosophy and Politics in Nazi Germany* (Cambridge, Mass.: Harvard University Press, 1992).
V. Spitz, *Doctors from Hell: The Horrific Account of Nazi Experiments on Humans.* (Boulder, Co: Sentient, 2005.
P. D. Stachura, ed. *Unemployment and the Great Depression in Weimar Germany* (London: Palgrave Macmillan, 1986).
P. Starr, *The Social Transformation of American Medicine* (New York: Basic Books, 1982).
R. Stevens, *American Medicine and the Public Interest: A History of Specialization* (Berkeley: U. of California Press, 1971).
W. Suess, *Der „Volkskoerper" im Krieg: Gesundheitspolitik, Gesundheitsverhaeltnisse und Krankenmord im nationalsozialistischen Deutschland, 1939–1945,* (Munich: R. Oldenbourg, 2003).
R. Swoch, *Aerztliche Standespolitik im Nationalsozialismus: Julius Hadrich und Karl Haedenkamp asl Beispiele* (Husum: Matthiesen Verlag, 2001).
H. Ten Have, *The Growth of Medical Knowledge* (Dordrecht: Kluwer Academic Publishers, 1990).
R. Wardhaugh, *An Introduction to Socioloinguistics: Fifth Edition* (Malden, MA: Blackwell, 2006).
P. Weindling, *Health, Race and German Politics Between National Unification and Nazism 1870–1945* (Cambridge: University Press, 1991).
J. Weiss, *Ideology of Death: Why the Holocaust Happened in Germany* (Chicago: Elephant Paperbacks, 1996).
R. Weikart, *From Darwin to Hitler: Evolutionary Ethics, Eugenics, and Racism in Germany* (New York: Palgrave, 2004).
M. Weinreich, *Hitler's Professors: The Part of Scholarship in Germany's Crimes Against the Jewish People* (New Haven: Yale University Press, 1999).
W. Weyers, *Death of Medicine in Nazi Germany: Dermatology and Dermatopathology under the Swastika* (Philadelphia: Ardor Scribendi, 1998).
J. Weiss, *The Fascist Tradition; Radical Right-Wing Extremism in Modern Europe* (New York: Harper & Row, 1967).
R. Wolin, *The Heidegger Controversy: A critical Reader* (Cambridge, Mass.: MIT Press, 1992).
G. Wolff *Deutsche Sprachgeschichte von den Anfaengen bis zur Gegenwart* (Tuebingen: A. Francke Verlag, 2004).
W. Wuttke-Groneberg, *Medizin im Nationalsozialismus: Ein Arbeitsbuch* (Tuebingen: Schwaebische, 1980).
J. Young, *Heidegger, Philosophy, Nazism* (Cambridge: University Press, 1997).
S. Zweig, *Vierundzwanzig Stunden Aus Dem Leben Einer Frau* (Frankfurt am Main: S. Fischer, 1983.
S. Zweig, *Twenty-four Hours in the Life of a Woman*, trans. Anthea Bell (London: Pushkin Press, 2003).
http://www.nobelprize.org/nobel_prizes/medicine/laureates/
http://www.almaz.com/nobel/medicine
http://www.webhealthcentre.com/surgcor/sc_doctor.asp
Unknown Author, "Der Arzt als Fuehrer und Erzieher" *Deutsch Aerzteblatt 92:* (1935) : 563–567.

MIX
Papier aus verantwortungsvollen Quellen
Paper from responsible sources
FSC® C105338

If you have any concerns about our products,
you can contact us on
ProductSafety@springernature.com

In case Publisher is established outside the EU,
the EU authorized representative is:
Springer Nature Customer Service Center GmbH
Europaplatz 3, 69115 Heidelberg, Germany

Printed by Libri Plureos GmbH
in Hamburg, Germany